The Vespers' T[rial]

ITALIANO CUCINA RUSTICA
WITH TRIAL TIPS FOR LAWYERS

A COOKBOOK FOR TRIAL LAWYERS

By "THE COOKIN' COUSINS"

THOMAS J. VESPER
DOMINIC J. VESPER, SR.

For Customer Assistance Call 1-800-328-4880

Mat #41662309

© 2014 Thomson/West

For authorization to photocopy, please contact the **Copyright Clearance Center** at 222 Rosewood Drive, Danvers, MA 01923, USA (978) 750-8400; fax (978) 646-8600 or **Copyright Services** at 610 Opperman Drive, Eagan, MN 55123, fax (651) 687-7551. Please outline the specific material involved, the number of copies you wish to distribute and the purpose or format of the use.

This publication was created to provide you with accurate and authoritative information concerning the subject matter covered; however, this publication was not necessarily prepared by persons licensed to practice law in a particular jurisdiction. The publisher is not engaged in rendering legal or other professional advice and this publication is not a substitute for the advice of an attorney. If you require legal or other expert advice, you should seek the services of a competent attorney or other professional.

ISBN 978–0–314–63500–6

BOLSTER BRIEFS AND SPEECHES WITH A FEW WELL-CHOSEN WORDS.

NEW EDITION!
Uncle Anthony's Unabridged Analogies, 4th: Quotes, Proverbs, Blessings & Toasts for Lawyers, Lecturers & Laypeople **by Thomas J. Vesper**

The latest edition of this timeless reference provides a unique collection of more than 31,000 useful proverbs, quotations, toasts, and other famous sayings, organized by topic and author and drawn from a wide range of trusted sources. Additionally, this updated volume now includes biographies for every author/source and a new section on movies about lawyers.

New sections added – including quotes ideal for court!

As specially requested by readers, author Thomas Vesper added a new section of compelling famous quotes on the right to a jury trial, ideal for presentations before a judge or jury that help you drive home your point in court. New sections of quotes for use in openings and eulogies – exceptional challenges for any writer or speaker – have also been added.

Collected over 40 years, this compilation of maxims, perfect zingers, and words of wisdom is an essential resource for lawyers and lecturers to use when writing and speaking on both everyday and legal topics, or for anyone looking to sum up an idea in a few well-chosen words.
One hardbound volume. #41531762

Don't miss these two additional titles for trial success!

Deposition Notebook, 4th by Thomas J. Vesper and Mark R. Kosieradzki makes it easy to organize your thoughts, strategies, and relevant materials for conducting efficient, effective depositions. This discovery storage system also serves as a standardized retrieval system, helping you build solid factual and evidentiary foundations that enhance your clients' chances of success.
Two looseleaf volumes, updated annually; three DVDs, replaced as needed. #14714598

Trial Notebook, 6th by Thomas J. Vesper is a redesigned and revised case management system that helps you understand, analyze, and monitor all stages of a lawsuit, including client interviews, case research, settlement negotiations, and the trial itself. It provides everything you need to work effectively and efficiently through even the most complex case.
Two looseleaf volumes, updated annually; three DVDs, replaced as needed. #13971917

For more information or to order:
go to **legalsolutions.thomsonreuters.com**
or call **1-800-344-5009**

© 2014 Thomson Reuters **MKT-6**

DEDICATION

There is an Italian saying: "AT THE TABLE ONE DOES NOT GROW OLD." When we stop and think of all the good times and endless moments of joy we have had with our families and friends, it has proven true. As long as we take the time to remember those whose chairs are now empty, then our family, our centuries' old traditions, and our Southern Italian recipes will never grow old.

This book is dedicated to our parents and Italian forebears.

Tom and I grew up in the Italian section of Camden, New Jersey. We both have fond memories, especially of our family and many family dinners. Our grandparents came to the United States in the early 1900s from La Provincias (provences) of Campobasso in the Regions of Abruzzi-Molise for the Nicolellas and Gallos and Bassilacata for the Vespers. The Nicolellas—Tom's mom, Carmella *nee* Nicolella, and her family—are from Riccia; and the Gallos—Dom's mom, Carmella *nee* Gallo, and her family—are from the next hill-town on the next hill over to the east of Riccia, named Gambatesa, in Southeastern Italia closer to the Adriatic than the Tyrrhenian Sea. The Vespers—Tom's dad, Rocco, and Dom's dad, Ferdinand—are from another even smaller town of Accettura, atop another hill with only two dirt roads (goat paths?) up and down. The Vesper side, whose name was originally Vespe, comes from the "South West" or the Toe of The Boot of Italy.

[GEOGRAPHIC NOTE: Italy's 1948 Consitution created 20 "Regions" or "Regiones," which are the first-level administrative divisions of Italy, i.e., autonomous entities with powers defined by the Constitution. Each region (except for the Aosta Valley) is divided into provinces, and there are 110 provincias, each with its own capital city or "citta." In Italy, a province is an administrative division between a city or municipality (comune) and a region (regione).]

Just to make it challenging, if you use a road map or atlas (which we had to on our several "road trips" through every region and most provincias d'Italia), "città" refers to big cities like Roma, Milano, and Napoli; smaller cities like Genova, Firenze, Torino, Bologna, Ferrara, etc.; and even the tiniest towns like Accettura, Riccia, Gambatesa, Portofino, Taormina, etc.; there is also a "comune" like"*Il comune di AccetturaIl comune di Portofino*," etc. A commune is Italy's basic unit of local government like a township or municipality in the USA.

In short, a "città" is also a "comune" but not always; but, "communes" are always a "città" because in Italy, there are some villages (not towns) that are local government units and therefore called "comuni" as in, e.g., "*comune di Pedesina*" (province of Sondrio, region Lombardia) with only 33 residents in an area of a few square miles.

Therefore, to be geographically pluperfect, Accettura is a tiny town and comune in the Province of Matera, in the Southern Region of Basilicata, 21 miles northwest of the Region's capital of Potenza, with a population of about 2,000 (not counting livestock); Riccia is a comune in the Province of Campobasso in the Region Molise, located about nine miles southeast of the Region's capital citta, Campobasso (see the overlap of names?). Gambatesa is a comune (municipality) in Provincia de Campobasso in the Region Molise, 12 miles southeast of Campobasso, and only one mile (as crows fly, NOT as cars wind up/down hills on narrow "roads"), with 1,654 residents within 26 sq. miles. Simply put: we are Southern Italians.

IN MEMORIAM

Dennis Vesper
(Born 1955 whom God called to Himself 2006)

Dennis Vesper, Ferdinand "Freddie" Vesper, Annette Vesper, and Dominic Vesper

IN MEMORIAM

(Ferdinand Vesper, Sr. & Rocco Vesper)

IN MEMORIAM

(Dominic "Tom" Vesper 1883 - 1967)

DEDICATION

Grandfather Domenico Antonio Vespe

Dedication

Tom and I were both named after our paternal grandfather. Now how did that happen? Well, let me explain. Our grandfather, Domenico Antonio Vespe, came to the United States in 1902 and settled in South Philadelphia with his sister Magdalena. Eventually, he moved "cross the river" (across the Delaware River) to the City of Camden, New Jersey, and was married to Giovannina Mattei and had seven children.

Dominic, as he liked to be called, unsuccessfully applied for many jobs in Camden, but he was very interested in working for the Pennsylvania Railroad, which was paying good wages at the time. However, he was denied employment at a Pennsylvania Rail Yard in South Camden because the Railroad at that time was not hiring Italians, but our grandfather was a very determined and resourceful man. He went to a "Pennsy" rail yard in North Camden, this time telling them his name was Thomas Vesper (with French accent to it). The Railroad hired him immediately; and thus, he was known as Tom and our family's last name was and forever will be Vesper (prounounced with no French "airs" or "heir" to the end—just an "ER" like in cook-ER or lawy-ER).

ACKNOWLEDGMENT

We would like to thank our unnamed muses and immediate family: Dom's Arlene, Dominic Jr, Anthony, Kristina Vesper Carey, Tom's Mary Alice, Maggie and Catie Vesper; Tom's father-in-law, Fran Trzuskowski, Esq., for his regular exchange of audio books and ideas for mixtures of vodka; and Tom's mother-in-law, Ann, for her many "pointers" (inside joke).

We must also thank Lisé Freking of Thomson Reuters for having the faith, confidence, and a large measure of patience to push us to "stop yakking about it" and to coach us on how to compile all of our recipes, collate the trial tips, and complete this written work and get it published.

Our deep appreciation to Glenn Ferguson, also of Thomson Reuters, for counselling, guiding, and expediting our raw opus onto beautiful final folios within this book.

We salute the Margate City Library staff, especially Mr. Jim Cahill, whose Italian dictionary, proofreading, and support were most helpful for us as we neared our "final" goal.

We also thank Mike Ferrara for his *bocconcini* (tid bits) of Italian history and fable.

Our gratitude is expressed to our mothers, who are both deceased but whose culinary inspirations have stayed in our hearts and memories forever: Carmella nee Gallo Vesper and Carmella nee Nicollela Vesper.

Table of Contents

	Page
INTRODUCTION: Three Steps and Recipes to Success at Culinary Art and Civil Jury Trials	1

Chapter 1. ANTIPASTI FREDDI (Multiple Cold Antipasto Dishes)
Part A. DOM'S RECIPES 11
Part B. TOM'S TRIAL TIPS: Presuit investigation and preparation 20

Chapter 2. ANTIPASTI CAULDO (Hot Appetizers)
Part A. DOM'S RECIPES 29
Part B. TOM'S TRIAL TIPS: Pleadings and written discovery 46

Chapter 3. ZUPPA (Soup)
Part A. DOM'S RECIPES 65
Part B. TOM'S TRIAL TIPS: Taking depositions 72

Chapter 4. PASTA OR "DOUGH" (Commonly "Macaroni, Macs, Noodles, Spaghetti")
Part A. DOM'S RECIPES 105
Part B. TOM'S TRIAL TIPS: Defending depositions 130

Chapter 5. INTERMEZZO (Short Dining Interlude to Cleanse And Refresh Your Palates)
Part A. DOM'S RECIPES 143
Part B. TOM'S TRIAL TIPS: Deposition & Trial Notebooks (discovery, trial, case evaluation and settlement) 162

Chapter 6. PESCE (Fish)
Part A. DOM'S RECIPES 181
Part B. TOM'S TRIAL TIPS: Jury selection 188

Chapter 7. LA VERDURA (Vegetables)
Part A. DOM'S RECIPES 207
Part B. TOM'S TRIAL TIPS: Opening statement 216

TABLE OF CONTENTS

Chapter 8. CARNE (Meat)
    Part A. DOM'S RECIPES   247
    Part B. TOM'S TRIAL TIPS: Direct and re-direct examination   256

Chapter 9. INSALATA (Salad)
    Part A. DOM'S RECIPES   287
    Part B. TOM'S TRIAL TIPS: Cross-examination   300

Chapter 10. DOLCE (Sweets/Desserts)
    Part A. ARLENE'S RECIPES   317
    Part B. TOM'S TRIAL TIPS: Summation   328

Chapter 11. APERITIVO (Aperitif) and DIGERENTE (Digestifs): Before and After Dinner Special Drinks
    Part A. TOM'S and DOM'S RECIPES   341
    Part B. TOM'S TRIAL TIPS: Negotiation, mediation and settlement   382

Chapter 12. SOME FINAL TOASTS TO TRIAL LAWYERS   425

Selected Bibliography   447

Index to Recipes

Index to Trial Tips

INTRODUCTION: Three Steps & Recipes to Success at Culinary Art & Civil Jury Trials

In this "Cookbook" we hope to give trial lawyers tips for both their kitchens and the civil courtroom. Every good cook knows that to make any "culinary delight" a pleasure for the palate, there are usually three steps to success: planning, preparation, and execution. For PROPER PLANNING, good cooks have an overall outline for their ultimate serving. Likewise, all good trial lawyers know that making a client's case understandable and compelling for a jury requires PREPARATION for the ultimate dish, as well as good, fresh ingedients. And to bring everything together for consumption, the cook must use GOOD COOKING TECHNIQUES.

In Latin, **florilegium** (plural *florilegia*) was a compilation of excerpts taken from other writings. The word is from Latin *flos* (flower) and *legere* (to gather): literally a gathering of flowers or collection of fine extracts from larger works. Romans, as with most everything, adapted from Greek *anthologia* or "anthology," the same etymological meaning. Medieval *florilegia* were systematic collections of extracts taken mainly from the writings of the Church Fathers from early Christian authors, pagan philosophers such as Aristotle, and sometimes classical writings. We have shortened some of the best excerpted trial tips from the *AAJ Trial Notebook* and *AAJ Deposition Notebook* to help trial lawyers better represent their clients in court.

We divided our cooking recipes/menu and a trial lawyer's agenda in a civil jury trial into twelve parts, with each part we have paired 12 tried (pun intended) and true litigation tips with corresponding tasty, rustica Italian recipes for delicious foods and interesting libations for family and friends of lawyers and non-lawyers alike. The following tasty, and we hope thought-provoking, analogs resulted:

Cooking Menu & Recipe Sections with Analogous Trial Lawyer Tips

1. Antipasti freddo (Cold appetizers)	Presuit investigation & preparation
2. Antipasti cauldo (Hot appetizers)	Pleadings & written discovery
3. Zuppa (Soup)	Taking depositions
4. Pasta	Defending depositions
5. Intermezzo (Interlude)	Notebooks (discovery & trial)

6. Pesce (Fish)	Jury selection/voir dire
7. La Verdura (Vegetables)	Opening statement
8. Carne (Meat)	Direct examination & re-direct
9. Insalata (Salad)	Cross-examination
10. Dolce (Dessert)	Summation
11. Special Drinks: Aperitifs & Digestifs	Negotiation, mediation & settlement
12. Toasts	Value & role of "Trial Lawyer"
Bocconcini Sources & Selected Bibliography	

Beginning in Chapter 1 and through to Chapter 11 we start each Trial Cookbook Chapter with fun recipes for success in the kitchen or dining room, and follow each meal course's set of food recipes with our analogous litigation "recipes" for trial lawyers to try or avoid at each stage of litigation to increase their likelihood of success in courtroom. Our final Chapter 12 is our salutes, toasts and blessings to you and yours.

Like our parents, grandparents, and Italian forebears, we do not take all tips or recipes as mathematically precise formulas. We give you herewith our best civil trial coaching and culinary counsel with the specific admonition to improvise and experiment and try your own variations of this cookbook's contents to fit your own tastes and those of your clients, judges, and juries, as well as *al dente* (to the teeth/taste) of your friends and family.

CONTENT AIDS AND EXTRAS: Whether you went to high school or law school, we assumed most readers have not been to the "culinary arts schools" we attended at the sides of our Southern Italian mothers, grandmothers, fathers, grandfathers, aunts, and uncles. Therefore, we included some translations, explanations, and speculations about dishes and drinks we enjoy making for our families. We hope you enjoy both the food and stories about our families, and the food, we recommend you try.

Each of our food and drink recipes has a suggestion: **"SERVES."** This is our rough estimate of the servings foreseeably to be consumed by what tort law calls "the reasonable man standard." Our Aunt Mary from Brooklyn would say, "if youz guys're hungry I'm gonna trow anudder box intada pot." What should serve six adults may only feed one or two young hungry teens. Be guided by your family and guests; take our suggested serving numbers *con un* *grano di sale* ("with a grain of salt." (pun intended)). We do not give **TIMES** such as Prep Time, Cook Time, Clean-Up Time, Total Time, for food. What might take Arlene 15 minutes is probably going to take our Hoboken friend Jerry Baker, Esq. all day.

BOCCONCINI: *Bocconcini* is Italian for "tid-bits." For each dish or drink, Cuz Tom includes one or two.

CUZ DOM & ME

PART A. A LA CUCINA—YOUR KITCHEN

By Dominic Vesper

I'm not a fan of kitchen gadgets and special equipment. The most important kitchen tools are sharp, good quality knives; well-made stainless steel pots; a good set of frying and sauté pans; and wooden spoons. Also, have a variety of spices and FRESH herbs.

By no stretch of the imagination am I a gourmet chef. I have no formal training. I am a "Home Cook" and enjoy cooking, especially for friends and family. I would have to thank my wife Arlene for any "formal" training I have had over the years. She has always encouraged me to cook and is my biggest and best critic. One of the first things she insisted was to keep the workspace clean and to remember that when I cook, I have to clean the kitchen when I'm finished. I think cooking is a form of art; the more creative you are, the more success you will have. When you read a typical recipe, and you do not like a certain ingredient, change it or delete it. People ask me what kind of wine I cook with, my reply is always the same: "I cook with the wine I like to drink."

You must remember there are four pieces of cutlery on any Italian table: fork, knife, spoon, and a loaf of Italian Bread. When I see people at my table using that fourth piece of cutlery to dip into my sauce or gravy, I know my meal is a success. Cuz Thomas, my brother Ferdinand aka "Freddy," and I have traveled throughout Italy and eaten in many regions. We found cuisine varies from region to region and each is credited with a certain technique or food preparation. My recipes are "rustica," or rustic, and from the regions of Abburzzi and Bassilcatta. These were the regions our grandparents came from in the early 1900s. I hope you enjoy this book and the recipes.

DOMINIC'S TIPS

1. Never rinse drained pasta. When this is done, all the starch is washed away and your sauce or gravy will not stick to the pasta.

2. Gravy is made with meat, sauce is NOT.

3. Always add your pasta to the pan the sauce is in and cook a minute or two. This helps the pasta to absorb the sauce.

4. Always remember to salt your pasta water.

5. Always keep one to two cups of pasta water; if your sauce seems dry add the pasta water.

6. Sharpen your knives often.

7. NEVER burn garlic; burnt, it tastes bitter. Remove it from the pan and replace with fresh.

8. Do not cook with any wine you wouldn't drink.

Bon Appetito!

DOMINIC

PART B. LA BAR LIQUORE E CANTINA CASA—YOUR HOME BAR & WINE CELLAR

Like Cuz Dom, I don't believe in "fancy-schmanzy" glassware or hi-tech "bar-tools." If you serve quality wines/spirits in clean glasses—we are used to jelly-jar-shaped water glasses—your friends and familia will enjoy savoring a good wine or libation with good food. Wine tastes just as fine in outlet crystal goblets as it does in Waterford stemware.

I. Wine Glasses vs. Crystal

Stemmed or stemless, crystal or glass, per piece or by the dozen, a basic selection of wine glasses for you and your guests is wise. Shape can affect appreciation of wine and spirits, but do not get carried away when you begin. Buy wine glasses of a clear glass or crystal that are not too fragile. As you get more interested in wines, explore other options. We say "itza nice" to have wider-bowl glasses for red wine (so it breathes) and smaller-bowl glass for whites. All you need to start a wine glass collection is a set of six red wine glasses and a set of four to six champagne flutes. Two tips:

1. Buy the varietal specific type glass of the varietal wine you enjoy the most and build your collection from there. If you love Pinot Noir, buy a Pinot Noir glass, for example.

2. Spend about the same amount of money per glass that you do on your bottle of wine.

Vino Rosso

Glasses for *vino rosso* (red wine) have rounder, wider bowls, which increases the rate of oxidation; as oxygen interacts with wine, the flavor and aroma are subtly altered. This oxidation is more noticeable with red wines, whose complex flavors are said to smooth out after being exposed to air. Red wine glasses have styles of their own, such as:

Bordeaux glass: tall with a broad bowl, and designed for full-bodied red wines like Cabernet Sauvignon and Syrah. It directs wine to the back of the mouth.

Burgundy glass: broader than a Bordeaux glass, it has a bigger bowl to collect aromas of more delicate red wines such as Pinot Noir. It directs wine to the tip of the tongue.

Vino Blanco and Spumante

White wine glasses vary in size and shape, from delicately tapered Champagne flutes, to wide, shallow "Chardonnay glasses." Different shapes accentuate unique characteristics of different wines. Wide-mouthed glasses act like red wine glasses, hastening oxidation altering the flavor of the wine.

White wines that are best served slightly oxidized are generally full-flavor wines, such as Italian Chardonnay from Piemonte or California Chardonnay. Lighter, fresher styles of whites, like Frascatti from Rome, do not need oxidation because it masks the delicate nuances of these *vino blancos*. Therefore, to preserve a crisp, clean flavor, many white wine glasses have smaller mouths, which reduces surface area and in turn, the rate of oxidization. For sparkling wines, like Prosecco, Asti, or Champagne, an even smaller glass-mouth is used to keep the wine sparkling longer in the glass.

Spumante or Champagne Stemware or Flutes

Champagne flutes have long stems with tall, narrow bowls on top. Their shape is to keep sparkling wine desirable during its consumption. The bowl itself is designed in a manner to help retain the signature carbonation of the drink. This occurs by reducing the surface area at the opening of the bowl. Also this design adds to the aesthetics of spumante, etc., allowing bubbles to travel further, giving a more pleasant visual appeal.

Sherry Glasses

Sherry glass or sherry copita (Spanish for cup) is drinkware generally used for serving aromatic alcoholic drinks, like sherry, port, aperitivos, liqueurs, and layered shooters. The copita, with its aroma-enhancing narrow taper, is a type of sherry glass.

Boccalinos

If you have Swiss guests, you might want to invest in a "boccalino" (a nozzle); it is a little ceramic mug (like a tiny pitcher) used in Ticino, Switzerland, to drink local wine (Merlot et al). OK, it's not usually stocked anywhere in South Jersey. . .but, it's Italian!

II. Home Bar Basic Glassware

Highball Glass

You'll see these tall, slender, sometimes ever-so-slightly flared glasses at most bars because they are so versatile; generally in 10 or 12 oz. range and often used for drinks not shaken (e.g., Bloody Marys, Gin & Tonics). These are great for summer straws and stir-sticks.

Martini Glass

A good martini glass is a must for a home bar. Look for the classic flared bowl that has become favored by martini traditionalists; sizes range from three to 12 ounces. Cuz Dom and I choose the smaller glasses because we tend to like stronger, more classic martinis, but you might want to choose the larger "birdfeeder" style preferred by my father-in-law Fran Trzuskowski . . . and for that matter most of my in-laws.

Champagne Flutes (For Cocktails)

Whether you prefer more of a taper or a coupe, celebrations call for champagne flutes! Drinking champagne out of another type of glass just "don't feel right, Cuz." You might like "the coupe-style" champagne glasses, aka "Marie

Antoinettes," that have a shallow bowl and are used for sparkling cocktails as well.

Old Fashioned Glass

At our homes, these are the glasses we reach for first. They are short, squatty glasses with thick bottoms that hold anywhere from six to ten ounces. They are very versatile and perfect for any drink "on the rocks." If you're a whisky or bourbon person, you already know these glasses are used for cocktails like Old Fashioneds, Negronis, or Manhattans.

III. <u>Essential Bar Tools</u>

There are some basic, inexpensive tools needed to make cocktails at your home bar. Some of these may already be in your kitchen; the rest can be bought within any budget.

Shakers: Cocktail & Boston Shakers

There are two basic types of shakers:

Cocktail or Traditional Shaker: A metal shaker with a tight-fitting top covering a strainer which fits onto a bar tin (top); they are available in many stylish designs.

Boston Shaker: This has a dual purpose: it is made up of a 16 ounce mixing glass and a larger, flat-bottomed bar tin (top). The glass can be used alone to stir drinks over ice, and the two pieces are used together for shaking ingredients with the tin fitting over the glass. The Boston Shaker is used by professional bartenders and requires a strainer.

Strainers: Hawthorne & Julep

Hawthorne Strainer: For drinks shaken or stirred with ice and served neat or over new ice, a strainer is needed to separate ice, fruits, herbs, or solids from the liquid. A strainer is needed with a Boston shaker because there is not one built in; a Hawthorne strainer is most common—a flat-topped, perforated metal device with wire coil around the perimeter that keeps the strainer in place. The short handle, and either two or four "thumbs" extending from the top and sides keep it in place and allow the bartender to use only one hand.

Julep Strainer: A perforated, stainless steel, shaped like a big soup spoon with holes; placed at an angle inside a mixing glass or bar tin while straining drinks into the glass.

IV. <u>Other Basic Bar Tools</u>

Among can openers, cutting board, cotton bar towels, bottle/can opener, bottle sealers, grater, ice tongs and scoops, juice squeezer/extractors, measuring cups, mixing glasses, and strainer, a good sharp knife is indispensable. Here are our suggested "bar basics":

Cork Screw: T-Types, screwpulls, double levers, prong types, lever-pull corkscrews, hand-held corkscrew machines, and big bar-screw cork pulling machines all work; but our "wine weapon of choice" is the "Waiter's Corkscrew" or "2-Step" corkscrew where the neck rest articulates to allow two "steps" to a cork-pull. This leverage more evenly applied to the cork moving out of the bottle with much less risk of breaking/crumbling.

Jigger: Jiggers are metal measuring devices usually with two cones, one on either end. The larger cone usually holds 1 ½ oz. and the smaller cone holds ¾ or 1 oz. The jigger is an essential tool that helps measure liquids precisely to create consistent cocktails. I can tell you with family and friends cuz Dom and I don't use jiggers—just our memory.

Bar Spoon: Not just a spoon, a bar spoon has a long shaft to reach bottom of tall glass, spiral handle for easy twisting, and tiny spoon bowl with holes for floating liquors. This type of spoon helps stir and layer drinks and with the sport of fishing cherries or olives out of a jar.

Muddler: A thick stick of wood, stainless steel, or plastic; used to mash ingredients in the bottom of a glass; also to mix sugars, bitters, and to extract juices and oils from fruit and mint. "Muddling" is an essential step in Old-Fashioneds, Mojitos, and Caipirinhas.

It's best to choose a thick muddler with a 1 ½" to 2" diameter at its widest point; this will give you more crushing and mixing power than the thinner muddlers.

Ice Bucket: Ice is key to any bar, and items like ice buckets, crushers, scoops, and tongs are helpful. Electric ice crushers work well, but to remove one more appliance, you can get an insulated ice crushing bag, sometimes called a "Lewis Bag," and whack it with your muddler to the consistency of ice needed. Talk about taking out your frustrations!

Electric Blender: A blender is necessary to prepare frozen drinks like Frozen Daiquiris and Margaritas, and they also crush ice and puree fruit.

Juicer: Most juicers yield the same results. They range from simple reamers to electric juicers. If you get a juicer, use it! Don't leave it sitting in the cupboard. Fresh fruit and vegetable juice make the best cocktails. We recommended fresh ingredients over bottled juices whenever possible. Your "bar patrons" will *"mille grazie"* you for your effort.

Propino tibi salutem! (I drink to the health of all of you!)
TOM VESPER

Chapter 1. ANTIPASTI FREDDI (Multiple Cold Antipasto Dishes)

PART A. DOM'S RECIPES

PROSCIUTTO AND MELONE
(Ham and Melon)

This appetizer is very refreshing and the sweetness of the melon with the saltiness of the prosciutto stimulates the taste buds. It is a great way to begin any meal. The success of this appetizer is the use of fresh ingredients.

INGREDIENTS (Serves 8):

1 Cantaloupe or honeydew melon

8 Slices of prosciutto (Italian ham)

DIRECTIONS:

Cut melon into 8 slices.

Lay one piece of prosciutto on each slice of melon.

BOCCONCINI: *Prosciutto* (BRA-SHOOT in South Jersey/Philly) is dry-cured Italian or Parma ham, usually sliced thin, served uncooked as *prosciutto crudo*; cooked ham is *prosciutto cotto*; Italian *prosciugare* means "to dry thoroughly; to extract juices from." Most are from Friuli in Northeast Region of Friuli-

Antipasti Freddi

Venezia Giulia, or Emilia (historic North Emilia-Romagna Region, sandwiched—no pun—between Veneto and Tuscano Regions). The best, most expensive are from pig or wild boar hams (hind leg/thigh); take 9—24 months depending on size. Cuz Dom makes and ages his own soppressata. Aging is an art: too warm = aging never begins and meat spoils; too dry = ruined meat. It needs damp + cool; summer is too hot. Winter is salami, prosciutto, soppressata time.

Sliced *prosciutto crudo* is often an antipasto, wrapped around *grissini* (breadsticks), or with melon; also an accompaniment to cooked spring vegetables, like asparagus or peas. It can be added to a simple pasta sauce made with cream or Tuscan dishes of tagliatelle and vegetables; also used in stuffings for other meats, like veal; or wrap around veal or steak, in a filled bread, or pizza topping. Prosciutto slices are difficult to cut and tend to shred and stick to one another, so either use very sharp knives/scissors or shred the best way—by hand. Prosciutto is great in sandwiches and Panini, like a Caprese salad.

Saltimbocca is an Italian veal dish where escalopes of veal are topped with a sage leaf before being wrapped in prosciutto and then pan-fried.

Culatello is a refined variety of prosciutto, made from heavier pigs, cut to a fraction of the normal prosciutto and aged; it may be wine cured. It is served as a starter along with slices of sweet melon or fresh figs, especially in Northern Italy on New Year's Eve.

The Vespers' Trial Cookbook

CARCIOFI ANTIPASTO
(Marinated Artichokes)

"Antipasto" literally means before a meal but not before the pasta. Antipastos are usually served before a special occasion dinner or holiday dinners. This antipasto is easy to make and is a very elegant addition to your meal.

INGREDIENTS (Serves 6 to 8):

3 (8 oz.) Jars of artichokes

2 (16 oz.) Mozzarella balls

3 Roasted Red Bell peppers cut into stripes or 1 (16 oz.) jar

1 Clove of garlic minced

1 (6 oz.) Can green pitted olives, drained

1 tsp dry basil

1 tsp Italian Seasoning

¼ cup Balsamic vinegar

½ cup Olive oil

DIRECTIONS:

Combine all ingredients and mix well. Refrigerate overnight.

Assemble on a bed of Romaine lettuce and serve at room temperature.

BOCCONCINI: The globe artichoke, aka "French artichoke" or "green artichoke," gets its name from Northern Italian words *articiocco articoclo* or Ligurian *cocali*, meaning "a pine cone." From the sunflower family, it is believed to be native to the Mediterranean and Canary Islands; of about 140 artichoke varieties, only 40 grow commercially.

According to an Aegean legend and praised in song by poet Quintus Horatius Flaccus, the first artichoke was a lovely young girl, Cynara, who lived on the island of Zinari. The god, Zeus was visiting his brother Poseidon and saw her; Zeus seized her, and he was so pleased with Cynara, he decided to make her a goddess, she agreed but soon missed her mother, grew homesick, and snuck back to Earth for a brief visit. Zeus found this to be ungoddess-like behavior, and he hurled her to Earth, transforming her into the plant we call artichoke. Greek philosopher/naturalist, Theophrastus (371-287 B.C.) first wrote of them being grown in Italy and Sicily. So, next time you bite into one's leafs, remember Ancient Greeks and Romans considered artichokes a delicacy and an aphrodisiac; in Greece, artichokes supposedly were effective in securing births of boys.

ANTIPASTO INSALATA
(Appetizer Salad)

This is one of my personal favorites, and you can make it as small or large as you like.

There are no rules for antipasto; use ingredients you like and be as creative as possible.

INGREDIENTS (Serves as many as you want):

Romaine Lettuce

Italian salami

Prosciutto

Roasted peppers

Olives

Anchovy Filets

Sharp provolone cheese

Plum tomatoes

Hard-boiled eggs

DIRECTIONS:

Arrange a bed of lettuce on a plate.

Arrange meats and remaining ingredients in any design/order you like. There are no rules to making antipasto. I like to serve this with a container of olive oil and a container of balsamic vinegar and everyone can fix their own dressing.

BOCCONCINI: France has *hors d'oeuvre*; Italy *antipasto* (singular) or *antipasti* (pl.). It can be hot or cold, cooked or raw. Antipasti (plural) can be served on individual plates, each artfully designed, or bite-size pieces on a plate to pass, or an elegant centerpiece "family style." For Home Cooks, it's a chance to embellish and have fun. An antipasto course can be the host's culinary valentine, a savory introduction to the feast to follow.

Many think antipasto is a dish served before a pasta course; this sometimes occurs, but it isn't the real meaning. Literally *antipasto* is Latin *"anti"* (before) and *"pastus"* (meal). Contrary to some beliefs, it is not common in Italy to have antipasto at home; from New Jersey to New Mexico kids and working parents come home hungry, and while waiting for lunch/dinner, they open the fridge and gobble a couple of slices of salami or cheese. In Italy, the beautifully prepared, arranged plates of sliced, cured meats, vegetables, fish, and patés we Americans associate with antipasti are reserved for special occasions.

ANTIPASTO TRADITION: In Milan, aperitif with antipasti is an institution. "Aperitif" is Latin *aperire* (to open). Aperitif is meant to open our appetite with a drink. Milanese drinking Campari, nibbling chips, olives, and peanuts, an hour or so before a meal is an essential to a good life. In Milano, it is unthinkable to start good meals with no aperitif. After Mass or before Sunday lunch, all bars in Milan are always busy serving Prosecco, Campari, Aperol, and various combinations of these with wine, seltzer, or juice.

CAPONATA
(Sweet and Sour Eggplant)

There are many versions of this dish that can be found in various parts of Italy. It is very rustic and can actually be served as a meatless main course. It is a hardy antipasto and goes well with all main courses.

INGREDIENTS (Serves 6 to 8):

4 or 5 Small eggplants (2 or 3 lbs)

5 Celery stalks chopped into ¼" slices

1 Medium Vidalia onion sliced thin

1 (28 oz.) Can Italian crushed tomatoes

¼ lb. Black olives pitted

¼ lb. Small green olives pitted

3 Tbsp Capers

3 Tbsp Chopped walnuts

3 Tbsp Raisins

½ cup Balsamic vinegar

1 Tbsp Sugar

Salt and pepper to taste

DIRECTIONS:

Peel and cube eggplant into 1" cubes. Place cubes in a colander, rinse, and drain. Place a dish on cubed eggplant to help drain dark bitter liquid for about 20 minutes.

Rinse eggplant and in a skillet sauté eggplant in hot oil for about 20 minutes, eggplant should be cooked but still firm. Remove eggplant and set aside.

In same skillet, sauté onions and celery in hot oil for about 20 minutes.

Add crushed tomatoes, salt and pepper to skillet;then add olives, capers, and eggplant;simmer for 15 minutes.

Add walnuts, raisins, vinegar, and sugar and simmer for an additional 15 minutes.

Mix well and transfer to a serving dish and let cool.

Refrigerate about an hour; serve at room temperature with a loaf of good Italian bread.

BOCCONCINI: Etymology of "caponata" is debatable. Some say it's Catalan, others say it's from *caupone* (sailors' taverns). We think this Sicilian antipasto relish is probably of Spanish birth. There are three theories:

Theory #1: Sicilian food authority Pino Correnti says the dish comes from Catalan word *caponada*, meaning a kind of relish. Spanish-Catalan relish (*caponada* or *capponata*) came from the *"cappone di galera,"* an ancient sailor's dish of biscuit soaked in oil and vinegar with chopped veggies, whose name referred to the capon (*'cappone'* in Italian) sailors ate on board ancient galleys. The Catalan word literally means "something tied together like vines."

Theory #2: Alberto Denti di Pirajno, a Sicilian gastronome, says the dish was born shipboard as a Spanish mariner's breakfast due to large amounts of vinegar used, which acted as a preservative.

Theory #3: Giuseppe Coria, author of an authoritative Sicilian cookbook, offers: the word comes from Latin *caupo* (tavern) where *cauponae* was served, i.e., "tavern food" for travelers.

Who cares? Whatever its true heritage, the caponata we eat today is worth travelling for.

TAPENADE or DIFFUSIONE DI OLIVA
(Italian Olive Paste or Olive Spread)

Tapenade is a rich olive spread very popular in Italy, throughout the Mediterranean, and a key ingredient in New Orleans' Muffaletta sandwiches. It's very easy to make at home with just a few simple ingredients. The hardest part is pitting the olives . . . if you must do so.

INGREDIENTS (1 Cup serves 4 to 6):

20 Pitted Kalamata olives, coarsely chopped

1 Tbsp rinsed, drained, and chopped capers

1 tsp fresh lemon juice

2 tsp olive oil

½ tsp anchovy paste (optional)

Fresh cracked black pepper

DIRECTIONS:

Combine Kalamata olives, capers, lemon juice, olive oil, anchovy paste, and pepper. Mix well.

Refrigerate and use within two weeks.

Use as a spread for crackers, sandwiches like Panini and muffaletta or as a condiment.

BOCCONCINI: Tapenade (Italians or Occitans say Top-hay-NAD) comes "advertised" as "a Provençal dish" from the Provençal word for capers (tapenas), but we are here to tell you informed home cooks/lawyers that the French—as they want to do—took a great Italian food and slapped their label on it as an *hors d'œuvre*. Olive-based spread with anchovies and/or vinegar are ubiquitous in Italian cuisine and documented in ancient Roman cookbooks thousands of years before the appearance of any French "tapenade" or (just to make this point) the French language itself! The earliest known "tapenade" recipe, *olivarum conditurae*, appeared in *Columella's De re Rustica*, written in the first century and, about 400AD, Marcus Gavius Apicius wrote in *De re coquinaria* ("On the Subject of Cooking") of olive spread mixed with "Garum" fish paste—very close copy.

Just to brag a bit more on Italians—the word Provençal, comes from Roman Empire's "provincia." The language of "the Provence" is really "Occitania as a whole"—i.e., "the entire territory of the old Provincia Romana and even Aquitaine." The term "Provencal" first came into fashion in Italy. Occitan, aka *Lenga d'òc* by native speakers, is a Romance language spoken in southern France, Italy's Occitan Valleys, Monaco, and Spain's Val d'Aran: the regions sometimes known unofficially as "Occitania." It is also spoken in *Guardia Piemontese* (Calabria, Italy). Occitan language descended from the spoken Latin language of the Roman Empire, as did other languages such as Catalan, Galician, Italian, Portuguese, Spanish, Romanian, and Sardinian; Occitan is an official language in Catalonia. So, remember that the foods called Provencal are really Italian.

PART B. TOM'S TRIAL TIPS: PRESUIT INVESTIGATION & PREPARATION

Presuit Investigation & Preparation of Plaintiff Personal Injury Cases

<u>**ANTIPASTI FREDDO, DITO ALIMENTARE, & SPUNTINO or cold appetizers, finger foods, & snacks**</u>

PRESUIT RECIPES FOR DISASTER: 12 QUICK & EASY STEPS THAT WILL DESTROY OR DIMINISH YOUR CLIENT'S CASE THROUGH AN INADEQUATE INITIAL CLIENT INTERVIEW OR PRETRIAL INVESTIGATION, DISCOVERY, & RESEARCH

"If You Don't Know Where You're Going, When You Get There You'll Be Lost"
—Yogi Berra

INTRODUCTION: HOW TO PREPARE YOUR TRIAL TABLE

My father Rocco used to tell me, "You can't win every case you try . . . but with very little effort, you can damn sure lose every case." These tips assume the attorney has either decided to accept the case, or investigate, that is, "screen" it to decide taking or declining. The beginning of every case is a "decision tree" resembling NYC subway maps. Critical decisions or nondecisions are made or not at initial interviews or initial phases of investigation that either set the course for success or doom the case to failure. Sometimes, the client and attorney just "don't see it coming," i.e., affirmative defenses that ultimately defeat the client's case at trial are invisible. It may be simply preserving a key piece(s) of evidence needed to prove a client's case; other times, a combination of your client being less than truthful, as well as the defense truly being a hidden trap.

Once a case is opened, pretrial investigation should not be only getting a police report. If witnesses, physical evidence, or incident scene need preserving, then pretrial work should go beyond reports, which often are incomplete inquiries/sloppy summaries. After reading/hearing client's initial version, if you decide a case isn't worth pursuing, clients should be instructed carefully and **in writing** their case is declined; they should be warned of time periods for formal Notices of Claim or within which to file suit.

The following are twelve (12) potential land mines to avoid stepping on if you have screened the client's case and decided to take it on at least investigate it.

I. ASSUME THE CLIENT'S CASE WILL SETTLE

> "Unilateral agreement is with yourself; if anyone else was involved, they wouldn't!"
> —R.C. Westmoreland (my partner)

If at the case outset you assume it will settle, you will do an injustice to yourself, your firm, and most important, your client. Starting with such assumption, you will take the "path of least resistance." Philosophically and practically, you will do the minimum investigation. Your staff also will work under this false assumption. The discipline and self-critical analysis needed will not enter preliminary research or evaluation. In these overly optimistic situations, the following fiasco occurs: the file languishes two years; then just before the Statute of Limitations runs out, someone decides to make settlement demand; said demand is rejected; a scramble ensues to file suit. The next false theory is then made: whatever discovery is needed to make the case better—liability, causation, damages—can be gotten through formal discovery. Rarely do plaintiff pipe dreams of "quick/easy settlement" come true; much better to assume every case even "absolute, 100% (apparent) winners" should be investigated and prepared as if it will go to a jury.

II. ASSUME THAT LIABILITY IS CLEAR

> "Y'can always tell out of town cars in Atlantic City, they're the ones with fenders"
> —Bob Burns (my investigator)

I refer to this mistaken conjecture as "The Big Bang in the Rear Theory." That is, the client heard/felt a big bang/crash and got rear-ended. This, to some lawyers and most clients, means clear liability. NOT! Even in "rear-enders," fault and/or proximate cause can be (or can be made) unclear. Ingenious claims' adjusters, defense attorneys, and their junk scientists will argue the client stopped short and/or injury was not caused by "Big Bang." In "obvious tripping hazards," the defense will be . . . the "obviousness" of said defect: the hazard was so "open and obvious" that plaintiff was careless; plaintiff was solely at fault (or sole proximate cause) for not seeing "obvious tripping/slipping/stepping hazard." In clear professional neglect cases where even freshmen law or medical students see clear deviations from well-recognized standards, the defense is "So what? . . . any alleged mistake did not cause plaintiff's damages, if any were in fact caused."

Never assume liability will be stipulated. Insofar as liability is concerned, if there are eye witnesses, preserve their testimony if possible. Have the eye witnesses, if at all possible, use scale diagrams or photographs to illustrate what they observed.

III. ASSUME THAT CAUSATION IS CLEAR AND UNCONTESTED

> "A pessimist is a lawyer who thinks a tough case can't be won. An optimist is the office manager who thinks the lawyer won't try to take the case."
> —Mike Huddy (my office manager)

Never assume because a doctor treats a host of injuries that every one of client's injury litany is, in treating doc's opinion, "probably caused by the traumatic event." It is very cost efficient and time saving when our associates, paralegals, or medical assistants contact treating doctors to determine if certain conditions are causally related.

Today's M.I.S.T. (Minor Impact Soft Tissue) defenses are used indiscriminately; you can never be certain an injury suffered in minor impact or "low property damage" auto crash will be uncontested. Vesper, "M.I.S.T.: A National Insurance Defense Strategy & How To Counter-attack, From A to Z," The Trial

Lawyer, (formerly Trial Diplomacy Journal) January-February 1999, Vol 22 No.1, p. 47-58

IV. ASSUME RELEVANT RECORDS/EXHIBITS WILL BE PRESERVED

"Always put off 'till tomorrow what you are going to make a mess of today."
—Nancy Cattie (my paralegal)

Never assume any report, photo, or record of any event will be kept for even 30 days let alone 2 years. Often, police and EMT audiotapes of radio communications are saved for limited time. Statements made over the radio by Police or EMTs can often assist in establishing liability, as well as a dramatic recreation of damages.

Most hotels and stores have security videotapes. In Atlantic City casino hotels, surveillance and security videotapes of various casino and hotel areas are usually kept 30 days. Immediately filing a Temporary Restraining Order or Order to Show Cause to preserve those tapes, a plaintiff's case can sometimes be established from defendant's own records. Do not hesitate to use presuit methods of discovery including de bene esse or "Before Action" depositions, TROs, and Orders to Show Cause. FRCP 27 (a).

V. ASSUME THE POLICE/INCIDENT REPORT IS COMPLETE, ACCURATE AND IDENTIFIES ALL WITNESSES AND ALL RELEVANT RECORDS

"Horse sense is that intuitive ability that keeps horses from betting on people."
—W.C. Fields

Often, police take photos not referred to in their reports; they talk to witnesses whose names/addresses are not reported; more often, there are witnesses with whom Police never talk because of insufficient time to do a thorough investigation.

If a case is serious to your client, serious effort should be made to "canvas the neighborhood" to find eye/earwitnesses not identified by police. Make some effort to see if "records" exist in addition to reports. "Paper trails" include: EMT/ER records, which may show how parties said events occurred; tow truck records may have scene photos; records from other officials "on scene"; newspaper, TV reporters, and photo/film crews.

VI. ASSUME ALL CLIENT HISTORIES ARE CONSISTENT

> "There are folks who make things happen, folks who watch things happen, and folks who don't have clue about what's happened!"
> —John Romano

Never assume your client was recorded/reported accurately in history or injury mechanism. Often, clients give EMT/ER/nurses/doctors or their family/treating doctors a rough sketch of events which haunts the case like Ghost of Christmas Past.

Often, misrecordings occur of what clients tell EMT or ER clerks/nurses/doctors. When histories are wrong, some effort should be made to correct them. Often, mistakes are easily explained as "typos"; other times, the record is defense's star witness. Better to know upfront if such "prior incorrect statements" exist. E.g., you must know if your client's recital of their preincident alcohol intake was recorded or any "AOB" (alcohol on breath) was observed rather than assume client's recall is accurate of sobriety at time.

VII. ASSUME THE CLIENT'S PAST MEDICAL HISTORY AND/OR LIFE EXPECTANCY ARE "NORMAL"

> "If life had a second edition, how would you correct the proofs?"
> —Mike Ferrara

Never assume because clients look healthy/young their past history is "clean" nor life expectancy "normal." Clients may have low life expectancy due to disease. Past history, esp. when claimed psychic/emotional residuals, must be studied. Costs of "prior meds" are dwarfed by time/money wasted on frivolous damage claim.

Plaintiffs with preexisting psychiatric problems will be painted with broad bias/bigotry brushes by defense. Due to preexisting psychiatric issues, current complaints will be dismissed out of hand. Unless plaintiff's prior mental health care providers are solid in their opinions as to aggravation of prior conditions, these cases are problematic.

Never assume a client has no prior claims. Attorneys can get records of prior claims from Central Insurance Index Bureau (CIB) whose telephone number is 212-669-0400. Avail yourself of that opportunity to be 100% certain of client's memories.

VIII. ASSUME ACCIDENT SCENE/SITE/INSTRUMENTALITY STAYS INTACT

> "There is nothing that can replace experience. It's the one thing that allows you to recognize a mistake when you have made it again."
> —Mike Maggiano

Never assume scenes will not change. Accident "scenes" are referred to by reconstruction experts as actual places where injuries/death occurred while vehicles and/or victims are present. "Accident site" is scene **after** vehicle(s)/victim(s) leave.

"Sites and scenes" never freeze in time. Accident sites change; fall spots in casino hotels get redecorated/replaced overnight; machines causing injury or work sites get dismantled and scrapped; amusement rides disassemble or move. If "accidents" need reconstruction, site/instrumentality must be preserved, at least, pictorially; as soon as possible, photos should be taken of site/scene; if necessary, reconstructions should be hired.

IX. ASSUME THE WITNESSES WILL REMAIN "STATIC" AND "ALIVE"

> "Nothing is quite as responsible for the good old days as a bad memory."
> —Groucho Marx

Never assume witnesses live at listed address. Witnesses move; some die. Those old or with little/no roots in town, and no reason to stay at their rental/mobile homes, should be "preserved," if possible, by pretrial video dep or signed, notarized statement.

X. ASSUME WITNESS' WRITTEN VERSIONS ARE CORRECT AS RECORDED

> "No person ever found perfect accuracy in news accounts of happenings he witnessed."
> —Walter Cronkite

Witness versions are short and incomplete. Witnesses are usually not shown scale drawings/diagrams to let them illustrate what they meant in written versions. A witness who originally believed your client was at fault may, on revisiting the scene and considering all facts, come to conclude they were wrong in their initial opinion.

Never assume favorable witnesses will stay favorable. After claims adjusters and other investigators confront a witness, the result may be inconsistent/unfavorable. Better to get first official sworn statement than to get the last version before/at trial.

XI. ASSUME YOU HAVE THE CORRECT SCALE

> "Man can never get lost on a straight road."
> —Charlie Chan

Never assume police rendered a scale drawing unless their drawing says "To Scale," and you or your investigator or expert actually corroborates accuracy of the "scale drawing." Mistaken scale can confuse all parties, all witnesses, and most trial attorneys.

In fall downs, differences in scale of few feet can be difference between good or "no cause" verdict. Photos/scale drawings for accurate models help prevent disasters with witnesses. Things out of scale can cause witnesses to be off scale and incorrect.

XII. ASSUME YOU HAVE THE RIGHT EXPERT

> "An expert came to town from an outlying village, where the people could outlie anyone else in the world!"
> —Will Rogers

Do not be fooled by CVs. I was; luckily, it did not diminish our case or verdict. One of our experts in a professional malpractice case had forged credentials! He was indicted for fraud and served a prison sentence including restitution of all expert fees.

Unless you personally know experts are who they say, you should have someone check credentials. Unless you know an expert has relevant experience, critically check their prior experience. Our friend, Mike Ferrara, has his "expert screen": explicitly asks if they have been "Daubertized," convicted, or license suspended. To avoid theoretically correct but impractical experts, I use both the well-credentialed plus "blue-collar-shirt-sleeve" experts like professional truck/bus/jitney drivers, hotel/restaurant managers, or experienced security guards. The jury gets both academia and real world proofs.

CONCLUSION

Just like cooking, you can spoil or burn or undercook anything. I am sure there are other methods and slopes to slip into instant failure in civil litigation, but like the old saying goes: "If you assume too much . . . you make an ASS of U and ME!"

un punto nel tempo non aspetti tempo

("a stitch in time save nine . . . and time")

Chapter 2. ANTIPASTI CAULDO (Hot Appetizers)

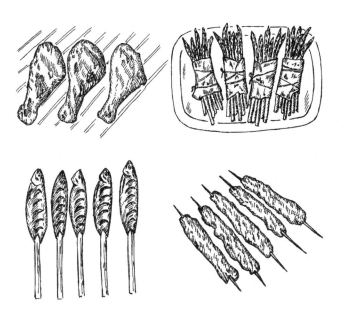

PART A. DOM'S RECIPES

BRUSHETTE
(Toasted Bread)

This appetizer is a great way to use day-old Italian bread. In villages and countrysides throughout Italy, you will find toasted day old bread with various spreads. This particular recipe makes use of garden fresh tomatoes and basil.

INGREDIENTS (Serves 4 to 6):

1 Loaf of day old Italian bread

4 or 5 Ripe tomatoes

¾ Cup fresh basil

4 or 5 Scallions

Antipasti Cauldo

4 Cloves garlic

1 Finely chopped chili pepper or red pepper flakes (optional)

Olive oil

Salt to taste

DIRECTIONS:

Slice bread about ¼ to ½" thick.

Lay bread on a sheet pan and toast it under the broiler on both sides until golden brown. Keep close watch making sure the bread does not burn.

Chop tomatoes, basil, garlic, and pepper very fine; add to a bowl.

Chop scallions and add to tomato mixture.

Add olive oil until well coated and toss until well mixed.

Put into refrigerator; after mixture has marinated in refrigerator for about an hour, spread on toast and arrange on a serving platter.

BOCCONCINI: Bruschetta's birth is in Italy (of course), but the exact region and year are unknown. Ancient Romans tested the quality of fresh-pressed olive oil by smearing it on a piece of fire-toasted bread for tasting; this custom is still practiced today. Some say oil-soaked bread was rubbed with a clove of garlic to bring out oils' flavors. Others say it's a "poor man's pannini/sandwich" for folks to revitalize stale bread with oil. The original, unadorned bruschetta was the poor man's version of garlic bread. As the hors d'oeuvre gained popularity, garlic and olive oil remained part of the recipe but the traditional Italian toppings of *alia e olio* on bruschetta were frequently replaced with sausage, cheese, pancetta, mushrooms, olive spread, and truffles.

The Vespers' Trial Cookbook

ARROSTO PEPERONE
(Roasted Peppers)

Roasted peppers are a treat when using with bread, cold meats, and in salads. My wife also uses leftover roast peppers to make pepper and egg sandwiches. They are versatile and very delicious.

INGREDIENTS (Serves 8):

6 Large Red Bell Peppers

Olive Oil

1 Clove garlic, minced

Salt to taste

DIRECTIONS:

Set pepper, stem up, on a sheet pan.

Place under broiler and broil until pepper is charred.

(NOTE: the skin of the pepper will be black in color)

Remove and place peppers in a paper bag for one hour.

Peel charred skin from pepper, cut in half, and remove stem, seeds, and ribs.

Cut in ½" strips and place in bowl, add garlic, and drizzle olive oil until well coated.

Add salt and pepper to taste; refrigerate until marinated, at least one hour.

BOCCONCINI: Peppers were found in prehistoric remains in Peru; so, peppers existed and were cultivated in Central and South America in primeval times. Columbus brought them back to Europe in 1493, and they were quickly adopted and cultivated. In fact, it was Europeans who christened their name. The only pepper known until that time was the black and white spice they sprinkled from pepper shakers. When Columbus brought dried peppers back from West Indies, Europeans said the fruit was "hotter than pepper of the Caucasus"—their table spice. The name "pepper" has stuck ever since.

In spite of similar names, our table pepper and my Cuz Dom's home grown sweet and hot peppers are not related. There are thousands of varieties of peppers, in a wide range of colors, flavors, shapes, heat levels, and sizes. From small compact plants, to giant monsters that can get over nine feet tall, with peppers ranging in size from a tiny fraction of an inch to over a foot long, and coming in nearly every color of the rainbow! Whatever color or size of "Bell Peppers" you roast or stuff—they will taste delicioso!

FRITTATA ala TOMASSO VESPER
(Vegetable Omelet)

<u>BOCCONCINI</u>: From *fritto* ("to fry"); originally a general term for cooking eggs in a skillet—from fried eggs to an omelet, to Italian equivalent of *tortilla de patatas* made with pasta instead of fried potato. Cuz Thomas thinks it's a "snack"—he eats at weird times and likes to throw leftovers into a pan. This dish is perfect if you, like Thomas, hate to throw away food. It's a thick, egg-based open omelet plus anything you like.

WHAT'S THE DIFF? There are four big differences between frittatas vs. conventional omelettes:

1. There is at least one optional ingredient in frittatas. There is no such thing as a frittata natural. Ingredients are added to beaten eggs while the eggs are still raw rather than laid over mostly cooked egg before folding like a conventional omelet. Eggs for frittata are beaten to get more air than traditional omelettes, to allow deeper filling and fluffier result.

2. The mixture is cooked over very low heat, more slowly than an omelet, at least five to fifteen minutes, until the underside is set but the top is still runny. The partly cooked frittata is not folded to enclose its contents like an omelet; instead it's either turned over in full, or grilled briefly under intense salamander to set top layer, or baked for about five minutes.

3. Unlike an omelet—generally served whole to one diner—frittata is usually divided into slices; served hot or cold, accompanied by fresh salads, bread, beans, olives, etc.

4. It's cooked very slowly in a large, usually cast-iron, frying pan and finished under a grill to set the top. The end product should be very moist.

Like one of the other popular cold recipes, *Torta di Riso* (Italian rice cakes), and lots of foods in Italy, it's often made to use up leftovers from other meals. It can be eaten for breakfast or lunch, is a popular cold picnic food recipe, and is also used for packed lunches.

This is the Tom Vesper (actually the Maggie Vesper) version of an Italian frittata recipe.

The most popular additions to the egg base are potatoes, spring onions, and cheese, but just about anything is fair game as long as it's properly cooked.

Cooking time for this recipe is short, so added ingredients will need to be cooked first.

Antipasti Cauldo

Vegetables should be diced into small pieces or, like zucchini, cut into rounds; then they should be boiled, steamed or sautéd until just tender. Maggie's recipe has mushrooms, peas and tomatoes. If using frozen vegetables (peas and sweetcorn are very good), make sure they're defrosted and lightly boiled.

If you want to add meat, make sure it's cooked, cut into small pieces, and if you want a bit more flavor, sauté meat in olive oil for a short time before adding it to the egg mixture.

Pasta can also be added as long as it is cooked and cut into pieces about an inch long. It's not unusual to find leftover cooked spaghetti as part of an Italian omelet.

Margaret Ann "Maggie" & Catherine Carmella "Catie" Vesper would EGGS-plain thus:

MAGGIE: Knock Knock

CATIE: Who's there!

MAGGIE: Four Eggs!

CATIE: Four Eggs who?

MAGGIE: Four EGGS- ample

INGREDIENTS (Serves 2 to 3):

4 Eggs (EGGS-actly enough for two)

5-6 Cherry tomatoes—halved

8-10 Button mushrooms—sliced

1 Cup green peas

Extra virgin olive oil

Salt and Pepper to taste—Paprika is optional

DIRECTIONS:

Preheat the oven.

In an oven proof frying pan, heat olive oil.

When hot, add the sliced mushrooms. Fry until the bottom is caramelised.

Add the green peas, salt, pepper and paprika and cook until done.

In a bowl, whisk the eggs with salt and pepper.

Add the egg to the pan and cook till the edges are done.

If you are using cheese, sprinkle on top.

Put the sliced tomatoes on top.

Transfer the pan to the oven and grill/bake for about four minutes or until the top is golden.

BOCCONCINI: Speaking of Italian omlettes—the fluffy omelette Americans are used to is a refined version of ancient food. The French word *omelet* came into use in mid-16th century, but *alumelle* and *alumete* in <u>Le Ménagier de Paris</u> (II, 5; or <u>Le Menagier</u>; is a French medieval guidebook for women) appeared in 1393. The "Founding Legend" of "The Annual Giant Easter Omelette of Bessières, Haute-Garonne" in Southwest France is as follows: when Napoleon Bonaparte and his army were marching about Southern France, they rested for the night near the little town of Bessières where Napoleon feasted on an omelette made by a local innkeeper. It was so good he made townspeople gather all the eggs in their village and make a huge omelette for his entire army the next day. It may not be in the Guinness' Book of World Records, but the folks in Bessieres claim "the biggest omelet in the world" is cooked every year the day after Easter.

FRITTATA ala SALSICCIA E SPINACI
(Sausage and Spinach Omlette)

INGREDIENTS (Serves 6):

2 Tbsp olive oil

4 Italian sausages, cooked and diced

3 Potatoes, diced

1 Medium onion, sliced

½ Red bell pepper, chopped

1 Cup baby spinach leaves, lightly chopped

1 Tomato, diced

8 Whole eggs

½ Cup skim milk

1/3 Cup grated parmesan cheese

½ tsp salt

¼ tsp pepper

½ tsp Mrs. Dash® garlic and herb seasoning

DIRECTIONS:

Preheat broiler.

Heat cast iron skillet with 1 Tbsp oil on stove.

Add onion and pepper; sauté over medium heat for four minutes.

Meanwhile, beat eggs, milk, and seasonings in bowl or large measuring cup.

Add potatoes to pan and salt and pepper to taste. Sauté another 6 minutes.

Add sausage to pan, sauté another minute.

Turn down heat to medium-low.

Add other Tbsp. oil, pour in egg mixture, and sprinkle spinach on top.

Cover and cook 10 minutes.

Remove lid, and with a rubber spatula, loosen egg from sides of pan.

Sprinkle tomato and cheese on top.

Put under broiler 6-8 inches from heat; broil 3-5 minutes until slightly brown and bubbly.

Cut into wedges and serve.

<u>BOCCONCINI</u>: (fra-TAT-TA in South Jersey) Cuz Dom and I have concluded that the frittata predated the French omelet. Why? Besides the fact we are admittedly, blatantly biased? The historic proof is: What could be easier than mixing vegetables or leftovers into eggs, scrambled into a meal? It just made sense to prehistoric cooks to make use of the protein in eggs as meat substitute to add to vegetables. Some historians say the word omelet comes from Roman epicure Apicius, who called his dish *"overmele,"* which was made in Ancient Rome with eggs with honey and pepper.

FRITTATA ala DOMENICO

When we were kids, a frittata was a real treat. My Nonna, grandmother Gallo, would make a HUGE Frittata in a large cast iron frying pan, thick and full of delicious meats and vegetables. I stumbled onto an Italian sandwich shop several years ago in South Philly and noticed Frittata on the menu. It was, without doubt, as good as my Nonna's. I immediately went to the cook and explained to her how delicious it was, and much to my surprise she told me her family was from the same Provincia as my grandparents. She explained to me this is the way Frittatas are made in her Provence in Italy. There are a few things you have to remember about an Italian Frittata; unlike an omelet: (A) it must be thick, about two inches, (B) it must be cooked in a 10" by 4" frying pan, and (C) you can't leave the stove until the Frittata is done.

INGREDIENTS (Serves 6 to 8):

12 Eggs beaten (add 2 Tbsp of water and your eggs will become fluffy when cooked)

½ lb. Fried Italian Sweet Sausage cut into ¼" slices

2 Medium-sized potatoes sliced into ¼" slices

1 Medium onion chopped

4 Red Bell peppers cut into strips

4 or 5 Stalks of fresh Asparagus, boiled until tender and cut into bite-size pieces

4 or 5 slices of Provolone cheese

2 Tbsp olive oil

2 Tbsp butter

Salt and Pepper to taste

DIRECTIONS:

Fry sausage in olive oil, remove, and set aside.

In the same pan you fried the sausage in, add butter and sauté potatoes, peppers, and onions and sauté on medium heat until done.

Add sliced sausage and asparagus.

Add beaten eggs.

Allow eggs to set, keep checking bottom of pan.

When eggs are set, cover pan with a round pizza pan and flip Frittata on pizza pan (this is not as difficult as it sounds, however, you must use a large enough round, flat pizza pan or plate).

Slide Frittata back into frying pan and cover top with cheese.

When cheese is melted and eggs are set at bottom, slide onto pizza pan/plate and serve.

FRITTATA ala DOMENICO, JUNIOR
("Egg Giambotta" or A Big Mess of Eggs)

There's an old Italian expression: *"hai fatto una frittata,"* which loosely translated means "you've made quite a mess" or a sequence of mistakes. Sounds a lot like what Oliver Hardy would say to Stanley Laurel or what I often say to Cuz Thomas: "well, Cuz, here's another fine mess you've gotten us into!"

This dish is my son, Dominic Junior's, favorite breakfast *giambotta* (big mess).

BASIC INGREDIENTS (Serves 6):

Use between 6-12 eggs.

8 is probably best; too many make it hard to flip unless you've cooked in Navy or Marine Corps Mess Halls.

If you have a broiler, you won't have to worry about flipping over your frittata. Just stick the pan under a low flame and remove when the frittata is golden.

Use a 10"-12" skillet or fry pan with thick bottom and round borders. A sturdy, nonstick pan makes it easier to detach the frittata without having to add extra butter or oil.

VEGETABLES: Fresh, sautéed or steamed lightly seasoned vegetables:

- Boiled or roasted potatoes
- Fresh greens
- Wild mushrooms
- Zucchini
- Asparagus
- Bell Peppers
- Artichokes

CHEESES: Good-quality cheeses are ideal for frittata:

- Melting cheeses—such as provolone, mozzarella, and emmenthal
- Parmigiano, grana, and Pecorino Romano
- Ricotta—for a lighter taste and texture

MEATS AND COLD CUTS: Cold cuts or air-cured meats:

Antipasti Cauldo

- Sopressata
- Salami
- Mortadella
- Prosciutto
- Ham

<u>BASIC DIRECTIONS:</u>

If you're not using leftovers, prepare all the ingredients to be added to your eggs by sautéing or roasting them, then put them aside and let cool. Usually, this mixture is poured into the same pan in which you sautéed your vegetables; add some more olive oil or butter before you cook the frittata.

Mix vegetables or other ingredients into your eggs, which should be salted, peppered, and lightly beaten with a fork.

Immediately pour this mixture into the hot pan; reduce heat to a moderate-to-low flame.

CAVEAT (WARNING): This next step can be tricky:

With the help of a spatula and a wooden fork, allow the upper, liquid part of the mixture to slip down below the solidified part, so all parts of the frittata are cooked.

Then, using just the spatula, lift the sides of the frittata and check that the bottom is not burning.

When you see the top is firm, pull the pan away from the flame, half cover it with a lid, and leave it that way for 30 seconds.

Shake the pan to be sure that it's not sticking to the bottom. If it does stick, gently detach it with a spatula. The frittata can now be turned over.

CORRAGIO! NON ESITATE ESSERE VELOCE! (Be brave! Do not hesitate, be quick!) If you want to use the traditional method for flipping the frittata over, you'll need to be careful and quick.

Use a flat dish larger than the pan, or a flat lid. Put one hand firmly on top of the lid and your other hand on the handle; quickly turn the whole arrangement upside down. Immediately slide the frittata—the golden-brown side will now appear on top—back into the pan to finish cooking the last few minutes.

If this is your first frittata, you may feel all your "moves" are a bit awkward, or you may find the mixture too high for the shallow pan. With "practice,

practice, practice," you will gain experience, and learn the best proportions and how to regulate the ingredients—e.g., the amount of eggs and cheese—to be sure your frittata does not wind up too dry.

This family-fun-feel-good-taste-good-and-healthy dish is worth perfecting!

<u>BOCCONCINI</u>: The Italian *"HAI FATTO UNA FRITTATA"* expression no doubt comes from the fact that it is often the case frittata is made on the spur of the moment: a last-minute decision when you don't have time to go shopping and your refrigerator seems empty. But, NONA YOU WORRY, all those odds, ends, and leftovers in your fridge can make for a great frittata. In fact, in Italy, sometimes before serving lunch or dinner, a small portion of the meal is purposely put aside for a frittata for the next day.

Cucina povera—the "humble cuisine" is what most of us innately love. Eggs are an essential part of the diet almost everywhere in the world; so, from China and Southeast Asia to Canada, from the tip of Argentina to Siberia some kind of frittata-like dish is being prepared. In Italy, mothers—and fathers!—make delicious frittate with leftover pasta (with or without sauce or seasoning). A frittata is a perfect way to entice children into eating vegetables (they're hidden); it can often be a complete meal in itself. It is usually tastier hours later, eaten at room temperature, or enjoyed the next day with a side of arugula. For a quick lunch, it can be served with sautéed greens, salami, or cheese.

If you store your frittata in the fridge, be sure to put it in an airtight plastic container as water and humidity can ruin the taste. Remember that any greens or veggies you add to your frittata should first be sautéed to eliminate most of the water. As for whether to use butter or extra-virgin olive oil, besides your personal preference, you should also consider which of those tastes marries best with the other ingredients you're using in the dish. Our personal choice—since Southern Italians use oil and not butter—is olive oil.

The Vespers' Trial Cookbook

POLENTA FRITTA
(Fried Polenta or Cornmeal)

POLENTA (we say POO-lend) is simply thick mush or cornmeal boiled into a porridge; *cucina povera* or "humble food" is eaten directly or baked, fried, or grilled. The word is from Latin *pollen* for fine flour, hulled and crushed grain/barley-meal. Typically served hot, it is a great winter-time comfort food. This recipe is a chilled, deep fried tasty change from french-fries. Follow Catie Vesper's use of extra light olive oil (not extra virgin olive oil) to fry—you'll get all the health benefits but less olive flavor in your polenta.

INGREDIENTS (Serves 8):

½ cup Extra Light Olive Oil, for frying

1 (24 oz.) Package of Instant Polenta

¼ cup Grated Parmesan

1 (25.25 oz.) Jar of Marinara sauce, warmed

Coarse Sea Salt

DIRECTIONS:

Bring 4½ cups of salted water to a rapid boil.

Add the polenta to the water by pouring slowly and stirring until mixture is thickened (this usually only takes about 1 minute).

Remove from heat.

Coat an 11" by 7" baking pan with a tsp of olive oil.

Pour cooked polenta into greased pan.

Cover and refrigerate until cold and firm, about 2 hours.

Cut the chilled polenta into 2" by 1" pieces.

In a large skillet, heat the olive oil for frying; working in small batches, fry the polenta.

Transfer the fried polenta to a serving patter. Sprinkle with salt and cheese.

Serve warm alongside any Marinara sauce or other favorite dipping sauce.

BOCCONCINI: Corn was not originally grown in Italy but came to Venice through Eastern trade routes just before Columbus discovered America in the early 1400s. Polenta was not made from corn until hundreds of years later when corn was introduced into Europe around 1650. *Pulemntum* was the staple of Roman soldiers, whose field ration consisted of two pounds of grain; they would toast the grain on a hot stone oven fire, crush it, and tuck it in their haversacks. When they had time, they would grind the grain to gruel and boil it into porridge or "mush." Soldiers could eat it in this form or let it harden into a semi-leavened cake. Over time, the basic ingredients in the preparation, millet and smelt, were replaced by barley. Polenta, when allowed to harden on a hot stone, is served as the first bread. What we know today as bread was unknown in ancient times because of poor milling methods and lack of yeast.

PART B. TOM'S TRIAL TIPS: PLEADINGS & WRITTEN DISCOVERY

AFFORDABLE APPETIZERS: CAR CRASH CASE COST CONTROL: SAVE COSTS: WAIT 'TIL YOU SEE THE WHITES OF THEIR EYES

I. INTRODUCTION AND CAVEATS

Today's computerized, Smart Phoned, i-padded pressure cooked environment see our courts demanding "instant offense"; micromanagers and Case Management Orders draw unrealistic time limits, "Lines of Death," or DEDs (Discovery End Dates) in sands of litigation. With ever escalating litigation expenses, saving pretrial costs is an absolute necessity for any plaintiff trial lawyer who has two or more cases being prepared for trial.

Let me begin with three important warnings to all practitioners: First, do not make it your primary, overriding goal to avoid costs on serious or catastrophic injury cases. When clients have serious/catastrophic injuries or suffer the ultimate injury—death—and you know a case involves substantial amounts of what is euphemistically called by some Legislatures "economic and non-economic losses," you should not artificially restrict yourself by handling such client cases on shoestrings or unreasonably limited budgets. All immediate efforts should be made to preserve relevant physical evidence—whether surveillance videotapes, vehicles, or physical evidence at scene. If you/client do not preserve critical evidence and later seek to pursue a product claim, attorney/

client may face a claim of spoliation of evidence with possible consequential liability or evidentiary problems.[1]

All efforts should be made to retain the best liability and/or causation experts whether in biomechanical or accident reconstruction fields. Remember: commercial trucking or bus accident reconstruction can be substantially different than motorcycle accident reconstruction, and both are different from a common "Car #1 vs. Car #2" auto collision case. A reconstructionist in one type crash may not be familiar with specific issues, different vehicle types. If your practice does not allow flexibility to spend money on case investigation immediately, you should seriously consider either entering into a joint venture with cocounsel who can finance such matters or referring said matters in the best interests of your client.[2] Do not take the following cost-saving advice as being a standard operating procedure or categorical imperative for all MVC cases.

Second warning to plaintiffs is some jurisdictions and judges are stricter/more conservative than others. Carefully consider procedural, evidentiary, substantive law of your jurisdiction before implementing one of my "hold your fire" trial tactics, like "shirt sleeve (non-technical) expert" or "rebuttal experts."

Our final caveat is that all personal injury trial lawyers must consider as a real "cost" the physical demands and financial burdens on them of handling an auto crash case. If you believe, as some, that a personal injury jury trial is terribly taxing on your health and "quality of life," it may be time for you to think about taking on a partner or establishing a referral relationship with a trial lawyer who is willing to pay emotional as well as financial costs for the clients if and when a trial is necessary. One remedy to alleviate excessive mental/physical costs is learn to enjoy the exercise. If you cannot develop a love for trying these cases, then at least try to learn to enjoy "the game" and improve your legal/advocacy skills from such exercises.[3]

Recognize and plan which costs can be delayed, defrayed, reduced, or avoided. This process of cost control is similar to what every infantryman learns in boot camp. It is what I was taught as a basic Marine rifleman at Parris Island: "fire control." I learned to conserve ammunition. For trial lawyers "the final

---

[1] Annotation, "Intentional spoliation of evidence, interfering with prospective civil action, as actionable," 70 ALR4th 984.

[2] "Trial By Joint Venture, Thomas J. Vesper," New Jersey Trial Lawyer, National Trial Lawyer, September 1993, p. 31.

[3] How to Be a Less-Stressed Litigator, Ashley Lipson, TRIAL, Jan 1993, V29, p. 38; Managing Stress, A.Elwork, TRIAL, Jul 1994, V30; Stress & Trial Lawyer, Can It Lead to Ethics Problems and Worse? Michael Ferrara,Jr., ATLA Paper, 1996, VII, p. 1931-40.

conflict" is trial. Therefore, saving costs until you literally see the whites of their (defense witnesses') eyes in court is how all of us should try to conserve costs in our garden variety cases. We repeat, this advice does NOT APPLY to the serious or catastrophic case where investigation costs should begin from the moment you are retained. The following are some ways to save money and cash flow in your more humble but nevertheless legitimate motor vehicle cases.

II. INVESTIGATION EXPENSES

A. Pay Now . . . Or Pay More Later

"A stitch in time saves nine" is true of personal injury cases. Many hours of wasted time and much expense can be avoided if immediate and inexpensive preliminary investigation is done to see whether or not there is a good case of liability. We cannot practice out of "armchairs." Rather than try to prove liability from a tort textbook or model jury charge, we must teach ourselves and our staffs to reconstruct and illustrate FACTUALLY "what the heck happened!" to best present our client's case to adjusters, supervisors, and/or committees of insurance claims executives or ultimately to a jury. We should be able to factually reconstruct how the crash occurred in a storyboard or caption by caption, split-second by split-second re-enactment of the collision sequence.

The time to start thinking about collision investigation is in the initial client interview. The more time you, your legal assistant, and in-house/subcontracted investigator spend getting an accurate description of circumstances surrounding and identity/whereabouts of any eye witnesses to a crash, the less time will be spent answering interrogatories, preparing for depositions, and floundering at trial for answers to liability questions.[4]

B. Get Your Entire "Team" Involved

A key to saving time and expenses is to get your staff involved in initial investigation and case screening. Any articulate, motivated adult with a sense of curiosity, camera, tape measure, and pad of witness statement forms with NCR copies can be shown how to take photos of a crash/fall-down scene, an injured client, or the damage in and outside vehicles. These skills are not mystical. The abilities to obtain accurate information or witness statements,

---

[4]Conducting Initial Interview: Deciding Which Case to Take, Rob Cartwright, Jr., ATLA Convention Paper, 1996, V. I, p. 817-824; Trial Considerations in Selecting Plaintiff's Case, Amato DeLuca, NCA College Paper, Oct 1997; Trial Considerations in Selecting a Plaintiff's Case, James R. Moriarty, NCA College Paper, March 1997.

take reusable relevant photographs, and make reasonably accurate scale drawings are skills which can be taught.[5]

Basic equipment for auto investigation is inexpensive. The 1,000 words saved by one snapshot means every PI office should have one or more cameras or dedicated i-Phones loaded and ready to photo client's injuries, outside/inside of cars, crash scenes, etc.

C. Basic Tools of Auto Crash Investigation

Here is some basic investigative equipment you should keep on hand:

- Camera & video camera (or dedicated i-Phone) with film, tripod, & lighting
- Ruler, yardstick, tape measure, measuring wheel, calculator
- Google Earth or other access to aerial photographs
- Maps, street directories, cross directories
- Modeling clay, plaster of paris, molding materials, or a carpenter's "contour gauge" for preserving and documenting impressions, holes, or elevations
- Plastic bags of various sizes and labels for evidence
- Toolbox with tools, flashlight, jack, and a "creeper" (to get under vehicles)
- Dictating machine, extra tapes, . . . and batteries
- Access to a good body/fender repair shop to document property damage
- Witness statement forms with carbon copies and instructions
- Pre-prepared diagram forms and graph paper
- Notary kit to notarize statements by witnesses
- Exhibit stickers with name, address, and telephone number of law firm
- Business cards and predrafted letters of introduction
- A written set of instructions for the investigator

---

[5]Investigating Auto Accidents, Larry Coben, TRIAL, March 1994, Vol. 30; Case Investigation, Charles Mathis, Jr., ATLA Convention Paper. 1993, Vol. I, p. 217-220.

D. Some Keys to Basic Automobile Collision Investigation

Here are basic issues to keep in mind during an auto negligence case investigation:

    Obstructions to sight lines of each driver

    "Second Impact" causes and effect

    Any cause(s) of intoxication or fatigue of each driver

    Any alleged/perceived mechanical failures causing/contributing

    Any employment, agency, or "errand" by any "at fault" driver

    Determine the POI (Point of Impact) of the vehicle

    Determine the POR (Point of Rest) of the vehicles

    Calculate time and distance for each driver from POFO (Point of First Observation) to POI (Point of Impact)

    Graph and diagram the time and distance calculations to scale

    Identify and interview all sight and sound or "eye and ear" witnesses

    Interview all police witnesses, including police photographers

    Interview all EMT and tow truck witnesses

    Canvass the "neighborhood" for any other witnesses

    Identify and reproduce all photos, video/audiotape (police/EMT tape logs) of the incident, scene, cars, victims

    Match up the client's injuries with directional forces and impacts of collision sequence

    Prepare to meet/refute the MIST (Minor Impact/Soft Tissue) defense

    Prepare to meet/refute the "Seat Belt Defense"

    Inspect and photograph all signs/signals/lines/traffic devices

    Determine the actual posted speed limit

    Determine the result of traffic violations charged

    Obtain any "admissions" by defendant at the scene, in traffic court, hospital, ER, statements to insurers, etc.

    Consider any potential Government Tort Claim Notice for unsafe road

    Determine "Prior Medical" and "Claims History" of client

Identify and preserve any "Black Box" or electronic crash data recording system which was in any of the vehicles involved

If necessary for you to reconstruct "what the heck happened?"

GO TO SCENE VIRTUALLY + ACTUALLY WITH CLIENT/ EYEWITNESS(ES) . . . AND ASAP!!

Yes, you can get a "good general overview" of the scene of a crash or a fall down by using Google Earth with client directing you to "x" spot. However, nothing substitutes for going to the actual site/scene and looking around the area for helpful "stuff."

Do not overlook the fact that police, EMTs, tow truck operators, or others on the scene, together with Emergency Room Physicians, often obtain "histories" from our clients or "other drivers" as to how the crash occurred. They also may have preserved on audio tapes their Fed.R.Evid. 801(1) "present sense impression" or 801(2) "excited utterance" from the scene. Therefore, obtain any police/EMT "tape logs" as soon as possible.

Also, do not overlook the modern fact of life that most commercial vehicles and almost all private cars/vans/SUVs are equipped with "black boxes" or electronic crash data recording systems which you must obtain, preserve, and encode in order to establish the speed and/or braking/steering conditions at the moment of impact.

III. INEXPENSIVE & HOMESPUN OR BLUE-COLLAR-SHIRT-SLEEVE EXPERT

A. Use Homespun Experts

Often, the best experts are uncredentialed but very practically experienced tradespeople—"School of Hard Knocks Expert." Caveat: in any catastrophic vehicular collision, you should not simply rely on police diagrams or police reconstruction of how collisions occur, nor should you exclusively rely on local mechanics for why brake systems or other mechanical parts fail. In a case where injuries are relatively minor and not serious, I found a welder can be as good and credible as any metallurgical/failure analyst expert or engineers . . . and a lot less costly. In a recent amusement ride tower collapse onto an amusement pier in Atlantic City, NJ, one local union welder with 30 years' experience determined and testified to the reason for the tower's collapse; to wit: over 50% of the welds were improper or nonexistent! That objective and demonstrable fact finding by an experienced welder avoided thousands of dollars in expert engineering costs in a case where the clients, by the Grace of God, sustained only sprains, strains, and shock.

The best place to find home-spun experts is often your own backyard: your own client base. Former clients, their parents, relatives, and employers have a wide range of expertise. You can develop a client database and expert database where your friends, clients, and local artisans are listed according to expertise. In auto cases where M.I.S.T. (Mild Impact Soft Tissue) defenses are raised, local body and fender repairmen with a Unibody machine that measures slight variations in body damage have the credibility and expertise to objectively explain severity of impact. At around $300, this can be just as effective as spending $3,000 for an engineer.[6]

Local community colleges are another excellent source of expertise. You will be surprised at some of the gold you will uncover in the untapped academic mines of local trade schools, community colleges, and universities. Retired professionals who teach in your local schools have a wealth of clinical and technical experience and expertise in engineering, biomechanics, medicine, and other forensic sciences.

It bears repetition: you must consider admissibility of the expert and each opinion. Any expert, including a "blue-collar, shirt sleeved, experience only," or Fed. R. Evid. 701 lay opinion witness must meet the threshold requirements of *Daubert* and *Kumho Tire*.[7]

B. Create a Revolving Cost Account

If you do not already have a line of credit or "floor plan" with some bank for your litigation costs, you should. Try to establish a line of credit for "costs" you must expend for your personal injury clients. In New Jersey, it is ethically permissible to "back charge" the client for any interest you actually pay for borrowed costs; remember, in your Retainer Agreement, to be sure you so advise your client in advance and in writing of your undertaking to borrow such costs and future pay back of any interest charged by commercial lenders.

C. Defer or Establish Credit Lines With Experts

If a case requires payment of expert fees for which you are "financially embarrassed" and unable to pay in full and "up front," then try to create an install-

---

[6]"M.I.S.T.: A National Insurance Defense Strategy & How To Counter-attack, From A to Z," Thomas J. Vesper, The Trial Lawyer, Jan-Feb 1999, V22 No.1, p. 47-58.

[7]*Daubert v. Merrell Dow Pharmaceuticals, Inc.*, 509 U.S. 579 (1993); *Kumho Tire Co., Ltd. V. Carmichael*, 526 U.S. 137 (1999).

ment plan or "credit line" with your expert. That is, try to get the expert to accept some monthly or periodic payment plan so you can obtain the expert's report, and the expert in turn can receive reasonable compensation for services rendered.

IV. DEPOSITION AND TRIAL EXHIBITS

In our practice, we find some of the best, least expensive demonstrative aides come out of "brain storming" meetings with our clients, witnesses, and people in our community. In pretrial preparation, our focus groups/mock juries with clients' and experts' input are a great source for improving "visual strategy" for trial.[8] Elementary, high school physics, college textbooks often have some of the best illustrations for explaining to a jury how an accident occurred, how an injury resulted, or how an injury is causing permanent pain.[9]

A. The Simple Answer: Use the Resources at Hand: Your Client Base

Have your office staff and clients alerted to your intended use of all resources at hand. Often, your clients, their family, friends, and relatives will have ideas for how to visually demonstrate various aspects of how the collision occurred or the resulting disabilities and losses of your client's enjoyments of life. Family albums, photographs, videotapes, and vacation souvenirs will often surface that are very useful in demonstrating to the jury the "before and after" status of the plaintiff's life, activities, and enjoyments.

B. Ten Backyard Exhibit Bargains: Dig a Little to Find Value for Your Dollars

Here is a suggested list of places to look for inexpensive demonstrative exhibits:

Google Earth: using "ground level" and a bird's eye view can give you a good idea of the area and may save time for your investigator(s); but do not use virtual reality as a lazy substitute for actually inspecting a scene yourself.

Aerial Photographs: Many municipal, county, state, and federal agencies have aerial photos of almost every square inch of their corner of the world. Also,

---

[8] Rodney Jew, "Tap the Visual Power of Your Demonstrative Evidence: Develop a Visual Strategy to Strengthen Your Case," ATLA Annual Convention Paper (1994).

[9] Cost Effective Demonstrative Evidence for New Lawyer, Linda Miller Atkinson, ATLA Convention Paper, 1993, VI, p. 951-6; Cost-Effective Demonstrative Evidence, Stephen Heninger, TRIAL, Sep 1994, V30; Cost-Effective Demonstrative Evidence, Virginia Van Valkenberg, ATLA Paper, May 1996; Creative and Innovative Ways to Use Demonstrative Evidence in Your Depositions, Michael Ferrara, ATLA Paper, Sep 1996; High Technology on a Low Budget, Donald H. Slavik, ATLA Paper, Sep 1996.

private companies will, with longitude and latitude, provide aerial photographs of almost any spot in the world.

Junkyards: Almost any type of car or car interior can be found.

Doctors' Office Handouts/Wall Hangings/Video Library: Color illustrations and videos with simple explanations of almost every operative procedure, PT, and common injury.

HO Scale Models: Almost any vehicle made can be purchased and used in miniaturized "docu-drama" video or HO scale reconstruction.

Community Colleges: Good sources for graphic artists, architectural surveyors, model builders, and medical illustrators.

Vo-Tech/Trade Schools/Unions: Good sources for inexpensive carpenters/builders of courtroom model/exhibits.

Power Point or Desktop Publishing Software: If you/staff are computer literate, make your own courtroom charts.

Enlarging Machines: Make little photographs into large court room charts.

Foam Core Board + Word Perfect: Like Jersey's line: Perfect Together, if you do not have enlargers, simply retype key testimony and make your own billboard size exhibit.

Newspaper libraries, children's book stores, and children's libraries are good sources of very understandable illustrations, maps, diagrams, etc.

V. CONSERVATION OF TRIAL COSTS aka "FIRE CONTROL"

A. Rating Your Case Inventory

At your client interview and case screening, if you rate potential range of gross value for your client's case, the costs can be assigned and predicted in a rough workable manner. You and your office manager get a rough idea of costs needed over the life of client's case. If you rate gross value of cases S, M, L, XL or Type 1, 2, 3, et seq., you can then assign reasonable ranges of expenses to help fix flexible and reasonable budget on client costs.

B. Take More "Home Videos" & Less De Bene Esse Videotaped Deps of Experts

To save trial costs and "ammo" until trial, in garden variety cases, **use nonprofessional videotaped deps** as permitted by federal and most state rules. We use our own video camera; and we **do not take de bene esse video**

deps before trial of experts. Once you video your expert and preserve testimony "in the can," you allow defense to show taped testimony to their experts. Thus, defense experts comment on your doctor's testimony. Also, videotapes (like food) get stale by time of trial. Try to convince doctor/expert to come in person or via Videoconferencing (e.g., by Courtroom Connect or Skype) during trial. As much as possible, wait until trial to schedule videotaped deps. Most judges are accommodating if doctor/expert cannot appear live, and video can be done at night after trial days. This satisfies most trial judges, but be sure to check the viability of this tactic in your trial vicinage. Scheduling your doctor thusly postpones cost until the absolute certainty trial has started, settlement is impossible, and you actually need the testimony.

C. Use Rebuttal Experts

Another cost saving plan is to use rebuttal witnesses rather than trying to anticipate and disprove defenses in your case in chief. In garden variety cases, if the defense threatens to use biomechanical/forensic experts to show injury could not have been caused, rather than trying to anticipate such a defense, use rebuttal witnesses. Use of rebuttal witnesses is an exercise in strategy requiring careful review of state/local rules. Rebuttal witnesses in some venues need not be disclosed, but if so, reports need not be supplied since their opinions depend on testimony of defense experts.[10] This tactic postpones time and costs until absolutely necessary. If defense chooses not to call its experts at trial, you do not need to prepare for and rebut them. But, remember to your due diligence whether your planned rebuttal will be permitted by your trial judge.

D. Synopsize Your Expert's Opinions

We have also found a written synopsis of what our expert has reported orally costs less and is more timely than waiting for an expert to supply a multipage typed document with appendix. In small/garden variety cases, getting oral opinions from treating doctors and having them report their opinion to you over the telephone, then synopsizing their opinion and in turn having them sign a copy of your letter to defense, is a cost-saving device and faster way to advise your adversary of the expert's proposed testimony. Depending on your court rules, you may want to consider this technique.

---

[10] "Credibility of witnesses, propriety, in federal ct action, of attack on witness' credibility by rebuttal evidence pertaining to cross-exam testimony on collateral matters," 60 ALR Fed 8; "Judicial notice, reception of evidence to contradict or rebut matters judicially noticed," 45 ALR 2d 1169.

VI. CONCLUSION

As plaintiff lawyers, we need to solve our people and dollars problems. Civil litigation should not become the "Sport of Kings" limited to the very rich. There is nothing we cannot accomplish with our collective imaginations, initiative, staff training, AAJ National Colleges of Advocacy, state TLAs and CLE, and forensic training.[11]

With the primary objective of achieving the best result for the client, it is nevertheless the case that in relatively small/medium size damages cases, it is not necessary to spend the same amount on litigation costs as in large/catastrophic cases. Central to this point is the fact that our client is a partner with us in prosecuting a lawsuit. If clients know up front their case will be handled within a reasonable budget and/or by borrowing money and by so doing you will maximize their net recovery, then such cost cutting/financing/deferring cost measures can be cooperatively conducted by you and your client.

Cost management is a judgment call for trial lawyers as to when a client's case crosses the line from one where costs should be strictly conserved to one where you should "pull out all the stops." Most cases we handle are not cost intensive. True art in personal injury trial practice is deciding which cases can be strictly cost budgeted as opposed to those which demand all our resources. I recommend as soon as possible some thoughtful and cooperative decisions be made by lawyer and client as to which of two cost allocation—1. "Damn the Torpedoes! Full Speed Ahead!" or 2. "Nice & Easy Does It"—is needed to conserve costs and still obtain the best result for client. After the art of case selection and differentiation of issues then, as always in trial, comes the true "science test" of our daily practice: the disciplined management and control of ongoing client costs.

KEEPING COSTS DOWN: EFFECTIVE WAYS TO REDUCE EXPERT COSTS

By: Dara A. Quattrone Esq., Partner, Westmoreland, Vesper, Quattrone & Beers, P.C.

INTRODUCTION

As full disclosure, I am the "fiscal conservative" among my partners. Like all good trial attorneys, I love to try cases, hate to lose, and will take no prisoners

---

[11] Beating Big Firm; How Little Guys Can Compete, G. Pillersdorf, ATLA Paper, 1995, V.I, p. 821-30; Managing Money in Office, R. Cloar, ATLA Paper, Sep 1996.

until I exhausted all avenues to assure my clients' success. How to "conserve" costs but prepare thoroughly? How to manage daily expenses of PI practice yet prepare for full frontal attack in trial? While experts are key to most premises, products, and negligent security claims, attorneys often rely on the expert's research and inspections as the only technical analysis done. That runs up case costs and may lead to erroneous conclusions. End-product expert analysis and reports will be more "Daubert proof," reliable, and less expensive by these tips:

1. INVESTIGATE YOUR CLIENTS' CASES EARLY

There is no greater first rule than to do initial fact investigation before you open your office file. Technical proofs later used by your expert to prove causation—photos of scene, preserving any perishable evidence (security video, etc.), interviewing witnesses, forensic exam of scene/product—should be done ASAP; send written demand to parties to preserve evidence and prevent spoliation. Complete medical records can be gotten months/years later—fact liability investigation can't. Don't delay! It may not seem like cost saving, but in long run, early costs insure success plus save time and costs on bad cases.

In certain cases, you may perform the initial investigation without any experts doing it. This is, provided you know what you are looking for. However, accident reconstruction and premises inspections should be done by a credible expert at earliest opportunity. We find many experts will agree to do a site inspection at reduced initial retainer if you ask. While their actual report may be months, even years away, it doesn't hurt to ask experts in advance for a reduced fee inspection and an "oral" unwritten preliminary report.

2. DO YOUR LEGAL RESEARCH BEFORE YOUR EXPERT'S WORK BEGINS

Remember that technical experts you retain are NOT legal experts. You must provide them with the legal standard within which their opinions must be formulated. The best example I can give involves the tragic death of a young man killed while walking on a sidewalk by a police vehicle, not in pursuit but on route to a call. I contacted an expert who had written "the book" about proper police procedures for pursuit who was initially impressed with the case. However, I also did the legal research and determined that the legal standard was not mere negligence but reckless conduct. Our expert then opined that he did not believe that level of conduct could be proved, and the case was declined.

3. DO YOUR OWN TECHNICAL & SOC (STANDARDS) RESEARCH

We credit the late Harry Philo, Esq. and Linda Atkinson, Esq. of Detroit, Michigan, for this recommendation. Not enough can be said for benefit of doing your own technical research. Not only do you save costs by doing so, it is really the best way to develop your trial themes and strategies. As the late Harry Philo, Esq. has pointed out, Prosser never mentioned safety in his analysis of tort law. Victim compensation is not the focus of tort law. To assure your clients will be fairly compensated for their injuries, you should not "assume" that your professional experts will know or review all applicable standards and doctrines which will most benefit your client.

Most standards are readily accessible either on the Internet or obtainable directly from trade associations or government publications.

Begin your technical research with the philosophy that any risk of serious injury or death is unacceptable if there is a reasonable means to have prevented or minimized that risk. A good starting point is industry standards themselves. All industries have their standards. This includes machinery, construction, carpets, automobiles, etc. In addition to industry minimum standards, there are government standards and professional standards to consider. Many of these standards are easily obtainable. For example:

a) BOCA (http://www.bocai.org/): this is issued every three years and defines the effective minimum requirements for safe construction.

b) ASME (www.asme.org/): American society of mechanical engineers safety standards.

c) OSHA (www.oshadata.com/): offers federal compliance and enforcement data, as well as business and consumer related databases.

d) ANSI/CE (www.safety link.com/): this site offer access to electrical product safety approval test labs and test standards.

e) CPSC (www.cpsc.gov/indexmain.html): offers recall information.

f) NHTSA (www.nhtsa.dot.gov/): air bags, crash test, and other auto related safety issues.

What you cannot get on the computer, you should be able to order directly through the associations or through a local library.

4. DETERMINE WHAT KIND OF EXPERT(S) YOU NEED

Know what kind of expert(s) you need and their costs BEFORE you undertake the case. As for "war stories," my best reason to heed this caveat comes from my experience: I was contacted by a referral source to represent a very credible man ("Mr J") who was injured on a casino elevator. Our office investigator—former casino security supervisor we call "Racehorse Russell—did a preliminary investigation and determined an incident report had been filed consistent with Mr. J's statement of events. A serious injury had been documented in the ER, the "history" was also consistent, and Mr. J had been out of work for several weeks since the "traumatic event" with no imminent return to work (RTW) date. We accepted the client referral. Should I have accepted? I put the case into suit to access documents not available presuit which would be needed by our expert. What I did not do is contact any expert early on. Later, I discovered elevator expertise is a specialty that most local P.E.s we use do not possess, and I discovered that fees for bringing the correct specialist (four hours away) to Atlantic City, NJ, for inspection and opinion would exceed 10% of the potential gross value of the case. That, in combination with our normal referral fee, made the client's case a losing proposition regardless of its outcome. Some cases are not conducive to "cutting corners"; in these cases, your initial analysis must be thorough to avoid making similar mistakes. If costs had been known in advance, both referring attorney and I could have explained this to the client up front.

To determine the technical field of the experts you need, consider the legal and factual defenses to liability and causation. Former police officers may be excellent accident reconstruction experts but not rebuttal expert to a biomechanical engineer if there are potential "lack of seatbelt," second impact, or low impact (MIST) analysis.

In a products case, if you foresee issues as to how your client used the product (assume there will be), make sure the engineer you hire has qualifications as a biomechanical humans factors/engineering expert. This type of foresight will eliminate the need to hire new rebuttal experts and incur duplicate review costs later in the litigation.

5. IN ADVANCE ESTABLISH A "BUDGET" WITH YOUR EXPERT

Some trial attorneys appear awkward discussing financial details that affect us and our clients' ultimate settlements. We should be "informed consumers" when we deal with experts; they should not have the upper hand in their role in litigation. We hire them, not the other way around. Experts have no everyday duty to us or our clients; they have a daily duty to put food on their tables. After a basic case overview, experts should be asked for anticipated fees. Based on their prior experience, this should not be difficult. Experts should also be told if anything arises by which their initial estimate is no longer justified, they are obligated to explain immediately why the initial budget can't be met.

6. DEFINE & FOCUS THE ROLE OF YOUR EXPERT

After a preliminary legal and factual case assessment leading to your decision to accept it, the initial role of the expert may be for an inspection. Once the product or property has been reviewed, experts must be told to sit back as you gather any needed facts through presuit or regular discovery. Experts do not get "gratis" standing to review anything at their discretion. A clear and defined role for scope of their review must be established.

The next phase of expert involvement comes during preparation of discovery requests and scheduling deps. Telephone calls with the expert about what documents they would like to see early on are most helpful framing discovery requests and ultimately eliminate the number of supplemental requests/interrogatories needed later in litigation. At that point, let the expert know you will be not needing their services again during the many months/years until all the requested documentation is collected. Do not "spoon feed" experts with drips of discovery. Wait to get the trial judge or case manager (judges seem to like managing vs. trying) to order all expert reports after all discovery is done. This avoids wasted expert time reviewing "partial" defense positions.

By giving your expert complete discovery and some "standards literature," you assure that you will not only get a report at less cost, but also a more effective, complete one.

7. PREPARE DOCUMENTS FOR EXPERT REVIEW

If you "throw a bunch of papers" at a reputable, well qualified expert, charging $250 to $500 per hour, you are guaranteed to pay double for "review & research" that in all likelihood was unnecessary cost probably for you paying their secretary/paralegal to collate and organize your mess of papers.

A valuable method of trial prep early in the case is my partner, Tom Vesper's, *AAJ Trial* or *Deposition Notebooks*. You/staff will have little/no problem using this system. When you send documents to your expert, prepare an index/table of contents (it may be discoverable but, so what!), eliminate duplicates, and put them in order of importance rather than the order received. Generally, we avoid giving experts our dep-summaries, which would be discoverable; but you can focus experts on relevant testimony by highlighting or underlining, and copying those pages and attaching them to transcripts. Make an exact copy of what you give experts so there is no question what was supplied/relied on by them.

We find document review time is dramatically shortened when documents are presented at one time, in concise, itemized way. If that means you/staff prepare three-ring binders of indexed documents with a complete, concise index, you save yourself and your client thousands of dollars, effectively preparing your trial notebook with your trial exhibits.

8. DEFINE FOR THE EXPERT WHAT SHOULD BE IN THE REPORT

At the point you seek an expert's report, if you gathered the standard of care documents through your technical research, the role of the expert is easily defined to say whether that legal/technical SOC was violated. Since we are not engineers or doctors, we find even after gathering applicable SOC, we can't just use them without some explanation as to relevancy. Beyond experts basing opinions on reasonable degree of probability or certainty in their field of expertise, ask the expert to clearly report the following:

1) What is the standard of care?

2) What data do you rely on to form the basis of your opinion as to what is a standard?

3) Has any "minimum safety standards been violated"? If so, which ones?

4) Has the standard of care (SOC) been violated (this is more than minimum standard)? Is there negligence or defect?

5) What facts/data do you rely on to form basis of your opinion as to negligence or defect?

6) Is there proximate cause between violation of SOC and damages sustained? Never take for granted your expert knows, by prior experience, that in products and negligence law, not only must expert opine how/why defendant's neglect caused product/premises to be unsafe; they also must define with specificity what the standard is. This is why giving experts technical research is vital. Don't let the expert or defense limit SOC to merely "what everybody else does" (unless, of course, everybody else does it better!). While SOC in general sense is reasonable care, or in product cases, to design a safe product without eliminating its usefulness, this standard should be supported with publications or "custom/practice" of the trade to avoid Daubert defenses.

9. FOCUS YOUR EXPERTS FOR ISSUES TO ADDRESS IN THEIR REPORT

At the time or very shortly after you submit documents to your expert for analysis and opinion, it is recommended you get on phone and talk with them. There is no better way to discuss strategies and perceived defense than by phone. It is also imperative you and your expert define the scope of their review and discuss the most relevant documents to utilize as the basis. For instance, as a practice, I send all dep transcripts and exhibits to an expert so there is no question as to the completeness of their basis. However, it will save the expert time, and save you costs, when you inform the expert in advance as to which transcripts are the most and least relevant to the issues they need to address.

Tell experts in advance to avoid asserting personal impressions, observations irrelevant to their findings, and lengthy recitations of facts not disputed. Reports need be clear and concise. You will not win any case because your report is longer than your adversary's.

10. READ THE EXPERT REPORT WHEN YOU GET IT

Do you find yourself going to end of reports to read conclusions? You see defendant was negligent, then elated, you forget to read the rest? Don't! When you get any report, check to make sure the expert recited a correct version of facts, a complete account of things reviewed, a citation of all relevant industry, government standards, and "guidelines" reviewed. Most important, the report provides an opinion and reasoning as to proximate cause. Some states say preliminary and draft reports are discoverable (Federal Rules do not); I have never heard a case lost because an expert corrected some typographical error within 24-48 hours of initial preparation; but I have seen cases lost where there was no expressed opinions of proximate cause and/or the expert failed to give either factual or scientific basis for opinions asserted, and therefore, "net opinion" was barred.

The best experts may not be the best writers. Never assume your engineer, recon, or other technical experts have mastered the judicial nuances of writing a comprehensive report. The faster any misquotes or misstatements are fixed, the better they and you will be.

11. CONSIDER ORAL REPORTS, ESPECIALLY AS REBUTTAL

When defense expert reports arrive, be sure your experts review, read, analyze, and have a chance to rebut defense's positions. Avoid sending documents without clear orders. If defense expert cites different standards/authorities than your expert, get them. ASAP! If contradicted fact, get relevant data to your expert for analysis. This often occurs in wage loss cases where your expert opines total disability, and defense argues less impairment. Don't wait for trial to find your expert willing to concede lower percentages and, if not, why. Once you get relevant added data, send defense report at same time for comment.

Most courts allow rebuttal but not when rebuttal testimony is merely an expert's response to defense expert testimony. Check local rules/law as to legal prerequisites for rebuttal. Questions to your expert may be simply: "Is there anything in defense report that needs rebuttal?" If yes, consider submitting rebuttals in form of a report summary.

Most courts allow attorneys to synopsize in letter an oral opinion in lieu of a full-blown expert report. This is useful when seeking rebuttal not needing recitation of everything previously reviewed and more analysis. It is less costly since you can get opinions by quick phone call, and your staff types it for expert signature. It helps to fax/email the proposed synopsis to expert and ask they sign an acknowledgment form.

12. CONSIDER USING "BLUE-COLLAR-SHIRT SLEEVE" EXPERT IN CONJUNCTION WITH THE "PEDIGREED PROFESSIONAL" EXPERT

In a wrongful death of an innocent driver, decapitated when a load of improperly loaded and fastened wood on a long bed tailor fell off and struck his car, a defense professional engineer gave testimony in quantum mechanics and energy kinematics to explain, but the federal judge and jury were most impressed with an Italian immigrant with a grade school education who was responsible for the truck fleet at a local lumber company. He had no degrees; what Sergio did have was 30 years "hands on" experience loading and directing others loading lumber onto trucks. He gave the jury a clear explanation how and why defendant's truck was loaded wrong. It was that simple. Millions of dollars later, we are happy we hired that yard foreman to explain that simple fact to the jury.

CONCLUSION

A separate book is needed for techniques of expert dep and trial prep; but to save costs, expert prep for dep/trial is not an area to cut corners. Always meet with your expert prior to their testimony with enough time to discuss the issues that will arise. With experts of little experience, try to meet at least day before the dep to review facts and opinions but most importantly legal standards to give opinions. Even experienced experts do not often grasp "possible vs. probable" difference. It is common nonlegal talk to call one's ideas "personal," but experts must be warned to refer to their opinions as **"professional NOT PERSONAL opinions"** in the strictest, fine-pointed formalized, legal jargon.

Like buying food for your family, you can save money without sacrificing quality. Fees are integral in most litigation, but I do not believe "get what you pay for" with experts. Effective cost reduction methods such as those I proposed not only help defray the ever increasing consultation costs trial attorneys must incur in our profession/business but my suggestions also guarantee a most definitive and sound report in the end.

De scegliere le parole giuste e il corretto –è molto importante!

("to choose the right and proper words and phrases is very important")

Chapter 3. ZUPPA (Soup)

PART A. DOM'S RECIPES

PASTA E FAGIOLE
(Pasta and Beans)

When we were kids we didn't eat meat every meal, not because we couldn't afford it, but because this was a traditional rustic meal. We ate this on Fridays because when we were growing up, Catholics were forbidden to eat meat on Friday. That church law was changed, but Tom and I still like a big bowl of Pasta e Fagiole for a Friday night dinner.

INGREDIENTS (Serves 6 to 8):

1 lb. Dry Cannellini or Great Northern Beans

1 (28 oz.) Can of Italian crushed tomatoes

Zuppa

½ lb. Orecchietti (pasta) cooked *al dente*

1 Clove garlic, minced

1 cup Chopped carrots

1 cup Chopped celery

1 Onion chopped

1 Tbsp Dry oregano

1 Tbsp Italian seasoning

Salt and pepper to taste

DIRECTIONS:

Soak beans overnight according to directions on package.

Drain and wash beans; cook in 3 quarts of salted water in covered pot for about one hour.

Add tomatoes, garlic, carrots, celery, and onion to beans; cook for one hour.

Add cooked pasta, oregano, Italian seasoning, salt, pepper; cook for another 15 minutes.

Taste and adjust seasonings and serve hot with grated cheese and Italian bread.

BOCCONCINI: *Fagiole* means "bean;" *fagiolini* means little beans. Pasta and beans, starch and protein all in one dish. Like lots of Italian favorites, this dish started as a "peasant dish" and it is our ultimate "comfort food." Often called "Pasta Fazool," there is musical reference for Dean Martin fans—his song: *"That's Amore"* has a verse: "When the stars make you drool just like pasta fazool."

PASTA E CECI
(Chickpeas or Ceci Beans and Pasta)

Ceci E Pasta was another Friday night dinner in our house when I was growing up. It was inexpensive to make, and with a good loaf of Italian bread and a glass of red wine, it was very satisfying. In some parts of Italy, this dish is prepared thicker with red sauce and served as a pasta course.

INGREDIENTS (Serves 4 to 6):

1 (12 oz.) Can of chickpeas, garbanzo beans, or ceci beans

1 (12 oz.) Can of chicken broth (home made is better)

½ Onion diced

½ Clove minced garlic

1 Tbsp Oregano

1 Tbsp Italian seasonings

1 Tbsp Basil

1 lb. Ditalini (or any small pasta you prefer)

2 Tbsp Olive oil

Salt and pepper to taste

DIRECTIONS:

Sauté onion and garlic in a heavy pot until they are wilted. Add broth and seasonings and cook for 10 minutes.

Cook pasta in boiling water until al dente; reserve pasta water and set aside.

Add chickpeas and cook for 10 more minutes.

Add cooked pasta to broth mixture and let these flavors marry for about five minutes.

If needed, add a cup of pasta water.

Serve with grated Pecorino Romano cheese and red pepper flakes.

BOCCONCINI: This soup dates back to ancient Roman times; in fact, Romans love it so much, they even enjoy eating it *freddo* (cold) during the summer. Every region and corner of Italy has its own version of this true everyman soup, which transcends class and season, a soup to nourish and sustain all. Someone called it "the Steve Buscemi of Soups" because it, like Buscemi "is a bit of a legend, but so low key you take him for granted, but love him so much more than all the fancy pants hogging the limelight."

ZUPPA DI SPINACI E RISO
(Spinach and Rice Soup)

This is a simple recipe but requires good homemade broth and fresh spinach. This is an example of another very humble dish enjoyed by Italians in small villages. I usually serve this dish on New Year's Day with roast pork.

INGREDIENTS (Serves 6 to 8):

4 quarts Water

2 or 3 Beef bones

½ Onion, chopped

1 lb. Fresh spinach

3 Stalks celery

3 Carrots diced

2 cups Boiled rice

Salt and pepper to taste

DIRECTIONS:

In a large pot, add beef bones, onion, celery, and carrots to 4 qts of water.

Cover and cook for 1½ hours over low flame.

Remove beef bones and set aside.

Steam spinach until tender.

Chop spinach and add to broth.

Add cooked rice to broth.

If there is any meat on the bones, remove to discard any fat and gristle.

Chop meat and add to broth and cook soup for 15 minutes.

Serve hot with grated Pecorino Romano cheese.

BOCCONCINI: KNOW YOUR RISO, RISOTTO, FROM YOUR RISONI & ORZO

Rice, riso, and risotto are grown grains. *Risoni* and *orzo* are pasta; *Orzo* (Italian for "barley" from Latin *hordeum*), and *risoni* (Italian for "big rice") are a form of short-cut pasta, shaped like grains of rice. *Riso* is the rice, *risotto* is the dish of rice.

A little History of Riso in Italy: exactly when rice was first introduced to Italy is hard to say. The best estimate is during the late middle Ages, around the 14th century. Rice got to Italy from trade with the East, probably on trading ships of Venetian or Genoese merchants. Rice quickly became a staple in the Po valley and spread to every part of Italy but never took such strong a hold as in Lombardy, Piedmonte, and the Veneto.

Types of Italian Rice: Italy grows short, barrel shaped rice; it is different from long-grain rice. Italians have four categories of riso based on grain size: comune, semifino, fino, and superfino. The superfino rice is the type most use for risotto, with Arborio being the most recognized outside of Italy.

Risotto: Risotto is an Italian rice dish made by briefly sautéing the rice in olive oil or butter (often with some onion), then adding a little bit of stock, stirring constantly until the rice absorbs the stock, then adding a bit more stock, stirring, adding, stirring, adding, until it's done. It usually takes between 20 and 30 minutes of stirring. When it's done, the rice is cooked through and bound in a wonderful creamy sauce that is made as the starch leaks out of the rice grains and combines with the stock. Risotto is best made with short and medium-grain rice, which is stickier than long-grain rice varieties. Three varieties are best suited to making risotto: Arborio, Carnaroli, and Vialone Nano. These produce the creamiest results. Of the three, Arborio, is the only one that is widely available in grocery stores in the United States.

Risotto alla Milanese is a famous Italian rice dish flavored with saffron. It resembles Spanish *paella*, which makes sense due to the Spanish rulership over Milan for nearly two centuries. In Piedmonte, it is not unusual to find risotto with truffles or red Barolo wine; in the Veneto—especially in City of Venice—seafood risotto is a mainstay, with risotto with sauteed eels a Christmas tradition. Risotto is very versatile and goes just as well flavored with cuttlefish ink (*Nero di Sepia*) or ham (*Prosciutto di San Danielle*) or butter and Parmigiano-Reggiano added just before serving (*Risotto Mantecato*), or wildfowl (*Risotto con la Quaglie*), or with plain old peas (*Risi e Bisi* or "rice and peas" which is a Veneto spring dish, flavored with pancetta). Whatever ingredients you and your family choose, cooking with riso or risotto will blend infinite flavor choices into one incredibly flavorful dish.

MINESTRONE CON POLPETTE
(Thick Vegetable Soup with Meatballs)

This is a very hearty soup and could serve as a main dish soup. At home we serve main-dish soups very frequently in the winter months.

INGREDIENTS (Serves 6 to 8):

1½ lbs Ground beef

½ cup Dry bread crumbs

1 egg

1 tsp Salt

½ tsp Pepper

2 Sprigs of fresh parsley, chopped

2 Tbsp Olive oil

8 cups Beef broth (you can use homemade, canned, or bouillon cubes)

1 (15 oz.) Can crushed tomatoes

1 Large onion, chopped

1 cup Carrots, sliced

1 cup Celery, sliced

1 Tbsp Oregano

1 Tbsp Basil

1 (15oz.) Can Cannelloni beans

½ lb. Orecchiette pasta, cooked al dente and drained

Salt and pepper to taste

DIRECTIONS:

Mix together beef, egg, bread crumbs, salt, pepper, and parsley.

Shape beef mixture into 1" meatballs.

Heat oil in a soup pot and brown meatballs; remove and set aside.

Add onion and sauté until limp; add beef broth, crushed tomatoes, beans, oregano, and basil.

Cover and simmer for 10 minutes.

Add celery and carrots and simmer until tender.

Salt and pepper to taste.

Add meatballs and pasta and heat through; about 5 minutes served hot with grated Pecorino Romano cheese.

BOCCONCINI: *"Polpetta"* is from "pulp" or *pulte*, ancient simple Roman porridge of spelt flour cooked in salt water; it morphed to describe any edible "ball," esp. meatball. Italian meatballs usually are main courses or in soup. Most are golf ball size, but where we come from—Abruzzo region, especially in Province of Teramo—meatballs are marble-size, called *polpettine*. *Minestrone*: The word for a thick vegetable soup, is from Italian *minestrone*, a form of *minestra*, "soup," or literally, "that which is served," from *minestrare*, "to serve."

My Aunt Mary Carlo from Brooklyn used to have a favorite saying about this soup: "May yer marriage be like **MINESTRONE or 'WEDDING SOUP'!**"

PART B. TOM'S TRIAL TIPS: TAKING DEPOSITIONS

Stir, Scoop Up, & Laddle Out Everything from Depositions: Innovative "New Wave" Techniques for Discovery & Deps

By: Tom Vesper & Mark Kosieradzki, coauthors of the AAJ Deposition Notebook
(With Special, Outstanding Written Assistance by: Phillip Miller & Paul Scoptur)

DEPOSING ADVERSE LAY & EXPERT WITNESSES: A DOZEN DO'S & DON'TS FROM A PLAINTIFF TRIAL LAWYER

INTRODUCTION TO "THE ART OF PLANNING, PREPPING & COOKING A DISCOVERY DEP"

Just as all trial lawyers, like all good cooks, have their own individual styles, each trial attorney develops a personal style for planning, preparing, then taking and defending discovery or de bene esse depositions. Notwithstanding this personalized or customized concept of conducting discovery, there are some basic methods and practical deposition procedures I believe can, and in some cases should, be adopted, adjusted, and applied by plaintiff trial attorneys in approaching and taking depositions of any adverse witnesses. These dozen tips are not "hard and fast" rules although the first five "do's and don'ts" do come pretty darn close to commandments in my law office.

I. DO PLAN, "CEREBRATE," AND FOCUS FOR EVERY DEP—DON'T JUST "WING IT!"

Whether you jot down a one page outline of ideas/issues/problems or whether you dig into the form books for a whole string of topics and/or reams of questions to be asked, you should have an overall discovery plan and an individual plan for each deposition you attend. Before you send out a notice for deposition, and certainly before you actually enter a deposition, you should have a "game plan" or written outline of objectives you seek to achieve at that particular deposition. As former ATLA President Ted Koskoff used to say: "Cerebrate! Think about the case!"

Without a general discovery plan and specific dep plan, you are risking too much wasted time and money. Without a plan, you may not focus on and achieve the definitive admissions or concessions you should. Without an evolving overall discovery strategy, you may lose sight of polestar objectives to achieve a fair resolution of your client's case.

As a suggestion, your deposition plan should be based upon the applicable law of the case you are prosecuting or defending. For example, in an auto collision case, the negligence of the defendant driver must be established. Therefore, you need to research all elements of the Model Jury Charges, as well as any other applicable statutory or case law. Establish a factual outline for questioning the defendant driver as to whether the rules of the road and/or the applicable law was/were followed or ignored. Also, review the up-to-date pleadings and factual discovery to prepare a factual chronology.

Likewise, in a fall-down case, when control of the property as well as reasonable maintenance are in question, you should prepare, by way of outline, a series of questions under each topic that will give a factual basis for establishing that the defendant owner and/or lessor and/or user of that particular property had some responsibility (legal duty) for and knew or should have known of the dangerous condition.

Three simple predeposition techniques and forms will improve any deposition:

A. **MAKE & UPDATE YOUR PLAN.** Write down and then put your

General-Overall Discovery Plan into the AAJ Deposition Notebook, or your own three-ring binder, or dep folder and refer to it before and after every discovery step.

B. **SPECIFY WHAT YOU WANT.** As my cousin Dom would say, "Call yer shots!" Put your deposition issues, areas of inquiry, or "contentions" into your "Death Star" Dep Notice (see below) so the witness and the defending attorneys know what "writings," documents, or things you want them to bring and also what issues you want them to be prepared to discuss. Thus, your Dep Notice also becomes your deposition outline to use to interrogate the witness.

C. **HAVE "THE GROUND RULES" HANDY.** Bring the Civil Practice Rules of Procedure with you, or prepare a "LIST OF COMMON DEP PROBLEMS" as the one contained in AAJ Deposition Notebook, or (better yet) include the "Ground Rules" or Dep Protocols and methods/penalties to address discovery abuses in your dep notices—type rules and sanctions into your Dep Notice. This may add a few pages and raise some eyebrows among your adversarial colleagues, but when a witness is told "Don't answer that" by a defending lawyer, and you cite to and direct the witness and lawyer to "re-read the Rule" that specifically forbids such conduct, your multipage dep notice will manifest its worth. (See below "DEP GROUND RULES or PROTOCOLS.")

II. DO PLAN "AFTER ACTIONS"—DON'T THINK "ALL'S WELL/ENDS WELL" AFTER DEPS!

I strongly recommend not only planning an outline of things to do for taking a deposition, but trial lawyers should also plan what they and their staff are going to do with the "stuff" produced after a deposition has been taken. Such an "after action/follow up" plan includes where the original deposition transcripts and/or copies are physically to be placed in the file or an archive; whether the lawyer, paralegal, or secretary is going to synopsize and/or digest the deposition transcript; where are the original exhibits and/or copies to be placed; and how to handle requests made at depositions. A dep synopsis or summary is simply a succinct restatement of key testimony. Synopsized deps are usually done with few sentences of verbatim testimony representing each page. Using a synopsis/summary for a large deposition transcript can enable the trial lawyer to "scan" quickly by reviewing several pages of summarized testimony.

A deposition digest on the other hand is a keyword index of issues and/or words and/or phrases that come up during the course of discovery. Such a case specific digest can be useful when a particular topic is discussed by a witness. It can be referred to by use of the digest. Then, as inconsistent statements are made by a witness during trial, the trial attorney can quickly confront the witness by use of the digest. The deposition digest addresses specific issues or keywords and phrases as opposed to a chronological synopsis of everything the witness has said in the order in which the witness said it.

Another after action item to plan for is what to do with exhibits that are marked, identified, and discussed during deposition. Copies should be attached to the transcripts by the court reporter. If they are not, some after action method needs to be put into place to insure that all deposition exhibits have been completely and accurately attached or cross-referenced for easy access before and during a trial. Whether you use three-ring deposition notebooks or duo-prong folders, some standard system should be employed.

III. DO PLAN TRIAL EXHIBITS BEFORE, DURING, AND AFTER DEPOSITION—DON'T AD LIB!

It can become important when a key witness is deposed that some visualization of that witness' testimony be prepared for trial. If you intend to use or discredit an important fact or expert witness, some tangible exhibit should be prepared so the jury can easily understand the point which is contested. For example, if the defendant driver is to be confronted with the fact that he had time and distance to avoid the collision, it may be necessary to prepare a scale diagram or an aerial photograph, or series photographs, to show the defendant driver during deposition. The defendant driver's "visualized" testimony can then be preserved to easily present to the jury at trial. If the defendant has made a prior inconsistent statement and at deposition is confronted with such statement, that prior statement should be marked and the inconsistency highlighted. At trial, such an exhibit can be enlarged and shown to the jury. Likewise with experts, if an expert opinion can be graphically illustrated and shown to be unscientific or ridiculous, do so at the deposition so that such exhibit can save time and effort for the jury at trial.

IV. DO ORGANIZE—DON'T JUST DHOW UP WITH A LEGAL PAD!

Whether you use folders, three-ring binders, or ATLA's Deposition Notebooks (see Tom Vesper, "What to Pack Up in Your 'Ole Kit Bag' for Discovery and Trial," Vol 25, 25th Special Anniversary Issue, American Journal of Trial Advocacy, Summer 2002, 1-25), you should try as best you can to organize all the necessary "dep stuff"—Q & A outlines, reference materials, exhibits, documents, witness statements, photos, pleadings, interrogatory answers, expert reports, etc.—into one reasonably usable mode of operation for the upcoming deposition and also for any follow-up depositions. It will make your discovery deposition much more effective if you have the materials and notes you need at your fingertips for instant use.

Especially in confrontation with an adverse witness, the organization of exhibits or documents needed to visualize, solidify, attack, or destroy the witness' recollection, opinion, methodology, or basis for opinion must be retrievable and at hand for instant use. To delay or cause a "time out" because an important document can not be found can destroy the rhythm of the examination. To not have the necessary photo/diagram for the witness to draw upon usually results with a marginally useful handmade, crossed out, smudged up pen or ink drawing. To not have readily available an interrogatory question/answer with which to confront the witness sends the message to both witness and the defending attorney that you are not prepared and not paying serious attention to this matter. Psychologically, as well as professionally, the better organized you are, the better the deposition will go for you, the examiner.

V. DO GO TO SCENES AND LEARN EXPERT'S "FIELD OF PLAY"—DON'T ASSUME ANYTHING!

To avoid the "Domino Effect of Depositions"—one bad, useless deposition falling into and after another bad, useless deposition—always go to the scene of the car crash, fall, or incident if at all possible in order to understand the area where the adverse witness was located. If the witness is an expert, always try to understand the "field of play." That is, like a chess match, you must know what resources the expert has at hand and what "moves" or opinions have been rendered and what "attacks" or criticisms are being made by the expert about your client's case or your expert's opinions. Therefore, you need to know the terminology used, the facts and authorities relied upon, and the methodology(s) employed by the expert to arrive at the ultimate conclusions. If the expert's foundational basis are incomplete, or include factual items or authoritative references which are not in your expert's possession, you must know and understand whether such "deficiencies" are relevant and significant. E.g., sometimes, a defense expert will conduct an ex parte test or demonstration, which may be very effective in trial if it is not rebutted. If an expert has a stronger or more supportable analysis or conclusion, you must decide how such an "imbalance of power" will effect your client's case. See below Tom Vesper, "When Your Ship Is Sinking: The Domino Theory of Depositions," Trial, July 1995.

VI. DO TAKE VIDEO DEPOSITIONS—DON'T OVERLOOK THE WITNESS' DEMEANOR!

I have come to believe in the principle I first heard expressed by my fellow trial lawyer, John Romano, to wit: important witnesses and sometimes even critical experts should be deposed and their demeanor and testimony captured on video. Videotaping often preserves their demeanor for the jury and the claims adjuster. It can also emphasize and dramatize the defendant's admission or concession. That is, the manner in which a witness or party admits fault or even refuses to admit fault may be shown and have much more effect upon the jury than simply reading a cold transcript.

By videotaping liability and damages witnesses in a catastrophic injury or death case, the adjuster can be sent the "video highlights" in the form of a videotape settlement brochure. I have found this to be very effective and instrumental in resolving cases.

In a recent trial, I know the majority of jurors were not at all satisfied with the cold reading of the deposition transcript of the defendant driver. They told the trial judge after their verdict that they would have preferred to have either seen the defendant testify live or on videotape. Remember that many younger jurors and even some of the older jurors today have become so impressed with TV news and "news magazines" that unless you have "film highlights" to show, they quickly become disinterested in what seems like a "sermon" or poetry "reading."

VII. DO PIN DOWN AND "EXHAUST" THE WITNESS—DON'T LET 'EM RUN 'N HIDE!

I learned from the AAJ Deposition Colleges that the key to getting a witness to divulge everything the witness knows is to be persistent and simply ask the deponent as to any specific point the following "Exhaustion Technique" or "Pin Down Questions":

Question 1: Have your told me everything you know about (X)?
Question 2: Regardless of the source, that is, from anything anyone has told you or anything you have read or anything you have sensed with your own personal observations, have you told me everything that you know about (X)?

Question 3: Now that you have told me everything you know, regardless of the source of your knowledge about (X), is there any person that could provide you with more information about (X)? If so, identify that person.

Question 4: Is there anything that you could look at that would provide you with more information about (X)?

Question 5: Is there any writing that you could read or look at that would provide you with more information about (X)?

Asking a witness whether there is any person, thing, or writing that could provide additional, or perhaps more accurate, information, you do two important things: you are providing yourself with other possible avenues of discovery if the witness reveals another possible source of information, or you are forever sealing that witness off from the claim there was something/someone else to have helped refresh recollection. Sealing off and pinning the witness down is very important in some cases to avoid surprises at trial.

VIII. DO SEPARATE FACTS FROM OPINIONS—DON'T LET 'EM FUDGE!

If a lay witness is testifying, be sure the deponent's testimony is factual and based on what the witness has sensed with his or her own five senses. If the witness is offering any conclusion, opinion, or summarization of what the witness claims to have observed, then you should try to separate the witness' opinion and/or reconstruction from the actual facts. E.g., if a witness gives an opinion that the defendant driver was not speeding or not driving carelessly, you need to separate that conclusion/opinion from factual observations the witness made. The lay opinion may or may not be admissible, but you must identify and delineate all opinions a lay witness holds or may offer to decide whether to use them affirmatively or defeat them if such opinions are unfounded and/or inadmissible.

IX. DO NAIL DOWN AND TOUCH ALL BASES—DON'T LEAVE 'EM ANY ESCAPE HATCH!

Whether a lay or expert witness gives an opinion, you must be persistent and be sure to enumerate every one of the facts, authorities, or other supports for their opinions.

I have found that a good technique to use when a witness gives an opinion is to actually make a list, show it to the witness to adopt, and mark it as a deposition exhibit. E.g., if a lay witness says the defendant driver was not speeding, I ask them to enumerate for me on a piece of paper all their reasons for saying such a thing. Sometimes, I write out this "laundry list" for them to expedite the deposition. After I have numbered each item, such as: 1) "I saw the car for a split second"; 2) "In that split second, I saw the car go from point A to point B"; 3) "I judged that going from point A to point B in that split second would have been in excess of 50 MPH"; and 4) "I have experience in gauging speeds because I was/am a traffic police officer, etc." After making a list of some or all of the facts, rationalizations, or reasons why they believe they have given an accurate opinion, I then sometimes list all the reasons why they could be wrong: 1) They were very excited; 2) They were distracted by doing something else at the moment their attention was drawn to the defendant's car; 3) They never rechecked any of their opinions and/or calculations; and 4) They really have never done anything like that before or since.

With expert witnesses, it is even more important that you be persistent and establish all of the facts or authoritative sources which form the foundation for their opinions. I strongly believe it is a good deposition exercise to have the expert follow along as you number each of the facts they claim support each of their specific opinions. Also ask them to enumerate and cite any and all authorities that support their methodology or opinions. Only by creating this 1, 2, 3, 4, 5 et seq. itemized list can your own experts and/or your rebuttal experts take apart the deponent's opinion. Sometimes, the very list you mark as an exhibit forms the model for showing the jury how wrong the witness was. To do this analysis brick-by-brick or point-by-point requires some perseverance by you in the deposition.

X. DO USE BRACKETING—DON'T LET 'EM EVADE ESTIMATING ANY MEASUREMENTS!

Whenever an adverse witness refuses to give an estimate or honestly struggles with a question that requires some type of measurement, you must try to "bracket" the witness. That is, whenever any witness says: "I just don't know how far the plaintiff's car was from me when I first saw it." Just ask for an outside and then an inside number, that is, a maximum and a minimum range. For example: "Well, I understand you don't know exactly how far in feet or in inches, but was it more than one foot? . . . more than one car length? . . . more than two car lengths? . . ." By extending up from a ridiculously low number the witness will ultimately give a reasonable estimate. Likewise, starting at an unreasonably high number and working down will also push the witness into giving up an estimate. Example: "You say you don't know how much income you earn from doing defense examinations for insurance companies, doctor? Well, let me ask, do you think you make $10 million? . . . what about $5 million? . . . what about $1 million? . . ."

It is virtually impossible for any person to avoid being bracketed between some high-low numbers. And the more they resist answering, the more ridiculous they become. Example: "You mean, sir, you can't tell us whether the time that elapsed between when you saw the plaintiff and the collision was more than one second . . . or less than one hour?" Usually, when the witness realizes he/she is in a vise-like stranglehold, they will concede that "I have no idea," or "I just do not know."

XI. DO USE DOCUMENTS TO CORRAL WITNESSES—DON'T LET 'EM FORGET!

It is often helpful to have prior statements the witness has given or, in the case of experts, prior articles or testimony which that expert has rendered in order to reign in the witness at deposition. By getting as much written material in advance of the dep as you possibly can, you may find some invaluable prior statement, writing, or publication which can be used to establish that the witness on a specific point is either being less than candid or totally inconsistent. For example, in the garden variety auto collision case, a statement to a police officer contained in a report or a signed or recorded statement to the claims adjuster, although not in writing, which the defendant driver now is refusing to admit was made or is being recanted can usually raise a credibility issue to be resolved about the defendant driver. Most police officers, investigators, and hopefully jurors recognize that statements made at the scene, with little time to reflect, are usually the most honest and accurate impressions a witness has about the events recalled. Likewise, in a products liability case, a prior article or advertisement from a manufacturer or manufacturer's representative to the effect that all possible considerations for a user's safety were taken into account can be used when confronting either the defendant expert or the defendant's corporate representative.

XII. DO SAVE SOME THINGS FOR TRIAL—BUT . . . DON'T SAVE EVERYTHING!

In every case, there are golden nuggets of information or impeachment material that is or may be unknown to the defense. Plaintiff trial lawyers should give some careful thought to conduct the dep in such a manner as to get maximum mileage out of these points with the adverse witness. You should consider letting the adverse witness climb out on a limb, which you might not want to saw off at the dep but rather wait for trial.

However, it may be that you or trial counsel will not get a chance to expose the adverse witness in as dramatic a fashion again because, by trial, the witness or defense may figure out what you were getting at with your dep line of questioning. Especially if you are taking a video deposition of an adverse witness, and the facial expressions or demeanor of the witness will definitely register surprise, anger, or some noticeable and discrediting reaction/emotion which will be apparent to the jury, then such a "golden moment" should not be postponed for the witness to be better prepared to be confronted. You may be able to generate a crisp, concise, and understandable series of questions where you can clearly demonstrate to the jury that the adverse witness testified falsely in the deposition. This approach may be tactically superior if available to you.

SELECTED BIBLIOGRAPHY

Atkinson, Linda Miller, "Depositions," Chapter 18, Vol 2, ATLA's Litigating Tort Cases, Thomson Reuters (2013).

Blackwell, Jerry and Burt, Ryan, "Keeping Discovery Focused: Budget Concerns and Theme Development," ATLA Seminar Paper, 1998 Winter Convention.

Fitzgerald, "Making a Record—How to Corral the Opposing Witness," ATLA Annual Convention Paper (1998).

Feldman, Michael H., "Winning Strategies for Deposing the Adverse Expert," Trial Magazine, January 2000, p. 83-87.

Hailey, Richard D., "Taking Witnesses to the Woodshed: Preparing Clients, Lay, and Expert Witnesses for Deposition and Trial," ATLA Annual Convention Paper (1994).

Hare, et al, Full Disclosure—Combating, Stonewalling and Other Discovery Abuses, (ATLA Press 1995).

Herr, David and Kempf, Richard, "Discovery of E-Email and Other Electronic Nuggets Buried in Your Opponent's Computer," The Trial Lawyer, Vol. 21, p. 374-379 (1998).

Kosieradzki, Mark, "Disarming the Rambo Litigator," AAJ Deposition College (1999).

Krehel, Greg, "Using Chronologies to Win Cases: Best Practices," The Trial Lawyer, Vol. 22, p. 334-340 (1999).

Lees, James, "Deposition Psychology: Channeling the Witness," ATLA Conv. (1997).

McLarty, Mary Alice, "Videotaped Depositions: When, Why and How" ATLA (1998).

Romano, John F., "From the Editor: Helpful Hints on Deposing Expert Witnesses," The Trial Lawyer, Vol. 22, pgs. 393-395 (1999).

Smalley, Bernard W., "Positioning Your Client and Witnesses: Witness Preparation and Control; What Say Can and Will be Used Against You," ATLA Convention (1998).

Starr, V. Hale, "Preparing Witnesses for Discovery and Deposition," Trial Diplomacy Journal, Vol. 21, p. 139-149 (1998).

Sykes, Robert B., "Abusive Deposition Tactics," Trial Magazine, pg. 30, (Sept. 1999).

Vesper, Thomas J. & Kosieradzki, Mark, The AAJ Deposition Notebook, 5th Edition, Thomson Reuters (2012).

Vesper, Thomas J., "10 Tips for Effective Depositions," Trial, August 2000, p. 36-39.

Vesper, Thomas J., "Deposing Defendant's Biomechanical Engineer in Auto Wreck, Neck & Back Injury Cases," PESI Absolute Litigator, Vol. IV, Mar 1999.

Watts, Mikal C., "Discovery Abuses—Ethics," ATLA Winter Convention (1998).

Wivell, Martha K., "Dealing With Discovery Abuses: Boilerplates, Stonewalls, and Boxcars—Decedents' Commonly Used Techniques for Evading Disclosure," Trial Advocacy College: Depositions (1999).

Zagnoli, Theresa, "Preparing Your Witness for Deposition," ATLA Convention (1997).

THE DOMINO PRINCIPLE OF DEPOSITIONS

By: Thomas J. Vesper, Esquire

I. INTRODUCTION: A TALE OF TWO DEPOSITIONS: ONE GOOD, THE OTHER BAD

Those who remember the Vietnam War recall "The Domino Principle." It went as follows: "if Vietnam falls, Southeast Asia falls, if Southeast Asia falls, there goes the whole enchilada!" Whether you believe in the Domino Principle as it affects foreign policy or national security, the Domino Principle does have an everyday application in our practice of taking discovery depositions. If one dep falls down and goes wrong, that fallen deposition usually leads to a chain of events or mistakes which may influence all future discovery and may, indeed, adversely impact the outcome of the trial.

A. The "Simple" Automobile Negligence Case Scale Drawing

In a case I once prepared for deposition and trial, our client was a passenger in an automobile that came around the last curve in an "S" curve, skidded on ice, and slid into the path of an oncoming truck. After coming through the last curve, the defendant car driver felt the car lose control, fishtail, skid, and then slide sideways across the center line and into the oncoming path of a fully loaded tractor trailer hauling gravel. The issue, insofar as the truck driver and the car driver, was their respective share of fault. A second equally important issue arose as to the responsibility of the county for improperly maintaining this stretch of roadway with potholes and ice. The potholes caused the road surface to ice up; and in addition, the County failed to sand or salt this "dangerous S curve" the weekend before a forecasted heavy snow and ice storm. This particular S curve was known to be "extremely dangerous" even when dry.

What should have been a simple matter of estimating feet, yards, car lengths, or football fields—the usual units of measure in an auto collision deposition—actually turned into a BIG MISTAKE that produced a domino effect of additional mistakes which almost caused the tort claim against the County to be summarily diminished for lack of causation. The defendant car driver was shown a one-page police diagram; then the defendant truck driver, our client, and several eye witnesses were also shown this same diagram. When asked to estimate how far from the point of impact (POI) the car was when the truck driver first saw the car skid and slide out of control, the truck driver said "three or four car lengths." The car driver and eye witnesses were asked the same question. Not merely relying upon what the truck driver had testified but also by referencing the police diagram, the car driver and eye witnesses also estimated "three or four car lengths." The plaintiff mercifully did not have a clear recollection. This is the span of time and distance which many reconstructionists refer to as "the triangle." In actual fact, the distance which the truck and car closed to the POI from the time the car first started to slide was probably 35 car lengths or two football fields or 500 feet. How could both defendant drivers underestimate this huge distance? How did this underestimation happen? The Domino Principle! One slight distortion, one little miscalculation, caused a chain reaction of mistakes.

In this case, the state trooper (a rookie at the time of the collision) drew the diagram. In order to save paper, the trooper drew his "scale diagram" (except for the distance of the road) onto one sheet of graph paper! The actual "S" curve, width of the road, and vehicle sizes were drawn to scale; but rather than use two sheets of paper to show the true scale distance between the last curve of the "S" curve and the actual point of impact (which was exactly 528 feet), the young trooper simply sketched the actual distance in the compressed space on one page of graph paper. Then, in order to illustrate the movement of the defendant's car, the trooper drew four scale model versions of the car over this distorted, out of scale, and shortened distance on the graph/diagram. The trooper showed the defendant's car coming through the last curve (V1-A), then starting to fishtail (V1-B), sliding sideways (V1-C), and at the point of impact with the truck (V1-D). Not surprisingly, on the trooper's diagram, the impression was that from the last bend in this road to the point of impact, the defendant car travelled a short distance of approximately four or five car lengths. In fact, this physical distance of the skid, fish-tailing, and slide was well over 150 yards.

B. The Sidewalk Patch of Ice "Nobody Saw" Before The Fall

In another case, I saw the Domino Principle lead several attorneys to reject a case that ultimately was settled for a very significant amount. At an Ocean City, NJ, "Senior Citizens Convalescent Center," aka Nursing Home, an elderly woman visiting a friend slipped on ice, fell, and broke her hip. The defense was simple: the ice was not caused by the resident center; it had accumulated "suddenly and without warning" over a very short period of time and, therefore, was a slippery condition of which they had no notice.

During the "Death Star" discovery dep I asked the DCR or Designated Corporate Representative of the convalescent center to draw a diagram of the scene. He did. I asked him to identify the area where my client had fallen. He did, anddescribed the walkway where our client fell as being "in the rear of the building." This building was a 30-minute drive from the law office where we were taking the deps. My client was present, and I asked her if she could identify the location. She said if we could return to the center, she could certainly find it. The "impression" the defendant's manager gave was this slip and fall had occurred in an out of the way, remote spot; this "back of the building" site was not an area within the everyday maintenance of the center, and our client, who was visiting a friend, had actually taken a "short cut." Instead of going to her friend's room by the interior hallways, she had taken a "short cut" across the rear parking lot from the main building to one of the wings. This "short cut" was via an outside area reserved for "employees only." It sounded as if our client was a trespasser. That "initial characterization" was not lost upon defense counsel.

Before the deposition was over, I asked if we could return with the manager to the center to compare his hand-drawn diagram to the actual scene and to orient some black and white photos from the manager's files. Over some very weak "objections" sprinkled with my repeated suggestions to return another day that was "more convenient to all concerned," the manager and defense counsel reluctantly agreed to this site inspection. Once at the scene, we all saw what the jury would not have seen had we simply relied on the manager's diagram and some cropped,close range black and white photos by an insurance adjuster. Our client had indeed taken a "shortcut," but it was one everyone at the center took on a daily basis. The subject concrete walkway/sidewalk crossed through a picnic and public area into which visitors had always been invited. This was not a private parking lot. There was "private parking" approximately 200 feet from the walkway, but curiously, this area was a great deal farther away than the DCR's diagram had made it appear. We also found something I had never thought to ask because I had never been to the scene. The manager's office, with a large picture window, actually overlooked and was 15 feet from the exact spot where my client had slipped and fallen on the ice. In order to get to his office, assuming he used the reserved parking spot with his name painted on it, hewould have had to cross that exact spot that morning. Additionally, we saw instantly, with Sherlock Holmes' deductive insight, the probable source of the ice: the sloped grounds and a drainpipe's run-off had left water stains on that particular area of the sidewalk. (These were not detectable with black and white photos) Water flow from surface and rainspout actually ended up covering the sidewalk which was below the level of the surrounding grounds. With this simple on-site inspection, the liability picture (no pun intended) came into focus without any expert.

II. HOW TO AVOID THE DOMINO PRINCIPLE

Since my earliest CLE days, I have always been taught that to truly understand a client's physical and emotional injury, you must "walk a mile in the client's shoes"—spend more than just a day doing this. You should try imagining a lifetime spent living the life your client has been left to live. As for liability, to truly understand how any incident or injury occurs, you must go to the scene. To take an accurate deposition, you should not only go to the scene but also try to duplicate the scene, not with photos that have distorted angles, colors, or close up focuses but with actual scale drawings and color photographs.

In the "simple" automobile collision referred to above, a scale drawing of the crash scene would have avoided the "Domino Depositions." Rather than relying on a distorted rendition by the state trooper, the witnesses would have been in a much better position to accurately estimate time and distance as it probably occurred during the crash sequence. The best way to avoid the Domino Principle affecting your own client is to have the client return with you to the scene and actually go through the collision sequence step-by-step.

As in the slip and fall injury referred to above, the simple act of going to the scene, with or without the client, and noting the important landmarks and particularly the source for the water and ice and the function and accessibility of the area's use will assist any trial lawyer in understanding the cause of the slippery condition and whether the client was an invitee, licensee, or trespasser. It also helps deflate defense claims that the area or condition of foreseeable danger was not under their immediate supervision, control, and ability to correct.

In any automobile collision, time and distance are the critical ingredients used to gauge the relative fault and legal responsibilities of the drivers. In order to fairly depose any eyewitness or participant, it is often important that the crash site be thoroughly inspected and totally reproduced with scale drawings and not just photographed. Without aerial photography, most photos will not depict the time and distance of the "triangle" of first sight or perception, reactions, braking, and impact. Preparing your client with photographs and no actual measurements or points of reference will be of very little assistance when, at the time of the deposition, your client is asked the usual questions: "When did you first see the defendant's car/truck?" "How far was the defendant's car/truck from you and/or the point of impact?" "What, if anything, did you do between the time you first saw the defendant and the ultimate impact?" Time and distance are critical ingredients in automobile negligence cases. Therefore, it should be a very basic step in preparing for depositions to obtain the exact measurements at the scene, the site line distances, and then compare the perception, reaction, and braking times. Only then can you analyze and prepare for either the defense of your client's deposition or the taking of a defendant driver or witness' deposition.

In a slip and fall case, there is usually some artificially created or poorly maintained condition that causes or contributes to cause our clients to fall. The relative obscurity of the condition or lack of warning thereof to our client needs to be illustrated. Do not simply rely upon photographs. Try to show in terms of time and distance that for a certain period of time and over a certain short distance your client did not have sufficient opportunity to make observations, or the client's angle or site line of observation was greatly diminished.

On the offensive side of premises liability depositions, try to show that the area is one that was under the supervision and control of the defendant or one where the defendant created a condition that would cause slipping hazards. Example: the supermarket produce isle where approximately 65 feet of open bin space is designed and stacked with leafy vegetables that foreseeably cause droppage; yet for that 65 foot floor area, there are only three plastic drop mats that are 10 feet long and do not sufficiently cover this entire droppage area.

Spatial and scaled analysis can become important even in the most obvious automobile or premises cases. To avoid the Domino Principle leading to an unjust or distorted result at trial, fight your battle for accurate recollection in your discovery depositions. To be successful in your discovery battles, prepare in advance just as you would for trial with as many accurate and demonstrative exhibits as you believe are necessary to assist the witness in accurately reflecting the events or conditions at the scene.

III. CONCLUSION

The lessons I learned early by trial and error were reaffirmed recently in the unsafe highway and tractor trailer collision I undertook. What had already occurred was the "Domino Principle of Depositions." The one bad deposition led to several repeated witness mistakes, and those led the accident reconstructionists for both sides having a wide range of ammunition against both drivers to dispute the accuracy of their recollections and the location of the damaged roadway and pooling water which froze and led to the head-on crash. Because of one distorted exhibit in the first deposition taken, not just one but several eyewitnesses were completely misled and accordingly gave mistaken testimony as to time and distance. Only in preparation for trial, after the defendant car driver was taken to the scene by her lawyer, along with our accident reconstructionist, were the events accurately recalculated. In the future when there are important issues of liability at stake, perhaps I will take depositions of eyewitnesses at the scene or at a minimum, so the witnesses may refresh their recollection, show them aerial photographs and scale drawings.

Avoid the Domino Principle by thoroughly preparing for your discovery depositions. Think visually. You can reduce the risk of making mental errors, miscalculations, or false assumptions in your analysis of the case by going to the scene. At a minimum have a scale drawing prepared by someone from your office who has been to the scene, is familiar with the area, and can discuss it in detail with you. Do not assume the police diagram is accurate. Do not let the dominos start to fall!

THE DEPOSITION "GROUND RULES" OR FEDERAL PROTOCOLS

By: Tom Vesper & Mark Kosieradzki

(excerpted from a much larger chapter in their *AAJ Deposition Notebook*, 4th Edition)

A. Why Set Any "Ground Rules"

Some attorneys scrupulously follow the rules, some have a more relaxed approach or "situational ethic" about the rules, and some litigators flat out ignore and/or abuse the rules. Before launching upon discovery depositions, it may avoid future problems to obtain the agreement and/or court order to follow the ground rules or "protocols" for taking depositions. The purpose for setting the protocol is not just to avoid unsightly and unprofessional arguments in front of clients and witnesses. One very important purpose is to assure everyone that when important witnesses are being deposed, they will be giving their honest testimony and not the defending lawyers' version of the truth. If your adversary will not agree, we recommend obtaining a court order; if for some reason the court will not order the protocols to be followed, then we recommend that the protocols be announced at the commencement of the first (and possibly every) discovery deposition. For your use, we provide a brief in support of a motion, court ordered stipulation, list of the protocols, and SAMPLE DEP NOTICE form with the FRCP included in the notice . . . in the AAJ Deposition Notebook, 5th Edition for you to bring to every depositions.

B. What Are The "Ground Rules"

To prevent any misunderstanding between counsel, plaintiff counsel should try to obtain consent from adversaries, at outset of discovery, to follow the protocol set forth immediately below for all depositions.

FEDERAL DEPOSITION PROTOCOL

(1) FOLLOW THE RULES. Dep shall be conducted in compliance with Federal Rules.

(2) PROPER OBJECTIONS. During all depositions counsel shall adhere strictly to Rule 30(d)(1) and (3). No objections may be made, except those which would be waived if not made under Rule 32(d)(3)(B) (errors and irregularities) and those necessary to assert a privilege, to enforce a limitation on evidence directed by the court, or to present a Rule 30(d) motion (to terminate bad-faith dep). Objections to form shall be stated "objections as to form." Any further explanation is inappropriate and prohibited. There shall be no speaking objections. An objection made by one party preserves the objection for all. Substantive objections are preserved by Rule 32(d)(3)(a) and are therefore unnecessary.

(3) INTERRUPTIONS. Neither a deponent nor counsel for a deponent may interrupt a deposition when a question is pending or a document is being reviewed except as permitted in Rule 30(d)(1).

(4) INSTRUCTIONS NOT TO ANSWER. A party may instruct a deponent not to answer only when necessary to preserve a privilege, to enforce a limitation on evidence directed by the court, or to present a motion pursuant to Rule 30(d)(3). Whenever counsel instructs a witness not to answer a question, he or she shall state on the record the specific reason for such an instruction, the specific question, part of a question, or manner of asking the question, upon which counsel is basing the instruction to answer the question.

(5) RULE 30(b)(6) DESIGNATED REPRESENTATIVES. A business entity responding to a Fed.R.Civ.P. 30(b)(6) notice of taking deposition shall designate proper individuals for the deposition and to ensure that the designated individuals are properly prepared to testify regarding the categories designated in the deposition notice. The deponent organization must immediately provide a substitute knowledgeable witness if the testifying designee is deficient in responding to the questions within the scope of the matters for which he/she has been designated. Any question that could reasonably be expected to produce relevant facts is permissible, including those outside the scope of inquiry designated in the Rule 30(b)(6) dep notice. Corporate designation of a witness for Rule 30(b)(6) does not prevent a non-30(b)(6) deposition of the same witness.

(6) VIDEOTAPED DISCOVERY DEPOSITIONS. Any depositions may be videotaped, in addition to being recorded stenographically.

C. Obstructive Deposition Tactics Are Prohibited

The landmark case of *Hall v. Clifton Percision*, 150 F.R.D. 525 (E.D, Pa. 1993) identified the obstructive deposition tactics that will not be allowed. The court said:

> The purpose of a deposition is to find out what a witness saw, heard or did—what the witness thinks. A deposition is meant to be a question and answer conversation between the deposing lawyer and the witness. There is no proper need for the witness's own lawyer to act as an intermediary, interpreting questions, deciding which questions the witness should answer, and helping the witness formulate the answers. The witness comes to the deposition to testify, not to indulge in a parody of Charlie McCarthy with lawyers coaching or bending the witness's words to mold a legally convenient record. It is the witness—not the lawyer—who is the witness.

The court went on to explain that:

> ". . . depositions are to be limited to what they were and are intended to be: question and answer sessions between a lawyer and a witness aimed at uncovering the facts in a lawsuit. When a deposition becomes something other than that because of strategic interruptions, suggestions, statements, and arguments of counsel, it not only becomes unnecessarily long, but it ceases to serve the purpose of the Federal Rules of Civil Procedure: to find and fix the truth." Hall, 150 F.R.D. at 527. (Emphasis added.)

The "Hall Standards" have been recognized by courts throughout the country. *Armstrong v. Hussmann Corp.*, 163 F.R.D. 299, 301-05 (E.D. Mo. 1995); *ML-Lee Acquisition Fund II, L.P. Litigation*, 848 F.Supp. 527, 567 (D. Del. 1994); *Bucher v. Richardson Hosp. Auth.*, 160 F.R.D. 88, 94 (N.D. Tex. 1994); *Holland v. Fisher*, 1994 WL 878780 (Mass. Super. Ct.); *Van Pilsum v. Iowa State Univ of Science & Tech.*, 152 F.R.D. 179, 180–81 (S.D. Iowa 1993); *Johnson v. Wayne Manor Apts*, 152 F.R.D. 56, 58–59 (E.D. Pa. 1993); *Deutschman v. Beneficial Corp.*, 132 F.R.D. 359 (D. Del. 1990); *In Re: Amezaga*, 195 B.R. 221 (Bankr. D.P.R. 1996); *Damaj v. Farmers Ins. Co.*, 164 F.R.D. 559 (N.D. Okla. 1995); *Bucher v. Richardson Hosp.*, 160 F.R.D. 88 (N.D. Tex. 1994); *Odone v. Croda*

Int'l, 170 F.R.D. 66 (D.D.C. 1997); Acri v. Golden Triangle Mgmt Acceptance Co., 142 Pitt. Legal J. 225 (Pa. Ct. 1994); Collins v. International Dairy Queen, Inc., WL 293314 (M.D.Ga. 1998); W.R. Grace & Co. v. Pullman Inc., 74 F.R.D.80 (D.C. Okla. 1977); Applied Telematics, Inc., v. Sprint Corp., WL 79237 (E.D. Pa, 1995), citing the International Union of Elec., Radio & Mach. Workers v. Westinghouse, 91 FRD (277, D.C. D.C. 1981); and Dickerson, The Law and Ethics of Civil Depositions, 57 Md.L.Rev. 273, 286 (1998) and Smith v. R. J. Reynolds Tobacco Co.,630 A.2d 820 at 826 n. 7 (N.J. Super. App. Div. 1993), a lawsuit seeking compensation from Reynolds for the plaintiff's lung cancer. The memo was from J. Michael Jordan, an attorney for R. J. Reynolds Tobacco Co., and it was uncovered in discovery.

These two statements illustrate the "Dark Side" of our American system of litigation . . . what many lawyers face every day in discovery—deliberate and premeditated attempts to obstruct and deny open and honest exchange of discovery . . . despite the letter and spirit of rules, there are still attorneys who believe "stonewalling" (refusal to disclose damaging information) is a legitimate if not morally acceptable litigation tactic. Some attorneys are pragmatic about their obstructionism: they see by forcing their opponents to compel discovery, some of their opponents do not follow up to get court orders to compel the obstructer to do the right thing! For an excellent treatise on the ways to avoid and address discovery abuse, I recommend Francis Hare, James Gilbert, Stuart Ollanik, Full Disclosure: Combating Stonewalling and Other Discovery Abuses, ATLA Press (1995).

It is not my purpose to solve all obstructive tactics, but there is a way to expose and discover "writings" which will better your chances of gaining full and open discovery from an organization. We call it "The Death Star" or FRCP 30(b)(6) Deposition.

D. Introduction to Federal Rule 34 Demand For Production

As in almost all complex litigation involving some form of organizational defendant, there are many "writings" which would help establish liability and perhaps even intentional wrongdoing. "It's all in the documents." The truth is often found within these "writings" or documents. The challenge is not only to identify the documents that are necessary to uncover the truth but also to compel complete production of those documents. Unfortunately, some of the traditional approaches to discovery—such as Federal Rule 34 Requests to Produce or written interrogatories—are often met with dilatory and/or evasive responses. The "Death Star" is a reference to the ultimate destructive weaponry in Star Wars, which would devour and destroy entire planets. This nickname is applied to forms provided in the AAJ Deposition Notebook . . .., because once the designated corporate representative (DCR) is produced, the dep becomes the ultimate discovery tool to begin the "paper chase" and expose bad-faith defenses and obstructionism . . . you should learn to use the Federal Rules to maximize your discovery of documents that exist or help expose the diversion, destruction, alteration, or spoliation thereof.

FRCP 34 provides for production, inspection, and copying of documents by parties to a lawsuit. The Federal Rule specifies the procedure and time requirements to be used when requesting the production of documents from a party. Pursuant to FRCP 34, the responding party must be given at least 30 days to assemble and produce the requested documents. If the responding party objects to any of the requested documents, those objections must be stated with particularity within 30 days after service.

Regarding the documents that are produced, the responding party has the obligation to:

- Produce the documents as kept in the usual course of business; or
- Organize the documents to correspond with the categories in the request; and
- Label the documents to correspond with the categories in the request.

The FRCP 34 production of documents requires the responding party to produce all documents that are in their control. "Control" is defined not only as possession, but as the legal right, authority, or practical ability to obtain the documents requested from a nonparty.

When FRCP 34 requests are met with responses that are evasive, filtered, and/or contain litanies of boiler plated pattern objections, it is necessary to establish an effective record of the impropriety to support a motion to compel.

E. Federal Rule 45—Depositions Compelling Nonparty Document Production

To the extent the documents sought are in the control of a nonparty, FRCP 30(b)(5) is inapplicable. FRCP 34 applies exclusively to parties to litigation. Testimony, as well as production of documents of things, by nonparties is governed by Fed.R.Civ. 45.10. When requesting documents from a nonparty, the appropriate vehicle is a subpoena or subpoena duces tecum. Testimony is compelled by a simple subpoena while the production of documents from nonparty is compelled with a subpoena duces tecum, or an "independent action" such as one pursuant to the Right to Know Laws, where a public entity is involved.

F. Federal Rule 30(b)(6)—Depositions of Witnesses Speaking on Behalf of Organizations

When attempting to establish the existence of documents as well as the completeness of the production responses, the question becomes whom do you depose? It is literally not possible to take the deposition of a corporation. In order to accurately discover institutional information, it is necessary to obtain that information from natural persons who can speak for the corporation. However, you may not know the identity of the appropriate witness within the organization. To this end, FRCP 30(b)(6) require an organization to designate and prepare persons authorized to speak on its behalf relative to specific inquiries. The advisory comments to both rules set forth the underlying policy that gave rise to the rule.

An FRCP 30(b)(6) deposition more efficiently produces the most appropriate party for questioning; curbs the elusive behavior of corporate agents who, one after another, know nothing about facts clearly available within the organization and suggest someone else has the requested knowledge; and reduces the number of depositions for which an organization's counsel must prepare agents and employees.

G. Pulling it All Together: The FRCP 30(b)(6) + 30(b)(5) + 34 Document Deposition aka "The Death Star Dep"

FRCP 34 is used to identify the categories of documents to be produced. FRCP 30(b)(6) can be used to define the persons who will identify the available documents and attest to the search for those documents. FRCP 30(b)(5) requires that person to produce the documents at the deposition.

By using in federal court the FRCP 30(b)(6) in conjunction with 30(b)(5) and Rule 34, it is possible to establish whether the documents produced are complete. Verification of completeness by opposing counsel is not adequate. Counsel does not have institutional knowledge of the client. Rather, counsel can only repeat what has been identified by the client. Further, there are attorneys who improperly believe it is their role to limit or obstruct their adversaries' access to information.

To the extent there are omissions with produced documents, the FRCP 30(b)(6) designee can be questioned to determine what was omitted and why. This provides an efficient and distinct advantage over the more common approach of requesting your opponent to produce documents under FRCP 34 alone, without a sworn witness to vouch for the authenticity and completeness of the documents produced.

The FRCP 30(b)(6) designation for the document production witness similarly follows:

Pursuant to Fed.R.Civ.P. 30(b)(6), Defendant is required to designate and fully prepare one or more officers, directors, managing agents, or other persons with the most knowledge concerning the following designated matters, whose consent to testify on its behalf and whom Defendant will fully prep to testify, regarding the following designated matters and as such information that is known or reasonably available to the organization:

1. The existence of the documents requested below pursuant to Fed.R.Civ.P. 34;

2. The electronic creation, duplication, and/or storage of the documents requested below pursuant to Fed.R.Civ.P. 34;

3. Any and all document retention/destruction policies that would relate to any of the documents requested below pursuant to Fed.R.Civ.P. 34;

4. The location of the documents requested below pursuant to Fed.R.Civ.P. 34;

5. The organization, indexing, and/or filing of the documents requested below pursuant to Fed.R.Civ.P. 34;

6. The method of search for the documents requested below per Fed.R.Civ.P. 34;

7. The completeness of the documents produced pursuant to Fed.R.Civ.P. 34; and

8. The authenticity of the documents produced pursuant to Fed.R.Civ.P. 34.

The primary purpose of the document production witness is to establish the completeness of the records. Once the produced documents are established as complete, additional witnesses may be examined as to the content of those records.

H. Duties Imposed By Federal Rule 30(b)(6)

The responding party has obligations under FRCP 30(b)(6) that differentiate this type of deposition from non-30(b)(6) depositions customarily used in civil proceedings.

Duty to Designate. In response to valid FRCP 30(b)(6) dep notice, a responding deponent organization must either designate one or more of its officers, directors, or managing agents to testify on its behalf or designate another person who consents to speak for the deponent. By designating someone pursuant to an FRCP 30(b)(6) dep notice, an organization indicates that the person has the authority to speak on behalf of the corporation with respect to the area within the notice of deposition . . . not only to facts but also to subjective beliefs and opinions. In specifying the consent requirement for persons not officers, directors, or managing agents, the rules allow an employee or other agent who has an independent or conflicting interest in the litigation to refuse to be deposed as a deponent's designee.

Duty to Substitute. The deponent organization must immediately provide a substitute knowledgeable witness if and when it becomes clear during a deposition that the testifying designee is deficient in responding to questions within the scope of the matters for which he or she has been designated. The fact that the initial designation was made in good faith is of no consequence.

Duty to Prepare. The deponent organization has a duty to "prepare the witness to testify to matters not only known by the deponent, but those that should be reasonably known by the designating party." Witnesses must be prepared to completely, knowledgeably, and unevasively provide binding answers to questions within the scope of the matters specified in the deposition notice. To permit otherwise would allow the responding corporation to sandbag the depositional process by conducting a half-hearted inquiry before the deposition but a thorough and vigorous one before the trial.

DCRs shall testify to matters known or reasonably available to the organization. The testimony elicited at FRCP 30(b)(6) dep represents the knowledge of the corporation, not of individual deponents. Thus, if deponent's DCRs have no personal knowledge about matters specified in the dep notice and for which they have been designated to testify, the organization must prepare them to give knowledgeable, binding answers; this duty goes beyond those matters in which witnesses had personal involvement.

It is the responsibility of the corporation to undertake a thorough investigation in response to FRCP 30(b)(6) dep notice. While corporate deps can require extensive prep, it is the organization's duty to so prepare: "[p]reparing for a Rule 30(b)(6) dep can be burdensome. However, this is merely the result of the concomitant obligation from the privilege of being able to use the corporate form in order to conduct business."

The corporation's responsibility is to prepare the witness to testify properly. If the Rule 30 witness is not knowledgeable about relevant facts, and the entity has failed to designate an available, knowledgeable, and readily identifiable witness, the appearance is, for all practical purposes, no appearance at all. If an unprepared witness is produced to testify in response to Rule 30 notice, the court can impose sanctions under Rule 37 ranging from attorney costs and fees to an entry of default judgment.

"Reasonably available" information includes all documents that a party has a legal right or authority or practical ability to get even if they are not in the deponent organization's physical possession and even if a nonparty to the action has possession of them. Dead or discharged personnel do not excuse inadequate knowledge by the witness nor do voluminous documents for which review is burdensome. A court may consider evidence withheld despite reasonable availability as similar to spoliation, which "should be sanctioned accordingly." An inadequately prepared designated witness will amount to an impermissible refusal to answer a question and sanctionable failure to appear.

The well-crafted FRCP 30(b)(6) notice identifies specific issues counsel seeks rather than designating a category of person which counsel "thinks" will be able to give data sought. By doing so, the burden shifts to witness producing party to come with necessary data.

I. Scope of Inquiry

FRCP 30(b)(6) cannot be used to limit what is asked of DCR at a dep. The description contained in both rules and the notice identifies the minimum to which the DCR must be prepared to testify, not the maximum. If an examiner asks questions outside the scope of the matters described in the notice, general dep rules govern, relevant questions may be asked, and no special protection is conferred on a deponent by virtue of the fact that the dep was noticed under FRCP 30(b)(6). Once a corporation has produced someone capable of speaking to matters described in a notice of deposition pursuant to FRCP 30(b)(6), the scope of inquiry is only guided by the general discovery standards of FRCP 26(b)(1). A witness is not excused from providing information that is relevant, or likely to lead to relevant information, simply because that person works for a corporation.

J. Conclusion

By integrating FRCP 30(b)(6) + 30(b)(5) + FRCP 34 into a single deposition notice, the adversary's lawyer is eliminated as an intermediary in formulating the true record of whether a document exists and is discoverable and reasonably available. By establishing the record through a party's own testimony, the court can make an informed decision on the propriety of the discovery request and response.

I. INTRODUCTION: ABCs, DON'T ASS-U-ME & BE A DUMMY!

Most discovery depositions today, unfortunately, are not done for witnesses to provide full disclosure and complete discovery. Discoverers who assume the adversary/witness will always follow the letter and spirit of our federal and state discovery rules are headed for a "dumming down dep." The three purposes for which many deponents and their "defending attorneys" prepare for prior to being deposed are as simple as the ABCs: (A) to AVOID disclosure, if at all possible; (B) to BURY WITH BS OR BEFUDDLE the examiner's efforts to obtain full disclosure; and (C) to COVER, CAMOUFLAGE, OR CONFUSE the full discovery of the most damaging factual and/or documentary truths.

II. KIPLING'S SIX SERVANTS: WWWWWH

Rudyard Kipling: "I have six honest serving men, they taught me all I know, their names are who and what and where, and why and when and how."

Using Kipling's six loyal servants (Who, What, Where, Why, When, & How) is not enough to break through intentional, premeditated (at worst), or careless/subconscious (at best) efforts to withhold facts. After "discovery deps" with strings of "who, what, where, why, when, how" questions, you may know what a witness knows or remembers at that time. But that is usually not enough. No defense attorney will lose sleep because you spend hours asking corporate representatives "who, what, where, why, when, how" questions; alone, they will unlikely change case value or increase odds of winning.

Avoiding DUMMY DEP requires a focused effort to reach specific goals critical to case outcome. This paper discusses only four techniques needed to avoid being "dummied"—that is, 1) The "Death Star," 2) Exhaustion, 3) Boxing In, and 4) "The Miller Mousetrap" to establish "SOC" or standards of conduct/care from defense witnesses. Each of these techniques has a special purpose; if used appropriately, and sequenced properly in a dep, the outcome will NOT be a "dummy dep" and often will produce exceptional results.

III. DEATH STAR: PULLING IT ALL TOGETHER: FRCP 30(b)(6) + 30(b)(2) + 34

FRCP 34 is used to identify categories of documents to be produced during discovery. FRCP 30(b)(6) can be used to define the persons who will identify available documents and attest to the search for those documents at a discovery dep. FRCP 30(b)(2) requires that person to produce materials designated in notice and accompanying the notice with RRCP 34 request deponent must produce "writings" and tangible things at deposition.

Using Rule 30(b)(6) with Rules 30(b)(2) and 34, it is possible to establish if documents produced are complete. Verification of completeness by opposing counsel is NEVER adequate. Counsel do not have institutional knowledge of the client. Rather, counsel can only repeat what has been identified by the client. Also, there are attorneys who improperly believe it is their rightful role to limit and obstruct access to information.

To the extent there are omissions in produced documents, FRCP 30(b)(6) designee can be questioned to define what was omitted and why. This is more efficient and distinctly advantageous than common methods of requesting opponents to produce documents per Rule 34 alone, without a sworn witness to vouch for authenticity and completeness.

The FRCP 30(b)(6) designation for the document production witness is as follows:

Per Fed.R.Civ.P. 30(b)(6), defendant is required to designate and fully prepare one or more officers, directors, managing agents, or other persons with "ALL or the most knowledge" concerning the following designated matters, whose consent to testify on its behalf and whom Defendant will fully prepare to testify, re the following designated matters and to information that is known or reasonably available to the organization:

1. The existence of the documents requested below pursuant to Fed.R.Civ.P. 34;

2. Electronic creation, duplication, and storage of the documents requested;

3. Any and all document retention/destruction policies that would relate to any of the documents requested below pursuant to Fed.R.Civ.P. 34;

4. The location of the documents requested below pursuant to Fed.R.Civ.P. 34;

5. Organization, indexing, and filing of documents requested pursuant to Fed.R.Civ.P. 34;

6. Method of search for the documents requested below pursuant to Fed.R.Civ.P. 34;

7. The completeness of the documents produced pursuant to Fed.R.Civ.P. 34; and

8. The authenticity of the documents produced pursuant to Fed.R.Civ.P. 34.

The primary purpose of document production witness is to establish the completeness of the records. Once produced documents are established as complete, additional witnesses may be examined as to the content of those records.

DUTIES IMPOSED BY FEDERAL RULE 30(b)(6)

The responding party has obligations under FRCP 30(b)(6) that differentiate this type of deposition from non-30(b)(6) depositions customarily used in civil proceedings.

1. Duty to Designate. In response to a FRCP 30(b)(6) deposition notice, the responding deponent entity or organization must either designate one/more of its officers, directors, or managing agents to testify on its behalf or designate another person who consents to speak for deponent. By designating someone per a FRCP 30(b)(6) deposition notice, an organization indicates such person has authority to speak on behalf of the corporation with respect to the area within the notice of deposition . . . not only to facts but also to subjective beliefs and opinions.
In specifying the consent requirement for persons who are not officers, directors, or managing agents, the rules allow an employee or other agent who has an independent or conflicting interest in the litigation to refuse to be deposed as a deponent's designee.

2. Duty to Substitute. The deponent organization must immediately provide a substitute knowledgeable witness if and when it becomes clear during a deposition that the testifying designee is deficient in responding to questions within the scope of the matters for which he or she has been designated. The fact that the initial designation was made in good faith is of no consequence.

3. Duty to Prepare. The deponent organization has a duty to "prepare the witness to testify to matters not only known by the deponent, but those that should be reasonably known by the designating party." Witnesses must be prepared to completely, knowledgeably, and unevasively provide

binding answers to questions within the scope of the matters specified in the deposition notice. To permit otherwise would allow the responding corporation to sandbag the depositional process by conducting a half-hearted inquiry before the deposition but a thorough and vigorous one before the trial.

A deponent's designated witnesses shall testify as to ALL matters known or reasonably available to the organization.

Testimony at FRCP 30(b)(6) deps represents the knowledge of the corporation, not of the individual deponents. Thus, if designees are not personally knowledgeable about matters specified in the dep notice and for which they have been designated to testify, the entity must prepare them to give knowledgeable, binding answers; this duty goes beyond matters about which the designated witness had personal involvement.

It is the responsibility of the corporation to undertake a thorough investigation in response to the FRCP 30(b)(6) deposition notice. While corporate depositions can require extensive preparation, it is the organization's duty to so prepare:

> [p]reparing for a Rule 30(b)(6) deposition can be burdensome. However, this is merely the result of the concomitant obligation from the privilege of being able to use the corporate form in order to conduct business.

"Reasonably available" info includes all documents a party has a legal right or authority or practical ability to get even if not in the deponent organization's physical possession, and even if nonparty to action has possession. Dead or discharged personnel do not excuse inadequate knowledge by designated witness nor do voluminous documents for which review is burdensome. A court may consider evidence is "withheld" despite reasonable availability as being similar to spoliation, which "should be sanctioned accordingly." Likewise, an inadequately prepared designated witness will amount to an impermissible refusal to answer a question and a sanctionable failure to appear.

Well-crafted FRCP 30(b)(6) notices identify the specific issues counsel wishes to explore rather than designating a category of person which counsel "thinks" will be able to provide info sought. By doing so, the burden is shifted to the witness producing party come with the necessary information.

SCOPE OF INQUIRY

FRCP 30(b)(6) cannot be used to limit what is asked of the designated witness at deposition. The description contained in both rules and notice identifies the minimum to which a witness must be prepared to testify, not maximum. If examiner asks questions outside the scope of the matters described in the notice, the general deposition rules govern so that relevant questions may be asked, and no special protection is conferred on a deponent by virtue of the fact that the deposition was noticed under R. 4:14-2(c) or FRCP 30(b)(6). Once a corporation has produced someone capable of speaking to matters described in a notice of deposition per R. 4:14-2(c) or FRCP 30(b)(6), the scope of the inquiry is only guided by the general discovery standards of R. 4:10-2 and FRCP 26(b)(1). A witness is not excused from providing information that is relevant, or likely to lead to relevant information, simply because that person works for a corporation.

TAKE THE "D" OUT OF DILATORY DISCOVERY DEFENSES

By combining FRCP 30(b)(6) + 30(b)(2) + FRCP 34 into one deposition notice, the adversary's "defensive" lawyer is eliminated as intermediary in formulating the true record of whether a document exists and, is discoverable and reasonably available. Dilatory discovery tactics such as deponent's attorney claiming "I don't have any documents in my file" or "I can't find anything you ask for" are snipped in bud. The only person(s) who can answer the questions about searching for data requested is/are the designated representative(s). By establishing the record through a party's own testimony, the court (and jury) can make informed decision on propriety of discovery request and response.

THE "MILLER MOUSE TRAP"

By: Tom Vesper & Mark Kosieradzki,

(excerpted from a much larger chapter in their *AAJ Deposition Notebook*, 4th Edition)

To avoid a "Dummy Dep" and reach the Valhalla of exceptional deps is to help persuade the jury and imbed rules of conduct and truths that allow justice to prevail. Proving standards of conduct by defense witnesses obviates the need or cost for plaintiff experts, changes defense's case evaluation, provides credible/persuasive trial testimony, and drives settlement favorably to you. Named for Phil Miller, Esq. Nashville, TN, the "Miller Mousetrap" help you reach "unreachable stars" by following 12 simple rules:

RULE 1. PLAN IN WRITING! Before any depositions—Analyze your case in writing.

Although it sounds premature, most case facts are known before deps. Organizing the entire case "in your head" is never as effective as putting pen to paper; and the more witnesses you have, the more difficult it can be to maintain focus and direction. Begin your analysis by listing the most probable case critical issues including defenses, juror attitudes that could sway deliberations, witnesses likely to be deposed, documents, and the anticipated sequence of discovery depositions.

A. "BEST CASE SCENARIO."

Write out any responses that take out defenses. After writing out and thinking about defenses, you will identify many that are not substantive but need to be rebutted nonetheless. Even "lame" defenses can have staying power or "legs"; they can often be defeated with opposition witness testimony if they are part of the discovery plan. "Defenses" should include potential negative juror conclusions or biases; such "jury bias" cannot be erased by simple rhetoric, metaphors, and analogies.

B. "SOUNDBITES."

Write out responses that will create a record (concise soundbite) for

— Opposition to motions for summary judgment

— Motions in limine

— Amendments for punitive damages

— Motions for Spoliation

— Mediation/Settlement Presentations

— Opening Statement

— Cross-examination

— Summation

C. "COMMON SENSE STANDARDS OF CONDUCT."

Identify standards of conduct important to your case. In most cases, there are commonsense, statutory, regulatory, or company policies that define what conduct is accepted, required, or the norm. "Is it important to hire safe drivers?" or "Is it important to protect a fetus from group B strep?" is unlikely to get a "no" response from any witness.

RULE 2. USE THE "MOUSETRAP" TO ESTABLISH STANDARD OF CONDUCT.

Step 1. HONOR THY STANDARD. Elicit testimony that specific SOC is important.

Step 2. EMPHASIZE THY RATIONALE. Elicit why standard is important.

Step 3. GIVE THY STANDARD A "COMMON SENSE NAME." Elicit a short, recognizable, common sense name or mantra for the standard or "rule" of conduct.

Step 4. MEMORIALIZE THY STANDARD. Elicit testimony that a particular standard of conduct has been the known standard of conduct for more than XX years.

Step 5. AGGRANDIZE THY STANDARD. Elicit why this standard is so important.

Step 6. UNIVERSALIZE THY STANDARD. Elicit testimony that this defendant expects others to comply with this standard.

Step 7. NONCOMPLIANCE ' NEGLIGENCE. Elicit testimony that not complying with this standard of conduct is negligent/unsafe/improper.

Step 8. NONCOMPLIANCE ' RECKLESS. Elicit testimony that not complying with this standard of conduct is reckless.

Step 9. REFOCUS THE CASE ON "THE BIG PICTURE." Make the case bigger than your client or the immediate parties.

Jurors can feel their time being wasted. They want to feel they are deciding something important. What in the case has broader implications? Is the case about a misdiagnosis by an ER doctor or ER doctor too disinterested to give good care? A bad truck driver or a company with 120% turnover a year that hires anyone? Mistakes by a nursing home aide or a company that ignores rules/regs and won't hire enough staff for needed work?

RULE 3. WRITE OUT & SEQUENCE. Write out key questions and resequence them for maximum effect. Cicero said, "Eloquence comes from the written word." Unpleasant truth is succinct; concise questions are not a natural part of attorney speech. Questioning "from the hip" is unlikely to have the persuasive power of questions that are written, parsed, and then sequenced and resequenced with other questions for maximum affect.

RULE 4. PREPARE FOR EVASIVENESS. Anticipate and have a written strategy to deal with evasive responses. Cicero: "If the truth were self-evident, eloquence would be unnecessary." To avoid the "dummy dep" and achieving an exceptional deposition, the truth will only become self-evident if we anticipate and plan for nonresponsive answers and devise alternate questions and strategic approaches to deal with them.

Avoiding "Dummy Deps" and taking exceptional deps are both within your grasp. Just like making an ordinary dish or drink into a memorable treat, you as the trial advocate can prepare properly and "serve" a great quote or series of admissions for trial.

SELECTED BIBLIOGRAPHY

AAJ Exchange "Taking Depositions: Experts, Lay Witnesses, and Corporate Representatives"—this CD has over 1,000 pages in pdf format including forms, motions, checklists, anddescriptions/examples of techniques from actual deps. For more info about ATLA Exchange, go online at http://www.exchange.atla.org or call 800-344-3023.

AAJ Deposition Notebook, 3d. edition, Thomas J. Vesper and Mark Kosieradzki (West Group 2006)—covers everything: organization, technique, forms, motions, and case law.

AAJ's Deposition College & Advanced Deposition College—educational programs are designed for plaintiff attorneys, combine substantive dep techniques; workshops give the opportunity to try new approaches. For more info on programs contact AAJ at http://www.atla.org/education/ncacal.aspx or call 202-965-3500, Ext. 335.

Brown, Peter Megaree, The Art of Questioning, Thirty Maxims of Cross Examination, MacMillan Publishing, New York, 1987.

Cicero, De Oratore, Harvard University Press, 1967, Translated by E.W. Sutton.

Friedman, Rick and Malone, Patrick, The Rules of the Road: A Plaintiff Lawyer's Guide to Proving Liability, Trial Guides Publications, 2005.

Haydock, Roger and Sonsteng John, Cross Examination: Trial Theories, Tactics, Techniques West Publishing Company.

come si fa a trovare la verità?

si deve guardare duro

("how do you find the truth? you must look hard")

Chapter 4. PASTA or "DOUGH" (Commonly "Macaroni, Macs, Noodles, Spaghetti")

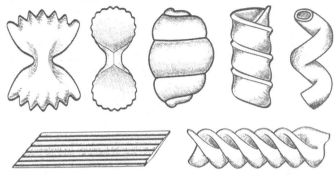

PART A. DOM'S RECIPES

PASTA FROM A to Z
(Just so you know the pasta varieties to cook & order)

LONG NOODLES or STRAND PASTA (made by extrusion, rolling & cutting)

Angel Hair	Extremely thin, long strands of pasta, available in both strands and nests; also called *Capelli d'angelo*
Barbina	Thin strands often coiled into nests; means "little beards"
Bigoli	Thick Venetian spaghetti with a rough surface to better absorb flavorful sauces, often made of buckwheat/whole wheat flour
Bucati	See Fusilli bucati; "holed rifles"
Bucatini	Thick spaghetti-like pasta with a hole running through the center; name comes from buco or "hole"; bucato means "pierced"
Capelli d'angelo	Synonym of capellini; coiled into nests or "Angel hair"
Capellini	The thinnest type of long pasta; literally "thin hair"
Chitarra	Spaghetti alla chitarra; long strands, which resemble spaghetti except they are square instead of round; means "guitar"
Ciriole	Thick strand pasta stretched until double thickness of spaghetti. It has a squared shape rather than round; small, thin "White Eel" in Tuscany and Umbria; Latin *cereus* or *ciriolus* means "candle"
Fedelini	Very thin spaghetti or "little faithful ones"

Pasta or "Dough"

Fusilli	Long, thick, corkscrew shaped pasta; solid or hollow. Hollow fusilli are called fusilli bucati. "Fusilli" is from fuso because traditionally it is spun by pressing and rolling a small rod over each thin pasta strip to wind them around it in a corkscrew shape, like a spindle; means "long rifles"
Fusilli bucati	Long coiled tubes that are hollow; "holed long rifles"
Fusilli lunghi	Longer fusilli; lunghi simply means "long"
Matriciani	Like perciatelli, but folded over rather than hollowed out; term Amatriciana or matriciana (Roman dialect) is a sauce for pasta that took its name from Amatrice, a town in provincia Rieti near Rome; the word now has come to mean "inn with a kitchen"
Pellizzoni	Thick spaghetti; "medium twines"
Perciatelli	Identical to bucatini; word comes from *perciare* or "to hollow"
Pici	Very thick, long, hand-rolled pasta, originates in Siena in Tuscany; in Montalcino it is called pinci; means "woodpecker"
Spaghetti	Long, thin, cylindrical pasta of Italian and Sicilian origin; made of semolina or flour + water. "little strings." Spaghetti is plural for "spaghetto," diminutive of spago, meaning "thin string or twine"
Spaghettini	Thin spaghetti; "small little twines"
Spaghettoni	Spaghetti that is extra thick or extra long; "long twines"
Vermicelli	Traditional pasta round that is thicker than spaghetti (in America, refers to a style thinner than spaghetti); "worms"
Vermicelloni	Thicker vermicelli or "large little worms"

RIBBON CUT PASTA (often rolled flat and then cut by hand or mechanically)

Bavette	Narrower version of tagliatelle; "little drip-thread"
Bavettine	Narrower version of bavette; "narrower drip-thread"
Chitarra	Lute-shaped pasta named for the Renaissance Era lute-shaped plucked instrument with 4-5 single, sometimes double, strings
Ciriole	Thicker version of chitarra; "lute"
Fettuccine	Ribbon of pasta about 6.5 mm wide; "little slices"
Fettuce	Wider version of fettuccine; "little slices"
Fettucelle	Narrower version of fettuccine; "little slices"
Lagane	Wide noodles
Lasagne	Very wide noodles often fluted edges: word for "cooking pot"
Lasagnette	Narrower version of lasagna. Little lasagna or "cooking pot"
Lasagnotte	Longer version of lasagna. Bigger lasagna or "cooking pot"
Linguettine	Narrower version of linguine or "little tongues"
Linguine	Flattened spaghetti; "little tongues"
Mafalde	Short rectangular ribbons; named for Princess Mafalda of Savoy
Mafaldine	Long ribbons with ruffled sides; "little Princess Mafalde"
Pappardelle	Thick flat ribbon; from "pappare" for "gobble up"
Pillus	Very thin ribbons typical of Sardinia
Pizzoccheri	Kind of short tagliatelle, a flat ribbon pasta, made with 80% buckwheat flour and 20% wheat flour; "delicatessen"
Reginette	Flat, wide, ribbon-shaped pasta, usually about ½" wide with wavy edges on both sides; means "little Queens" and is also called Mafaldine, or simply, Mafalda
Sagnarelli	Rectangular ribbons with fluted edges like little sheets of paper; with zig zag edges; great pasta to use with a creamy sauce
Scialatelli/scilatielli	Homemade long spaghetti with a twisted long spiral; "shawl"

Spaghetti alla chitarra	Like spaghetti, but square not round, made of egg and flour; named for a guitar-like device used to cut pasta, which has a wood frame strung with metal wires, pasta sheets are pressed onto the wires, which are "strummed" so the slivers of pasta fall through
Stringozzi	Similar to shoelaces; "shoestring-like"
Tagliatelle	Ribbon, narrower than fettuccine; Italian *tagliare* means "to cut"
Taglierini	Thinner version of tagliatelle; from tagliare, meaning "to cut"
Trenette	Narrow, thick tagliatelle, ridged on one side, from Liguria
Tripoline	Thick ribbon ridged on one side

TUBULAR, SHORT-CUT EXTRUDED PASTA

Bocconcini	Medium sized tube pasta like elicoidali and tufoli; has a 3/8" diameter and the ridges on the surface are slightly curved around the tube. Its length ranges from 1 3/8 to 1 ½"; "mouthful"
Bucatini	Thick spaghetti shaped pasta hollow in center, like a thin sipping straw; name comes from buco or "hole"; bucato means "pierced"
Calamarata	Wide ring shaped pasta; means "squid-like"
Calamaretti	"Little squids"
Cannelloni	Large stuffable cylinder or tube pasta; "large reeds"
Canneroni	Shorter version of cannelloni, ½" diameter, ¾" long; "reeds"
Cannolicchi	Short, straight tube with a wide grooved surface; "reeds"
Cavatappi	Corkscrew-shaped macaroni; "corkscrews"
Cellentani	See Cavatappi; tube twisted to resembles shape of a corkscrew
Chifferi	Short and wide macaroni; "croissant" or elbow macaroni
Chifferini	A smaller version of chifferi pasta
Ditalini	Short tubes; "small thimbles"
Elbows	Not table manners, but the most common tube pasta shape; See Gomiti; narrow tube with semicircular curved shape, 1" long
Elicoidali	Medium sized slightly ribbed tube pasta; its ribs are corked as opposed to rigatoni's helicoidal ribs; "helix"
Fagioloni	Short narrow tube; "large beans"
Fideuà	Short and thin tubes. Fideuá is not really a type of pasta, it's a Spanish dish similar to paella but made with pasta instead of rice
Garganelli	Like penne, egg pasta in square shape rolled into a tube, but "flap" is visible where one corner of square adheres to rest; its unusual name is Latin *gargala* for trachea, similar to English "gargle"
Gemelli	Single S-shaped strand of pasta twisted in a loose spiral; "twins"
Gomiti	Bent tubes; "elbows"
Macaroni	Macaroni is "Medican" (American) term re any narrow short tube pasta; straight or curved, varying widths; common type is Elbow Macaroni; from Italian *maccheroni* a Greek food made of barley
Maccheroncelli	Hollow tube-shape, less thick than a pencil; "small maccheroni"
Magliette	Short, curved tube pasta; "links"
Maltagliati	Short, wide egg pasta with irregular/diagonally cut ends, seen all over Italy; prominent in regional Italian cuisines; "roughly cut"
Manicotti	Large stuffable ridged tubes; pl. of *manicotto* "muff" or "sleeves"
Marziani	Short spirals; "martians" refers to antennae of cartoon martians
Mezzani pasta	Short curved tube; "half-size" pastas
Mezze penne	Short version of penne; "half-pens"
Mezzi bombardoni	Wide short tubes; "half bombards"

Pasta or "Dough"

Mezzi paccheri	Wide hollowed out tube of pasta, a shorter version of paccheri; same diameter as paccheri but is only 1 1/4" in length
Mezzi rigatoni	Short, slightly curved tube pasta about 5/8" long, 1/2" diameter; due to the short length, the slight curve is barely noticeable
Mostaccioli	Smooth, ridgeless penne; penne lisce; "moustache-like" things
Paccheri	Large tube pasta; prepared with sauce atop or stuffed; "slaps" for the slapping sound made when it is eaten.
Pasta al ceppo	Sheet pasta similar in shape to a cinnamon stick "log-type" pasta
Penne	Medium length tubes without ridges, cut diagonally at both ends. "Pens" (after a quill pen)
Penne rigate	Penne with ridged sides; "lined pens"
Penne lisce	Penne with smooth sides' "smooth pens"
Penne zita	Wider version of penne; "pens"
Pennine rigate	Thinner than pennette; rigate means ridge; also smooth or "lisce"
Pennette	Short thin version of penne; "little pens"
Pennoni	Wider and thicker version of penne; it is a tubed pasta with a diagonal cut on both ends' "pennants"
Perciatelli	Long tube pasta with a hollowed out center; about double the thickness of spaghetti; from *perciare* or "to hollow"
Reginelle	Pasta like penne; slightly longer, smaller in diameter; sometimes named for its wide, flat, wavy edge ribbons named reginette; "little Queens"; not to be confused with the flat ribboned Reginette
Rigatoncini	Smaller version of rigatoni "small large lined ones"
Rigatoni	Medium-large tube with square-cut ends, sometimes slightly curved; "large lined ones"
Sagne Incannulate	Sagne 'ncannulate; long tube formed of twisted ribbon or ringlets
Spaccatelle	Short curved Sicilian tube pasta shaped like a half circle; "break"
Spirali	Tube which spirals round; "spirals"
Spiralini	More tightly coiled fusilli; "little spirals"
Trenne	Penne shaped as a triangle; "triangular"
Trennette	Smaller version of trenne; "small triangle"
Tortiglioni	Narrower rigatoni; "spirals"
Tufoli	Ridged rigatoni, 3/8" diameter, slightly curved, 2" long; "tube"
Ziti	Narrow hose-like tubes smaller than rigatoni, larger than mezzani ziti "rigati" are lined/ridged; "lesci" smooth; Zito is "bridegroom"
Ziti—Cut	Ziti 1/4" in diameter; available cut short lengths of 1½" to 3" and also available in long lengths of 10". The shorter lengths are sometimes found with a slight curve to them.
Ziti—Long	Ziti available in long lengths of approximately 10"; also available cut to shorter lengths of 2" to 3".
Zitoni	Wider ziti; "large bridegroom"

FANCY DECORATIVE SHAPED PASTA

Campanelle	Flat bell-shaped pasta with frilly edge on one end; "little bells"
Capunti	Short convex ovals shaped like an open empty pea pod or canoe
Casarecce	Short lengths rolled in s-shape. Casereccio means "homemade"
Cavatelli	Short, solid lengths. From the verb cavare meaning "to hollow"
Cencioni	Petal shaped, slight curve with rough convex side; "large rags"
Conchiglie	Seashell shaped; "shells"
Conchiglioni	Large, stuffable seashell shaped; "large shells"

Corzetti	Genoese "Curzetti; flat figure-eight stamped; "corsetry"
Creste di galli	Short, curved, and ruffled; "cock's comb"
Croxetti	Flat coin-shape discs stamped with coats of arms; "little crosses"
Farfalle	Bow tie or butterfly shaped; "butterflies"
Farfalloni	Larger bow ties; "large butterflies"
Fiorentine	Grooved cut tubes; "florentine"
Fiori	Shaped like a flower; "flowers"
Foglie d'ulivo	Shaped like an olive leaf; "olive leaves"
Gigli	Cone or flower shaped; "lilies"
Gramigna	Short curled lengths of pasta; "infesting weed," esp. scutch-grass
Lanterne	Curved ridges; "lanterns"
Lumache	Snailshell-shaped pieces; "snails"
Lumaconi	Large snailshell-shaped pieces; "large snails"
Maltagliati	Flat roughly cut triangles; "badly cut"
Mandala	Designed for French pasta maker Panzani to deal with overcooking; name refers to "mandalas"
Orecchiette	Bowl or ear-shaped pasta; "little ears"
Pipe	Similar to Lumaconi but lines run its length; "smoking pipe"
Quadrefiore	Square with rippled edges from quadro "square," fiore "flower"
Radiatori	Shaped like "radiators;" created in 1960's by industrial designer; often used same as rotelle/fusilli; shape works well in thick sauce
Ricciolini	Short wide noodles with a 90-degree twist; "very little curls"
Ricciutelle	Short spiralled noodles; "little curls"
Rotelle	Wagon wheel-shaped pasta; "little wheels"
Rotini	Two-edged spiral, tightly wound, some brands are three-edged, like fusilli, but tighter helix, i.e., with a smaller pitch; helix or corkscrew-shaped pasta; name is from the Italian word for "twists"; not to be confused with rotelle ("wagon wheel" pasta)
Sorprese	Bell shaped pasta creased on one side + ruffled edge; "surprise"
Sorprese Lisce	Bell shaped pasta creased on one side with ruffled edge; larger version of Sorprese; "smooth surprise"
Strozzapreti	Rolled across their width; "priest-chokers" or "priest-stranglers"
Torchio	Torch shaped; "winepress"
Trofie	Tiny dumplings, specialty of Recco in Liguria; "trophy"

TINY OR MINUTE PASTA

Acini di pepe	Bead-like pasta; "peppercorns"
Alfabeto	Pasta shaped as letters of the alphabet; "alphabet"
Anelli	Small rings of pasta (not the same as Calamaretti); "rings"
Anellini	Smaller version of anelli; "little rings"
Couscous	Grain-like pasta, common in North Africa and Europe (esp. France)
Conchigliette	Small shell-shaped pasta; "little shells"
Corallini	Small short tubes of pasta; "little corals"
Ditali	Small short tubes; "thimbles"
Ditalini	Smaller versions of ditali; "little thimbles"
Farfalline	Small bow tie-shaped pasta; "little butterflies" ("bow tie" in Italian is *cravatta a farfalla*, "butterfly tie")
Fideos	Pasta made with eggs, flour and water; Spanish means "noodle"
Filini	Smaller version of fideos 12-15 mm long; means "little threads"

PASTA OR "DOUGH"

Fregula	Bead-like pasta from Sardinia; "little fragments"
Funghini	Small mushroom-shaped pasta; "little mushrooms"
Grattini	Small irregular shaped; smaller than Grattoni; "little Grains"
Grattoni	Large granular, irregular shaped pasta; "grains."
Midolline	Flat teardrop or melon-seed shape, like Orzo but wider; "soaked"
Occhi di pernice	Very small rings of pasta; "partridge's eyes"
Orzo (also, risoni)	Rice shaped pasta; "barley"
Pastina	Small spheres; same/smaller than acini di pepe; "little pasta"
Pearl Pasta	Spheres slightly larger than acini di pepe
Puntine	Smaller version of Risi
Quadrettini	Small flat squares of pasta; "little squares"
Risi	Smaller version of orzo; "little rice"
Seme di melone	Small seed-shaped pasta; "melon seeds"
Stelle	Small star-shaped pasta; "stars"
Stelline	Smaller version of stele; "little stars"
Stortini	Smaller version of elbow macaroni; "little crooked ones"

IRREGULAR SHAPED PASTA

Cappelli del prete	"Priest's hats"
Gnocchi	Thick, soft dumplings; made from semolina, ordinary wheat flour and egg, cheese, potato, and bread crumbs or similar ingredients. "Lumps" derives from nocchio, a knot in wood, or nocca ("knuckle"), or gnocco ("dumpling")
Passatelli	Made of bread crumbs, eggs, grated Parmesan cheese, lemon, and nutmeg; cooked in chicken broth; typical of Pesaro e Urbino in North Marche, and North Italy, e.g., Emilia Romagna; "elderly"

STUFFED PASTA

Agnolotti	Semicircular pockets; can be stuffed with ricotta or mix of cheese and meats or pureed vegetables; origin of the name may be from name *Angelot* from Montferrat, Piedmonte, said to be inventor of recipe, or from Latin *Anellus*, referring to ring-shaped material, or a diminutive of old word "Angel"; was also Giotto's nickname
Anolini	Stuffed pasta from Parma, like ravioli, but half-moon shaped; not to be confused with agnolotti; served in broth during holidays
Cannelloni	Rolls of pasta with various fillings, usually cooked in an oven; "big little canes"
Cappelletti	Square of dough, filled with minced meat, closed into a triangle "little Alpine caps/hats"
Casoncelli/casonsèi	Stuffed pasta of Lombardy; various fillings; from casa "house"
Casunziei	Stuffed pasta typical of Veneto area; various fillings; from "casa" Fagottini "Purse" or bundle of pasta, made from a round of dough gathered into a ball-shaped bundle, often stuffed with ricotta and fresh pear; "Little cloth bundles"
Maultasche	Pasta stuffed with meat and spinach common in southern Germany or Northern Italy and Italian Alps; "mouth pocket"
Mezzelune	Semicircular pockets; about 2.5 in. diameter; "half-moons"
Occhi di lupo	Large, penne-shaped pasta that is stuffed; "ribbed wolf eyes"
Pansotti	Stuffed 2" square folded in half from one corner to opposite forming triangle; edges may be straight/pinked; "pot-bellied"

Pierogi	<u>NOT Italian</u>; homage to Trzuskowskis; unleavened dough dumplings stuffed with various fixings; *pierogi* has proto-Slavic root in "pir" (festivity); West/East Slavic word; "pie"
Ravioli	Square 3x3 cm pasta envelope, stuffed with cheese, ground meat, pureed vegetables, or mixtures; possibly from rapa or "turnip"
Raviolini	Larger version of ravioli
Ravioletti	Smaller version of ravioli
Sacchettini	Round, similar to fagottini; also may use ravioli stuffing; small square of pasta around the stuffing and twisted; "little sacks"
Sacchettoni	"Large little sacks"
Tortelli (Anolini)	Stuffed pasta made with filling on a 2" circle of pasta and then folding the pasta in half to form a half circle; "little pies"
Tortellini	Ring-shaped, stuffed with a mix of meat and cheese; "little pies"
Tortelloni	Round or rectangular, like ravioli, usually stuffed with cheese and veggie mixture; a larger variety of tortellini; "large little pies"

IT'S IM-PASTA-ABLE: WHAT'S THE DIFF?
Understand the Different Functions of Different Pasta Shapes

There are 600 different types of pasta; even if you think that most of them are the result of Renaisance Italy's city-states, provencias, regional preferences or mass-marketing decisions that leaves a lot of variation to explain. We have seen some research on why there are so many different pasta shapes and when you might choose one or the other. Understanding pasta shape functions; general taxonomy splits pasta up into categories:

1. **SHEETS:** are made for dishes like lasagna that are prepared as casseroles or pies, rather than a dish eaten from a bowl with a fork. Some have ruffles for sauce retention.

2. **STRANDS:** are pretty simple, but the main variation among them is thickness.

    A. **THIN STRANDS:** are meant for light sauces, like an angel hair with olive oil and garlic, or thin tomato sauce; otherwise, the strands get lost in the sauce, and you don't get their texture at all. Also, with thin strands, the lubrication provided by thinner and oil-based sauces helps keep the strands from sticking together.

    B. **THICK STRANDS:** are meant for heavy sauces. The reason it's Fettucine Alfredo not Angel Hair Alfredo: angel hair in Alfredo would never be noticed.

    C. **SPAGHETTI:** in-middle, nice all-purpose pasta. If you are detail-oriented, you can look for square spaghetti, with slightly more surface area for sauce to stick to.

3. **TUBES:** for tubes and shapes, the main variation is also by size.

    A. **VERY SMALL TUBES:** ditalini, and small shapes, like orzo or even alphabet pasta, are meant for soup. Some authorities make distinctions between pasta for soup and pasta for broth, but I won't get into that here.

    B. **BIGGER TUBES:** the bigger the shape/tube, the heartier the sauce you can serve it with. E.g., Rigatoni is good with a bolognese because the tubes are big enough to fill with sauce and ground meat. Note: spaghetti bolognese is not served in Italy.

4. **SMALL & LARGE SHAPES:** like strands and tubes, shapes also vary in

size. Large shells, are stuffed. Giant shells are also often baked; generally possible with larger pastas like ziti. They won't fall apart after being in a hot oven. Ravioli and tortellini are stuffed too, and their size is dictated by the same considerations above.

Additional considerations:

RIDGES: In general, larger pastas are good for heartier sauces; but you can modify the stick-to-it-ness of sauce by picking ridged or unridged. E.g., bolognese with fine chunks of meat in tomato puree: get ridged pasta; thick sauces will stick easier to the outside.

SMOOTHNESS: On the other hand, if the pasta is smooth, it can move more easily in an oil-based sauce. So serve penne with pesto.

OPEN vs. CLOSED SHAPES: Most pasta shapes that come to our minds, like wagon wheels, have nowhere for sauce to get trapped. But there are a few shapes, like tiny shells, or campanelle, that let even a thin sauce into each bite, if that's what you want.

CURVED vs. STRAIGHT SHAPES. Curved shapes are better for pasta dishes meant to be eaten like a casserole, e.g., macaroni and cheese. Our kids have made this with penne; it's harder to eat—without breaking up pieces, you can't fit them in your mouth as easy. Curved shapes get the right amount of pasta into a smaller/easier chew, like casseroles do.

Final tips on how to choose between different pasta shapes:

SIZE MATTERS: In general, the bigger the pasta, the heartier/heavier the sauce you can serve it with. Very small shapes go in soup.

GO TUBULAR: Tubes have the ability to hold small chunks of tomato, meat, or other flavorful sauce add-ins. Sort of like impromptu stuffing. Strands make sense in smoother sauces, or dishes where something is served alongside the pasta (e.g., clams).

TAKE CHANCES: Experiment not only with different sizes of the same pasta, but also other variables (shapes, ridges, pasta cut) to achieve different culinary experiences.

Rigatoni Bolognese: a thick, tomato and meat sauce, large shapes stand up well to this sauce, and allow the sauce to infiltrate inside. Ridges provide even sauce adhesion.

Fettucine Alfredo: the thick strands stand up to the heavy cream and cheese sauce; you eat pasta in a sauce, not vice versa. Tubes or other shapes don't improve surface area.

Linguine alle vongole: the flat, medium-width strands with clams, olive oil, white wine sauce are able to move around easily in the sauce; since the flavors of the sauce are relatively subtle, the linguine stand up to it just fine (one thing I'm not sure about is why linguine are used instead of, say, spaghetti. Though note that linguine, being flat, have a higher ratio of volume to surface area).

PASTA PUTTANESCA or "Sauce of the Harlot" (Spicy Pasta)

VESPER FAMILIA: This sauce is the very first (good tasting dish) mastered by my Cuz Thomas. In fact, when he was invited to his first *Wagilia* (Vigil or Christmas Eve in Poland) with his soon-to-be in-laws, he brought this sauce to use with pasta or calamari. It remains a big hit in the Trzuskowski family whatever feast day dinner is being served.

INGREDIENTS (Serves 6):

2 Tbsp Olive oil

4 Anchovy fillets, chopped

1 large can Whole Italian tomatoes

2 (7.7 fluid oz.) Jars of Cappers

3 (16 oz.) Jars of Greek dried olives (with or without pits)

2 Tbsp Fresh basil, chopped

Pinch of Crushed red pepper

1 Clove Garlic, minced

DIRECTIONS:

Heat oil in a medium skillet over low heat.

Add garlic and anchovies, cook for 3 minutes until anchovies dissolve.

Add the tomatoes and red pepper.

Heat to simmering over medium heat, break up tomatoes with a spoon.

Cook until sauce is reduced, about 10 minutes.

Serve over 1 lb of pasta cooked al dente.

BOCCONCINI: Quick, very tasty red sauce, takes 15 minutes from start to table. This is said to have been created and enjoyed by "working women" of Naples "in between" liaisons.

Caper, caper bush aka "Flinders Rose"; a perennial plant known for its edible flower buds (capers), used as seasoning, and its fruit (caper berry); both are consumed pickled; traced back to Latin *capparis*, "caper." Ancient Greco-Romans used it as "carminative" (herb preventing formation of gas in gastrointestines or facilitating its expulsion). In Biblical times, the caper berry

Pasta or "Dough"

was apparently supposed to have aphrodisiac properties; the Hebrew word *abiyyonah* for caperberry is closely linked to the Hebrew root word meaning "desire."

GNOCCHI CON DOLCE PATATA
(Sweetpotato Gnocchi)

Pair this with butter or your favorite Alfredo sauce. This recipe can also be made with butternut, Hubbard, or almost any cultivated squash instead of the sweet potatoes.

VESPER FAMILIA: Tom's in-laws will never forget his "christening" their new blue-tiled kitchen in ubiquitous white flour dust from his homemade-in-their-home gnocchi.

INGREDIENTS (Serves 6):

2 (8 oz.) Cans sweet potatoes or yams or squash

1 Clove garlic, pressed

½ tsp Salt

½ tsp Ground nutmeg

1 Egg

2 cups All-purpose flour

DIRECTIONS:

Preheat oven to 350° F (175° C).

Bake sweet potatoes 30 minutes or until soft to the touch. Remove from the oven and let cool.

Once potatoes are cool enough to work with, remove peels and mash/press them through a ricer into large bowl.

Blend in garlic, salt, nutmeg, and egg.

Mix in flour a little at time until dough is soft. Use more/less flour as needed (just like making homemade pasta).

Bring a large pot of lightly salted water to a boil.

While waiting, make the gnocchi. On a floured surface, roll the dough out in several long snakes; cut into 1" sections. (IF you like creativity you can shape these little dough knots with your thumb—this can be VERY SEXY (see *Godfather III* gnocchi scene)—drop pieces into boiling salted water; let them to cook until they float to the surface. Remove floating pieces with slotted spoon; keep warm in a serving dish. Serve with butter, thyme butter, cream, or Alfredo sauce.

Pasta or "Dough"

HOW DO YOU MAKE THYME BUTTER?

Take a stick or two of butter; melt it in a pan with two to four sprigs of thyme. Attsa all ya do.

<u>BOCCONCINI</u>: *Gnocchi* comes from *nocchio*, Italian for "a knot in wood," or *nocca* meaning "knuckle." Its origin is Roman legions during the expansion of the empire into the European continent, and 2,000 years later, each country had its own specific type of small dumpling, but the ancient gnocchi is their common ancestor. In Roman times, the gnocchi were made with semolina porridge-like dough mixed with eggs; after the potato was introduced to Europe in the 16th century, potato gnocchi became popular in Abruzzo.

PESTO SAUCE
(Basil and Pine Nuts Sauce)

VESPER FAMILIA: This Italian favorite originates in Northern Italy; so, as Cuz Tom and I learned growing up in SOUTH Camden, in SOUTH Jersey and having our many relatives living in "The Fatherland of SOUTH Philadelphia," it was a shock when we first realized anyone from NORTH Italy could cook! MADONNA! They cooked some great pasta, with saucy sauces, like this classic our wives, Arlene and Mary Alice, love.

INGREDIENTS (Serves 6):

2 cups Fresh basil leaves

½ to 1 cup Fresh parsley

2 Cloves garlic

2-3 Tbsp Capers if you have them or throw in some chives instead

¼ cup Pine nuts or walnuts (I have used both and they are equally good)

½ cup Grated parmesan cheese

½ cup Olive oil

1 Tbsp Lemon juice

DIRECTIONS:

Put all of the above in a blender and puree until thick and smoot

BOCCONCINI: the sauce originated in Genoa in the Liguria region of Northern Italy (pesto genovese). The name is from the Genoese word *pestâ* (Italian: *pestare*), meaning "to pound or crush," referring to the original method of preparation, with marble mortar and wooden pestle. The ingredients in traditional pesto are ground with circular motion of the pestle in the mortar. This Latin word also gave rise to the English word "pestle."Just so you know: ancient Romans thought basil would only grow if you screamed wild curses and shouted while you were sowing the basil seeds. I'm not sure, but I think my Uncle Fred taught his son, my Cuz Dom, a few Italian incantations for "basil growth.

PASTA CON DI NOCI
(Pasta with Walnuts and Bread Crumbs)

This dish is defiantly from Abruzzi because both my Nona Gallo, and Tom's mother Carmella Nicolella Vesper, would make this dish on special occasions, especially on *"Vigilia di Natale"* or Christmas Eve. This pasta dish is not complicated and another example of how to make use of simple and fresh ingredients.

INGREDIENTS (Serves 4 to 6):

½ cup Olive oil

1 Tbsp Butter

1 Clove of garlic chopped

8 oz. Chopped walnuts

½ cup Seasoned Italian breadcrumbs

1 lb. Cooked spaghetti, al dente

2 Tbsp Chopped parsley

Salt and pepper to taste

Red Pepper flakes (optional)

DIRECTIONS:

Add oil to heavy pot, when oil is hot; add butter and sauté garlic, about one minute.

Add walnuts and continue to cook until walnuts are toasted, about five minutes.

Drain spaghetti and reserve about a cup of pasta water.

Add spaghetti to walnut mixture (remember, when making dishes like this you should always add cooked pasta to this sauce so the flavors can incorporate together).

Toss in mixture about five minutes and add breadcrumbs and toss another minute or so.

If sauce seems a little dry add some pasta water.

Add salt, pepper, and pepper flakes and serve with grated cheese.

BOCCONCINI:

Myth& Medicine: according to legend, the walnut originated when Baccus, Greek god of wine and ecstasy, fell in love with Carya, youngest of three daughters of Dion, king of Loconia. When the jealous elder sisters tried to stop the two lovers meeting, Bacchus turned them into stones and his beloved into a walnut tree.

Roman Magic: Walnuts were valued by Romans for both medicinal and magical uses. Romans believed eating walnuts improved fertility or fecundity; this started the Mediterranean custom of throwing walnuts at weddings. In parts of Italy, a three-chambered walnut in your pocket is still considered protection from witches and lightning. Putting a walnut under a chair will prevent a witch from rising and is, therefore, an excellent witch-detection device.

European Medicine: "Doctrine of Signatures" was key to 17th century European herbal medicine; it held plant parts physically resembled human body parts to which they should be medically applied. The walnut was a "signature" of a human head; the kernel representing a brain; ground walnut husk was prescribed for head wounds; eating walnuts was a cure for mentally ill. Note: modern biochemists found walnuts contain high concentrations of serotonin, a compound important to transmit signals between neurons in human brain.

FETTUCINE ALA RICOTTA
(Pasta with Ricotta)

My grandfather, Luco Gallo, was diagnosed with a deceased Gall Bladder when he was in his early fifties. The doctor informed him that he could not eat red gravy because of this condition. What was my grandmother Antionetta to do? Luco loved pasta and usually ate it three times a week for dinner. She cooked his pasta al dente and added fresh Ricotta Cheese with parsley and grated cheese. He loved it and continues to eat pasta three times a week until he died at the age of 89. I have a variation to this recipe that my family loves. I hope you enjoy this one.

INGREDIENTS (Serves 4 to 6):

1 lb. Fettuccine

2 cups Heavy cream

2 Tbsp Ricotta cheese

5 Tbsp Grated Pecorino Romano cheese

2 Tbsp Chopped Parsley

1 Clove garlic minced

4 Tbsp butter, softened

$1/4$ tsp Salt + $1/4$ tsp Black pepper

DIRECTIONS:

Boil pasta in salted water until al dente, drain.

In a deep frying pan over medium heat, melt the butter.

Sauté garlic about three minutes, do not burn.

Add the Ricotta cheese and stir with a wooden spoon until well incorporated.

Slowly add cream stirring with wooden spoon until well mixed.

Cook until mixture is bubbling.

Add salt and pepper.

Cook for about one minute and add pasta to cream mixture.

Reduce heat to low, add grated cheese, and toss Pasta until well coated.

BOCCONCINI: Ricotta—pronounced Rah-GOT in South Jersey—means "recooked." It is an Italian cheese made from sheep, cow, goat, or Italian water buffalo milk whey leftover from the production of cheese. The origins of Ricotta cheese date back to Latin and Mediterranean history when it is believed to have been created in the Roman countryside as travelers cooked their food in big kettles over open fires. The product was cooked twice to extract the cheese from the buttermilk.

ZUCCARRELLI RISOTTO
Risotto alla Zucca
(Sweet Pumpkin and Salty Parmesan Combined Into Risotto Pasta With Ricotta)

Zucca is a slang term for "hard head." That was our cuz, Joseph "ZUKE" Zuccarrelli—the best football player in our family—rail thin, wiry, strong as a steel cable, the fastest most fearless kick-off and punt returner we ever saw wearing a leather Green andWhite helmet (no face-mask) for Camden Catholic High varsity. My father, Rocco, used to say he "coulda been a professional lightweight boxer, if he just limited his opponents to one at a time." And, our Cuz Zuke loved to eat risotto with any type of sauce.

INGREDIENTS (Serves 6):

5 cups of salt-reduced chicken stock

1 sprig fresh rosemary

1 tbs olive oil

40g or 1 ½ oz. of butter

1 brown onion, finely chopped

2 garlic cloves, crushed

1 ½ cups of arborio rice

450g or 16 oz. of butternut pumpkin, peeled, seeded, cut into 1.5cm pieces

1 cup shredded parmesan

2 tbs chopped fresh continental parsley

Shaved parmesan, to serve

DIRECTIONS:

Bring the stock and rosemary to a boil in a medium saucepan over high heat.

Reduce heat and hold at a gentle simmer.

Heat the oil and half the butter in a large saucepan over medium heat.

Cook the onion and garlic, stirring for five minutes or until soft and translucent.

Add the rice and cook, stirring for two to three minutes or until grains appear slightly glassy.

Stir in the pumpkin.

Add one ladleful (about ½ cup) of simmering stock to rice mixture and stir with a wooden spoon until the liquid is absorbed.

Add stock, one ladleful at a time, stirring constantly, allowing the liquid to absorb before adding the next ladleful.

Continue 20 minutes or until the rice is tender yet firm to the bite and risotto is creamy.

Remove from heat.

Stir in shredded parmesan, parsley and remaining butter. Season with salt and pepper.

Divide risotto into serving bowls. Top with shaved parmesan and season with pepper.

BOCCONCINI: in the U.S., pumpkins go hand in hand with fall holidays (Halloween and Thanksgiving) and the supernatural. To wit: the folk tale carriage of *Cinderella*; Linus' Great Pumpkin in Charles M. Schulz's comic strip *Peanuts*, In the *Harry Potter* novels, pumpkin juice is a favorite drink of students of Hogwart's School of Witchcraft and Wizardry; the pumpkin thrown by the "Headless Horseman" in Washington Irving's *The Legend of Sleepy Hollow*; Tim Burton's *The Nightmare Before Christmas*, the main character, Jack Skellington, is "the Pumpkin King," and I have to give some credit to the Irish for bringing Jack-O-Lanterns to our families.

In tribute to my Irish mother-in-law, Ann Fleming Trzuskowski, I repeat the legend: The practice of Jack-O-Lanterns at Halloween started centuries ago from an Irish myth about a man called "Stingy Jack." As the story goes, Stingy Jack invited the Devil to have a drink with him. Jack didn't want to pay, so he convinced the Devil to turn himself into a coin Jack could use to buy their drinks. Once the Devil did so, Jack decided to keep the money and put it into his pocket next to a silver cross, which prevented the Devil from changing back. Jack later freed the Devil, with the condition he would not bother Jack for one year and that, should Jack die, he would not claim his soul. The next year, Jack again tricked the Devil into climbing into a tree to pick a piece of fruit, and while he was up in the tree, Jack carved a sign of the cross into the tree's bark so the Devil could not come down until the Devil promised Jack not to bother him for 10 more years. Soon, Jack died. As the legend goes, God did not allow such wicked souls into Heaven. The Devil, upset by Jack's tricks, kept his word not to claim his soul and did not allow Jack into Hell—the Devil sent Jack off into the dark night with only a burning coal to light his way. Jack put the coal into a carved out turnip and has roamed the Earth with it ever since. The Irish called this ghostly figure "Jack of the Lantern" and then simply "Jack-O-Lantern."

Joseph "Zuke" Zuccarrelli

PART B. TOM'S TRIAL TIPS: DEFENDING DEPOSITIONS

"PRIMO PIATTI:" THE TRIAL STARTS WITH PLAINTIFF'S DEPOSITION: HOW TO BETTER PREP FOR PLAINTIFF DEP + DIRECT + REDIRECT THREE-PRONGS or TRIPLE PLAY OF DEP PREP to BULLET PROOF PLAINTIFF

THE TRIAL OF ANY PERSONAL INJURY CASE STARTS WITH PLAINTIFF'S DME (DEFENSE MEDICAL EXAM DEPOSITION) & THE PLAINTIFF'S DISCOVERY DEPOSITION: HOW TO BETTER PREP FOR THE DEFENSE MEDICAL EXAMINATION PLAINTIFF DEP + DIRECT + REDIRECT "THE TRIPLE PLAY OF DEP PREP" TO BULLET PROOF THE PLAINTIFF

THERE IS NO SUCH THING AS "IME" or INDEPENDENT MEDICAL EXAMINER.

More and more, the insurance industry employs medical experts, and groups that almost always act more like advocates and often less than objectively. At times, these "professional experts" act unscientifically to examine injured plaintiffs and render opinions on the nature, extent, and permanency of the injuries in question, andthe etiology, proximate causation of each "alleged injury"; they also opine on the exacerbation *vel nom* of preexisting medical conditions.

It is important that these paid experts for the defense are labelled correctly—they are DME's defense medical examiners. They are not IMEs because they are not "independent" in the sense that they have been appointed by the court or have no interest in the outcome. They are not chosen by the court to be impartial; they are not unaware of their role and for the side they are working for; they also know that they will not be hired for future work if their opinions are not "acceptable" to the insurance company that hires them. Their forensic "independence" therefore is not a label which plaintiffs' counsel should ever allow anyone to adopt, especially in trial with an impressionable jury who might believe such expert is truly "independent" and therefore more credible than the treating doctors.

The DME Doctor is much smarter and much more credible than any insurance defense attorney. They have the medical expertise to support their opinions or at least sound as if they and their medical opinions are "scientifically" reliable; and they seem to be fair and objective, and so they are many times found credible by jurors. The rhetorical question arises: would you as the legal representative for your injured client ever let your client talk with any defense attorney or any insurance adjuster alone and without you present? And since you would not allow such a situation, why allow your clients to go unescorted to a DME? If you can't be present, then someone from your office should be with the client. Why? Well, if for no other reason than to make your clients feel more at ease and comfortable rather than nervously vulnerable and literally facing a defense examiner unprotected and without any witness.

Therefore, to prepare the client for this very first step in the "discovery" process, I recommend

1. PREP yourself
2. PREP your staff
3. PREP your client

1. PREPARING YOURSELF FOR THE "DME MESS"

To best prepare the plaintiff, it is best to prepare yourself as plaintiff lawyer. You need to really see the fact that DME is like an unofficial, unrecorded deposition by the defense doctor. It needs to be approached and prepared as if you were sending your client into a formal discovery deposition. That is, you should prepare a checklist or set of written instructions for your clients so they can be better prepared for their interrogation by the DME doctor and DME staff who often have a multipage questionnaire with a long list of written questions which are often redundant of the written interrogatories. For the client to hand write answers which, if they are inconsistent or can be made to "appear" inconsistent with interrogatory answers, will be an unnecessary risk to place the plaintiff into.

You, unlike the naïve, inexperienced plaintiff, know full well that most common DME findings are: NO-NO-NO: NO "Objective Signs" of any injury, NO "Causation," and NO Permanency.

Sometimes, there is a "scientific" finding by the DME of NO "CREDIBILITY" on the part of plaintiffs due to alleged "findings" I call the "DME MESS"—"Malingering, Exaggerating, Symptom Magnifying, Symptom Inconsistency." "Inconsistent Symptoms" really means the DME is saying YOUR CLIENT IS NOT HONEST!

Pasta or "Dough"

To best prepare yourself for the DME of your client, you need to prepare the following:

1. A letter of instruction to your client.
2. A letter to your adversary and also the DME "setting down the rules" for the DME.
3. A DME "escort" needs to be prepared to go with your client, to be your deputy, your eyes and ears.

The letter to the client can simply set forth the following advice:

1. Where and when to go for the DME.
2. What this "IME" or "DME" thing is all about.
3. Warn the client of "video surveillance" cameras that some DMEs use.
4. Warn the client what to expect from the DME.
5. What to bring to the DME.
6. What to remember to say to the DME.
7. What NOT to say or do at the DME.
8. IF someone from your office will accompany them.
9. When you will prepare them—either in person or telephonically for this DME.
10. Finally, warn the client what will happen if they cancel or do not show up.

The letter to your adversary and the DME can include the following:

1. Acknowledgement of the DME (NOT to be called IME in any future communication).
2. Confirmation of the time and place and examiner.
3. Questionnaires will NOT be answered unless you receive them in advance.
4. Documents will not be reproduced which defense already received in discovery; unless they have been properly requested per FRCP there will be no "production" other than the client.
5. Nature of "Accident" (Incident is better choice of words) is already set forth in the pleadings and interrogatory answers and depositions, and thus should not be re-examined.

6. Prior Medical Hx (History)—this should also have been set forth in discovery, but a list of "priors" will be provided with the client and your law firm's representative.

7. Current Medical Hx (History)—also should be part of written discovery already exchanged; but an extra copy will be provided.

8. Medical Authorizations—do NOT let your client sign anyone's authorizations unless according to court rules/orders.

9. Diagnostic Testing—there will be no invasive testing or filming without prior notice.

10. Designated Representative of Plaintiff—that is, your employee will accompany the plaintiff to the DME office and also be present as a witness during the examination.

11. Tape/Video Recording—if your jurisdiction allows it, advise the adversary that film and/or audio recording will be made and an unedited copy supplied to the adversary.

12. No-exam Fees/Costs—if for any reason the DME cancels the exam there will be costs assessed for the client's time and also your agent.

13. Waiting Time—advise how long your client will wait before leaving.

14. Failure to Comply—if DME/staff do not follow the ground rules you may terminate DME.

15. Spoliation—no notes or recordings by the DME or DME staff should be destroyed or lost.

16. Notification of DME Identity—if the DME doctor specified as the examiner is not to be the examiner, then you insist on notification.

2. PREPARING YOUR STAFF FOR DMEs

Your office staff needs to know your "DME SOP," i.e., when the adversary sends a letter with DME date and place; what form letters will be sent to your client, adversary, DME, et al; and what "Phone PR" or client communication need to be set up. Will you prepare clients with a set of videotaped instructions (there are available on the market several excellent videotape tutorials for clients and lawyers on what to expect and how to prepare for a DME). Will you or your legal assistants meet in person, by live video-conference, or by telephone with the client and the "DME escort" to prepare them for the DME? What you need your staff to remind clients to bring with them for a DME?

3. PREPARING YOUR CLIENT FOR THE DME—JUST LIKE CLIENT DEP PREP.

You and your staff should prepare your client FOR THE STANDARD DME QUESTIONS:

- HOW DID THE ACCIDENT HAPPEN?
- WHAT, IF ANY, PRIOR INJURIES OR CONDITIONS DID YOU HAVE?
- WHAT ARE YOUR PRESENT COMPLAINTS?
- WHAT DISABILITIES/IMPAIRMENTS OF "ADL" (Activities of Daily Living)?

HOW DID THE ACCIDENT HAPPEN? I recommend you give the client a copy of either or both their signed statement to police or their sworn answers to interrogatory/deposition questions about the CAR WRECK, or HEAD-ON COLLISION, or T-BONE CRASH, or SLIP AND FALL, or INCIDENT; rarely are clients injured by random "accidents"—usually a mechanism of injury occurred as a result of neglect or reckless conduct. Such "avoidable incidents" should not be trivialized as "accidents."

WHAT, IF ANY, PRIOR INJURIES/CONDITIONS DID YOU HAVE? Herein lies an opportunity for the defense and/or the DME to do intentional mischief—if the client honestly forgets some minor incident in their past—even if it did not result in a serious or permanent injury; it gives the defense a "plausible argument" that the plaintiff was being dishonest at the DME and hiding" something from the DME, judge, and jury. To avoid such "historic credibility traps," have your clients complete and unedited medical history of prior medical conditions, treatment thereof, and any prior injuries and treatment; especially important in "causation cases" is history of any prior medical filming—X-ray, MRI, CT, etc.

WHAT ARE YOUR PRESENT COMPLAINTS? Here, like with the use of the colloquial "accident," there is for me a prelude to paranoia—if you ask it enough times, you get people to adopt the words in a question as a fact they embrace. Thus, if plaintiff has "complaints of . . ." and "more complaints of . . ." or if "plaintiff is complaining of . . .," then it seems like the plaintiff is indeed a "COMPLAINER." Remember to instruct your client of three things:

A. Do not adopt or co-op defense words "COMPLAIN, COMPLAINT . . . COMPLAINING."

B. Use your List—the "4 Steps of Pain" List to describe your SYMPTOMS, PHYSICAL PROBLEMS, PAINS (See below The 4 Steps of Pain).

C. Do not ad lib—USE YOUR LIST, READ YOUR LIST, GIVE THE DME YOUR LIST.

WHAT DISABILITIES/IMPAIRMENTS OF "ADL" (Activities of Daily Living)? As with the "Physical Problems" List, the "Lost Enjoyments" List allows plaintiffs to prioritize the lost enjoyments of their individual lives. As with the 4 Steps of Pain List, the clients need to be reminded to:

A. Not adopt the defense words.

B. Use your "Lost Enjoyments" List which is prioritized with those most objectively important.

C. Do not ad lib—USE YOUR LIST, READ YOUR LIST, GIVE DME YOUR LIST

REHEARSE THE DME: Last, but not least in importance, for any plaintiff lawyers is to REHEARSE with your clients for the DEPOSITION or the DME.

THE "TRIPLE THREAT" OR TRINITY OF DEP/TRIAL PREP

By: Tom Vesper & Mark Kosieradzki,

(excerpted from a much larger chapter in their *AAJ Deposition Notebook, 4th Edition*)

CLE courses such as AAJ's Deposition Colleges have taught me how to help clients improve their demeanor, increase their confident ability to handle difficult questions, and turn their lengthy, lifeless litany and stream-of-consciousness complaints into interesting, positive, credible descriptions of their lives. We now use "The Triple Threat" or "The Trinity of Witness Preparation." First, I encourage clients to write out and use notes. Second, I show them how to use a structured outline to answer stock defense questions; e.g., following a 4-step method of describing physical pain and preparing a "Top 10" list of ways their lives have been significantly affected by their injuries. Third, I encourage role-playing.

I. FIRST THREAT: CLIENT NOTES, DIAGRAMS & TIME LINES

A. Client Notes

- SHORT & SPECIFIC
- LEGIBLE HAND WRITTEN OR PRINTED
- CLIENT'S OWN LANGUAGE

- "SUITABLE FOR FRAMING"
- CLIENT "CLIFF NOTES." Using handwritten notes eliminate/reduces client's (and my) fear he/she will make mistakes about important facts. E.g., in every case, our clients need to answer questions about their "present problems" and "things they can no longer do or no longer do as well." Deponents can easily address questions about who said/did what, when, where, and to/with whom when reading notes. Clients can do this easily if they know in advance they can use notes. And if the client is foreign-born (many of my clients speak English as a second language), he or she will find it a great relief to have personal notes in their familiar, native tongue.

B. Client Diagrams

- BE ACCURATE Re SCALE, PLACING "X" + DATE of INCIDENT
- REVISIT THE SCENE/SITE WITH CLIENT
- USE AERIALS or AVAILABLE DIAGRAMS/PHOTOS
- PREP FOR TIME/DISTANCE/SPEED + CHECK THE MATH
- CLIENT "ART WORK" & DIAGRAMS. In any auto case where time and distance are crucial details, clients can make a hand-drawn map with notations to be used as ready and reliable reference. In any slip/trip/step and fall down case, clients need to be able to reconstruct visually and then recount what happened and where it happened. Accurate location of "point of impact" or "place where" fall occurred is critical. To be mistaken/incorrect in reconstructing any traumatic event can be devastating. It has been our experience that confident, well prepared clients, armed with predrawn diagram, scale drawing, premarked photos, or aerial photo, always do better than a witness unfamiliar with scene, diagram, floor plans, or photos of scene or who tries to start artistic career at their dep with no practice or rehearsals.

C. Client Time Lines

- CHECK FOR "CONFLICTS"—BE ACCURATE + CHRONOLOGICAL
- OBJECTIVE, NONINFLAMMATORY REPORT OF EVENTS
- USE ALL SOURCES OF DATES/TIMES—INCLUDING DEFENSE
- CONSISTENT CALENDARS or LISTINGS or "LINES"
- SYMBOLS, CIRCLES, & STARS

- REVIEW ALL DATES WITH CLIENT
- KISS = Keep IT SIMPLE Silly!
- CLIENT CALENDAR OF EVENTS. In cases with many critical times/dates, we encourage all clients to prepare in advance (with/without our typing support) and use these "Time Lines" during their depositions. This engenders confidence as well as a more error-free deposition.

II. SECOND THREAT: STRUCTURE NOT "FREE FALL"

A. Structure The "Four Steps of Pain"

- QUALITY—HOWZIT FEEL?
- QUANTITY—HOW OFTEN?
- DURATION—HOW LONG LASTING?
- RELIEF—WHADDAYADO FOR IT?
- STRUCTURE: THE 4 STEPS OF PAIN OUTLINE. I make it easy for the client to get to the gist of their complaints by using a "Four-Step Pain Outline." It asks about the following:
    1. Quality. Describe what the pain feels like. Don't just say "it hurts." I force clients to think of their own descriptive terms for their feelings and sensations of pain/discomfort.
    2. Quantity. Tell how often during the day or the week the pain occurs.
    3. Duration. Describe how long each occurrence of the pain lasts.
    4. Relief. Explain what, if any, medicine or home therapy helps to relieve the pain.

Outlining these four questions in his/her own handwriting makes clients more confident when describing their situation, whether it involves one or a dozen injuries. I tell clients when they prepare the "Top 10" list to set out in clear, simple terms the things lost or impaired as a result of their injuries. Armed with this list, my clients are much more confident answering the ubiquitous defense question "Tell me what, if anything, you cannot do at all, or cannot do as well as you did before?"

You may think these "cheat sheets" are discoverable. You're right. In fact, I encourage defense counsel to review and mark them as exhibits. Notes only emphasize my client's testimony.

Do not fear that using notes makes your client look "less credible." I would rather have a relaxed, confident client testify than one who is anxious, upset, and frozen with fear that he/she might misstate or forget something important. I prefer clients speak clearly about what is most important to them rather than force them to rely on their memory, which may be weakened by stress or fatigue.

Handwritten notes are best with a client who tends to ramble, like the Whiner. I have found that keeping the notes short—usually just two pages—helps them remain, as the politicians say, "on message."

B. Structure The $64, $64.50, and $65 Questions

1. The $64 Question

- PRIORITIZE "LIST OF FAVORITE THINGS"
- PRIORITIZE ADL
- SHORTEN & SUMMARIZE
- USE CLIENT'S "FIRST LANGUAGE"
- INSIST ON LIST BEING DEP EXHIBIT
- PREP CLIENT FOR "TYPICAL DAY/WEEKEND"

The $64 Question is "THE ONE BURNING QUESTION" jurors want answered: What are significant effect(s) has your injury(s) had upon your life and your family relationships? Clients must be prepared to address this in interrogatory answers and deps. We recommend they have written answers to interrogatories AND a short, legible prewritten structured list, prioritized for their ready reference.

2. The $64.50 Question

- PREP CLIENT FOR "TYPICAL DAY/WEEKEND"

The $64.50 Question is the logical extension of ultimate $64 Question, to wit: What do you do with yourself during a typical day/weekend? As with present physical problems and effects on their lives, each client must be ready to answer this Q in dep, mediation, arbitration, or trial.

3. The $65 Question

- CONSCIOUSLY AVOIDED BUT UNCONSCIOUSLY ASKED

The $65 Question is my name for "THE UNASKED QUESTION" most jurors unconsciously want answered: "What will plaintiff do with money?" or "What good will money do for plaintiff?"

We as trial lawyers for injured clients or survivors of wrongful death must be prepared to answer or suggest an answer to this unspoken question in our clients' answers to interrogatories, depositions, and trial testimony. A painful example of this unasked question is in the wrongful death of a child: in many such cases, there are very well-meaning jurors who will ask silently or out loud "How will money help to replace this child?" For a rather simplistic economic example, if an injured and permanently disabled plaintiff needs to have household assistance or substituted services, then the actual cost or economic "replacement value" for the plaintiff to go out and buy or repay people to help him/her is the answer to the $65 question—the plaintiff could use X amount of money to be able to live a normal life.

III. THIRD THREAT: ROLE-PLAYING

- IT'S THE CLIENT'S ROLE . . . NOT OURS
- IT'S THE CLIENT'S INTERPRETATION THAT WILL BE SEEN
- IT'S EASY IF IT'S NECESSARY & IMPORTANT TO CLIENT
- IT'S EFFECTIVE IF PRACTICED BY CLIENT

ROLE-PLAYING. This can be done inexpensively or expensively. Expensive—which saves a lot of your time—is to hire a jury consultant to perform a complete professional overhaul of clients' appearance, grooming, speech, and demeanor. We work with several jury consultants and find they are often useful and, in some cases, extraordinarily helpful. Good ones make clients more likeable, better witnesses.

The inexpensive approach involves you and your staff meeting with problem clients and finding a role model for them to imitate. Believe it or not, this works. If, for instance, a client tends to ramble, ask who they most admire as honest, straight-talking, and succinct. Tell them to imitate that person. I ask clients who are prone to whining to think of a brave, stoic person they know of and respect. Clients often find role models in their own family, American history, books, television, or movies. The source doesn't matter. What's important is the role model is a good one and that the client can play that role.

I had two elderly clients, both incorrigible "Ramblers." They could not answer any question in less than 100 words and regularly went off-track. They too were frustrated with their inability to reverse this trend. I asked each who they most respected, their ideal of tight-lipped, concise speaker. I expected the Husband, a Baby Boomer, to name terse-talking Jack Webb from the old TV series *Dragnet*. Instead, he chose Superman, who was strong, fearless, and always said the most in few words. Wife chose Golda Meir. With little practice—less than one hour—this elderly couple dramatically changed how they handled questions. Each became a better witness.

Another time, my staff and I tried over four hours—using videotape, mirrors, and demonstrations—to convince one Whiner that his long, drawn-out monody of his problems was excessive and irritating. Despite our best efforts, he continued to whine. Finally, I learned he was an opera singer. I asked him to think about the toughest, most stoic character he could play. I thought sure he would select an Italian opera hero with much coraggio. But to my surprise, he said he'd always admired the movie characters John Wayne played: men who, despite bullets, shrapnel, arrows, spears, and whatever else was thrown at them, always picked themselves up and "got 'er job done." I asked could he play such a role? He could and did. He turned himself from John Whine into John Wayne. And his deposition was a masterpiece.

IV. "ALL IN THE FAMILY" or CLIENT "BACKUP"

- IMMEDIATE FAMILY
- FRIENDS
- ADVISERS

As with any performance, contest, or public exhibition, a deposition is like a trial in open court. The people being deposed are being put "on display." Most of the people being questioned have a sense of being "all alone." Many, if not all, deponents feel some pressure on or sense of importance about their testimony. Often, their memories are challenged, meanings critiqued, motives criticized, and the merits of their claims condemned. People unused to the deposition process can get "stage fright." Lawyers tend to believe they are champions for their clients, and they are. But even champs need to have "backups" and friends "in their corner." Our clients have longer, deeper relationships with family and friends than they do with us and our legal team. Therefore, we encourage all our clients to bring someone with them to sit in the dep room, with whom they have a special and close relationship of trust and confidence.

Clients who do have family or friend sitting with them during deposition or trial appear to be (and may in fact be) more confident and relaxed. Whether the "backup" is a spouse, child, lover, sports coach, karate sensei, rabbi, or spiritual guru, if the person sitting in the room is giving off "good vibes" for the client, then that person is an asset to be used for the best interest of your client. In my opinion, having one or two close friends/family sitting in with clients during the dep results in two very positive effects on clients' cases, their settlement or jury verdict value, and our attorney-client relationships:

1. It puts clients at ease by creating a friendlier atmosphere and another source of facts; and

2. It sends a message to the opposition: this client has a life with friends and a "support group."

V. AT TRIAL: THE REAL CONTEST IS AFOOT + THE JURY IS KEEPING SCORE

- CALL FOR "BACKUP"
- PRACTICE RELAXATION TECHNIQUES
- STAGE REHEARSAL(S)
- PREP FOR THE "DAYLIGHT" IN THE DEFENSE
- THE ART OF REDIRECT

As discussed above, always have family and friends with the client to provide moral support and help during the stress of trial. We invite our clients to bring family and close friends who not only help fetch coffee/tea/water but also can be very helpful during jury selection due to their community contacts.

As with any physically challenging contest (combat?), try to teach your client to take some type of deep breathing, stretching, or calming exercise(s) that work, before starting up to the witness stand. A relaxed and calm witness is usually a more effective witness: calm, not careless or unconcerned; confident, not arrogant; authoritative, not condescending; assured in the truth of the accuracy of their memory, not cocky or smug.

Before trial or dep, be sure client understands every defense has "holes." Prime your client for any such "openings" in the defense, through which the theme of your client's truths may flow.

Finally, be sure to reinforce the fact that your client is confident in the knowledge that "even if they make a bad mistake" you can correct it on redirect examination. They should not feel that they are going to be "trapped" on cross-examination and let swinging in the breeze with no ability to explain or fully describe their answers or prior deposition/interrogatory answers. That is what trial lawyers call "The Art of Re-direct Examination." And that is a subject for another paper at another Seminar.

EPILOGUE: TRIPLE PLAY/TRIPLE THREATS WORK

These three rather simple techniques—notes, structured lists, and role-playing—really do work. I have seen the results with my own clients, with the clients of colleagues, and with the work of jury consultants. So the next time your clients are having difficulty saying what they need to say, tell them to take notes, make an outline, and finally pick a role model to play. Then tell them: Break a leg!

difendere e proteggere i deboli è non facile

("defending and protecting the weak is not an easy job")

Chapter 5. INTERMEZZO (Short Dining Interlude to Cleanse And Refresh Your Palates)

PART A. TOM'S & DOM'S RECIPES

WHAT'S THE DIFF? ICE CREAM, GELATO, SORBET & GRANITA

Ice Cream—custard base of milk, cream, sugar, and egg yolks. Churning this as it cools gives it a smooth texture and puts air in ice cream for a light-textured, creamy result.

Gelato—starts with similar ice cream custard base, but it's churned slower and frozen at a slightly warmer temp; slow churning puts in less air, so gelato is denser. A higher freezing temperature means gelato stays silkier and softer; also more likely for gelato to use a lower proportion of cream and eggs (or none at all) so main flavor ingredient shines through.

Intermezzo

Sorbet—dairy and egg-free, made from fruit juice or flavored water and simple syrup; churned like ice cream to give it a soft and snowy texture (sherbet usually contains some amount of milk or cream in addition to the fruit juice).

Granita—granitas are just like sorbets except they're made by hand; their liquid base is poured into a shallow dish and frozen. At intervals the base is stirred to break up the ice crystals as they form. The result is a frozen dessert with a coarse and flaky texture.

Sorbetto is usually a dessert. An intermezzo is a palate cleanser. These two sharp-tasting ices are a bit of both and highlight our love of Campari, my Cuz Dom's homemade limoncello, and citrus flavors. Enjoy a "clean-up" of your taste buds between courses, or let these two recipes be your light touches to finish off any good, rich meal.

The Vespers' Trial Cookbook

COMPARI SORBETTO

<u>BOCCONCINI</u>: Campari was invented in 1860 by Italian (of course), Gaspare Campari in Novara, in the Piedmont region of Northwest Italy, west of Milano. It was originally colored with carmine dye, from crushed cochineal insects (yuck!), which gave the drink its distinctive red color. In 2006, Gruppo Campari ceased using the carmine dye in its production. *Molto Grazie Gruppo!*

<u>INGREDIENTS</u> (Serves 2):

4 to 5 Pink grapefruits, juice of

4 oz. Sugar

½ cup Campari

4-5 Drops of Angostura bitters

<u>DIRECTIONS</u>:

Mix together all ingredients until sugar dissolves.

Churn in an ice cream maker, according to manufacturer's instructions.

LIMONCELLO MINT SORBETTO

VESPER FAMILIA: my Cuz Dom makes THE BEST limoncello (see below), and good sorbet makes a great intermezzo, and the lemon and mint in this will cleanse the palette and the addition of limoncello will keep it from getting too hard in the freezer.

BOCCONCINI: limoncello is an Italian lemon liqueur mainly produced in Southern Italy (close to where Cuz Dom and I are from), especially in the region around the Gulf of Naples, the Sorrentine Peninsula, coast of Amalfi and islands of Procida, Ischia, and Capri. Traditionally, it is made from zest of Femminello St. Teresa lemons aka Sorrento lemons or Sfusato Lemons. Limoncello is the second most popular liqueur in Italy.

The exact origin of limoncello is hard to pin down between the anecdotes and legends. Its paternity is claimed by sorrentini, amalfitani, and capresi. Capri, businessman Massimo Canale, Azzurra landlady Maria Antonia Farace, the big families of Sorrento, or the fishermen of Amalfi; Cuz Dom and I like the story that claims the recipe was born inside an Italian monastery or convent to delight the monks and/or nuns between prayers.

INGREDIENTS (Serves 6):

2 cups Water

1 1/3 cups Granulated white sugar

½ cup Limoncello (Italian liqueur)

1 cup Fresh lemon juice (about 6 large lemons)

½ cup Fresh mint, chopped

DIRECTIONS:

Combine the water and sugar in a sauce pan.

Cook over medium-high heat until the sugar melts.

Turn off the heat and add the limoncello, lemon juice, and mint.

Stir; cover and chill.

Strain through a fine sieve into a bowl; discard the solids. Pour into the freezer can of an ice-cream maker; freeze per manufacturer's directions.

Spoon sorbet into a freezer-safe container; cover and freeze until firm; make in advance.

LIMONCELLO MINT SORBETTO WITH FRESH BLACKBERRIES

INGREDIENTS (Serves 4):

2 cups Water

1 1/3 cups Granulated white sugar

½ cup Limoncello

1 cup Fresh lemon juice (about 6 large lemons)

½ cup Fresh mint, chopped

2 cups Blackberries

Lemon slices (optional)

DIRECTIONS:

Combine the water, sugar, and limoncello in a saucepan over medium-high heat; bring to a boil, stirring until sugar dissolves.

Remove from heat; add lemon juice and mint. Cover and chill.

Strain juice mixture through a sieve into a bowl; discard solids. Pour mixture into the freezer can of an ice-cream freezer; freeze according to manufacturer's instructions.

Spoon sorbet into a freezer-safe container; cover and freeze one hour or until firm. Serve with blackberries; garnish with lemon slices, if desired.

If you don't want to use limoncello, you can substitute ½ cup of lemonade.

BOCCONCINI: blackberries are also called bramble, brummel, brambleberry, and bly. Their origin is hard to trace since blackberries' 40 species proliferate all over the globe, but it is likely the first were in Asia, North or South America, or in Europe. Greeks and Romans used blackberries in medicine, and Native Americans used them for food, medicine, and to dye animal skins. Blackberries were considered wild, so in the early days, they were not cultivated, and those who wanted the berries would travel to a bush and gather them. Blackberry development is relatively modern and done mostly in America. Judge Logan began to breed blackberries in California and introduced "Loganberries," a relative of blackberries, in 1880.

Medicinal history: blackberries have been used to treat bowel problems and fever for more than 2,000 years. The berry was not often used in medicinal applications but the root, bark, and leaf were; they were boiled in water and given as medicine for whooping cough and bites from venomous creatures, boils, and sore throats. In 1771, it was documented that blackberry decoctions would cure ulcers.

Folklore: blackberries were thought to protect against spells and curses if gathered during a certain phase of the moon. Children with hernias were known to pass through an arched area in the bramble to cure them. Boils were supposed to be cured when the sufferer crawled through the brambles (more likely the thorns lanced the boils).

Other uses: Native Americans used blackberry canes and vines to make twine; the bushes were often planted around European villages to offer protection against enemies and large wild animals. The berries have been used to make an indigo or purple dye.

The Vespers' Trial Cookbook

STRAWBERRY SORBETTO

<u>BOCCONCINI</u>: "Sorbet" is from the Italian verb *sorbire* (to imbibe). One story says Marco Polo brought the recipe back to Italy from China in the late 13th century, as written in *The Travels of Marco Polo*. Another story is Roman Emperor Nero invented sorbet in the 1st century AD when he had runners along the Appian Way pass buckets of snow hand over hand from the mountains to his banquet where it was mixed with honey and wine. The frozen dessert is said to have been brought to France in 1533 by Catherine de' Medici when she left Italy to marry the Duke of Orleans, later King Henry II of France.

<u>INGREDIENTS</u> (Serves 4):

1/3 cup Water

1/3 cup Granulated white sugar

2½ cups or 1lb. (454 grams) Fresh or frozen unsweetened strawberries

1 Tbsp Lemon juice

1 Tbsp Grand Marnier or other liqueur (optional)

<u>DIRECTIONS</u>:

Add sugar and water in a small saucepan, over low heat.

Stir until the sugar is completely dissolved (about three to five minutes).

Boil the mixture for one minute then remove from heat.

Pour the sugar syrup into a heatproof container.

Place in the refrigerator until completely chilled (about an hour or so).

In the meantime, thaw the frozen strawberries and put the thawed strawberries in a food processor; process until berries are pureed.

Transfer to a large bowl and add the lemon juice and liqueur (if using).

Refrigerate until mixture is thoroughly chilled.

If using fresh strawberries, puree the berries in food processor, transfer to a large bowl, add the lemon juice and liqueur (if using), and place in the refrigerator until chilled.

Once the simple syrup and pureed strawberries are completely chilled, combine simple syrup with the pureed strawberries.

Transfer the mixture to your ice cream machine and process. Once made, transfer sorbet to chilled container; store in freezer.

If you do not have ice cream machine, pour mixture into 8" or 9" stainless steel pan (sorbets freeze faster), cover with plastic wrap, put in freezer. When the sorbet is 100% frozen (3-4 hours), remove from freezer, let stand at room temp until partially thawed. Transfer partly thawed sorbet to processor, and puree to break up large ice crystals on sorbet (this gives sorbet its fluffy texture). Put sorbet back into pan and refreeze for at least 3 hours up to several days.

The Vespers' Trial Cookbook

LEMONE GRANITA ALLA SICILIANO

VESPER FAMILIA: Our good friend, Paisano and Godfather to my first born, Mike Ferarra, Esq., love this traditional Sicilian delicacy.

BOCCONCINI: *Granita* means what it sounds like—granite or stone. The granulated ice-dessert, *la granite*, was brought to Sicily by the Arabs, whose sherbert was an iced drink flavored with fruit juices or rosewater. In the Middle Ages, the *nevaroli* (meaning ice or snow-gatherers) had the important job of harvesting snows of Mt. Etna and other mountain ranges; the Sicilian nobility then bought the mounds of ice during the summer months, mixing in the juice of the island's lemons to make this perfect thirst-quencher.

INGREDIENTS (Serves 2 to 4):

½ cup (3 ½ oz.) Granulated sugar

Zest of 1 Lemon

½ cup freshly squeezed lemon juice (from about 4 lemons)

DIRECTIONS:

Whir the sugar and lemon zest together in a food processor for about 20 seconds until the sugar is moist and fragrant.

Transfer the lemon sugar to a small saucepan and add 1 cup water.

Bring to a simmer, stirring to dissolve the sugar completely.

Remove the lemon syrup from the heat and cool to room temperature.

Add the lemon juice and transfer to a freezer-safe pan.

Freeze for 2-3 hours, scraping and stirring with a fork every half hour or so to give the granita a flaky but smooth consistency. Scoop and serve.

MINT JULEP GRANITA

VESPER FAMILIA: This is my Mary Alice's favorite "Kentucky Derby Party" cooler.

BOCCONCINI: OK, so what's a "julep"? The origin of the mint julep, goes back further than 1938, which is the year it started to be "drink du jour" of the Kentucky Derby at Churchill Downs. The word "julep" comes from ancient Persian *gulab*, denoting a sweetened rosewater (the *gulab jamun* served at an Indian restaurant is made with such a syrup). In classic Arabic, the word became *julab*. Then it crossed into Latin as *julapium*. Throughout medieval Europe, variants of the name came to mean variety of medicinal syrups, generally flavored with herbal essences. The 17th-century poet John Milton described "spirits of balm and fragrant syrups" called "juleps," and by 1755, English dictionaries were defining the term as an "extemporaneous form of medicine, made of simple and compound water sweetened, serving for a vehicle to other forms not so convenient to take alone."

How did a centuries-old *"julapium"* medicine get transformed into a deliciously minty and modern cocktail? Well, as with many of our most treasured beverages—Coca-Cola and G&Ts—what began as a restorative tonic was quickly adopted for more recreational purposes. By early 1800s, using sugar water and Mentha spicata, aka spearmint, to make spirituous liquors more palatable was commonplace in "Ole Virginny." As many of the early Virginians crossed the Appalachians into Kentucky, it was only natural they'd make their restorative juleps with the most plentiful liquor at hand—bourbon. The drinks were consumed at any social, warm-weather gathering that merited a little extra cocktail-based cheer, celebrated horse races in Louisville most prominent among them.

INGREDIENTS (Serves 2 to 4):

¾ cup Sugar

1 cup packed Mint leaves, plus mint sprigs for garnish

¼ cup Bourbon, preferably Four Roses

½ tsp Crème de Menthe

DIRECTIONS:

Bring sugar and 1½ cups water to a boil in a 1 qt. saucepan; cook, stirring until sugar is dissolved, about 1 minute.

Remove from heat and add 1 cup mint leaves.

Let sit until room temperature, then chill 30 minutes.

Strain syrup into 9" x 13" baking dish, discard mint; stir in bourbon and Crème de Menthe.

Cover with plastic wrap and place in the freezer.

Using the tines of a fork, stir the mixture every 30 minutes, scraping edges and breaking up any ice chunks as mixture freezes, until granita is slushy and frozen, about 3 hours.

Scoop into chilled serving glasses and garnish with mint sprigs.

The Vespers' Trial Cookbook
GRAPEFRUIT CAMPARI GRANITA

BOCCONCINI: grapefruit, aka "The Forbidden Fruit," is a hybrid subtropical citrus tree known for its sour to semi-sweet fruit; it was an 18th century hybrid first bred in Barbados. One story of the fruit's origins is that a "Captain Shaddock" brought pomelo seeds to Jamaica and bred the first fruit; but, it probably originated as a naturally occurring hybrid. This "forbidden fruit" was first documented in 1750 by a Welshman, Rev. Griffith Hughes, who described specimens in *The Natural History of Barbados*. Today, the grapefruit is called one of the "Seven Wonders of Barbados."

Ruby Red grapefruit: the 1929 Ruby Red patent had real commercial success, which came after the discovery of a red grapefruit growing on a pink variety. Only with Ruby Reds did grapefruits become agricultural successes. Reds even became Texas' symbolic fruit where "inferior" whites were eliminated; only reds were grown for decades. The Rio Red variety is current (2007) Texas grapefruits with registered trademarks Rio Star and Ruby-Sweet, also sometimes promoted as "Reddest" and "Texas Choice."

Campari was invented in 1860 by Italian (of course), Gaspare Campari in Novara, in the Piedmont region of Northwest Italy, west of Milano; originally colored with carmine dye, from crushed cochineal insects, which gave it its distinctive red color. In 2006, Gruppo Campari ceased using the carmine dye in its production.

INGREDIENTS (Serves 4 to 6):

2 cups freshly squeezed Ruby Red grapefruit juice

½ cup Campari

½ cup Sugar

½ Vanilla bean split lengthwise, seeds scraped and reserved

DIRECTIONS:

Purée juice, Campari, sugar, vanilla seeds, and $1/3$ oz. and the smaller cone holds $3/4$ cup water in a blender.

Pour into a 9" x 13" baking dish, cover with plastic wrap, and place in the freezer.

Using the tines of a fork, stir the mixture every 30 minutes, scraping edges and breaking up any ice chunks as mixture freezes, until granita is slushy and frozen, about 3 hours.

Intermezzo

Scoop into chilled serving glasses.

The Vespers' Trial Cookbook

WHITE WINE OR CHAMPAGNE GRANITA

VESPER FAMILIA: Mary Alice Vesper is a big fan of anything with champagne in it.

BOCCONCINI: Prosecco is an Italian sparkling wine, generally a dry or extra dry wine, and made from Glera ("Prosecco") grapes which initially grew near the village of Prosecco on the Karst hills north of Trieste and was then known as Puccino. The name is derived from the Italian village. DOC prosecco was produced in the regions of Veneto and Friuli Venezia Giulia, as far back as Roman times. In the 18th century, cultivation of Glera expanded throughout the hills of Veneto and Friuli.

INGREDIENTS (Serves 4):

2 cups Full-bodied white wine

½ cup unsweetened Apple juice

⅓ cup Water

½ cup Sugar

Dried Apple slices, for serving

DIRECTIONS:

Place white wine (or Proseca or champagne), juice, sugar, and ⅓ oz. and the smaller cone holds ¾ cup water in a bowl.

Whisk until sugar is completely dissolved, about 2 minutes.

Pour into a 9" x 13" baking dish, cover with plastic wrap, and place in the freezer.

Using the tines of a fork, stir the mixture every 30 minutes, scraping edges and breaking up any ice chunks as mixture freezes, until granita is slushy and frozen, about 3 hours.

Scoop into chilled serving glasses and top with apple slices, if you like.

THE VESPERS' TRIAL COOKBOOK

SHERRY CARDAMOM GRANITA

VESPER FAMILIA: as Mary Alice Vesper says: "KISS it! Keep it Simple Silly!" You can also make this with puree of plain ginger if you can't/don't want to find cardamom.

BOCCONCINI: Cardamom or cardamon refers to several plants of the ginger family. The word "cardamom" comes from the Latin *cardamomum*, which was the name for an Indian spice plant. Guatemala is the biggest producer and exporter of this spice in the world, followed by India. It is the world's third most expensive spice by weight, outstripped in value only by saffron and vanilla.

BACKGROUND: this delicately sweet, lightly spiced, sherry-based granita makes a very refreshing palate cleanser for your intermezzo.

INGREDIENTS (Serves 4):

2/3 cup Sugar

1 Tbsp Loose black tea

6 Cardamom pods, lightly crushed

Zest and juice of 1 lemon

½ cup Amontillado sherry

DIRECTIONS:

Bring sugar, tea, and 2/3 oz. and the smaller cone holds 3/4 cup water to a boil in a 1 qt. saucepan over high heat.

Cook, stirring, until sugar is dissolved, about 1 minute.

Add cardamom and lemon zest; let cool completely.

Strain syrup into a 9" x 13" baking dish.

Stir in lemon juice, sherry, and 1 cup water.

Cover with plastic wrap and place in the freezer.

Using the tines of a fork, stir the mixture every 30 minutes, scraping edges and breaking up any ice chunks as mixture freezes, until granita is slushy and frozen, about 3 hours.

Scoop into chilled serving glasses.

Intermezzo

PART B. TOM'S TRIAL TIPS: DEPOSITION & TRIAL NOTEBOOKS (DISCOVERY, TRIAL, CASE EVALUATION AND SETTLEMENT)

CLEANSE YOUR DISCOVERY & TRIAL PALATES WITH MOUSETRAPS AND DEATH STARS, NEW RECIPES, AND TACTICS FOR DEPS: BIGGER & BETTER SETTLEMENT & DEP NOTEBOOKS

I. INTRO TO THE NEWEST DEP NOTEBOOK: BIGGER & BETTER

This will orient plaintiff trial lawyers to the newest litigation weaponry (proven successful in actual litigation) and methods to help you be a "triple threat"—in discovery, settlement, and trial. The new "weaponry" involve interchangeable use of BIGGER (2 volume) Vesper & Kosieradzki Deposition Notebook 3rd ed. and (2 volume) Vesper Trial Notebook 5th ed.

BETTER than prior editions, the new Settlement Notebook—with its fresh forms and sample presentations—has innovative settlement, discovery, and litigation strategies that are incorporated in both Trial and Deposition Notebooks. This is an introductory preview of the Deposition Notebook 3rd ed. and Trial Notebook 5th ed. for settlement strategy, preparing settlement presentations, preparation and taking of depositions, as well as focusing your overall discovery and trial preparation.

Most lawyers today are experts at "litigation." They do everything (especially some of our hourly brethren) prior to trial. But few "litigators" have actual jury trial experience. "Jim Bob" Moriarty, a trial lawyer from Houston, Texas, refers to the trial lawyer's job of "litigating" as akin to a "condenser." Just as a condenser in a refrigerator takes out hot air, the trial lawyer's job is to remove the "hot air" from the pretrial litigation process: compress and avoid unnecessary time delays or wasted motions. John Romano from Florida says: "today (for many reasons, not least of which is financial self-motivation), insurance companies are less willing to make fair settlement offers and more willing to force every case to trial and/or appeal; and, plaintiff "trial lawyers" (for reasons, not the least of which are financial self-preservation) are less likely to try cases and more likely to mediate/arbitrate." I concur. But there is a method to reach resolution in shorter time + with better results. If you shorten your client's "time line" to settlement and/or trial, you will succeed in your law practice by satisfying—if not enthralling—your clients.

Organizing your thoughts, strategies, and materials needed to conduct an efficient and effective settlement presentation, discovery, and trial begins with an overall "file sense" of order and ongoing organizational framework (or "toolbox" or "cookbook") in which to store then retrieve data. Case files should be standardized to quickly yet accurately review in segments. E.g., a good case filing system is where all correspondence is date stamped in chronological order in one clip/folder/binder et seq.; all investigation materials filed chronologically and indexed; all medical records filed chronologically or by subject or treatment modality or health care provider with an indexed covering page/cumulative table of contents; and pleadings and discovery likewise date/Bates stamped and kept in chronological and/or procedural order and indexed. This standardized and indexed case file allows for quick manual or computer review of the file so thoughts and plans can be formulated for taking/defending any issue during discovery or trial.

II. WHAT'S WITH ALL THESE "MOUSETRAPS AND DEATH STARS"?

These nicknamed techniques are innovative ways for plaintiff trial lawyers to fight fairly for our clients to achieve full unobstructed discovery (the "Death Star" Dep Notice) and acceptance of responsibility by wrongdoers (the "Miller Mousetrap").

The "DEATH STAR" DEPOSITION NOTICE, invented by Mark Kosieradzki, Esq., from Minneapolis, MN, coauthor of AAJ Deposition Notebook, named for the Star Wars sci-fi movie ultimate weapon which destroyed entire planets. The "Death Star" technique is fully explained in the Deposition Notebook. It is one of the best ways to use Federal Rules and equivalent state rules to uncover relevant documents; how and why they were originally created, used, filed; and then for purposes of litigation how they were located, copied (edited? hidden? or deleted?), and produced for the deposition.

The "MILLER MOUSETRAP" is a series of questions by Phil Miller, Esq. of Nashville, TN, which lead defendant (individual/corporate) into admitting personal or corporate responsibility and possibly recklessness. The line of questions (Form 3E, Phil Miller's "Mousetrap" Questions for Establishing Responsibility/Reckless Conduct), and a sample outline for trucking company representative (Form 3F, Phil Miller Mousetrap Sample Question Outline in a Trucking Co. Deposition), and actual dep transcript of "Miller Mousetrap" Qs asked of a witness (Form 3G, Miller's "Mousetrap" Q & A From an Excerpted Deposition Transcript) are all available in the Deposition Notebook.

The "DEPOSITION PROTOCOLS:" The Ground Rules We Should All Follow is another brainchild of my ATLA (now AAJ) sidekick Mark Kosieradzki. With some lawyers, it is necessary/helpful to take the time to repeat all the "ground rules" by which we conduct ourselves during depositions. This we do prior to taking depositions, at the very start of discovery by asking the adversary to agree in advance to the rules or what we like to call "Protocols" for depositions. If the adversary will not agree in advance, there is always the option to file a motion for a court order to make the Protocols compulsory on all counsel. Likewise, if a new attorney—or the same obstinate one(s)—appear for and act up at the deposition in bad faith, ignorance, or intentional disregard of the rules, then rereading on the record your understanding of the standards of conduct for depositions may have a curative effect upon the obstructive/obstinate attorney(s) and helps cast a favorable light upon your repute with your client, your staff, the witness, and the court reporter. The Deposition Notebook (Sec. IV & App. Form 9B) has a full explanation, form of motion, and brief in support of these "Deposition Protocols" [Sec. IV & App. 9B].

III. HOW CAN YOU FOCUS AND TEST DRIVE YOUR CASES?

There is an old Italian proverb: "A man who chases two chickens always loses both." Often, focus groups and/or mock juries are not thought of until after discovery has been substantially completed, and the case is on the trial list. Outstanding trial lawyers and jury consultants advocate "focusing" your trial themes long before a trial date is given out by modern day civil case management computers. Focusing on dispositive issues for trial can be done before or shortly after complaint is filed. The issues, themes, and phrases identified by "real people" who make up real juries help direct and focus discovery.

The Trial and Deposition Notebooks both provide an instructional, operational framework and a depository for the forms, notes, ideas, and strategies gathered and generated by using focus groups or mock juries. The Focus/Mock Jury Section with its eight subtabs will assist trial lawyers and support staff to focus the goals of discovery, as well as trial.

This organized method and framework for conducting a focus group/mock jury allows you to plan, record, and preserve the ideas generated from focus group/mock jury exercises. The Deposition and Trial Notebooks are both supplemented with an entire section, color coded with three large yellow tabs and eight smaller yellow subtabs for conducting focus groups and mock juries.

Optimally, you should begin to focus your client's case from the initial interview and the moment you begin to prepare the complaint to be filed. By seeing what issues are important to focus/mock jurors, you can draft more pointed discovery requests. At an early stage in the litigation process, if you and your client become better oriented upon your objective and how to achieve same, there may be a tremendous savings in time, money, and emotional stress.

IV. IMPORTANT QUESTIONS A TO Z BY PLAINTIFF LAWYERS

The newest Settlement, Dep, and Trial Notebook systems, as revised and used, will help answer the following self-critical analyses:

A. Will These New Notebooks Help Me Settle Cases?

Today, almost all civil trial calendars are overshadowed by ADR/CDR (Alternative/Complimentary Dispute Resolution) proceedings. There are more settlement proceedings—be it telephone negotiations, judicial settlement conferences, arbitrations, or mediations—than there are jury trials. However, by preparing the best trial proofs and trial presentations, and having all the data at your fingertips for any settlement discussion at any time or place, you are better able to engage in any form of negotiation or settlement hearing. The Settlement Section of both Trial and Deposition Notebooks provides a ready-made, working portfolio to take with you to any meeting with clients, adjusters, defense council, etc. Your entire Settlement Section can be kept separate in Volume 2 of the Notebooks and used as a cumulative and growing "Settlement Book" into which everything that can help the settlement overview, accumulation of positive proofs, and the final settlement briefs or presentations can be stored and kept "on the front burner" and "at the ready" in your three ring Settlement Notebook at all times.

The Settlement Section will help make any case—large, complex, or relatively simple and straitforward—easily digestible and presentable. Having every bit of Settlement Data that supports your Settlement Briefs/Letters/Power Point presentations laid out and tabulated in easily retrievable format sends the right message (you're ready) to the right people (clients, adjusters, supervisors, defense counsel, arbitrator/mediators, trial judge) at the right time (whenever and wherever you confront the issue of settlement).

B. Will They Help Improve My "Bottom Line"?

Time is a precious commodity. Your time is money. The Notebooks will save both your time and your clients' money. Once the Settlement, Dep, and/or Trial Notebooks are prepared by your staff, you will save inordinate amounts of wasted time digging for information. Everything you need will be in one easily reviewable location. Your mediation/arbitration, dep, or trial prep time will be reduced, and therefore, more time can be spent researching legal issues, thinking of creative ways to express yourself, or discussing the case with your clients and witnesses.

The new Notebooks help avoid mistakes or duplications of effort which cost money. They help focus settlement strategies/presentations, discovery, and scheduling witnesses for trial, thus preventing wasted time, unnecessary travel, and standby expenses.

C. Will They Save Me Time?

Self-evident features: once either Notebook is prepared, you need not reorganize your file for the next dep or discovery step, ADR/CDR (Alternative/Complimentary Dispute Resolution) or trial. Notwithstanding litigation delays, you will be ready. After a quick review of and orientation to the cumulative discovery in the Deposition Notebook and a quick pretrial check of the various sections in the Settlement Section and your Trial Notebook, you will be properly prepared to arbitrate/mediate/try your case.

D. Can These Notebooks Be Delegated to My Staff/Associates?

With the Guide in both Notebooks, any lawyer, paralegal, or secretary can understand how to begin, set up, and update your Settlement, Dep, and Trial Notebooks. The Guide to each notebook (excluding focus group and settlement articles and forms in Appendix) can be read in a half-hour. After a few "trial runs," your staff will be accomplished users. By ongoing use of Trial and Dep Notebooks, both can be adapted to your personal style.

E. Will They Improve My Case File Organization?

"Historically, there are three ideas involved in a profession: organization, learning, and a spirit of public service. These are essential. The remaining idea of gaining a livelihood is incidental." Roscoe Pound "What Is a Profession," 19 Notre Dame L. 203, 204 (1944). Both Notebooks are organized to find and retrieve data quickly and easily for pretrial discovery, settlement conferences, preparation, or trial. The 2-volume Trial & Deposition Notebooks are laid out in main color-coded tabbed and numbered sections:

I.   THE MAIN DEP NOTEBOOK—VOLUME 1

1. Plan
2. Research
3. Q&A Outline
4. Notice/Stips/Instructions
5. Data Base
6. Dep Rules
7. Notes/Summary
8. Originals
9. Things To Do

II. DEP NOTEBOOK ARCHIVE—VOL 1—contains three sets of tabs for completed deps:

1. Summary
2. Notes
3. Originals

III. SETTLEMENT section—VOL 2—has three sets of large tabs + 16 subdivisions/tabs to view all facets of settlement strategy, data + store settlement briefs/presentations:

   A. Overview (with eight subdivisions/tabs)
   1. Strategy
   2. Case Evaluation
   3. Jury Verdict Research
   4. Settlement History
   5. Fee Shifting
   6. ADR/CDR
   7. Liens
   8. Recovery Management

   B. Settlement Data (with eight subdivision/tabs)
   1. Plaintiff Background
   2. Liability

3. Injury(s)
4. Economic Loss
5. "Human Loss"
6. $64 Question
7. Consortium
8. Punitive/Bad Faith/Fee Shift

C. Settlement Briefs & Presentations

IV. FOCUS GROUP section—VOL. 2—has three large tabs with eight subtabs for conducting and storing information and ideas gathered from focus groups/mock jury research:

A. Ideas
B. Focus/Mock Juries (with eight subdivisions/tabs)
   1. Focus Plan
   2. Confidentiality Forms
   3. Jurors' Background Data
   4. Jury Questions
   5. Minutes/Notes
   6. Lessons Learned
   7. Visual Strategy
   8. Trial Prep/To Do
C. Notes

The 2-volume Trial Notebook is set out in nine color-coded divisions. The first set of seven dividers and subdividers are contained in Volume 1:

VOLUME 1 of the TRIAL NOTEBOOK

I. Pre Trial Management
II. Preparation
III. Legal Research
IV. Trial
V. Trial Ideas

VI. Discovery

VII. Post-Trial Proceedings

VOLUME 2 of the TRIAL NOTEBOOK

Volume 2 of the Trial Notebook contains the same organizational dividers and subdividers/tabs as Volume 2 of the Deposition Notebook (see above).

VIII. Concept/Focus

IX. Settlement Section

Each of nine Trial Notebook's main divisions has subtabs for every aspect of settlement, focus group/mock jury pretrial preparation, and trial. Both Notebook systems are color coordinated, thereby allowing easy access into separate subsections and cross-referencing from Dep Notebook into Trial Notebook. Both provide easy filing and retrieval systems.

F. Will These Notebooks Affect How I am Perceived?

If organized and well prepared, you will be confident. If confident, you will be seen as a worthy, formidable adversary. Being organized and well prepared will assist how your clients, witnesses, adversaries, and arbitrators/mediators/trial judges perceive you.

G. Will They Improve My Negotiation/Settlement Skills?

The Trial & Deposition Notebooks provide valuable insights on settlement strategy, some better negotiation techniques, how to have better mediations with a law firm "Mediation Policy," what makes insurance companies settle (or not), land mines to avoid in mediation, and how to avoid settlement malpractice. Some Settlement articles include: 1) WHY YOU NEED A CASE SPECIFIC SETTLEMENT STRATEGY; 2) WHAT NOT TO CONSIDER WHEN PLANNING SETTLEMENT STRATEGY: NEEDS BASED NEGOTIATION; 3) WHAT "GENERALLY" YOU SHOULD CONSIDER—HIGH GROUND & RISK; 4) A SCIENCE TO SETTLEMENT? YES . . . CHAOS!; 5) WHAT DO INSURANCE COMPANIES USE? . . . COMPUTERS!; 6) WHAT MAKES INSURANCE COMPANIES SETTLE . . . OR NOT?; 7) WHAT ARE THE "LAND MINES" IN MEDIATION—AND HOW TO AVOID THEM; 8) HOW TO HAVE BETTER MEDIATIONS; 9) WHAT ABOUT HIGH-LOW SETTLEMENT AGREEMENTS?; 10) THE EIGHT AREAS OF SETTLEMENT MALPRACTICE; 11) THE "LAND MINES" IN RECOVERY MANAGEMENT; 12) FAQs (Frequently Asked Questions) About Structured Settlements.

H. Will They Improve My Discovery Skills?

With more time to reflect alone and with clients on settlement presentation, discovery, trial, witnesses, and evidence, you will be more persuasive. Your skills will improve. Saving unnecessary time searching for facts, materials, avoiding "Paper Chases," and reducing your "warm up" time, you will be a better prepared and confident advocate.

I. Will They Improve My Trial Skills?

With better control over legal research, trial proofs, exhibits, and witness materials for direct and cross, your effortlessness, self-assurance, and poise in trial will noticeably improve.

J. Will The Dep & Trial Notebooks Be Expensive?

Deposition Notebooks and Trial Notebooks are available through Thomson Reuters. Considering your/your staff's time and unnecessary expense saved and the favorable client relationships and peer approval to be gained, this price is miniscule.

K. Can They Be Recycled/Reused?

Another cost savings is the fact the letter size 3-ring binders and plastic color-coded tabs can be reused for any of your settlement presentations, discovery, or trials. The letter size forms in the Notebooks can be reordered from Thomson Reuters and kept in your office supply. If you have a busy litigation practice, you might want to have several extra binders and sets of dividers and forms.

L. Can They Improve My Existing System(s)?

If you already have a "settlement/deposition/trial book/folder system" that is working perfectly, then you probably have a very good system for your style of advocacy. But even "the best" offensive or defensive plan can be improved upon and updated. If you already have your own system for settlement, pretrial discovery, and trial, be it with trial folders, clips, or two/three ring binders, take the time to look at the Notebooks and adapt some of their up-to-date features to your litigation and trial prep systems.

M. Does The Settlement Notebook Have Forms I Can Use?

The Settlement section of both Notebooks contains a helpful checklist and outline for evaluating and briefing a plaintiff's personal injury case. There are also helpful Samples of demand letters, settlement briefs, and CD settlement presentations.

N. Will These Notebooks Help Reduce Stress?

The Trial & Deposition Notebooks both help reduce stress. Their use will reduce stress upon you and your staff to prepare for, monitor, and follow discovery and prepare for and conduct trial. As a very important side effect, these notebooks will also reduce the trial and deposition stresses upon your clients and witnesses.

Use of a visible system of notes/papers somehow sends the unspoken message to any client, deponent, or trial witness that you have the situation well in hand. Notebooks will reduce witness anxiety. Like the keystone in an arch, a well-organized litigation system "puts it together" in eyes of clients and witnesses. Your Notebooks will be a sedative for frayed nerves of clients or inexperienced witness. Even experienced expert witnesses—doctors, engineers, etc.—respond favorably. They sense you are not going to waste their time with unnecessary pretrial preparation or embarrass them in court. Most trial judges are less reluctant to try cases if they sense the trial lawyer is truly prepared to proceed to verdict. Your Notebooks can be your "calling cards" to the judiciary.

O. What is The Importance of Organizing For Settlement?

The Trial & Deposition Notebooks both have a self-contained and removable Settlement Section which allows you and your client to discuss, record, and store information necessary to evaluate the client's case and plan and decide upon a strategy to achieve a fair value. Both Notebooks provide a checklist with subdividers and tabs which can be very useful in assembling, organizing, and storing the data needed for any type of settlement presentation—a settlement demand letter, settlement brief (do not call them "brochures"—it is too disparaging of your work product), arbitration/mediation statement, or video/CD/DVD presentation.

This system for planning, discussing, and conducting case evaluation and settlement presentations and conferences allows you to plan and preserve all settlement demands/offers, as well as the data needed to intelligently and fairly discuss settlement with the client, adversaries, or neutral arbitrators/mediators/judges.

P. Why is an Overall Settlement Strategy Important?

While the task of a plaintiff trial lawyer is very complex, it can be dissected into four component and far from simplistic settlement processes: 1) The First Phase is "Case Evaluation"—to recognize and evaluate the facts and circumstances of the plaintiff's case; 2) The Second Phase is "Liability Insurance & Risk Analysis"—to recognize the "risk factors" and settlement concerns of the liability carrier(s); 3) The Third Phase is the "Settlement Presentation"—to prepare a settlement presentation or position which will motivate the insurer/self-insured to make a reasonable and acceptable settlement offer; 4) The Fourth and Final Phase is "Recovery Management"—to plan and consider how plaintiff clients will maximize their net recoveries and if necessary address the safe future use of their net settlement dollars. Without a considered and overall settlement strategy, you and your client will be left to a reactionary role in the process.

Q. Does The Deposition Notebook Have Forms I Can Use?

As you can see from the itemization below, there are numerous helpful forms to use, reuse, and adapt to your standard deposition and discovery procedures. Included among these are John Romano's "5 Silver Bullets" (For Defense Experts); the "Miller Mousetrap" (Phil Miller's Line of Questions for Establishing Responsibility and/or Reckless Conduct); Mark Kosieradzki's "Death Star" (Dep Notice & Outline to compel a Designated Representative/FRCP 30 (b)(6) Witness to Produce and explain origins and evolutions of documents); and practical dep tips for clients, experts, and lawyers:

APPENDIX 1A—OUTLINE FOR DEP Q & A OF MOTOR VEHICLE DRIVER
APPENDIX 1B—ALTERNATIVE Q & A OF MOTOR VEHICLE DRIVER
APPENDIX 2—OUTLINE FOR DEPOSITION Q & A OF PROPERTY OWNER
APPENDIX 3A—OUTLINE FOR DEPOSITION Q & A OF EXPERT WITNESS
APPENDIX 3B—JOHN ROMANO'S 5 SILVER BULLETS vs DEFENSE EXPERTS
APPENDIX 3C—JIM PERDUE'S 5 CROSS-EXAM Qs FOR DEFENSE DOCTORS
APPENDIX 3D—HARRY PHILO's 5 STEPS RE PRODUCT/PREMISES SAFETY
APPENDIX 3E—PHIL MILLER'S "MOUSETRAP" QUESTIONS TO ESTABLISH RESPONSIBILITY AND/OR RECKLESS CONDUCT
APPENDIX 3F—PHIL MILLER'S "MOUSETRAP" SAMPLE Q&A OUTLINE
APPENDIX 3G—PHIL MILLER'S "MOUSETRAP" Q&A FROM ACTUAL DEP APPENDIX 4A—GENERAL NOTICE TO DEP WITH DOCUMENTS—STATE
APPENDIX 4B1—FEDERAL GENERAL NOTICE TO TAKE DEP ORAL EXAM
APPENDIX 4B2—FED DEP ATTACHMENT OF "WRITINGS" TO BE PRODUCED
APPENDIX 5A—STATE COURT NOTICE TO DEP MVA DEFENDANT DRIVER
APPENDIX 5B—FEDERAL NOTICE DEP AN MVA DEFENDANT—FRCP 30(a)
APPENDIX 6A—STATE COURT NOTICE TO DEPOSE A DESIGNATED REP
APPENDIX 6B—FRCP 30(b)(6) NOTICE OF DEP OF CORP, GOVT AGENCY
APPENDIX 6C—FRCP 30(b)(6) ALTERNATIVE NOTICE OF VIDEO DEP RE DEFENSE CONTENTIONS—FRCP 30(b)(6)

APPENDIX 6D—ALTERNATE DEATH STAR VIDEO DEP FRCP 30 (b)(6)
APPENDIX 6E—FRCP 30 (b)(6) WITNESS Q & A
APPENDIX 6F—FRCP 30 (b) (6) E-DISCOVERY/IT (InfoTechnology) DEP NOTICE
APPENDIX 6G—FRCP 34 REQUEST PRODUCTION of E-DOCUMENTS/THINGS
APPENDIX 6H—SAMPLE EDD DATA PRESERVATION LETTER TO CLIENT
APPENDIX 6I—SAMPLE EDD DATA PRESERVATION LETTER TO 3rd PARTY
APPENDIX 7A—STATE COURT SUBPOENA FOR DEPOSITION
APPENDIX 7B1—FRCP45(d)(1) DEP SUBPOENA TO TESTIFY/PRODUCE
APPENDIX 7B2—DEP NOTICE ATTACHMENT OF "WRITINGS" TO PRODUCE
APPENDIX 7C—ALTERNATIVE DEP NOTICE TO TAKE VIDEO DEP—FRCP 45
APPENDIX 8A—STATE COURT NOTICE TO TAKE A VIDEOTAPE DEP
APPENDIX 8B—FEDERAL NOTICE TO TAKE A VIDEO DEP-FRCP 30(b)(2)
APPENDIX 8C—ALTERNATIVE NOTICE TO TAKE VIDEO FRCP 30(b)(6) DEP
APPENDIX 8D1—MOTION TO TAKE A TELEPHONE DEP—FRCP 30 (b)(7)
APPENDIX 8D2—ORDER TO TAKE A TELEPHONE DEP—FRCP 30 (b)(7)
APPENDIX 8E1—MOTION FOR VIDEO CONFERENCE DEP OF REMOTE LOCATION WITNESS
APPENDIX 8E2—ORDER TO TAKE VIDEO CONFERENCE DEPOSITION OF A DEPONENT FROM A REMOTE LOCATION—FRCP 30 (b)(7)
APPENDIX 9A—THE USUAL STIPULATIONS
APPENDIX 9B—THE DEPOSITION PROTOCOLS
APPENDIX 10—IRVING YOUNGER'S NINE OBJECTIONS TO FORM
APPENDIX 11—GENERAL INTRODUCTORY INSTRUCTIONS TO DEPONENT
APPENDIX 12—SPECIAL INTRODUCTORY INSTRUCTIONS TO DEPONENT
APPENDIX 13—STANDING INSTRUCTIONS FOR COURT REPORTERS
APPENDIX 14A—COMMON DEP PROBLEMS & RULES FOR FAIR DISCOVERY
APPENDIX 14B—PLAINTIFF'S BRIEF IN SUPPORT OF DEP PROTOCOL
APPENDIX 14C—STIPULATION & ORDER FOR DEPOSITION PROTOCOL
APPENDIX 15A—SUGGESTIONS FOR CLIENT DISCOVERY DEPOSITION
APPENDIX 15B—12 COMMON "PITFALLS" IN PLAINTIFF DEPS + ANTIDOTES
APPENDIX 15C—SUGGESTIONS FOR PROPERLY GIVING YOUR TESTIMONY
APPENDIX 16—HELPFUL TIPS FOR WITNESSES IN VIDEOTAPE DEPS
APPENDIX 17—VIDEO TIPS FOR TRIAL LAWYERS
APPENDIX 18—EXPERT WITNESS DEPOSITION CAVEATS

R. How Will My Discovery Be Better Organized?

Whenever the opposition deposes your client, or you depose an important witness, the use of a standard procedure allows you, defense, court reporter, all parties to be effectively and efficiently involved in dep process from beginning through the follow-up phase. Whether you take deps or propound epistolary discovery by interrogatories, requests to produce, requests to admit, etc., your overall goals and/or "targets of opportunity" and follow up requests should be in a central location for easy access and review.

An organized litigation system allows getting any requested data in a professional and orderly manner. To give yourself such a modus operandi is the key.

Intermezzo

Providing yourself with a tabbed three ring Deposition Notebook and organized three ring Trial Notebook for trial preparation is a long term time saver and a helpful device to help pursue your discovery efforts and also prepare for trial testimony of the deponent.

S. What's The Difference: Deposition Notebook vs. Folders?

Normally, a "dep folder" consists of a duo-pronged folder with dep notice, photocopied dep outlines from form books, handwritten notes, and yellow legal pad tossed in with driving directions, "weapons of choice" for most lawyers. Whether you divide a single dep folder into subparts with inserts, use tabs, or sectional dividers or slightly more expensive three part folder/notebook depends on personal style. But there is a more organized and efficient approach to deposition and discovery practice: AAJ Deposition Notebook. Difference is that between a musket and a machine gun: you can create one folder per dep (like loading and reloading old time muskets for each shot); or you/your staff can load, update, and accumulate your Dep Notebook (like having all the ammo you will need in your machine gun, always loaded and ready to use).

T. How is The Settlement Notebook System Set Up?

Both Trial and Dep Notebooks' Settlement Sections are made to be removed and put in a separate binder, used at mediations/arbitrations. The three large, bright green dividers to store all input/plans for evaluation, settlement, recovery management of client's net proceeds, outline settlement package/presentations, and settlement briefs or demand letters.

IX(A).	SETTLEMENT OVERVIEW (AND EIGHT SUBDIVISION TABS)
IX(B).	SETTLEMENT DATA (AND EIGHT SUBDIVISION TABS)
IX(C).	SETTLEMENT BRIEFS & PRESENTATIONS

The first large divider in Settlement Section—IX(A), SETTLEMENT OVERVIEW—has eight bright green subdividers for you to strategize, evaluate, record settlement offers/demands, participate in ADR/CDR (alternative/complimentary dispute resolution) proceedings such as mediation/arbitration, calculate liens, and consider the net recovery and management thereof for the best interests of your client. These eight bright green subdividers will help keep the overall settlement goals of the client at hand at all times:

1. STRATEGY

2. CASE EVALUATION

3. JURY VERDICT RESEARCH

4. SETTLEMENT HISTORY

5. FEE SHIFTING

6. ADR/CDR

7. LIENS

8. RECOVERY MANAGEMENT

The next section—IX(B), SETTLEMENT DATA—contains another eight bright green subdividers for you/your staff to use to gather all the raw data, and plan and prepare the exhibits and/or PPT slides to use for an effective settlement brochure or presentation. As the facts, documents, and exhibits develop during discovery, clean and marked copies can and should be placed in one or more of the eight subdividers in order to begin to formulate the structure of what will become the ultimate "position paper," that is, the Settlement Brief, Videotape, and CD for your client. These eight tabs will help you and your staff to collect, prioritize, sequence, and arrange this data within the overall process of the presentation of settlement demand and negotiation:

1. PLAINTIFF BACKGROUND

2. LIABILITY

3. INJURY(S)

4. ECONOMIC LOSS

5. "HUMAN LOSS"

6. $64 QUESTION

7. CONSORTIUM

8. PUNITIVE/BAD FAITH/FEE SHIFT

The last section and divider—IX(C), BRIEFS & PRESENTATIONS—is simply a central place to store your final settlement "package"—whether a demand letter, settlement brief (avoid the retail merchandizing term "brochure"), or Power Point presentation. All position papers, exhibits, videotapes, CDs, and DVDs dealing with any party's settlement position should be stored in this part of your Notebook.

U. How is The Focus Group Section Set Up?

This entire self-contained Focus Group Section with its eight subdividers or smaller tabs is provided for your use while planning, conducting, and following up after conducting focus groups. Even in seemingly straightforward and obvious cases of clear 100% liability, the ingenuity of liability insurance companies has become such that discovery and trial may be necessary to achieve fair and reasonable compensation for our clients. Often, the issues raised by the defense as to comparative fault, "other causes," or even outright accusations of malingering are issues we can and should focus upon as early as possible during the discovery and pretrial phase of litigation.

Trial & Deposition Notebook's Focus Group Guides explain reasons for and the general procedure by which focus groups/mock juries should be conducted. The following is a summary of "How to Do It" Guide for Conducting Focus Groups with the Notebooks to keep your plans, ideas, and strategies refined from the process of using focus/mock juries:

Tab 1	Focus Plan for "The Jury Project"
Tab 2	Confidentiality Forms
Tab 3	Jurors' Background Data
Tab 4	Jury Questions
Tab 5	Minutes/Notes
Tab 6	Lessons Learned
Tab 7	Visual Strategy
Tab 8	Trial Prep/To Do

V. Does The Focus Group Section Have Forms I Can Use?

The Focus Group Section in both Notebooks has every form you need to conduct your own focus group with or without a professional jury consultant.

W. How is The New Deposition Notebook Set Up?

A better way of approaching discovery and deposing a key witness is to use a three ring binder Deposition Notebook and incorporate the following 10 tabs or dividers:

1. PREP: Deposition Plan and Preparation Notes.

2. OUTLINE: An Overview of Areas of Inquiry.

3. NOTICE: The Dep Notice/Subpoena With Attachments.

4. STIPS: The "Usual Stipulations."

5. THE WITNESS: Instructions to Give Before Dep. Over two dozen sample instructions are provided for you to use to properly instruct and "box in" a deponent.

6. THE COURT REPORTER: Written Instructions for Shorthand Reporters. There are a list of standard written instructions which include standing requests that any time a witness is told "Not to answer a question," that the record be noted and a separate list of such instructions be made for you for the purpose of a Motion to Compel. Also, requests for additional information not available at the dep should be made as a separate "Request List" and provided to all counsel expeditiously by the Court Reporter.

7. DEP RULES: Court Rules & Applicable Case Law. It is helpful to have a summary of some of the more common or fragrant violations of professional conduct during depositions. Having case law at your fingertips in your Dep Notebook is often helpful to defuse a hostile deposition environment.

8. DATABASE: Case Database of Facts and Impeachment Data.

9. TO DO: Things to Do & Notes.

10. ORIGINALS: The Original Transcript and Exhibits.

11. AN ARCHIVE SYSTEM: Where to Put the Completed Discovery.

X. Does The Trial Notebook Have Forms I Can Use?

The Trial Notebook has almost a hundred useful forms to prep and try a plaintiff's case.

Y. How is The New Trial Notebook Set Up?

The organization of the 2-volume Trial Notebook is set out in nine color-coded divisions.

The first set of seven dividers and subdividers are contained in Volume 1:

I. Pre Trial Management

II. Preparation

III. Legal Research

IV. Trial

V. Trial Ideas

VI. Discovery

VII. Post-Trial Proceedings

Volume 2 of the Trial Notebook contains the same organizational dividers and subdividers/tabs as Volume 2 of the Deposition Notebook (see above).

VIII. Concept/Focus

IX. Settlement Section

Each of these nine Trial Notebook's main divisions has subtabs for every aspect of settlement, focus group/mock jury pretrial preparation, and trial. Both Dep & Trial Notebooks systems are color coordinated and allow easy access into separate tabbed subsections and cross-referencing from the Dep Notebook into the Trial Notebook. Both provide easy filing and retrieval system for your staff.

Z. Are These Notebooks Just For New Lawyers?

In a one syllable answer: No! We never stop learning in our professional lives as trial lawyers. Our destiny is to continue to fight our best fight for our clients' sake, with the best litigation weapons at hand. Even old pilots use checklists before takeoff. To do our best preparation for settlement presentations, discovery, depositions, and trial, the use of the Dep and Trial Notebook tabs can be a checklist for you and your staff regardless of your level of experience. Having better, faster grasp of all the data needed for conducting a dep, opening statement, arbitration, or settlement negotiation can benefit trial lawyers of any age and level of trial expertise. Although you may have your own settlement, deposition, focus group, and trial systems, using a standardized set of tabs and dividers, you and your staff can adapt and improve upon your long standing procedures.

CONCLUSION: CHOOSE YOUR NEW WAVE LITIGATION WEAPONS

You may be a linear-type logical thinker who moves methodically like a freight train or a creative stream-of-consciousness type who moves easily from one good idea to another. Whatever your style of settlement presentation, discovery, or trial, you need some form of blueprint or notes of your concepts, some "magazine" or "ammunition clip" in which to put your settlement and litigation bullets, and storehouse for your settlement, discovery, or trial work product. That blueprint/magazine/arsenal/storehouse can be the Deposition & Trial Notebooks. If you have no plan, others will impose their own image of the case. If you have an imprecise plan, others will seek to distort the issues of your client's case.

Whatever your settlement, litigation, or trial system, you will have the right tool for the right job if your system is well organized, easily understandable, and quickly transportable to arb/settlement/mediation/conference sites and dep/court rooms. That way, when you reach these sites, you will be able to retrieve all your specs and plans from your tool box.

Using the Deposition & Trial Notebooks in three ring binders, important materials needed for settlement, discovery, and trial prep are gathered and organized in a fashion you can use effectively any time. In settlement, your raw data and settlement presentations are always at hand and prearranged. In discovery, using preprinted instructions for your clients and deponents and having pretyped "ground rules" for adverse attorneys in the form of Notices, Attachment/Schedule of Documents to Produce, "Usual Stips," and "Rules of Fair Play" (annotated with case citations) are things you can standardize in your office, reuse, and recycle. Likewise, in preparation for trial, having a standardized arsenal of pretyped forms, e.g., Tracking Control Form, Things to Do, Trial Calendar, Juror Demographic Worksheet, and Evidence Log.

The battle lines in personal injury litigation have been drawn. Insurance companies and self-insureds are not willing to make reasonable offers without discovery, mediations, and trials. The time you and your staff spend now organizing and systematizing your settlement and litigation weaponry will pay big dividends in the future time you save preparing for, taking, and following up on settlement conferences, depositions, and preparing for trial. The weapons are there for you to use.

May "The Force" (of your AAJ Trial & Deposition Notebooks) be with you and the "cleansing" of your discovery and trial palates be useful for you and your clients! Tom Vesper

mantenere i vostri coltelli affilati ea portata di mano

("keep your knives sharp and close at hand")

Chapter 6. PESCE (Fish)

PART A. DOM'S RECIPES

MERLUZZO DI POMODORA
(Whiting in Tomato Sauce)

This dish is a favorite of mine, and I also serve this on Christmas Eve. The secret to this dish is the freshness of the fish. Merluzzo (meaning "cod") or whiting; it is a mild white fish and, when gently simmered and allowed to absorb the sauce, it is very delicious.

INGREDIENTS (Serves 4):

2 lbs Whiting fish, cleaned, heads and tails removed, DO NOT filet

1 Clove Garlic

2 Tbsp Parsley

1 (16 oz.) Can chopped Plum tomatoes

1 Small onion, thinly sliced

Olive oil (enough to just cover the bottom of the pan)

1 Tbsp Dry oregano

1 Tbsp dry Basil

1 Tbsp dry Tarragon

¼ cup Red wine

Salt, pepper and red pepper flakes to taste

DIRECTIONS:

Cut fish cross-wise in half.

In large fry pan, add olive oil; sauté garlic and onions until wilted; DO NOT BURN garlic.

Add tomatoes, parsley, salt and pepper, basil, oregano, and wine.

Cover fry pan; cook over low flame and simmer for about 10 minutes.

Add fish to the pan, cover, and gently simmer 10-15 minutes or until fish is done.

Taste and adjust seasonings

BOCCONCINI: Cod and codfish have many genera and species, e.g., haddock, pollack, ling, whiting, and other food fishes similar or related to cod, e.g., rock cod, tomcod. The North Atlantic *Gadus morhua* is very important as a food fish. One suggested origin for its name is the Old English cod(d) or "bag," because of the fish's appearance.

Cod has been an important economic commodity in international markets ever since the Viking period, around 800 AD. Norwegians traveled with dried cod; and cod markets developed in Southern Europe and lasted over 1,000 years. Portuguese began fishing cod in the 15th century and called it "clip fish." Basques allegedly discovered the Canadian fishing banks before Columbus discovered America. William Pitt the Elder claimed cod was "British gold." Our North American east coast developed in part due to the vast cod stocks. New England cities are located near cod fishing grounds, and the fish was so important to Massachusetts, the state's House of Representatives hung a wood carving of a codfish, called "The Sacred Cod of Massachusetts," in its chambers. Since then, use of salt, dried and salted cod (clip fish or "klippfisk" in Norway) has been exported around the world.

COZZE POMODORO
(Mussles in Tomato Sauce)

My grandchildren Dominic and Samantha stayed at our house because their parents were going to a restaurant for dinner. On this particular evening, we were having some family and friends for dinner. A bowl of mussels was on our table; the kids informed me, "we only like clams, Pop Pop." I looked, I smiled, and said: "Well kids, these are 'Italian Clams,' try 'em, I think you'll like 'em." They not only liked them, they almost ate the entire bowl. To this day, they will not eat mussels without tomato sauce.

INGREDIENTS (Serves 4 to 6):

3 lbs Mussels

Olive oil (just enough to cover bottom of a large pot that is large enough to hold mussels)

2 Cloves garlic

1 (16 oz.) Can crushed tomatoes

1 Tbsp Dry oregano

1 Tbsp Dry basil

1 cup Red wine

Salt and pepper

Red pepper flakes

Few Sprigs of fresh chopped parsley

DIRECTIONS:

Soak mussels in a bowl of cold water for 30 minutes (this helps purge the mussels of sand before cooking).

Clean mussels and be sure to scrub shell and remove beards from mussels.

Add oil and sauté garlic in the large pot.

Add tomatoes, wine, and seasonings.

Simmer for about 20 minutes.

After it simmers, raise the heat and bring to a boil and add mussels.

Cover the pot and stir occasionally until mussels are opened and cooked.

Mussels are done when they appear plump and juicy.

Serve with a large loaf of Italian bread.

BOCCONCINI: Both muscles in our bodies and mussels from the sea take their name from the Italians' common house mouse. The ancient Romans thought body muscles that appeared and disappeared as when men competed in athletic games and then rested, resembled tiny mice appearing and disappearing also; little dark mice were thought to resemble the dark colored marine bivalves Romans serve at banquets. Both the muscle and the mussel were named *musculus* or "little mouse." Mussel is spelled differently because this makes it easier to distinguish it from the human muscle.

Mussels are one of the oldest species still on the earth today with evidence of their existence dating back to the very beginning of time. Cultured mussels have been around for nearly 900 years, since the 12th century, when a shipwrecked Scottish sailor off the coast of France placed poles with netting in the water to catch fish, and he noticed that mussels had attached themselves to the poles. This has become today's "Bouchot method" of harvesting or *moule de bouchot*. Bouchot is a word in the local dialect for a submerged trap used to capture eels.

CALAMARI POMODORA
(Squid Stewed in Tomatoes)

I make this dish every Christmas Eve, and it is part of my Seven Fish Dinner, which is a traditional Christmas Eve dinner for Italians. When we were first served this dish I was very young. My brothers and sister wondered why we were being served "fishing bait." However, once we tasted the stew we loved it and have been eating it every since.

INGREDIENTS (Serves 4 to 6):

3 lbs Squid, cleaned and cut into ¼" rings

Olive oil (enough to cover bottom of pan)

¼ cup Red wine

1 Clove garlic, crushed and minced

1 Small onion, chopped

2 (28 oz.) Cans Italian style crushed tomatoes

4 Potatoes, diced

1¼ cup Frozen petite peas

2 tsp Dry basil

2 tsp Dry oregano

2 tsp Dry Tarragon

Salt and pepper to taste

DIRECTIONS:

Cover bottom of a large heavy pan with olive oil and add wine.

Add garlic and sauté 5 minutes on medium heat

Add tomatoes and cook for 5 more minutes.

Add squid, potatoes, basil, and oregano. Reduce heat to low; cover and cook until Potatoes are tender; approximately 1 hour.

Add peas during the last 15 minutes of cooking.

When done, add extra dash of oregano and basil.

BOCCONCINI: Calamaro or calamari is from Latin *calamrium*, pen-case, relating to a reed pen and thus the "ink" a squid secretes. Calamari (squid or cuttlefish) is not to be confused with polipo (octopus) or scungilli (conch). Squid is a favorite all over Italy. Squid, octopus, and cuttlefish all are molluscs known as Cephalopods, from a Greek word meaning "head-footed."

Calamari or Squid: with their stream-lined, torpedo-shaped body, excellent eyesight, and active swimming lifestyle, seem to be more like fish than to other molluscs. Unlike cuttlefish, which are mostly solitary, squid often move about in shoals. They lack the internal chalky bone of cuttlefish, relying instead on a thin membrane called the pen for support. Squid squirt a cloud of black ink into the water to help mask their escape.

Octopus: Octopi use jet propulsion and also may cloud the water with ink to escape its predators. Most octopi do not present a threat, but the blue-ringed octopus is lethal to humans; several species occur in Australian waters.

Cuttlefish: Well-known for spectacular color and skin texture changes which can indicate their mood. Cuttlefish have eight arms and two tentacles. When feeding on crustaceans and fish, two tentacles quickly snatch the prey which is drawn towards the beak-like mouth beneath the arms. The cuttlebone, well-known to beach goers, is a porous internal structure used by the cuttlefish to control its buoyancy. When dried, the so-called "cuttlebone" is sometimes given to caged birds as a source of calcium and essential salts and minerals.

TILAPIA CON POMODORA
(Tilapia with Tomatoes)

Tilapia has become a very popular fish in recent years. It is a good substitute for flounder, sole, or haddock. My family prefers this fish, especially this recipe.

INGREDIENTS (Serves 4 to 6):

6 Tilapia filets

3 Fresh tomatoes, chopped

1 Small onion, chopped

1 Clove garlic, minced

1 tsp Dry oregano

1 Tbsp Chopped parsley

2 Tbsp Olive oil

2 Tbsp Butter

Juice of ½ Lemon

Salt and Pepper to taste

DIRECTIONS:

Mix tomatoes, onion, and parsley together.

Add olive oil, lemon juice, and oregano to tomato mixture and mix well.

Lay fillets in a baking dish greased with the butter.

Add salt and pepper to taste.

Spoon tomato mixture on each fillet.

Broil about 8 minutes or until done. Fish will flake with a fork when done.

BOCCONCINI: FOR PETE'S SAKE! Tilapia is the Latinized word thiape for "fish"; a common name for a hundred species of "cichlid fish of tilapiine cichlid tribe." Mainly freshwater, they inhabit shallow streams, ponds, rivers, and lakes and are important in Africa and the Levant in both aquaculture and aquaponics. It's first "ID" was in the Tomb of Nakht, 1500 BC, which has a tilapia hieroglyph above the head of the central figure. Tilapia is also called "St. Peter's Fish" because it was one of three types of fish caught in Biblical times from the Sea of Galilee. They were called musht, or "St. Peter's fish," from the story in Gospel of Matthew about the Apostle Peter catching a fish that carried a coin in its mouth.

PART B. TOM'S TRIAL TIPS: JURY SELECTION

A LIGHTER BUT IMPORTANT TRIAL SERVING—JURY (DE)SELECTION: A FRESH SERVING OF THE BEST "1 QUESTION" VOIR DIRE QUESTIONS: SOME VERY TELLING OPEN ENDED VOIR DIRE QUESTIONS

(A few of many voir dire questions compiled by Tom Vesper & Jerry Baker for NJAJ in 2012 and incorporated into the complete Voir Dire Chapter of Tom Vesper's *AAJ Trial Notebook*)

With invaluable insights and input from the following:

<u>Trial Consultants</u>

Lisa Blue, Esq (Trial Lawyer & Trial/Jury Consultant)

Amy Singer (Trial/Jury Consultant)

Rob Hirschhorn (Trial/Jury Consultant)

Phil Miller, Esq (Trial Lawyer & Trial/Discovery/Jury Consultant)

INTRODUCTION

It always comes up whenever trial consultants talk with trial lawyers; it is the one question with 1,000 different answers, the ubiquitous voir dire question, the "Holy Grail" of all trial lawyers and jury consultants: IF YOU CAN ONLY ASK ONE QUESTION IN VOIR DIRE, WHAT SHOULD IT BE?

The "Top 3" Voir Dire questions, according to my coauthor, friend Gerald Baker, are:

1. Other than a family member, who is the person you most admire, and who is the person that you least admire, and why?

2. Do you think there should be a cap or upper limit in the amount of damages that a person can recover from a lawsuit? Please explain why or why not?

3. Please share with us how you felt when you just learned that you were chosen to sit on a case where the trial deals with a [motor vehicle, fall down, etc.] incident?

TOM VESPER, Esq. (Trial Lawyer, Jury/Trial Consultant)

What are your thoughts or feelings about the homeless?

JERRY BAKER, Esq.

If you had to choose between money and friends, which would you choose and why?

LISA BLUE, Esq. (Jury & Trial Consultant)

1. If you ask a person who knows you best what three adjectives would he use describe you?
2. If were hurt by the negligence of another would you sue?
3. If up to you, would you limit the amount of money a person could collect in lawsuit?
4. Which way do you lean—lawyers create more problems for society OR lawyers solve more problems than they create?
5. If you were my client would you want someone on this jury just like you?

AMY SINGER (Jury Consultant)

Instead of what do you think, always begin with: What are your thoughts or feelings?

If they say "I think," it's a cognitive decision; If they say "I feel," . . . it's an emotional decision.

My favorite question: Are lawsuits good or bad for society? Why?

10 IDEAS: SNAKES, STAKES, SEINFELD & TIPS TO CONNECT WITH JURY

DOES REPTILE THEORY CURE THE SEINFELD SYNDROME AND INDIFFERENCE OF OTHERWISE NICE JURORS AND TRIAL LAWYERS CONNECTING WITH THE JURY

I. AN ANTIDOTE FOR APATHY?

In a paper first presented at AAJ's Mega-Seminar in Las Vegas, Nevada (1997) and republished for AAJ Case Workshop Programs and OJB (Overcoming

Juror Bias), my friend Greg Cusimano wrote of "The Top 4 Juror Attitudes That Turn Otherwise Nice Jurors Hostile." I agree with Greg on the Top Four Juror Attitudes constantly arising in deliberations of personal injury juries: (1) Accountability & Personal Responsibility, (2) An Unwillingness to Compensate Tort Victims, (3) The Rationalization that "Stuff Happens," and (4) The Focus of Super Critical Fault Finding on the Part of Plaintiffs.

Competing for consideration in jury selection methodology is the David Ball and Don Keenan Reptile Theory, which is bottomed on the fact that the reptilian part of our human brains has the capacity to understand on a subliminal level the emotion of fear. How to use fear-factor in framing questions for jury selection is not the purpose of this chapter. Rather, I will try to raise some concepts to help lawyers better connect and communicate with the jury panel and also try to elicit honest responses to questions that reveal bias or lack thereof.

At times, I feel like the neurotic protagonist in the movie "As Good As It Gets," when Jack Nicholson says, "I'm drowning here and you're describing the water!" Let me try to describe some of the "Nice Jurors" who hurt our clients. On May 14, 1998, I along with 76 million TV viewers watched "The Finale" or "Final Episode of Seinfeld" and saw the "New York Four"—Jerry, Kramer, George, and Elaine. These characters were humorous but an all too real mug shot of the character traits of today's young, upwardly mobile jurors.

The working title for this historic show was "A Tough Nut To Crack" to throw off outsiders about the contents of the episode. After finally striking a deal with NBC over their sitcom pilot, Jerry and George are faced with having to leave New York City for California. Before doing so, they decide to take NBC's private jet to Paris with Elaine and Kramer for one "last hurrah." Unfortunately, Kramer causes engine troubles by hopping up and down on the plane while trying to get water out of his ears, nearly killing the four friends in a crash. They make an emergency landing in the small, fictional town of Latham, Massachusetts. While in Latham, waiting for the plane to be repaired, they witness an overweight man getting carjacked at gunpoint. Instead of helping him, they crack jokes about his size while Kramer films it all on his camcorder then they proceed to walk away. The victim notices this and tells the reporting officer. The "New York Four" are then taken into custody for violating the Good Samaritan law that requires bystanders to help in such a situation.

After a lengthy trial, bringing back many characters from past shows as character witnesses testifying against the group for their "selfish" acts from throughout the series, the four are found guilty and sentenced to a year in prison for the crime of criminal indifference. I came away with a phrase I now use to refer to the Generation X and Y Juror's attitude: I call it the "Seinfeld Syndrome." The criminal indifference of the Seinfeld cast of misanthropes seemed to me to be a large part of a condition (or lack thereof) that infected the social conscience (or lack thereof) of many young jurors who are Generation X'ers (now in their 40s) and Y'ers in their late 20s, early 30s, and soon to be "40 Something's" by 2010. These individual jurors have a palpable indifference to the plight of anyone and everyone except the most horribly, objectively provable, damaged plaintiff. Even in the most catastrophic case, they do not believe in monetary compensation for any intangible yet legally compensable damages. To these indifferent jurors, "money solves nothing."

In 1998, I coined the phrase and wrote about this "new attitude" infecting civil juries in America—"Seinfield Syndrome: The Indifference of Otherwise Nice Jurors," Trial, October 1998, p. 38-43. However, criminal indifference is not now limited to people between the ages "20 to 40 something." I am sad to report that this virus has spread! It now typifies the social conscience (or lack thereof) of many jurors despite their age. More jurors of all ages now have an irrational indifference to anyone's plight except those most undeniably and catastrophically damaged plaintiffs. In a 2000 study quoted by Jim Lees, "almost 30% of people polled are not willing to award money damages for pain and suffering under any circumstances . . . and that is regardless of the law given to them by the judge." I have listened to jurors say that anyone seriously injured by a negligent party should be "fairly made whole" by getting "their lost wages and medical bills paid . . . and that's all! Special (economic damages) yes, but nothing for pain and suffering (non-economic damages)!"

Greg Cusimano and David Wenner have researched, written, and lectured extensively about "The Top Four Juror Attitudes That Turn Otherwise Nice Jurors Hostile" and Overcoming Juror Bias (OJB). We should read their papers, attend AAJ's OJB Colleges/Seminars, Case Workshops, and conduct as many focus/mock juries as possible to identify jury biases in your cases. But even without formal study or research, any trial lawyer who has tried any injury case in the past 10 or 20 years will agree there is "hostility" in some civil jurors.

"The Top 4 Juror Attitudes" which constantly arise in the deliberations of personal injury juries: (1) Accountability & Personal Responsibility, (2) Unwillingness to Compensate Tort Victims, (3) Rationalization that "Stuff Happens," and (4) Focus of Super Critical Fault Finding on the Part of

Plaintiffs. Many jurors seem to somehow reverse the characterization of "victim" and now empathize and identify with corporate defendants as "victims" of our civil justice system. This national skepticism and hostility of jurors has me and all my colleagues groping for reasons and cures or antidotes for this disease.

After dozens of NCA Trial Colleges, AAJ Case Workshops, and hundreds of focus groups/mock jury trials over the past 20 years, I still cannot explain exactly why some younger jurors have such bias towards wrongdoers and harbor such prejudice against the tort victim. Certainly, culture, education, the recent "medical malpractice crisis," and the media have something to do with this present mind set. There are no definitive answers to the riddle: "How do trial lawyers get such jurors to connect and empathize with plaintiff?" No "magic bullets" will kill this virus. Generalizations and "demographic" stereotyping are not helpful. However, having made that disclaimer, permit me now to generalize and offer some observations and theories which were recently gathered from an outstanding staff and several trial lawyers who participated with me in a 2003 New Jersey Institute for Continuing Legal Education seminar about case evaluation and settlement and the 2007 and 2010 ATLA-NJ (now NJAJ) Tom & Jerry Seminar About Voir Dire. We used research funded and conducted by my departed friend Rich Halpern, former President of The Halpern Group, in Springfield, N.J., had gathered over 20 years of case data. His database was code named "Paradox," and it contained significant information concerning effective modalities for "influencing the decision making of jurors" and also is highly predictive of how individual liability carriers and self-insureds evaluate cases and what "dirty tricks" they used in negotiation, mediation, and trial. Similarly, Joe DiGangi at Elite Settlements has his own proprietary data base or "book" on various carriers' and self-insureds' strategies and tactics.

TEN VOIR DIRE IDEAS TO "STAKE" YOUR VOIR DIRE

Some of these ideas have been formulated by trial lawyers and jury consultants; some of the strategies I have successfully used to counteract this Seinfeld Syndrome. The prescription for cure, as I reported in 1998, can be both simple and complex. The simplest antidote is to accept that such jurors will never change their apathy to civil justice by use of any trial advocacy, and since they are incurably prejudiced, they must be challenged and excused. This assumes one can successfully identify all "bad witches" from "good witches" and have enough time or peremptory challenges to "DING DONG . . . kill (ALL) the wicked witches" and exclude them from serving jury duty in our clients' cases. My court imposed restrictions upon attorney-conducted voir dire (we have none in New Jersey!), and a reluctance to stereotype people leads me to suggest, with no absolute guarantee for efficacy, the following approaches to cure a Seinfeld Syndrome:

(1) USE "7 STAKES" TO MAKE THE CASE "UP CLOSE & PERSONAL."

To impress upon the jury that some issue is meaningful to them, we should all be mindful of "The Seven Stakes." That is, to "connect" with jurors—or anyone—we know from psychologist Abraham Maslow there are "Seven Stakes" which explain what drives people, what people want, and what is "at stake" if people, like jurors, do not get it.

"Great stories place these basic needs in jeopardy in order to raise the level of concern and identification with the jury.

a. Survival. This is a basic instinct common to all mammals. We all want to survive and will go to great lengths to do so. We identify with the life-and-death stakes. The conflict is always clear, involving us, and bringing ultimate identification to the situation. This is why in wrongful death cases, the jury does not need to be motivated to understand the matter involved is very serious and of important consequence to the plaintiff family.

b. Safety and security. People need to feel they are in a place that is safe, secure, and protective. This is the safe haven or a place to call home.

c. Love and belonging. People need to connect, and it is natural to desire a sense of family. This can take the form of yearning for a nuclear family or a sense of community. This can also include the search for a mate or the need to belong to someone.

d. Self-esteem and self-respect. People desire to be looked up to and recognized for their skills and contributions. This includes the need for confidence and reward.

e. The Need to Know and Understand. We are born with a sense of curiosity. We have a natural desire to know how things work and are on a constant quest for knowledge.

f. Aesthetic need. People have a need for balance or being connected to something greater than themselves. It is a recognized need although perhaps the least universal.

g. Self-actualization. We have a need to express who we are by actualizing our talents, skills, and abilities. That need comes alive in a story for someone people find worth rooting for." Jacob Virgil, "Psychologically Preparing the Witness to Connect with the Jury," ATLA Annual Convention Paper, 2001. (HELP!)

Whether you are discussing liability or damages, you should make some reference to the fact that the issue does impact upon the "stakes" (1. Survival, 2. Safety, 3. Love & Belonging, 4. Self-Esteem/Respect, etc) of the client and on an analogous and/or subconscious basis also potentially would impact upon each of the individual jurors, their families and loved ones.

(2) THE LAWS OF OUR LAND. Establish to the jury at the very outset that their law has been broken. The tortfeasor has broken the individual citizen's own rules, laws, code of conduct, or some higher law. Jim Lees calls them "Rules of Civilization." If you can demonstrate to a Gen X'er that some life-saving safety standard or "minimum standard" of acceptable conduct was in fact violated, and if the Gen X'er believes that law is important, then you have a better chance of winning liability and collecting a full and fair recovery.

(3) THE "CIRCLE OF LIFE." Bring each juror and their family's welfare, or the juror's own basic instinct for self-preservation or the safety of anyone of value, into the great "Circle of Life." That is, demonstrate how the laws or rules that were violated are actually important to the juror's own life. "What goes around comes around" can be more meaningful to self-centered jurors than a judge's instruction about deterrent value of our common law of torts.

(4) MAKE A DIFFERENCE. Motivate, demonstrate, and convince jurors that the money they award will make a meaningful difference in the situation of the plaintiff: it should be a real and positive difference, not just a "reward for being victimized." My partner Dara Quattrone obtained a fair award for an elderly woman who injured her back in a trip/fall in an Atlantic City casino. After the verdict, jurors told Dara they hoped she would tell our client to spend the money to hire someone to drive the client around to visit her favorite grandchildren. We ask all our clients prior to answering interrogatories, deposition, or trial what we call the "$65 Question": what would you do with a monetary award or settlement? The answer to that query may be more important than the preliminary $64 Question. (See Suggestion (4) below for the $64 Question.)

(5) STRUCTURE HUMAN (NONECONOMIC) DAMAGES PROOFS & ARGUMENTS. Show the quality of life the client, client's spouse and family had prior to the injury, which has now been upset or destroyed. That goes a long way toward supporting the medical proofs of a serious personal injury. This is what we call the "$64 Question": Tell me all the ways your injury(ies) significantly affect/ed your life. We get our clients, their close relatives and friends to write lists in their own handwriting of all of the "enjoyments of life" that have been totally lost or impaired. Many times, the clients like to hold their lists in their hands while they are being deposed so when the inevitable defense attorney question is posed ("Now have you told me/us all of your present problems/complaints?), the client can authoritatively unfold and scan their notes. The courtroom version of the song "These Are (Were) a Few of My Favorite Things" can be impressive even to a young juror with no family but with a "Few Favorite Things" on his/her own personal agenda.

Avoid phrases such as "pain and suffering" or "non-economic damages." Jurors in New Jersey and all states have been brainwashed and conditioned by past and recent insurance propaganda to recoil from the terms "pain and suffering." At the outset, prepare jurors for the "human damages" of our clients. It is not enough today to simply recite, itemize, or draw upon colored charts the minutes/hours/days of pain. Seinfeld Jurors want to know "The Bottom Line": exactly and honestly how is the pain/suffering actually having an effect upon the individual plaintiff's life and plaintiff's family. I use an argument in summation analogizing a person's permanent injury to the sale of a home: the ground or lot is worth something; the house/residence unit, with its brick and mortar, is worth something in real estate markets; even furnishings have monetary value, but the love, care, and memories that went into the home is what human (noneconomic) damages are about.

(6) VOIR DIRE. There is much more importance today than ever before on good voir dire. Try to cite for your trial judges AAJ, Jury Verdict Research, National Jury Project studies that show 30% to 35% of Americans, regardless of the law, will not award money for pain and suffering. That reality must be addressed by you and the trial judge in voir dire, whether judge-conducted through use of Supplemental Juror Questionnaires (SJQs) or whether your jurisdiction allows attorney-conducted voir dire. Today, for reasons I will leave to the social scientists, a significant number of eligible jurors do not belong on any civil jury, which, fairly and without preconceived ideas, must award monetary damages to plaintiffs wrongfully injured.

(7) CREDIBILITY OF CLIENTS. Credibility of our clients is now more than ever THE key ingredient in any personal injury case. Proving a demonstrable injury does not mean the client's complaints are valid. In personal injury cases, plaintiffs are routinely attacked by the defense as malingerers, fakes, and liars for a variety of trumped up, boiler-plated reasons. The two most popular current defense attacks upon plaintiffs' credibility are: 1) The M.I.S.T. (Mild Impact Soft Tissue) Defense of "just a widdle bump, therefor no one could get hurt from such mild impact"; and/or 2) No Objective Signs of Injury. The later defense tactic is usually accompanied by some self-professed "IME" defense doctor who after looking at "the films" and conducting a 15-minute "drive-by" exam concludes "there must be some secondary gain" going on with plaintiff because there are "no objective signs" or "inconsistent" complaints. The M.I.S.T. defense is an insidious attempt by Allstate, State Farm, and other insurers to drive up the costs of litigating "soft tissue cases" in order to discourage the plaintiff bar from accepting representation of legitimate clients who unfortunately are not involved in car crashes with extensive property damages. When your client's credibility is squarely put in issue, consider calling "character witnesses." Fed. R. Evid. 608. When defense medical experts say our clients are "faking/exaggerating" the severity/extent of their injuries, we must bring the real treating doctors as well as character witnesses to support the client's character for truth and honesty.

Also consider proving the "Few Favorite Things" the client has given up for the sake of this alleged charade. According to Dr. Nelson Hendler, creator of one of the best objective "pain validity tests" for real "pain," most humans enjoy eating, sleeping, sex, play, and (if lucky) their work. Mensana Diagnostics Corp. Pain Validity Test, Mensana Diagnostics Corp., Newark, Del; Hendler & Kozikowowski, "Overlooked Physical Diagnosis in Chronic Pain Patients Involved in Litigation," Pychosomatics (1994); Hendler, "Validating and Treating the Complaint of Chronic Back Pain: The Mensana Clinic Approach," Ch 20 in Clinical Neurosurgery, Vol. 35, p. 385-397, Harvard University, 1989. Proving your client has lost one or more of these "enjoyments of life" helps most jurors to discount paid character assassinations as baseless ad hominem attacks.

(8) GUARD OUR CREDIBILITY AS TRIAL LAWYERS. From the start of all our trials, let the jury know we are the "good guys." Present all the facts in a credible and competent manner. Do not allow any defense attorney to impugn our integrity in any way in the courtroom. The defense really has the best of it in today's climate. After all, if the jury thinks all lawyers are liars, it will not matter to the defense that our profession is despised because they have NO BURDEN OF PROOF. When a trial judge scolds both sides in a case for any infraction, the only detrimental effect is to the party with the burden of persuasion. Be scrupulously careful and candid at all times. Be professional in your courtroom manner. Be careful not to appear to be "over reaching." In our trial presentations and in any public forum, we must convey to the jury and public at large that what we are about is not a big verdict or a little verdict but a fair verdict.

(9) DO NOT REFER TO "MISTAKES." Many jurors do not associate a mistake with something for which someone should be held legally responsible. It is better to phrase the issue of negligence as a violation of minimal written standards, or a disregard of unwritten but long established customs or practices, or failure to follow basic rules of civilization. A flagrant breach of accepted rules of behavior has more impact upon jurors than "unintentional, careless breaches of the reasonable man standard" or a careless "mistake" like disregarding a red light.

(10) DO NOT DIFFUSE THE FACT. Giving too much detail in the very beginning of our opening statements, we sometimes give too much information about our clients' cases. This "diffusion" psychologically results in a mixed and confusing message rather than the clear "bullet points" the jurors need. Sticking to the basics and giving the jury enough information to form a positive view of our client is a better preparation for them to assimilate and frame all the issues in their newly imprinted memory banks. E.g., jury studies show introducing plaintiff as "John was A GOOD FATHER" has more impact and staying power to listeners than "John was a 35 year old, single parent who worked hard as a mechanic to raise three boys as a good father." Some lawyers think every uttered statement of fact must have a preamble, factual predicate or string of case citations. Don't scatter your message and leave jurors unclear about your points.

(11) USE BLUE COLLAR/SHIRT-SLEEVE LOCAL EXPERTS. A good auto mechanic wearing greasy overalls can be as effective, as knowledgable, and even more credible product liability defect expert than the stable of GM, Ford, or Chrysler auto design engineers. To some Seinfeld Jurors, "street smarts" counts a lot when judging credibility of a witness. Some snobby Seinfeld types in upper class venues may also believe that only a "college degreed" expert can speak with intelligence. If so, "cover all bases" for some of the more cynical citizens in our jury boxes, and consider finding both a highly credentialed, degreed expert, and a good experienced "shirt sleeve expert." Example: any college anatomy and physiology teacher prior to and with plaintiff's treating orthopedic specialist can clearly and convincingly explain in general medical terms how the parts of the body work and the general problems occur when neck/back/leg muscles get torn. Having an anatomy professor briefly but understandably introduce jurors to the area and function of the human anatomy that is in dispute makes for a very powerful and synergistic presentation. The basic anatomy/physiology lesson gives jurors an ability to better understand the pedigreed and professional witnesses. In fall down cases, most good, experienced carpenters along with a safety engineer can effectively describe tripping hazards that result from faulty construction or lack of good maintenance. Vesper, "Saving Money on Accident Reconstruction," New Jersey Trial Lawyer, National Trial Lawyer, July 1992, p. 44.

II. WHAT ARE THE BEST TECHNIQUES TO "CONNECT WITH A JURY?

Long before I met my first jury consultant, years before I first knew about focus groups, jury demographics, and mock/shadow juries, I knew my Italian family—mother, father, aunts, uncles, and cousins—had an unlimited and irrepressible amount of "connections" with people. They each accumulated in their collective lifetimes an unfathomable wealth of stories stuffed with lessons and wisdom about how to "connect" with another human being. Before I enrolled in any NCA College, OJB or Overcoming Jury Bias Seminars, or Jury Workshops, and even prior to my first trial, I would rehearse and/or "test" my openings and closings in front of the toughest jury I knew—my own family. Asked for or not, they always told me whether my case selection, legal logic, or proofs made sense; always demanded I explain things confusing to them; and unmercifully criticized whenever my word selection sounded "lika Bigga Shot." With all my family's "support" and sage skepticism, one message remains in my trial bag of memories. No matter who I represent, the damages, or the facts, my family's overriding concern was always: "tell me more about the kind of person Mr./Mrs. is/was."

Today's defense strategy is one of finding "gaps" and driving wedges into plaintiff's cases. These "gaps" can be manufactured, imagined, or real defects in the liability, causation, or damages. The defense will attack the credibility, character, and complaints of all plaintiffs. The plaintiff's character is often assailed by defense medical examiners who question plaintiff's "secondary gain," exaggerated symptomatology, or motive to malinger. Credibility of the plaintiff's version of "traumatic event" is attacked when prior inconsistent statements in police, hospital, or medical reports or depositions can be found or created. Plaintiffs' "complaints" are treated with disdain and cynicism by the defense, who labels almost every plaintiff reported symptom as "subjective" and therefore frivolous. Even catastrophic injuries are "independently" evaluated as having little or no "permanency" or little reason to justify more than a trifle of lifetime care.

In personal injury trials, one constant remains despite an escalating amount of technological assistance available to trial lawyers for communicating to juries: a "serious" injury to the dignity of the individual plaintiff will usually result in serious interest by jurors. Whatever technological advancements we use for trial, we should never lose sight of the simple fact that it is the injured, the deceased, and the survivors of the wrongful death victim who are the keys to "connecting" their case with the jury. From focus groups, seeing jury trials, verdicts, and posttrial interviews, I believe there are at least a dozen meaningful ways to improve your "connection" with today's jurors:

A. Look 'em Straight in The Eye! Make Eye Contact

One immediate improvement to any interpersonal connection is to MAKE EYE CONTACT. If we do nothing else but look at jurors when we speak to them, we will go a long way toward gaining their trust and confidence. Actor James Cagney once described the best way to connect with an audience: "Stand up straight and tall on your own two feet, look 'em straight in eye, and tell the truth!" Good advice for every lawyer.

B. "Get Along By Going Along"

Jury consultant Rodney Jew likes to say, "To get along you must go along." Try as much as possible to look and sound like the real people on the jury. Alternatively, if you would be honestly "faking it" to look and sound like the jurors, then at least try to look and sound like someone, such as the judge, with whom the jurors do place trust and confidence.

C. Watch The Clients' Demeanor and Appearance

Plaintiffs are THE MOST IMPORTANT DEMONSTRATIVE EXHIBIT in any trial. Not only the center of jurors' attention, they are the center of attack and main targets for our adversaries. Knowing this, we plaintiff advocates must insure our clients make as credible an appearance during the entire trial and as believable a witness as possible. Clients must realize their "testimony" begins the first moment jurors see them and right up until the final verdict is rendered. Jurors will always watch the plaintiff and plaintiff's family to "spot" something which they either can "connect" or relate with or something they can tell the other jurors is "phony."

A bad client always trumps a great exhibit. In a recent legal malpractice trial, we prepared what our jury consultant and I believed to be a very clear, convincing, and credible time line. We believed our color-coded chronology easily showed all the mistakes defendant lawyer had made. After the verdict, the jurors told me that many of them did not understand our color code or the significance of the chronology of letters and telephone calls. However, they quickly found that the defendant lawyer was "guilty of malpractice" because they "just did not believe him from the get-go!" They immediately decided he was not honest. When we called defendant to the witness stand as our very first witness, he couldn't answer a single simple question without rambling and trying to make himself look genius. The jury thus decided he was unbelievable—"not a good lawyer." A positive and/or negative first impression can outweigh and trump any exhibit.

D. Use Anchors

Anchoring is a storytelling/communicating technique. You can get the jury to associate a certain part of the court room, or a particular exhibit, with a recurring theme or issue in the case. If you have one chart that outlines the economic damages, you should use that one chart every time you talk about those elements of damage. An example of an outstanding and unforgettable visual exhibit in a death case, Murray Ogborn "anchored" the testimony of a little girl to a single red rose the child brought to court and put on plaintiff's counsel table in the presence of the jury.

Sound can be an anchor. The first time I ever used "teleconferencing" was in a jury trial in 1985 for a woman who slipped on the contents of a broken bottle in an Acme supermarket. After the defense doctor testified and the defense rested, I requested the judge allow me a single rebuttal witness on one "surprise" opinion given by the defense examiner: on cross-examination it was his board-certified orthopedic opinion that as my client aged, the vertebrae in her spine would actually "settle like a new house." Therefore, he concluded her injured spine and her painful daily suffering would subside. In order to rebut this "junk" prognosis, I requested the recall of the treating doctor to rebut the defense doctor's medical theory of "spinal structural settlement." The judge and defense agreed to telephonic rebuttal rather than prolong the trial. The treating doctor's rebuttal testimony was on the phone in the jury's presence. What several jurors remember best about that doctor's rebuttal testimony was his immediate reaction when I read to him the defense expert's testimony that his patient's herniated and/or bulging disc would actually get better over time as she got older and her spine "would settle like a house." His laugh was instantaneous and memorable. It filled the entire court room. He laughed for only a few seconds, but it seemed like an hour. His laugh was so wonderful it became infectious. The judge and several jurors started to chuckle, cover their faces, and shake silently. After his laughter stopped, he said, "He's joking. His opinion is not really funny, because if he had been given such an absurd prognosis to his own patient he would surely be sued and probably lose his license to practice medicine . . . he's crazy." He went on to explain medically how the spine of any 35 year old woman or man would not "settle like a house," but rather, by the time my client was in her 50s, she would in all certainty suffer severe arthritis and much more serious problems with her back. The rebuttal medical explanation was not as effective as the doctor's laugh. His piercing laugh awoke in the jurors something they took into the jury deliberation room with them when it came time to discuss the credibility of the defense expert. They concluded it was not only silly junk science; it was despicably arrogant for anyone to suggest that a severe injury would just spontaneously go on and heal itself over time.

E. Make "Contact" and Use "Mirroring" in Voir Dire and Opening

The first formal and direct contact we as trial lawyers have with jurors is during voir dire and/or opening. It is then that we need to look directly at and speak clearly to each juror. With today's latest computer technology, court reporters are equipped with stenographic machines that can show, on a computer screen, each word of Q and A as they are spoken. This is often helpful when a witness tries to quibble over a phrase or wording. It helps the interrogator to quote the witness verbatim. What is important to remember with this new transcription technology is that we do not allow it to distract us from one of the most important personal interchanges and confrontations that can occur during a deposition or trial. That is, a face-to-face, eye-to-eye confrontation by the trial lawyer with the witness. The demeanor of witnesses, how they answer a question, how quickly or slowly they respond, how they look, where they look, how long it takes to answer, are human elements that do not show up on the computer screen.

While I strongly urge all trial attorneys to become computer literate and utilize up to date technology, especially real-time transcription, I would also caution all trial lawyers not to fall into the trap of becoming hypnotized by the pretty colored words on the computer laptop screen. If you are only looking at the computer screen, you will not see a witness look aside or look at his/her notes or make some indication with their eyes or face that there is more to their answer than what simply appears in the computerized transcript.

F. Concentrate On and Develop Damages—Availability Bias

The availability of data can influence perception. Jurors often mistakenly equate the availability of information with frequency, probability, and causality. David Wenner and Greg Cusimano suggest whatever most occupies juror attention during the trial will most influence what jurors focus on during deliberations and disproportionately use in rendering a verdict. Wenner, David A. and Cusimano, Gregory S., "Combating Juror Bias," TRIAL, June 2000, p.30.

A good rule of thumb is if your trial proofs are focused on the defendant's conduct, jurors will focus on that conduct in deciding the case. In contrast, if the trial focuses on causation, jurors likely will focus on causation. Likewise, if jurors focus on the plaintiff's conduct during trial, they will focus on the plaintiff during deliberation. That does not mean plaintiff trial lawyers can ignore our plaintiff's conduct if it is in issue or should we not inoculate against defenses. On the contrary, it just means that we should try to focus of the case and the jurors' attention on defendant's conduct and the damages we seek to recover for our client.

G. Shorten Your Trials—"Less is More"

Try to save time and move your case along "while ingratiating not aggravating" the jurors. One of the biggest criticisms from judges and jurors about the presentation of some trial lawyers is "they waste a lot of time." In direct examination, it is important for the plaintiff's advocate to use exhibits/demos or "demonstratives" in a crisp and expeditious manner, with little or no "wasted time." One frequent criticism easy to avoid is the "marking ritual." Handing an exhibit/demo (or worse, a series of exhibits) to the court clerk/reporter for placement of a sticker and inscription of a number is not exactly high drama for the jury. It is like watching paint dry for the jurors to watch mind-numbing ministerial misdirections of a witness' testimony. The scattered attention of such time warps also distracts and upsets some witnesses. Another common faux pas is to introduce a witness—usually an expert—who has a slide show, video program, or some other electronic audio visual aids presentation without first testing to see if the machinery will work. This usually produces "dead time" in court or another unnecessary "break" for the jury while court room attendants, lawyers, and "techies" try to get the exhibit/demo to work.

The best effect produced by the expeditious use of an exhibit/demo during direct examination is to have everyone in the courtroom, including the adversary, openly admit or secretly admire the conservation of time that was achieved. The use of the exhibit/demo, whatever its form, should result in less time for the witness being on the stand and therefore less time for the jurors to be involved with that witness. Rather than have the jury read or listen to a witness reading over long entries in medical records, some trial attorneys expedite the presentation by hiring nurses or using the hospital personnel to read summaries or synopsized charts of the records pursuant to Fed. R. Evid. 1006.

Another common time saver is using a photograph or scale diagram to describe what some-thing looked like rather than waste time having the witness describe a scene or object in minute detail. Having a witness describe or narrate what is being shown in a videotape, such as a "Day in the Life" video, may be a more dynamic and efficient use of the witness' and jury's time rather than simply showing the jury a silent movie or video and having the witness on direct exam orally testify and elaborate in detail to what has been or will be seen by the jury. Of course, some evidentiary foundation testimony and interest-peaking preliminaries are a necessary and proper use of the witness on direct before the exhibit/demo is shown to the jury. However, if the judge and jury are rolling their eyes and whispering to themselves "GET ON WITH IT! . . . SHOW US ALREADY!" then your preview of coming attractions has lost its appeal. The prelude should not preempt the exhibit/demo; overtures should never overwhelm main events.

H. "Ya Gotta Know The Territory!" Use Local Jargon and History

To motivate jurors to "connect" with your client and client's case themes and analyze the issues you present by way of exhibits/demos during trial, you should talk to them in ways and with word pictures and phrases they are used to and understand. "You gotta know the territory." What particular customs and traditions are practiced by the people in the trial venue which may be useful to explain some issue of the trial? You can use words and phrases and stories and analogies which are known to the local population. E.g., anyone visiting Atlantic City, NJ, from another state or even outside of Atlantic County is a "shoobie" (nickname given to train travelers around the pre-WWI era who carried their lunches in a shoe box). Therefore, if the witness is not from Atlantic City, referring to the witness as a "shoobie" will make a mental connection for an Atlantic County jury. Another example, in a negligent security or trip/fall/step down case, is to get the jurors to think about the experiences they, or their family or acquaintances, have had—or have not had—with similar well known premises sites in the local area.

I. Use Jury Views, Demonstrations, and Exhibits

In addition to using Power Point and WordPerfect for charts, graphs, and diagrams to project to the jury, there is still something to be said for the good, old fashioned flip chart, photo, or foam core backed diagram. The ability of jurors to touch, feel, and use the exhibits in the jury deliberation room is a consideration you should make whether or not you also utilize computer or audiovisual assistance in illustrating your exhibits to the jury during the trial.

J. On Liability Refer to "Choices" Not "Mistakes"

Whenever there is any accusation that plaintiff was contributorily/comparatively at fault for the happening of a traumatic event, try to marshal and present all of the defendant's "choices," options, or prior decision making. If you show that the "choices" made by the defendant went into a foreseeable and CONSCIOUS course of prior conduct, that may very well demonstrate how easily preventable and yet inevitable the injury was by reason of the defendant's conduct alone. By showing the jury all of the choices a defendant had to prevent the harm to the plaintiff, as compared with only a few, if any real opportunities or "choices" which were available to the plaintiff, the jury starts to sense that the overwhelming weight of (dare I say personal?) "responsibility" is upon the defendant.

K. Understate and Control Emotion

As a great trial lawyer-turned-judge Joseph Rodriguez used to teach, "Don't get emotional or passionate with the jury UNTIL YOU EARN THE RIGHT TO DO SO." We must slowly build our credibility with the momentum of our trial presentation. We can no longer assume that young jurors today will be outraged by an opening statement that outlines a tragic incident which was recklessly caused. Younger jurors have a lower threshold for outrage. Why? I do not know for certain (although I do have some personal theories). I will leave that for some later analysts.

CONCLUSION

Let us pray "Generation Next"—today's high school seniors and college students—is growing up to believe in our Constitution, the rules and principles of law, and the equitable precept of responsibility for full, fair, and reasonable compensation by those found to be at fault. Hopefully, our next wave of jurors are not a "Total No Fault" or "Capped" generation which believes economic loss should be insured against by plaintiffs (in the push for national No Fault or euphemistically "Choice Auto Insurance"), and "non- economic" losses should be capped at arbitrary numbers or ignored and absorbed by the innocent as another bit of conservative "tough love" or "that's life" philosophy.

With each client, one case at a time, one public speaking opportunity at a time, WE EACH must educate the public to be more informed and less indifferent to their role as cornerstone of our American democracy and 7th Amendment guaranteed right to fair and impartial civil jury.

As Justice William Blackstone said over 200 years ago:

> Trial by jury is a privilege of the highest and most beneficial nature and our most important guardian of public and private liberty. Our liberties cannot but subsist so long as this palladium remains sacred and inviolate, not only from all open attacks, but also from all secret machinations which may sap and undermine it.

My mother Carmella and her entire family were born in a small town in the hills of Abruzzi in Italy. My mother, father, and their brothers and sisters had very little formal education. But they understood people on a very deep yet basic level. They had amazing reservoirs of practical, everyday experience. Each had an abundance of good common sense. The things they wanted to know about are the same things today's jurors want to know about although perhaps in a more "modern" and abbreviated presentation. They want to know what kind of person plaintiff really is or was. To present our clients and their character, credibility, and complaints to a jury, we need to remember what is important to juries. It is still the type of person, not the type of glitzy technological advancements in communication employed by the trial lawyer, which will "connect" and carry the day. When viewing experts, it is still basic honesty and trustworthiness of the expert's methods, analysis, and conclusions, as well as the expert's manner of explaining opinions, that is important to jurors and not the number of slides or Power Point illustrations.

In addition to and more important than any audiovisual aide, THE most powerful trial exhibits in my opinion in any court room are still the plaintiff and the plaintiff's lawyer. Some say their importance is not necessarily in that order. A client's personality, the likeability and credibility of the plaintiff, the ability to engender empathy and not contempt, scorn, or skepticism are all factors that cannot be created with a scale model or photograph, videotape, or computer. Our ability as the plaintiff's trial attorney to practice the ABCs of advocacy (accuracy, brevity, and credibility) are still intangibles that will "connect" us with the jury. Those intangible "human connections" cannot be created or engendered in another human being through oratory, lap tops, or high tech trial exhibits.

Pesce

se si sceglie o meno, farlo con saggezza

("whether you choose or not, do so wisely" in Italian)

Chapter 7. LA VERDURA (Vegetables)

PART A. DOM'S RECIPES

GIAMBOTTA ZUCCHINI
(Zucchini Stew)

Giambotta (pronounce gee-OM-BUTTA) according to my nonna means "anything and everything." Zucchini can be found in all parts of Italy and is prepared in many different ways. This dish is especially good when using fresh-picked vegetables. I like to make this dish in the summer when I can use vegetables from my garden. This can be served as a side dish or main course.

INGREDIENTS (Serves 6):

4 Small Zucchini cut in ½" slices

2 Large potatoes cut in half, then cut in ½" slices

1 clove Garlic, chopped

1 Large onion, sliced

2 Green bell peppers, sliced in to stripes

4 Large tomatoes, chopped

4 Basil leaves, chopped

1 Tbsp Dry oregano

¼ cup Olive oil

Salt and pepper

Red pepper flakes

DIRECTIONS:

Add oil to heavy pan and sauté garlic and onion until just wilted, about 3 minutes.

Add chopped tomatoes and cook about 5 minutes.

Add remaining ingredients; cover pot and simmer on low heat.

When potatoes are done stew is ready to serve.

Serve with grated cheese and plenty of Italian bread.

BOCCONCINI: Zucchini is named for Italian *zucchina* (small pumpkin). Culinary-wise, it is a vegetable, which means it is usually cooked and presented as a savory dish or side dish; botanically, zucchini is immature fruit—swollen ovary of zucchini flower. Just so you know: August 8th is National Zucchini Day, if you would like to join Cuz Dom and I celebrating this versatile green veggie and all the delicious dishes to make with it; plan a healthy dinner with it! Grill it, bake it into bread, and add it to a salad. *Buon appétito! Mangiare tutto quello che vuoi e godere* (eat all you want and enjoy).

SCAROLA CON FAGIOLI
(Escarole and Beans)

This was without a doubt my father's favorite dish. I remember, when we didn't eat meat on Friday, my father would bring home a fresh baked loaf of Italian Bread just before we sat down for a delicious meal of escarole and beans. My mother usually served some kind of fish with this dish.

INGREDIENTS (Serves 4 to 6):

1 Large head escarole, well washed and coarsely chopped

¼ cup Olive oil

2 Cloves garlic, smashed and chopped

1 (15 oz.) Can cannelloni beans

Pinch of Red Pepper Flakes

Salt and pepper to taste

DIRECTIONS:

Make sure escarole is thoroughly washed because there will be sand between the leaves.

Boil escarole in salted water until tender; about 15 to 20 minutes.

Drain and set aside.

In a large frying pan, brown on medium heat sauté garlic until wilted.

Add beans with their liquid until heated.

Add Escarole, salt, pepper, and red pepper flakes.

Stir with a wooden spoon until well mixed and cook for 10 minutes.

This is a great side to just about anything.

BOCCONCINI: called "Skee-ya-DOLE" in both South and North Jersey. Escarole is like a "bad hair day lettuce"; it is a leafy green vegetable, a variety of endive whose leaves are broader, paler, and less bitter than other members of the endive family which is related to the daisy family. Sometimes called broad-leafed endive, escarole has broad, curly green leaves and a slightly bitter flavor. Its name in Latin was *escariola*, from Latin *escarius* meaning "of food." It is also a reference to money or cash, as in "That's a lot of skya-dole."

RISO CON LA VERZA
(Savoy Cabbage with Rice)

Many people are not familiar with this vegetable. Verza, *cavolo verza* or Savoy cabbage is a "savory" member of the cabbage family and has a sweeter taste than regular cabbage. This is another example of an Italian rustic dish. It is a great accompaniment to roast pork or ham.

INGREDIENTS (Serves 4 to 6):

1 Medium size, large-head Savoy cabbage

¼ cup Olive oil

4 Cloves garlic, chopped

1 cup Rice

1 Onion, cut in half and sliced thin

1 Tbsp Dry Basil

Salt and Pepper to taste

DIRECTIONS:

Clean cabbage, discarding the dark green outer leaves. Pull leaves from stem and make sure you cut the stem out and discard.

Chop cabbage into bite size pieces; boil in salted water about 15-20 minutes until tender.

Boil one cup of rice, which will yield 2 cups of cooked rice. Set aside.

In a large frying pan, add oil and sauté garlic and onion over medium heat until wilted.

Add cooked cabbage, turning until it is well coated, and cook for 10 minutes.

Add rice, basil, salt, and pepper and turn with a wooden spoon until well mixed.

Cook an additional 5 minutes and serve.

BOCCONCINI: Cavolo Verza, or Savoy Cabbage, is called "The Prince of Winter Vegetables." If the Italian summer means tomatoes, eggplant, and peppers, the Italian winter means cabbages, in many varieties. Historically cabbages were (like everything else in Italy) regional, and in the North, you would have found primarily head cabbages, both *Cavolo Cappuccio*, the smooth-leaved heads that are green or purple, and *Cavolo Verza* or Savoy Cabbage, the green-to-purple headed cabbage some people also call *Cavolo di Milano*, with its bright, wrinkly, almost bubbly leaves. In comparison to dishes made with smooth-leafed cabbage, the texture of a dish with Savoy cabbage feels airier, at least to us, because of the bubbly structure of the leaves.

PEPERONE CON RIPIENO
(Stuffed Peppers)

This was one of my Aunt Carmella's (Thomas's mother) specialties. She told me it was a dish she brought from her home in Riccia, Italy. My wife and I were visiting my Aunt Carmella one evening and she had just taken the peppers out of the oven. She was waiting for Thomas (as always late) to stop in for dinner; but, he was already an hour late. Well, he never showed up, so I ate the peppers. They were delicious! This is a great side dish with roasted meat or chicken.

INGREDIENTS (Serves 4):

4 Medium size Bell Peppers

4 cups Day-old Italian Bread

$1/4$ cup Raisins

$1/4$ cup Walnuts, chopped

1 Egg

$1/4$ tsp Italian seasoning

Salt and pepper to taste

DIRECTIONS:

Cut off top of peppers and wash and remove seeds (peppers will resemble a bowl). Set aside.

Wet bread (do not soak) and squeeze to remove any excess water.

Tear bread into small pieces and put in a large bowl.

Beat egg and add to bread.

Add remaining ingredients and mix together (I use my hands) until all ingredients are distributed.

Fill each pepper with bread mixture.

Put the stuffed peppers on baking sheet/pan; bake at 350° F for 50-60 minutes or until peppers are tender.

BOCCONCINI: *Ripieno* means "stuffed" or "to stuff." Most people think peppers are vegetables, but peppers are fruit because they grow from a flowering plant and contain seeds. Red, orange, and yellow bell peppers are actually very ripe green bell peppers; and red bell peppers are sweeter than green ones because bell peppers sweeten as they ripen. In fact, green bell peppers are the most popular type of peppers sold in the USA even though red bell peppers have more than twice the vitamin C as their "younger" green pepper relatives.

RAPINI CON SALSICCIA E FAGIOLI
(Broccoli Rabe with Sausage and Beans)

Rapini is another word for broccoli rabe. This rabe or rapini is absolutely one of my favorite vegetables. It has become considerably popular because it is sold on a variety of sandwiches. This recipe is actually a main entrée in my home, and my son Anthony usually walks out with any leftovers.

INGREDIENTS (Serves 4 to 6):

2 lbs Broccoli Rabe

1 lb Italian sausage

1 (15 oz.) can Cannalli beans

¼ cup Olive oil

3 Cloves garlic, chopped

Salt and pepper to taste

Dash of red pepper flakes (optional)

DIRECTIONS:

Cut thick stems from rabes and clean to remove any discolored leaves.

Boil rabe in water until tender.

In a large pan, add oil and sausage and fry until done. Remove and set aside.

Cut sausage into ½ slices.

In the same pan, add beans, oil, and garlic. Sauté for 5 minutes.

Add rabe, salt, and pepper. Sauté 10 minutes, turning rabe to make sure all are well mixed.

Serve hot with a large loaf of bread.

BOCCONCINI: Rapini or broccoli rabe is also spelled raab. It is a green cruciferous vegetable, and its edible parts are the leaves, buds, and stems. The buds somewhat resemble broccoli but do not form a large head. It has a slightly bitter taste and is particularly associated with Italian and Portuguese cuisines. In Italy, it is called *cime di rapa* ("turnip tops"), and in Naples *friarielli*.

PART B. TOM'S TRIAL TIPS: YOUR OPENING STATEMENT

ESSENTIAL NUTRIENTS OF TRIAL—GOOD, CLEAR, GREEN OPENING SEQUENCING YOUR OPENING: COMMUNICATION IS WHAT IS HEARD, . . . NOT WHAT IS SAID

By: Mark Kosieradzki

INTRODUCTION TO THE INTRODUCTION TO TRIAL—OPENING STATEMENT

We present the prima facie case; it's air tight . . . Defense verdict. Why? Because there is more to persuading fact finders than presenting a one-sided prima facie case. Jurors do not decide cases based on reality; they base decisions on their perceptions of reality. It is important to understand the sources affecting perceptions, including the beliefs and preconceptions they bring to court. Understanding forensic psychological principles that emerge from studies of decision-making processes of jurors, as well as persuasion strategies used successfully for centuries, should be considered in structuring the trial.

HOW IS INFORMATION PROCESSED

It is human nature to have preconceptions. All info is processed based on individual life experiences. "People's judgments about fault and compensation, like other social judgments, are shaped by who we are: our life experiences and attitudes, our habits of mind, our intuitions about how the world works and how it ought to work, and our received wisdom about who is responsible for what in given situations." As people receive new info, they immediately test it against their model of reality. They define/interpret info in terms of life experience (knowledge base) and use inferences (judgmental heuristics) to explain what they do not know, based on what they know. Conclusions they reach are a result of either accepting the info, confirming/enhancing their model, or rejecting the information as being inconsistent with the model.

THE INFERENCE TOOLS (HEURISTICS)

Hindsight Principle: Once people know outcome of a sequence of events, they give greater significance to precipitating events than would have given in foresight.

Issue Framing Principle: Info is interpreted based on how choices are presented to them.

Information Availability Principle: People rely on info which most readily comes to mind.

Prototype Principle: People use known models of how events should occur and will categorize new info based on perceived resemblance to known information.

Monocausality: People will look for simple explanations of new information.

Mutation Principle: Facts will be mutated to fit into a known model.

UNDERSTANDING THE INFERENCE TOOLS (HEURISTICS)

Hindsight and issue framing are the most powerful influences of after-the-fact perceptions of brand new information. People will use information to explain what happened. Hindsight bias is one of the most consistently replicated effects in the cognitive psychology literature and has been proven resistant to attempts to reduce its impact. Once jurors determine what questions they want answered, they will use information they have available to them either by life experience or from trial (Information Availability Principle) to categorize the new information into known models of how events should occur (Prototype Principle). They will look for simple explanations for what/why something happened (Monocausality). New data will be categorized, based on perceived resemblances to known information (Representative Principle), or the new data will mutate to fit into a known model (Norm Principle).

ATLA JURY BIAS PROJECT: UNSPOKEN DEFENSE THEMES

As part of their life experience, jurors have developed preconceptions or biases which will influence their processing of new information. Under the guidance of the great Greg Cusimono and David Wenner, ATLA has studied the prevalent preconceptions (biases) which influence juror decisionmaking process. Four biases found by Cusimono & Wenner will underlie the focus of this paper: Suspicion, personal responsibility, stuff happens, and victimization.

1. Suspicion Bias

"These are greedy plaintiffs, with a greedy lawyer, suing someone for big money."

Lawyers as a group are generally not loved by our society. Cusimono/Wenner found the general public to have strong anti-lawyer/anti-lawsuits attitudes:

- 78% believe there are too many lawsuits.
- 68% believe lawyers encourage people to file unnecessary lawsuits.
- 54.8% believe lawsuits are lottery with too many people striking it rich.

It is generally believed among the public that lawyers cannot be trusted and will say whatever it takes to win. The good news is the public does not necessarily discriminate against plaintiff's lawyers. They distrust all lawyers. In fact, 66% of the public have a more favorable view of lawyers who represent individuals than corporations.

2. Personal Responsibility Bias

Personal responsibility is a corollary to the belief most lawsuits are frivolous. Jurors want plaintiffs to accept responsibility for their own conduct and consequently for what happened. Assuming the trial lawyer successfully clears the suspicion bias hurdles, allowing the jury to conclude that neither the lawyer nor her client has brought a "frivolous" case, the lawyer must now face the psychological principle of "fundamental attribution." The more seriously injured the accident victim, the more anxious jurors become about the prospect of suffering the same fate. By subconsciously believing "I would have acted differently," the juror can blame the plaintiff and eliminate the fact that the same fate could occur to them or their loved ones.

3. Stuff Happens Bias

A second corollary to frivolous lawsuit bias is some events are not caused by the fault of anyone. Simply: "Stuff happens." Certain things occur regardless of conduct of persons involved. The underlying psychological process is that all persons, no matter how well intentioned, are involved in conduct which "accidently" results in some form of damage. A more critical analysis reveals a significant percentage of the American public which believes, regardless of the jury instruction, fault requires intent to harm.

4. Victimization Bias

The term "victim" does not necessarily mean plaintiff. 51% of white males believe defendants in civil lawsuits are the victim. As a result of the belief there are too many frivolous suits, there is a preexisting belief the defendant did nothing wrong.

STORYTELLING

In the course of a trial, jurors are presented with countless facts, technical terms, and concepts, often spanning days, weeks, and months. Facts which would otherwise be meaningless if not placed in some context. Without an organizational frame work, it would be impossible for them to make sense of all the information they receive. The opening statement provides that context. By the end of the opening statements, jurors have decided "almost immutably" what the case is about. Thus, the opening establishes how jurors will process/interpret the information which is presented throughout the trial.

Jurors will look for a story. If they do not hear one, they will create a story to make sense of evidence. By presenting the opening in the form of a story, jurors have an organizational framework to evaluate, organize, and remember facts. However, in order to be effective, the story must recognize the information processing principles jurors will use. Despite judicial instructions to the contrary, jurors begin considering life experience (facts not in evidence) and formulating opinions before deliberations. The story the jurors use will correspond to what they know (believe) about how people act and react in the real world. Therefore, to be effective, the story will not only have to account for the evidence but also fit with the jurors' life experiences.

As a general rule, "jurors think of themselves not as fixers and balancers of harm, but deciders of right and wrong." Although significant injuries are required in prosecution of a case, damage alone is not the key factor in themes that drive successful cases. Rather, exposure of defendant's bad conduct is the driving force. The greatest risk to a defendant is an angry jury. Jurors who are angered are often motivated to punish, to make social statements, or to get revenge. Holding a wrongdoer accountable is a much more effective motivator than compensating someone for being harmed.

It is not enough to focus on a defendant's negligent act alone. We have learned from our jury research that jurors are seldom motivated by someone's "mistake" or an "accident." Rather, the focus must expose why defendant acted negligently. What were the circumstances that gave rise to the conduct? What decision making was involved? This analysis often reveals the underlying corporate malfeasance and/or administrative indifference that explains why the negligence occurred.

By exposing the underlying reasons for negligence, the jury realizes that the injury will happen again to someone else unless they do something. The jury will understand that the case is not about an unfortunate accident. The case is about a disaster that was waiting to happen. The jury will understand that the defendant could have easily averted the disaster by doing the right thing in the first place. It is through this knowledge that the jury becomes motivated to make a statement with their award. Making the case bigger than one event, bigger than one family's loss, the defendant's risk is magnified. Therefore, the story must focus on the choices defendant made that result in the events that led to this lawsuit.

Jurors will look for applicable rules (Information Availability Principle) to evaluate the choices the defendant made. If those rules are not part of their life experience, they need to learn the rules as part of the story of the case.

HOW TO TELL A STORY: FOUR STORYTELLING RULES

Phillip Miller articulates the fundamental principles for a story to be effective. (1) The story must integrate and account for evidence acquired during trial (coverage). The greater the coverage, the more acceptable the story is as an explanation of evidence. (2) The story must be plausible. If the story does not correspond to a juror's knowledge about what typically happens in his or her world, or contradicts that knowledge, the story will fail. (3) The story must be complete. If the story is missing information, the jury will fill in those gaps with inferences based on their life experiences. (4) The story needs to provide the best fit for the verdict. The jurors will be faced with alternative stories. If the story does not correspond to the issues they need to resolve in the verdict, the story will fail.

The Story needs to be about people, not facts. However, factual details/descriptions help jurors characterize key story characters. Factual details/descriptions are used to describe the scene and circumstances of the key elements of the story. Details of the physical surrounding bring the story to life. But the story must be about the people and the choices they made.

Every story requires conflict. A conflict is a change, decision, or dispute which is the basis of the attribution of fault. The story will need to identify the choices the defendant made and the time in which those choices were made. Example: the choices the manufacturer made in the years before the injury.

In order to make the best fit, the story will need to make the defense story irrelevant or implausible; not by argument but rather by a presentation of facts which neutralizes the defense. Facts, when appropriately sequenced, are the most persuasive form of argument. Jurors are most persuaded by facts which cause them to reach conclusions on their own.

Every story needs a theme. Themes are not catchy phrases. They are the overriding principle which permeates the trial. We know jurors view themselves as the deciders of right and wrong. Therefore, our themes should respond to their view of their role. Theme of right and wrong or good vs. evil will resonate. When the case is not about what happened but why, jurors become motivated to make a statement.

The sequence of the presentation is critical to information processing and fault attribution mechanisms used by all persons. It is known that jurors will immediately start constructing their own story and attribution of fault simultaneously with the delivery of your story. It is also known that the more a defendant deviates from the jurors view of acceptable behavior, the greater the damage award. Therefore, focus needs to be directed at the defendant at the outset of the story.

Point of view controls the scenes of the story and the perception of the listeners. "Point of view is about whose 'eyes' are used to describe the action of the story." Point of view in a story affects how listeners asses responsibility and blame. By determining which character will be the focus of the story, the storyteller controls the jurors' focus.

The tense of the story, past or present, impacts the jurors' perception of the events as the story unfolds. Past tense creates a story about something that has already happened, something the listener can do nothing about. Present tense brings the listener into the story whose ending is not inevitable.

CONCLUSION

Communication is what is heard, not just what is said. A persuasive opening statement is much more than a recitation of the facts which will be presented at trial. How information is presented directly impacts how people interpret information. Presentation is more than rhetorical devices. Presentation requires an understanding of how people process information and what preconceptions they bring to the decision making process. With that understanding, rhetorical tools can be used to enable listeners to organize and retain information and to motivate them in their decision-making process.

OPENING: DOs & DON'Ts OF STORYTELLING & THEME CREATION

(Short excerpt from Opening Statement Chapter of Tom Vesper's AAJ Trial Notebook)

I. INTRODUCTION: MY PHILOSOPHY: THIS IS GUADALCANAL!

I firmly believe that the trial of any case must be looked at as a whole since every part of a trial relates to every other in a "seamless web." Although different aspects of a trial can be studied separately, I believe the plaintiff's opening statement is the most important element of a trial. Storytelling relates to opening statement and each individual witness and exhibit. Each trial, like a great tapestry, has a series of themes, story lines, and small evidentiary threads that are woven into one final story—the summation. Your overall theme should be enunciated and each "story line" or "thread" set up and foretold in your opening. Plaintiff's opening statement is the psychological "turning point" or "Guadalcanal" of the trial process.

While some refer to me with the same assigned agnomen of the battleship USS North Carolina ("the Show Boat"), and some call my settlement briefs syrupy, sentimental, and hokey, I nevertheless believe whether you are dramatic or understated, emotional or expressionless, sensitive or stoic, subtle or simplistic, double breasted, three or two piece suited, regardless of your approach, you should practice your art according to your conscience. Your own good philosophical and religious beliefs, in accordance with the ethics of our profession, should be your safety and navigational lights. You should KNOW YOURSELF (all your personal and professional strengths and weaknesses) and then . . . BE YOURSELF (comfortable with what you are doing) and then . . . TELL THE TRUE STORY! Tell your client's story the way you would tell your children about their grandparents or great-grandparents.

I will suggest storytelling techniques I recommend (Positive Thoughts) and conduct I discourage (Negative Thoughts). Some trial lawyers, young and old, will not agree with all my ideas or methods. This is natural for our individualistic discipline as trial advocates. Advocacy is three-dimensional, life scale art of applied psychology, marketing, and morality. We must communicate effectively and convincingly our client's rightful positions. Techniques and content are very subjective. They will vary with the personality, lifestyle, and life experiences of the individual lawyer. What I prefer is not necessarily "RIGHT" for you, but it may give some ideas for you to adapt/follow.

As a trial lawyer, you live your life in the pursuit of justice and fairness for your clients. You improve the human condition by the exercise of democracy in the courtroom. We must never forget our role in court and our important mission in the civil arena. Despite the urgings of some statistic-sensitive, calendar-conscious, and micro-managed and overcontrolled judges; despite the assembly-line mentality of some administrative AOC personnel; and in the insensitive and skeptical face of a hardened defense bar and an entrenched "hard line" insurance adjuster, our duty is clear: to obtain full and fair compensation for our clients. Plaintiff trial lawyers, above all professionals in our system of justice, have the unique and heavy responsibility to maintain, protect, and recover just compensation for the dignitary interests of each individual we represent. Plaintiff trial advocacy is, as Plato wrote, "the most noble of professions."

II. SOME STORYTELLING TECHNIQUES

A plaintiff's trial attorney should be aware of the following psychological principles and acting techniques.

A. Primacy and Recency

(1) Primacy: Highly familiar issues tend toward primacy. That is, when the issue is familiar, the side presented first tends to be more persuasive. Lana, R.E., "Familiarity and the Order of Presentation of Persuasive Communications," J. Abnorm. Soc. Psychol., 1961, 573-577.

(2) Recency: When moderately unfamiliar issues are presented, they tend toward recency. That is, if the issue is moderately unfamiliar and requires explanation and thought, the side heard last tends to be more persuasive. Lana, R.E., "Interest, Media and Order Effects in Persuasive Communications," J. Psychol. 1963, 56, 9-13. See also James Fitzgerald, "Opening Statements, A Presentation" 1989 National College of Advocacy, Basic Course in Trial Advocacy, ATLA, Des Moines, Iowa 1989.

With respect to an opening statement, when a plaintiff's attorney does not make an issue or a "story line" familiar to the jury, that attorney fails to utilize the advantageous position as the first speaker and the psychological principle of primacy. For example, a wrongful death case or any serious personal injury case where the cause of the death or serious injury is a product failure could be a case about "safety." Therefore, the unfamiliar issue, for instance, a fork lift design for a roll bar, or lack of a guard on a machine, will become familiar by use of layman's concept of "safety." The position heard first, therefore, the plaintiff, will have a psychological advantage.

When plaintiff's counsel fails to reduce unfamiliar issues to familiar issues, the defense automatically gets the advantage of the psychological principle of recency. Defense counsel will talk about the moderately unfamiliar matters such as structural fork lift components, roll bars, engineering concepts, engineering judgments, manufacturing processes, etc. By explaining all of these "moderately unfamiliar issues" and doing so last in their opening statement, the defense is likely to be much more persuasive than plaintiff's counsel because the jury will rely upon the defendant's explanation for their guidance throughout the trial. As said above, studies have shown that when heard last, a moderately unfamiliar argument or issue is more persuasive. Therefore, it is the responsibility of plaintiff's counsel to make issues highly familiar and to simplify all unfamiliar issues and deal with them in advance of the defense.

B. Recall and Recognition

Trial is a learning process. A jury must be taught before they can be persuaded; they must be interested in what you teach before they can be taught. When people learn facts, they will remember them. Scientists and educators measure memory from tests of recall and recognition.

(1) Recall requires a person to explain what he has learned by producing the correct response without any demonstrative aid. Recall is tested by essay examination. Mednick, S., *Learning*, Prentice-Hall, Inc., NJ. Trial attorneys expect and/or hope jurors will recall their openings. Trial lawyers expect jurors to recall facts in trial, but relying on recall alone, some, not all, jurors will be able to recall a specific fact or opening point of discussion in a jury room. Assuming 70% of what you present is "learned" at time of its presentation, studies show in 20 minutes recall drops to a bit more than 50%; a day later, only 20% is recalled; the percentage of recall continues to drop down to 10% after two days.

(2) Recognition represents ability to discriminate what one has learned from other materials. It is a matter of identification. Recognition memory is tested by multiple choice and fill-in-the-blank tests.

If one assumes a jury learns a fact in opening and is tested immediately in a recognition test, studies show that recognition memory will test at 100% at the time of its presentation; 96% 20 minutes later; one hour later, it still tests at 96%; one day later, 78%; two days later, recognition memory tests at 72%.

Psychological studies verified this recognition and recall principle. Luh, C.W., Psychol. Monogr. 1922, 31, No. 142.

Remember these two teaching principles. Do not rely solely upon a verbal presentation of information in your opening statement or in the other parts of your trial. If you do, the recall of jurors will be relatively low. A jury cannot be expected to recall all of your client's important facts. If, however, you provide demonstrative aids in opening, such as blackboards, models, etc., the jury can recognize important facts or points of discussion as they are introduced during the trial. There will be enhanced learning, and memory of the facts supporting your position will be greatly improved.

C. Excite the Little Child Within Us All

When children are small, they are easily delighted by having stories told to them. Toddlers light up when we begin to perform a creation of imaginary characters with sound effects and pantomime. Eyes wide apart, young kids absorb information like sponges. Often, they clamor for more data. This is called "filling the gaps." Remember to avoid leaving "gaps" in your opening storytelling.

Children of all ages understand and remember stories. Jurors decide cases based on stories told, heard, remembered, and understood. As Gerry Spence has explained:

> Of course it is all storytelling—nothing more. It is the experience of the tribe around the fire, the primordial genes excited, listening, the shivers racing up your back to the place where the scalp is made, and then the breathless climax, and the sadness and the tears with the dying of the embers, and the silence. . . . The problem is that we, as lawyers, have forgotten how to speak to ordinary folks . . . lawyers long ago abandoned ordinary English. Worse, their minds have been smashed and serialized, and their brain cells restacked so that they no longer can explode in every direction—with joy, love, and rage. They cannot see in the many colors of feeling. The passion is gone, replaced with the deadly droning of the intellect. And the sounds we make are all alike, like machines mumbling and grinding away, because what was once free—the stuff of storytelling—has become rigid.

Gerry Spence, ABA Journal, April 1986

D. Neurolinguistic Programming

Communications experts studying the impact on how messages are received will explain that there are three primary channels of delivery: verbal (with words), vocal (how a message is delivered), and nonverbal (facial expressions, eye movements, body language). Experts say that the actual words used only count for 10% of the impact. The vocal message, that is, our inflection and the use of voice as an instrument of communication, accounts for 40% of the impact of any story told. By far, the most important impact or aspect of a message comes from nonverbal communication (50%).

E. Priorities for Storytellers: Men vs. Women

Certain communication principles we must remember when delivering our opening and throughout trial. Jurors pay more attention to behaviors that fit their initial view of a new acquaintance, but they also interpret behaviors to fit their first impression and may therefore completely ignore contradictory information. Research suggests that for male jurors, the most important traits are confidence, efficiency, sincerity, and friendliness of the speaker. Female jurors value these traits in a different order of priority: friendliness, sincerity, efficiency, and confidence. Sannito & McGovern, Courtroom Psychology for Lawyers, p182 (1985); see also John A. Call, "How Do You Like Me So Far?" Trial, p. 72 (Aug 1995).

F. "The Four Minute Drill"

One concept plaintiff trial attorneys should note is what social scientists call "The Four Minute Drill": most people in a social setting develop first impression within four minutes of initial encounters. In juror communication techniques, this means you must tell your main story to jurors as early as possible. Whether in opening, direct exam of every witness, qualifications/voir dire of experts, or in cross-examination, try to get your client's message to the jury in a short introductory statement or question.

G. The Present Tense

Use action words and present tense when we communicate to the jury. A story happening now in "real time" has the listener participating in it. "Imagine Joe stopped at a corner when struck from . . . ." This is less effective than "Imagine Joe sitting in his car at stop light at Vine & Broad, thinking of coming home to his children and suddenly his body is catapulted forward as defendant rams his motionless car from behind."

H. Memory Organization Packages—MOPs

Roger Shank in Tell Me A Story says memory is made of "MOPs or memory organization packages." A MOP covers a context-dependent aspect of memory like taking a trip or eating dessert. A MOP can be a set of scenes, each covering visually defined boundaries that might occur in a variety of combinations, such as going to a hospital ER, confronting the desk attendant, and arguing over insurance coverage.

Most male lawyers have experienced the embarrassment of thinking (or actually finding) our fly has been left unzipped in public. When in direct or cross-examination of witnesses, we should try to elicit affirmative responses to descriptions that will produce MOPs in the jurors' minds consistent with the client's theme.

I. Anchoring

There is a storytelling and communicating technique called "anchoring." That is, get the jury to associate a certain part of the court room, or a particular exhibit, with a recurring theme or issue in the case. If you have one chart that outlines the economic damages, you should use that one chart every time you talk of those elements of damage. Example: an outstanding, unforgettable visual exhibit in a death case, Murray Ogborn "anchored" the testimony of a little girl with a single red rose which the child brought to court and placed upon the plaintiff's counsel table in the presence of the jury.

III. 101 IDEATIONS ABOUT THE OPENING STATEMENT

A. Fifty Positive Thoughts

1. Remember: "This is Guadalcanal!"
2. Remember the importance of opening: Primacy!
3. Use natural motivational analysis:

    (a) What natural motivation must this jury find for plaintiff on liability/damages?

    (b) What natural motivation must this jury find against plaintiff on liability/damages?

    (c) What natural motivation must jury find for each defendant on liability/damages?

(d) What natural motivation must jury find against each defendant on fault/damages?

4. Be honest and sensitive

5. Structure and analyze your presentation . . . especially concentrate on DAMAGES

6. Know Yourself, Be Yourself, Tell the True Story

7. Know your territory (venue + jury venire attitude)

8. Know your case

9. Know the law

10. Properly prepare in advance of trial . . .

(Excerpt from Opening Statement Chapter of Tom Vesper's *AAJ Trial Notebook*)

B. Fifty Negative Thoughts

1. "We are often experts at mimicking mediocrity." DON'T BE A "DOOFUS"!

2. Don't disclaim your credibility

3. Don't say ". . . is not to be considered evidence"

4. Don't make salutations and reintroductions in the first four minutes of opening

5. Don't lose "home court advantage" . . . DON'T SHORT CHANGE DAMAGES!

6. Don't hesitate to consult another experienced/Certified Civil Trial Attorney

7. Don't forget your locality, the local people, folklore, and customs

8. Don't start to prep the night before/morning of

9. Don't allow distractions during your opening; e.g.: "Watch your 60" or back-side at all times: audience, adversaries, court personnel

10. Don't be timid or afraid . . .

The Vespers' Trial Cookbook

(Excerpt from Opening Statement Chapter of Tom Vesper's *AAJ Trial Notebook*)

IV. WHAT TO DO BEFORE YOUR PLAINTIFF'S OPENING STATEMENT

A. Sensitivity Training

Sensitize yourself or settle the case! Walk around your client's home and talk to your client at his/her leisure for at least one hour. Make this house call more than 30 days before trial.

B. Five Easy Pieces

1. Take complete history of plaintiff: family, education, work, social activities.
2. Meet and talk with family, friends, coworkers, and neighbors.
3. Visit the home.
4. Consult experienced trial attorney + use "team"/mock jury to evaluate case.
5. Use a Trial Notebook.

V. CONCLUSION

Murray Ogborn's "Storytelling Throughout Trial" is an excellent article of how each phase of trial, beginning with voir dire, opening, direct exam, cross examination, and final argument, should incorporate storytelling techniques. As Murray explains:

> Unlike nursery rhymes, fairy tales, novels, even works of non-fiction, the trial is a compelling story which does not leave the audience merely contemplating and reflecting. This story, that is the trial message of a trial lawyer, must incite the listeners to act. They must find for the plaintiff.

Murray Ogborn, "Storytelling Throughout Trial," Trial, 63-65 (August 1995)

In my opinion, the best way to create a case theme and then build short stories or novellas around the theme is to visit the client at home. "Walking a mile in someone's shoes" works. Unless you try to fit into your client's moccasin for just a brief reflection, you will never understand your client's case or true themes in the client's life. If we can simply try, as much as possible, to live the life of our clients in physical and emotional circumstances their injuries left them, we will more easily find the theme and easily thereafter develop each part of the trial as a separate story around that central theme.

Storytelling and opening statements are not impossible or overly complex if you follow the advice of a truly great storyteller—James Cagney:

"Stand up straight on your own two feet,

look the audience in their eyes,

and

TELL THE TRUTH!"

OPENING STATEMENT—"Sequencing" for Success

POWER POINT—The Do's & Don'ts

MARK & MAD DOG: PPT OPENING: IS THE FORCE WITH YOU?

By: Mark Kosieradzki & Tom Vesper

I. INTRODUCTION

The purpose of this paper is to point out some important concepts to remember when preparing for and using PowerPoint for opening statements and show some basic, intermediate, and advanced PowerPoint mistakes to avoid. If the reader is not yet familiar with PowerPoint, there are references which can help any trial lawyer or paralegal in preparing a PowerPoint presentation for jury trial, focus Group, business meeting, or seminar. See the selected bibliography below.

A. The PowerPoint is Not The Opening, It is Just Another Tool

It is important to recognize that the PowerPoint is not THE opening statement. An opening by the plaintiff's lawyer is still a personal communication between the lawyer and the individual jurors. It is a very important initial impression created by the plaintiff lawyer on behalf of the injured plaintiff. The plaintiff lawyer's primary mission is to establish the client's, case's, and lawyer's credibility. As David Ball teaches, the "worthwhileness" of the client needs to be proven before jurors will award damages. David Ball, Ball on Damages, NITA (2003). Using PowerPoint should complement the trial lawyer in establishing credibility, worthwhileness, and a favorable impression of the merits of the case. Using PowerPoint is not a substitute for the art of styling, structuring, and delivering an opening statement.

B. Why Use a Six Shooter When a Light Saber is At Hand

In a very practical way, PowerPoint presentation can save time, help the jury understand, and help the trial lawyer persuade. Rather than writing out points/facts on a blackboard, instead of drawing diagrams on artists' pads, and in lieu of fumbling through stacks of photographs or x-rays, every trial lawyer has the availability of an instant and inexpensive graphics and art department in the form of a PowerPoint program. The very act of preparing PowerPoint slides will force the trial lawyer to organize the concepts and points of the opening. Additionally, use of PowerPoint will keep the trial lawyer on course and keep the opening "tight" and to the point (no pun intended). Just as we all (or some of us at least) have graduated from carbon paper to word processors, from typewriters to computer keyboards, from chalk to erasable markers, we now have a very valuable piece of weaponry in our advocacy arsenal.

". . ., the opening statement traditionally is a word story—it is an abstract of the case that will come—not a visual summary. The lawyer who creates the word story traditionally plays the role of a good magazine editor or abridger, cutting the story down to its core words. Yet if people do learn better from pictures or from the combination of pictures and words, why should we limit the lawyer to the role of editor?" P. Zwier & T.C. Galligan, Technology and Opening Statements: "A Bridge to the Virtual Trial of the Twenty-First Century," 67 TENN. L. REV., 523, at 526-27 (Spring 2000).

For the plaintiff trial lawyer, a PowerPoint opening can be very persuasive, especially in a complex case.

"Only about 10% of information delivered verbally is remembered after three days. Twice as much information delivered in a silent visual format is remembered after three days. 85% of information delivered visually and verbally is remembered after three days. E.S. Strong, Technology Tools in the Courtroom: How to Use Them and How to Oppose Them, 11 PRAC. LITIG. 15, 17 (Jan. 2000).

C. Some Will Sense and Fear "The Force"

Defense attorneys know the strength and persuasive power of PowerPoint. The presentation will focus jurors on evidence plaintiff considers key. For defense attorneys, the power of any technology like PPT, just as any powerful exhibits, is a threat. PPT in openings can emphasize selected pieces of evidence at expense of others, and thus, the risk of "unfair prejudice," misleading or confusing the jury, is always an argument for them to raise to bar such advocacy. Their arguments will be no different than if you try to show photos in your opening. E.S. Strong, *Technology Tools in the Courtroom: How to Use Them and How to Oppose Them*, 11 PRAC. LITIG. 15, 17 (Jan. 2000).

Some conservative and/or inexperienced trial judges may sense potential appellate issues and may hesitate to permit attorneys to utilize any demonstrative evidence or PowerPoint in opening statements. However, as Bruce Stern advises:

> A PowerPoint presentation can be basically broken down into two different types of slides. The first is simply the use of words and bullet points to be used as an outline during the opening statement. The second type of slide contains not only words, but also photographs, drawings, copies of books and documents, the originals of which will ultimately be moved into evidence during the course of the trial.

Bruce Stern, "Use of PowerPoint in Opening Statement," ATLA Seminar Paper (2002).

Few trial judges will refuse an attorney's request to use a blackboard, easel or large pad of paper to write on during opening. Thus, if you can write things out during an opening, certainly, you should be permitted to use prepared "boards" or PPT slides containing the same; but use of PPT slides depicting videotaped testimony, documents, or pictures that will be introduced during the trial may be a more complex issue. In the federal courts and many states, attorneys are required before trial to exchange exhibits that they intend to use in trial (aka PIX Pretrial Information Exchanges). Often, evidentiary hearings or motions in limine take place to rule on admissibility of these documents.

Most courts require disclosure of any visual aid or exhibit to be used in opening. Therefore, you can print out your PPT for the adversary and trial judge. In anticipation of objections, if you intend to use PowerPoint slides, regardless of their content, they should be exchanged before trial so that the court can rule on any objections.

D. In The Wrong Hands PowerPoint Will Be Your Death Star

Most of today's school children have seen PowerPoint presentations. A recent survey asked people how many PPT presentations they saw an average week. Most did not see that many PPTs per week, but they would see 30-50 per year. A large number (44%) of respondents would see two or more per week or 100 PPT presentations a year. Dave Paradi, *Summary of Annoying PPTt Survey of subscribers to Communicating Using Technology Newsletter*, at www.communicateusingtechnology.com, Sept. 2003.

Assume most jurors will be highly critical of "annoying" PPT presentations. In same survey, a high percentage of presentations suffered from problems that annoy audiences: 41.5% respondents said more than 40% of PPTs they see have "annoying elements." This survey shows how wide-spread "annoying Power Point" problem is and how much of an issue this can be for trial lawyers. Microsoft's statistics indicate there are 400 million copies of Microsoft Office installed and 30 million PPT presentations done each day. The increased reliance on PPT tool for communicating a message has not worked as well as hoped given the results of the survey. It is clear that many PPT presenters need help structure their presentations, especially the crucial text aspect. Question: Of those presentations you see, what % are done poorly (suffer from one or more problems)?

More than 50% 28.9%
0–5%	13.8%
41–50%	12.6%
31–40%	11.3%
16–20%	8.8%
21–25%	8.8%
26–30%	7.5%
6–10%	5.0%
11–15%	3.1%

Dave Paradi, Summary of the Annoying PowerPoint Survey of subscribers to Communicating Using Technology Newsletter, reported at www.communicateusingtechnology.com, Sept. 2003.

II. BEWARE OF THE "DARK SIDE": MISTAKES TO AVOID

A. Beginner's Mistakes

For the "beginner" trial lawyer PowerPoint user, there are some basic mistakes which have been made repeatedly by PowerPoint users which must be avoided.

In the same survey, people reported the most annoying things about the bad PowerPoint presentations. The three most annoying PowerPoint blunders are the following:

1. Reading the slides. When a speaker reads the written text of any slide most people are offended either consciously because they think the speaker does not trust them to read, or unconsciously because they sense a needless and wasteful repetition.

2. Conspicuity: Words too small to read or hard to see because of color. As with any exhibit, a trial lawyer must be sure the jury can see what is to be shown. If the printed words are too small for the jury to see and read easily the jury will simply give up and not try to read any of the written material. Many middle-aged people need reading glasses. Remember that fact and make sure any text is readable.

CAVEAT: Color can be a Killer. As we know from the teaching of Rodney Jew, the guru of visual strategy, the easiest color combinations to see are black on white or black on red based yellow. Use of light colors like reds, yellows, and grays on white background will not be easily seen by jurors sitting a distance away from the graphic.

3. Using full sentences vs. bullet points. Most folks look for a PPT presentation to save time and effort. By using full sentences instead of bullet points the reader again senses that their time is being wasted and the presentation itself is burdensome, tiring, and clumsy.

It is clear from responses to the survey that the most annoying aspect of bad PowerPoint slides is the ineffective use of text, not the use of graphics or multimedia. Therefore, it is most important that the trial lawyer focus on getting short, relevant, and readable text on slides then add to each point with what they say. Simply reading PPT slides jammed with text is an insult to the audience, and the results indicate that by doing this, presenters are severely damaging the message they are trying to deliver.

In creating a PowerPoint opening, do not let the presentation overwhelm the message you are trying to deliver. Seth Godin cautions:

> If all you want to do is create a file of facts and figures, then cancel the meeting and send it in a report. Do it in PowerPoint if you want, but it is not a presentation, it's a report. It will contain whatever you write down, but don't imagine for a second that you're powerfully communicating any

ideas. Communication is about getting others to adopt your point of view, and to help them understand why you're so excited (or sad, optimistic or whatever else you are). Unless you are an amazing writer, it is awfully hard to do that in a report.

> When you show up to give a presentation, people want to use both parts of their brain . . . they use the right side to judge the way you talk, . . . dress . . . your body language.
>
>> You can wreck a communication process with lousy logic or unsupportive facts, but you cannot complete it without a motion. Logic is not enough. If all it took were logic, no one would smoke cigarettes . . ..
>>
>>> PowerPoint presents an amazing opportunity. You could use the screen to talk emotionally to the audience's right brain (through their eyes) and your words can go through the audience's ears to talk to their left brain.
>>>
>>> That is what Steven Spielberg does. It seems to work for him.

Seth Godin, "Really Bad PowerPoint (and how to avoid it)" (Zoom, Inc. 2000) at http://www.SethGodin.com.

B. Intermediate Mistakes

Intermediate or advanced PPT users have a "Dark Side" to their PowerPoint force: a tendency to "do a lot" or "jazz up" the presentation. These annoying traits refer to the technical aspects of the PPT as opposed to fundamental mistakes with the text of the slides. Six most annoying media features of PowerPoint presentations are:

1. UFOs. Using text or graphics that move, fly, or zoom is distracting to jurors. It does not impress most people and will annoy/irritate a large majority of your jurors.

2. Sound effects. As with flying objects, use of sound effects distracts/annoys.

3. Data overload or chart gridlock. Many people surveyed found diagrams and charts were too complex to understand. Too much/many information, detail, colors, and too many ideas illustrated will not only be annoying, but also may in fact confuse jurors.

4. No flow or purpose. If jury cannot quickly decipher logic/reason for the PPT they quickly dismiss it as irrelevant "window dressing." Jumping around, having no order to presentation, and coming to no logical end will

cause your PPT presentation to be critically disclaimed. This factor alone accounted for 40% complaints of survey group.

5. Font flood and irrelevant graphics. Using too many different fonts distracts readers; using graphics that do not fit or relate to subject matter of the slide our items that accounted for approximately 20% of the negative criticism of the surveyed group.

6. Poor quality video/audio. Although the survey found this to be an annoyance to 5% of people questioned, the lack of good quality audio/video can be very damaging to a plaintiffs opening. If jurors cannot see/hear what is important for them to see/hear that aspect of plaintiffs case may be totally unknown or worse misunderstood by jurors. A poor video/audio presentation may result in what jury consultants refer to as "gaps." That is, jurors who have in their minds a gap or a lack of information or detail on an issue important to them—regardless of whether they have missed it or it was missing in the opening—they will likely fill the gap with their own imagination and experience.

The actual survey results were as follows:

Q1: What are three most annoying things about bad PPT presentation/slides you have seen?

The speaker read the slides to us 60.4%
Text so small I couldn't read it 50.9%
Full sentences instead of bullet points 47.8%
Slides hard to see because of color choice 37.1%
Moving/flying text or graphics 24.5%
Annoying use of sounds 22.0%
Overly complex diagrams or charts 22.0%
No flow of ideas—jumped around too much 18.9%
No clear purpose of the presentation 18.2%
Too many fonts used 12.6%
Graphic that did not fit the topic of slide 6.3%
Poor quality video or audio segment 5.0%

(Total 325.8% because people were asked to select three options, and some selected more than three) Dave Paradi, Summary of the Annoying PowerPoint Survey of subscribers to Communicating Using Technology Newsletter, at www.communicateusingtechnology.com, Sept. 2003.

Q2: What other things annoy you about PowerPoint presentations (presenters)?

This free form question in Paradi "Annoying PowerPoint Survey" had 94 of 159 respondents (59%) adding comments. Three common themes emerged comments:

1. Poor Preparation—People are very annoyed when the presenter does not even think about the structure of the presentation, simply copying text of a report onto slides. PPT should support the message, not substitute for the presenter or a more detailed handout. Presenters need to connect with the audience instead of hiding behind the slides.

2. Balance of Slide Elements—People find too much text or too much fancy graphics and multimedia a big turn off. These two extremes do not work well. A balanced approach is called for—text to give context for audience's understanding of what the presenter will next speak about, and graphics and multimedia to touch their emotions.

3. Not Knowing How to Use the Technology—If presenters are going to use technology during a presentation, they should learn how to set it up, start it so it looks professional and smoothly move between slides. Awkward use of PPT and presentation technology was mentioned a number of times as detracting from the message being delivered.

In comments, many respondents were passionate about the sins committed by presenters. Most see the PPT as being a useful tool but far too often misused. Dave Paradi, Summary of the Annoying PowerPoint Survey of subscribers to Communicating Using Technology Newsletter, at www.communicateusingtechnology.com, Sept. 2003.

III. LET THE JURY USE "THE FORCE"

A. Avoid Mistakes Re Color, Symbols, Text, and Words

The basic components of communication in trial, in order of their juror impact are:

1. color
2. pictures
3. symbols/icons
4. printed words

5. spoken words

Jurors perceive color and pictures before symbols and icons; they will perceive symbols and icons before words. Therefore, to communicate more effectively with PowerPoint in opening, plaintiff lawyers must first get the jury's attention and then tap into their emotions, beliefs, and life experiences. The most effective way of doing this is to combine the various modes of communication. Spoken words alone are NOT enough. Visual slides/exhibits will help, but slides/exhibits which are not strategically linked in the opening may not connect with or be of use to the jurors. Integrated PowerPoint slides/exhibits with spoken and written words provide the most effective means of conveying important information to the jury.

Plaintiff trial lawyers who rely only, or primarily, on their own spoken words in openings to impart critical information to the jury rely too heavily on the most ineffective and least impactful communication tool. To communicate effectively in the courtroom, it is necessary to present openings visually as well as orally. Therefore, in using PowerPoint, just as with any exhibit, you must select colors, shapes, images, pictures, symbols, and icons with the same care as words and understand the unique advantages of each.

1. Color. Color helps make information memorable; it increases attention and retention. It grabs the eye first—before pictures, symbols, or words. Color should be used judiciously to draw attention to key information, enhance the visibility and legibility of exhibits, and reinforce thematic connections (with color-coding and color symbolism). Text should appear in the most legible or visible color combinations. (Black text on white is most legible because it provides the greatest value contrast; black text on yellow is most visible, because yellow is the most readily perceived hue.) Colors that cannot be distinguished by color-blind viewers should not be used to show key distinctions. (About 8% of males, for example, are unable to distinguish red and green; and half of those who are color blind do not know it.) Colors may have a variety of connotations and evoke either positive or negative responses among different groups of people. It is critical to use colors that evoke appropriate responses from jurors.

2. Pictures. Like colors, pictures grab jurors' attention before symbols or words. They evoke an immediate emotional response. Inherently more memorable than words, pictures increase jurors' recall of information. The old adage is true: The right picture equals a thousand words.

3. Symbols and icons. Symbols and icons identify and help discriminate among

topics. They reduce the amount of text that needs to be read, increase information scanning and retrieval speed, and augment readability of information for those with limited linguistic skills.

4. Printed words. Words are excellent for naming concepts and things, defining terms, classifying elements, and allowing discussion of abstractions. Words on exhibits are best kept few and simple, to enable jurors to readily grasp them. Text items are ideally presented in groups of three, as people tend to remember things in threes. A neutral title should identify each exhibit (letting the jurors know what they are looking at). A subtitle that is a rhetorical question should stimulate jurors to scan information on the exhibit to determine a response. Rhetorical questions increase jurors' involvement by stimulating a higher level of information processing. Printed words, together with supporting visual images, can isolate key concepts and keep them in jurors' view, to ensure the concepts + their significance, are not missed.

5. Spoken words. Spoken words, on the other hand, although often the primary or only communication vehicle used to convey key concepts in trial, are not always the most effective. If jurors are even briefly distracted, they may miss key portions of spoken testimony (particularly if a witness rambles). Even if jurors hear the crucial words, they may overlook their importance, unless the oral testimony is reinforced with strategic exhibits. Rodney Jew, "Motivating The Jurors: A New Paradigm for Trial Communication," ATLA Paper 1998

B. Avoid "Perspicuity/Conspicuity" Problems

There have been many papers, lectures, and entire seminars dedicated to the production of exhibits/demos which are visible and understandable to jurors. Jurors, like any human beings, process information both consciously and unconsciously.

How Do Jurors Process Information?

1. Conscious, analytical processing involves searching for, sorting, and weighing information to arrive at a decision. Jurors engage in this process only if they are sufficiently motivated to do so. Jurors become motivated to analyze case issues if they perceive the issues as relevant to their own personal life experiences. To maintain their motivation, jurors must have:

    a. Access to what they view as adequate information;

    b. The intellectual capacity and skill to process the information; and

    c. Methods, provided by the lawyers and experts, to code the messages (including visual representations, metaphors, comparisons, etc.) If jurors cannot find any direct comparison in their own life experience for the concepts presented, they may lose motivation and stop searching for information. Responding irrationally, they may fall back on the closest comparisons they can find in their own experience, and thus bring irrelevant information into the decision process.

2. Lawyers must assume, jurors will apply some unconscious and conscious reasoning to the case issues. With unconscious reasoning, jurors tend to generate their own series of rules for categorizing data. They may take mental shortcuts, which can make their thinking inaccessible to correction. Although they may use intuitive reasoning in place of more objective reasoning, they will believe their conclusions are accurate. The unconscious process occurs in response to:

   a. A fact pattern that does not personally motivate the jurors; or

   b. Overwhelming or confusing information. "Rodney Jew, Motivating The Jurors: A New Paradigm for Trial Communication," ATLA Paper 1998

Another preliminary consideration for using PPT slides during an opening is for the trial lawyer to project and imagine what the local jurors in the trial venue will bring with them as far as general background attitudes and beliefs and what will the physical setup be like in the actual courtroom. As the saying goes, "Ya gotta know the territory!" An example of juror bias regarding PPT slides/exhibits would be if planned slide/exhibit used an image, symbol, or phrase which the local population had come to strongly associate or identify with in a positive way—such as a business logo, symbol, or slogan well respected in the community—then that slide/exhibit would have more impact than a slide/exhibit which created a negative reaction amongst locals—such as a symbol or slogan used in a bad local TV advertisement.

What Factors Affect Jurors' Perceptions and Response?

Juror perceptions and response are affected by following:

1. Socioeconomic filters and personal life experience. Preexisting beliefs held by the cultural group and the individual affect how jurors see and hear a case, what they are willing to believe, and what they decide.

2. Attention level and memory capacity. A lawyer's ability to sustain and direct jurors' attention and help jurors remember the case's key points is critical to a successful presentation. Many variables "such as fatigue, anx-

iety, age, amount and variety of stimulation" can affect jurors' attention to, and retention of, key information.

3. Physical considerations. Lawyers must also take into account environmental conditions in the courtroom (spatial layout, sources of lighting, and so forth), jurors' aural and visual acuity (affected by age, fatigue, color blindness, and so on), and the legibility of exhibits. Rodney Jew, "Motivating The Jurors: aA New Paradigm for Trial Communication," supra.

Understanding how jurors process information, and some of the factors that may affect jurors' perceptions and response, is a prerequisite to planning a strategy for trial and particularly opening statement. Strategic use of a PPT slide/exhibit should address two other questions:

1. What do the jurors want to know about the case, and
2. How can the plaintiff trial lawyer help jurors understand by using the PPT slide(s).

Easiest way to test if your PowerPoints are perceptible and comprehensible is to try it out with a focus group or mock jury. Another way is to check the courtroom in advance and put yourself in the juror's seats to see if the PowerPoint slides are clear.

C. Remember to Enhance and Anchor Your PowerPoint Opening

When planning the use of PowerPoint slides, consider what will be important for the jury to refer to when they hear the testimony and evaluate the witnesses during trial and then what will be important for them AFTER summations for them to conduct their deliberations. Try to prepare slides that will be used during the trial and also your summation and which will help the jurors to decide issues in favor of your client. For example, on the issue of liability, it is always useful to give the jury some type of scale drawing, model, or aerial photograph of the scene of a vehicular crash. Such an exhibit will usually be referred to by the investigating police officer and eyewitnesses to illustrate the evidence found at the scene or the happening of the crash.

Conversely, the use of a "rough sketch" which is not to scale, or the use of a distorted photograph which leaves out or confuses issues of liability, would be a relatively useless PowerPoint slide during the direct exam of the investigating officer or eyewitnesses and therefore should NOT be used in the PowerPoint opening.

Another way to approach the planning and preparation of useful PowerPoint slides is to conduct a focus group or other brain-storming session to decide what piece of tangible evidence will help the jury to resolve any issue about which the witness will be challenged. For example, if you can reasonably predict that the defense will make a foreseeable argument that an eyewitness to an auto crash did not have sufficient time to see what they claim to have witnessed, it would be useful for the jury to see in the PowerPoint opening slide that from a scale drawing or aerial photograph the distance over which the cars moved while the witness was at an unobstructed vantage point.

Planning the slides for opening which will used during direct examination with witnesses in an integrated and interesting manner will usually result in an expansion of the jurors' interest in your overall proofs. One approach to an overall visual strategy is to try to remember the "set up, link and payoff" method of demonstrations. Without going into this very deliberate and thoughtful process for which days of ATLA Colleges are dedicated, it is a good introduction to the new lawyer and reminder to the veterans that each PowerPoint slide or trial exhibit/demo should be tied into an overall case strategy. Included in any case strategy should be some attempt to "link" or "anchor" PowerPoint slides/exhibits/demos, that is, to use slides/exhibits on a subject of liability which complement each other and the testimony of the liability witnesses.

A classic example is for an eyewitness' diagram to be "linked" in the Power Point slide show to another exhibit/demo, such as computerized reenactments the vehicular crash reconstruction expert will use to explain the cause of the collision. The slides/exhibits used in openings on one subject, such as liability, may also be "setups" for the "payoff" exhibit/demo during trial. That is, the PowerPoint slides of photos, diagrams, x-rays, and anatomical models of the injuries used by plaintiff's counsel in opening as "setups" for the direct examination and "payoff" computerization, video reenactment, or chart by the plaintiff's damages expert.

Building an Effective Case Strategy

Exhibits not linked to oral testimony and to visual presentation as a whole can confuse jurors. Such exhibits may present a lot of information but fail to show jurors how to pull all information together to support the case.

If jurors lack the guidance they need to arrive at a conclusion through logical analysis, they are likely to pursue their own tracks of intuitive reasoning and arrive at erroneous conclusions that are not open to revision.

It is, therefore, essential to give not only data but also a context in which to fit the data into "a system for interpreting it." All experts' testimony must be linked in a unified structure; experts must be prepared, before trial, to fit their testimony into the overall schema. This key structure requires more than just oral link—it needs visual support. If overall structure is weak or lacking, jurors may miss key points of testimony or view experts' opinions as disjointed or unbalanced.

1. The Building Blocks

In a strategic presentation, each exhibit is assigned one or more strategic functions within a tight but dynamic framework. An exhibit must:

a. Convey critical, credible content, and help jurors tie all content together and navigate the case roadmap;

b. Support the affirmative case, or neutralize issues ("land mines") that may work against the case; and

c. Function in one or more of a series of setups and payoffs that together build the case. Within each setup and payoff, an exhibit may function as:

   (i). Anchor;

   (ii). Link; or

   (iii). Payoff.

The concept of the setup and payoff is critical.

2. The Setup and Payoff

Anchor and link exhibits together can be a setup for a payoff exhibit. Payoff exhibit is an exhibit that delivers a critical concept. The anchor and link precede the payoff and pave the way for jurors to fully get the impact of the payoff concept. Rodney Jew, supra.

D. Do Not Let The Stormtroopers Capture Your PowerPoint

A good PPT opening slide show is one not captured by your opposition and used as a weapon against you. A bad thing that can occur is having your PPT slide/exhibit turned around and used in a negative fashion during the defense opening, cross-exam, or summation. Example: if one point in opening is to establish the witness was in a good position to see the event, then the PPT photo(s) used should not be so confusing or ill prepared that the defense can use it (them) in their opening or cross-examination to argue with the witness about whether there appears to be some tree or other sight obstruction between the crash site and the witness' vantage point.

To avoid PPT "backfires" and make it an effective part of your opening, it is necessary to plan an overall effective case strategy integrating and "linking" slides/exhibits into a unified case structure. To develop such an integrated strategy of testimony and exhibit/demos, there is no better primer than Rodney Jew's ATLA paper "A Motivating the Jurors: A New Paradigm for Trial Communication," supra.

An important practical tip during and after opening is to be prepared to object to any effort by defense to alter or change PPT slides/exhibits/demos used in opening. E.g., many times, a witness creates a drawing or annotates a prepared diagram/photo. Witness may simply mark "X" for point of impact. Then on cross-exam, the opponent may try to get the witness to alter the exhibit by erasing, moving, enlarging "X" or adding another "X" or marking on the exhibit. DO NOT ALLOW this tactic to dilute what was illustrated clearly in PPT opening slides/exhibits.

One way to preempt such tactic is to move the actual exhibit into evidence during discovery dep (hopefully with no objections) and then renew the application to the trial judge in advance of the openings. This will allow the plaintiff attorney to meet and address any objections to the PowerPoint slide/exhibit's admissibility by the defense before the opening statements.

IV. PREPARE YOURSELF AND YOUR STAFF FOR "THE FORCE"

If you/staff are unfamiliar with PPT, it is an easy software package to learn without any professional help. You/your staff can take a short course to learn. While "PowerPoint for Dummies" and video training tapes may help, a short one day hands-on course on PPT is more effective. Read NITA's book, Power Point for Litigators. D.C. Siemer et al., PowerPoint for Litigators: How to Create Demonstrative Exhibits and Illustrative Aids for Trial, Mediation, Arbitration and Appeal, NITA (2000).

Some basic equipment you/your staff need for an effective PPT opening:

1. laptop
2. extension cord
3. screen
4. projector
5. bright bulb (some bulbs are not "bright" enough for "lights on" use)

6. wireless mouse

In courtroom logistics, your laptop computer can be put on a table or stand facing you, in front of, but facing away from jurors so it can only be seen by you. If you are opening without a helper, the projector can be set next to your laptop. The screen can be behind/above you so jurors can easily view it. Using a hands free mouse, the PPT opening is effectively an artist's canvas.

V. CONCLUSION

Cuz Dominic says: "too many spices kills the taste . . . most folks like meat and potatoes . . . that's it!" To paraphrase Microsoft Survey: trial lawyers need to take steps to properly train themselves and staff in the use of PPT to make more effective, persuasive, and meaningful opening statements. Clearly, PPT tool is a good one; it is use of the tool that is being criticized by audiences. Some lawyers have used PPT as a substitute for themselves and think the slides are the presentation instead of the PPT supporting the presentation they must deliver. Dave Paradi, Summary of the Annoying PowerPoint Survey of subscribers to Communicating Using Technology Newsletter, reported at www.communicateusingtechnology.com, Sept. 2003.

le prime impressioni sono impressioni durevoli

("first impressions are lasting impressions")

godere il rinvigorimento delle nostre bevande e la dolcezza del nostro cibo!

("enjoy the invigoration of our drinks and sweetness of our foods!")

Chapter 8. CARNE (Meat)

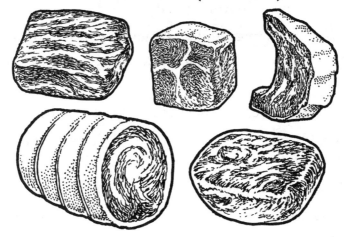

PART A. DOM'S RECIPES

PORCHETTA ARROSTO
(Roast Loin of Pork)

Roast pork is enjoyed throughout Italy, and a variety of wines and seasonings are used, depending on the region. My family enjoys roast pork because it is less fatty than other meats and very moist. They also like hot pork sandwiches the next day.

INGREDIENTS (Serves 8):

5 lbs Boneless Pork Loin

1 Tbsp Onion powder

1 Tbsp Garlic powder

1 Tbsp Lemon Pepper

1 Tbsp Paprika

1 Tbsp Dry mustard

Dry Red wine

DIRECTIONS:

Sprinkle all seasonings on lean side of pork.

Rub pork so all seasonings are well mixed.

Place Pork in airtight container and add enough wine to cover half the pork.

Close the airtight container and place in refrigerator and marinate pork over night.

Remove pork from marinade and roast in a baking dish or pan at 350° F.

After 15 minutes, add enough marinade to cover bottom of pan. If pan becomes dry, add just enough water to cover bottom.

Remember, the bottom of the pan will be used to make your *au jus* gravy.

When pork reaches internal temperature of 155° F, remove from oven and place on a dish to rest.

Pork should rest at least 15 minutes so the meat retains all its juices.

While roasting pan is still hot, add the remaining marinade and scrape with wooden spoon.

Those bits of meat at the bottom of the pan you are scrapping contain all of the flavor you will need for the *au jus*.

After you have scraped the pan, place the marinade in a small sauté pan and cook on medium

heat. You can add water to increase the amount of au jus aujus. If you prefer a thicker gravy, you can add a thickening agent.

After the pork has rested, slice and serve (with a glass of red wine, of course).

BOCCONCINI: Porchetta is from the word porco, or pork. Porchetta originated in Lazio, and its history dates back to the Roman Empire. This is known because its processing methods are even mentioned in some works by scholars and artists as far back as 400 BC. It was said to be the favorite dish of Emperor Nero. As far back as Roman times, the preparation and seasoning of the pig, including slow roasting it on a spit over a wood burning fire, has remained the same as today.

SALSICCIA CON PEPERONI ALLA SCALOPPINI
(Sausage Cut Thin with Peppers)

This recipe actually came about by accident. My son was having a party; at the last minute, he asked me to bring sausage and peppers to his party. I didn't think I had enough sausage; I put this dish together and was a big hit. Every time someone is having a party, I am TOLD to bring Sausage Scaloppini and Peppers.

INGREDIENTS (Serves 6 to 8):

1 1/4 lbs good Italian sausage

1 (28 oz. can) Italian style crushed tomatoes

4 Bell Peppers—seeds and core removed—cut into 1/4" strips

1 large onion, sliced

1 clove Garlic, cut in half

1/4 cup Dry red wine

8 oz. Mushrooms, sliced

Olive Oil

1 tsp Dry oregano

1 tsp Dry basil

½ tsp Garlic powder

Salt and pepper

DIRECTIONS:

Fry or bake sausage until brown and slightly pink inside.

When sausage has cooled, slice on a bias, about ½" slices, set aside (that's *scaloppini*).

In a pot over medium heat, add olive oil just to cover the bottom of pan.

When oil is hot, add onions, garlic & peppers; sauté for about 8 minutes; add mushrooms; cook for 2 more minutes.

When garlic turns golden brown, remove and discard.

Add wine and cook for 2 more minutes.

Add tomatoes and sausage and stir until well mixed. Bring to a gentle simmer and partially cover with lid; stir occasionally. Make sure mixture does not burn on bottom.

After about 30 minutes, add oregano, basil, garlic powder, salt, and pepper, and continue to cook. When bell peppers are done, adjust seasoning, remove from heat, and serve.

A good accompaniment is Aborio rice or any rice you like, a good loaf of Italian bread +a glass of Red Wine.

<u>BOCCONCINI</u>: Scaloppini (plural diminutive of scaloppa means literally "a small scallop;" it also refers to thinly sliced cuts of meat. Salsiccia and sausage derive from the Latin *salsus* which means "something salted." Salsiccia is almost 3,000 years old: goat sausages are mentioned in Homer's *The Odyssey* written by Homer more than 2,700 years ago: "These goat sausages sizzling here in the fire—we packed them with fat and blood to have for supper. Now, whoever wins this bout and proves the stronger, let that man step up and take his pick of the lot!" Which reminds me: did you know sausages were called "bangers" by the British "Tommies" during WWI because they contained so much water they exploded when fried. And if you don't poke some fork holes into your salsiccia, yours will GO BANG too!

POLO ALLA CACCIATORA
(Chicken Cacciatora "in the Hunter's Style")

This was originally made with wild rabbit or wild foul. Chicken was added, and it is a popular meal in most households. My kids love this with a side of rice and loaf of Italian bread.

INGREDIENTS (Serves 4 to 6):

1 Frying Chicken, cut into pieces

1 Medium Onion, cut in half and then sliced

2 Bell Peppers, cut into strips

8 oz. fresh Mushrooms

2 cloves Garlic, crushed and minced

1 cup Olive Oil

¼ cup Dry Red Wine

½ tsp Dry Basil

½ tsp Dry Oregano

1 (28 oz.) can Italian Crushed Tomatoes

1 cup Flour

1 tsp Salt

¼ tsp Black pepper

DIRECTIONS:

Wash chicken and pat dry with paper towels.

Mix salt, pepper, and flour together, and dredge chicken pieces until well coated.

In a deep 10" frying pan, sear chicken pieces until golden brown.

Remove chicken pieces and set aside.

Add onion, peppers, mushrooms, and garlic to pan; sauté until soft, not completely cooked.

Add wine and cook for 5 minutes.

Return chicken to pan. Add crushed tomatoes, basil, oregano, salt, and pepper to taste.

Cover pan and simmer for about 1 hour. Turn chicken occasionally.

Serve hot with a dry red wine and a large loaf of Italian Bread.

BOCCONCINI: *Cacciatore* means "hunter" in Italian, "alla cacciatora" means a meal prepared "hunter-style" with tomatoes, onions, herbs, often bell pepper, and sometimes wine. Beware: if you are in Gainesville, Georgia, "The Chicken Capital of the World,"' it is against the law to eat chicken with a fork. And, in "The First State" the Blue Hen chicken, noted for its fighting ability, is the official state bird of Delaware.

The Vespers' Trial Cookbook

AGNELLO ARROSTO
(Roast Leg of Lamb)

Roast Lamb is a favorite, especially for Easter dinner. If you have never eaten lamb, I suggest you try this recipe.

INGREDIENTS (Serves 6):

1 (3 or 4 lb) Leg of lamb

1 cup Dry red wine

1 clove Garlic, minced

1 tsp Dry Basil

½ tsp Rosemary

½ tsp Cracked black pepper

DIRECTIONS:

In a shallow pan (large enough to hold lamb) add wine, garlic, basil, rosemary, and pepper.

Cover and marinate for 12 hours, turning lamb after 6 hours.

In a roasting pan, place lamb fat side up on a rack and roast in a 350° F oven until meat thermometer reaches 155° F about 1½ hours.

While lamb is roasting, pour the marinade and 2 cups of water into a pan and simmer for 20 minutes.

Remove lamb from pan and set on cutting board and allow to rest for 15-20 minutes.

Reheat marinade until just before boiling and pour in roasting pan.

Scrape pan with wooden spoon and continue to deglaze pan until all bits of drippings are loose. This will become a rich gravy.

Slice lamb and serve with gravy.

BOCCONCINI: for our family of Italians, Easter without lamb on our table is hard to imagine. Pasqua (Easter) is the most important religious celebration of the year in Italy. The tradition of eating lamb at Pasqua (Easter) is strongly rooted in history. The lamb ("agnello,") is an important symbol in many religions, but especially Christianity. The image of the lamb appears in the most treasured Renaissance masterpieces; the lamb is seen in many ecclesiastical images and secular emblems, seals, and flags. The custom of eating lamb at important religious feasts goes back thousands of years, spanning many cultures and religions, especially in the regions around the Mediterranean Sea.

In Italy, the most prized lamb for Easter is the *agnello da latte* (milk-fed lamb)—in the regions of Lazio and Abruzzo, it's also called *abbacchio*—which is a four-week-old lamb, exclusively nourished by its mother's milk. At the market, these lambs usually weigh less than 20 pounds, and the meat has a light pink color and an exquisite taste.

VITELLA SCOLOPPINI
(Veal in Tomato Sauce)

Veal can be cooked in any type of sauce desired. This particular recipe is very rustic because it can be a complete dinner or served with a side of pasta or rice. It especially goes well with a loaf of Italian bread and a glass of red wine.

INGREDIENTS (Serves 4 to 6):

2 lbs Veal cutlets

2 Tbsp Butter

2 Tbsp Olive oil

½ cup Red wine

4 large Bell peppers

1 Onion, chopped

1 (15 oz.) can Crushed tomatoes

½ tsp Oregano

½ tsp Basil

Salt and pepper to taste

DIRECTIONS:

Cut veal into 2" pieces.

Heat frying pan, add oil, and melt butter.

Brown veal, remove and set aside.

Add wine and deglaze pan.

Add peppers and onion and sauté until wilted.

Add tomatoes, oregano, salt, pepper, and basil and simmer for 15 minutes.

Add veal and simmer additional 15 minutes. Serve hot with plenty of Italian bread!

BOCCONCINI: There are five types of veal:

(1) Bob veal: from calves slaughtered when only a few days old (70-100 lb. to 150 lb.)

(2) Milk-fed, Formula-fed veal: from calves that are raised on a nutritionally complete milk formula supplement. The meat color is ivory or creamy

pink with a firm, fine, and velvety appearance. Usually slaughtered when they reach 18–20 weeks of age

(3) Non-formula-fed, "red" or "grain-fed" veal: from calves raised on grain, hay, other solid food, in addition to milk; meat is darker, and some additional marbling and fat may be apparent. Usually marketed as calf, rather than veal, at 22–26 weeks of age

(4) Rosé veal: calves reared on farms in association with UK RSPCA's Freedom Food program; name comes from pink color, a result of calves, slaughtered around 35 weeks

(5) Free-raised veal: calves are raised in the pasture, have unlimited access to mother's milk and pasture grasses; not administered hormones or antibiotics. These conditions replicate those used to raise authentic pasture-raised veal; meat is rich pink color. Free-raised veal is lower in fat than other veal; calves slaughtered at about 24 weeks of age.

PART B. TOM'S TRIAL TIPS: DIRECT & RE-DIRECT EXAMINATION

SPEAKING OF MEAT & POTATOES–WHERE'S DA BEEF?"—MEATY PARTS OF CASES –DIRECT EXAMINATION & REBUTTAL

I. GENERAL DIFFERENCES BETWEEN DIRECT AND CROSS

In general, direct examination is a building process. Cross-examination, for the most part, is or turns out to be a destructive or dismantling process. Herbert Stern, "Three Techniques of Cross-Examination," 16 Trial Dip. J. 2, p. 49.

Cross-examination can constructively obtain helpful admissions or neutralize an opposing witness. But cross-exam usually involves the art of dismantling of credibility, observation testimony, or opinions of the opposing witness. Contrary thereto, direct exam is the sequential unfolding and dynamic documentation of plaintiff's theme, story, and theory of the case. Sometimes, a case proceeds point-by-point; sometimes, it plays out chronologically; most times, it is helter skelter due to the availability of witnesses. Individually, each direct witness, "friendly" or hostile, is made to disclose to the finders of fact their factual recollections, impressions, or opinions of events. Cumulatively, direct examination portrays the plaintiff's case in a mosaic art form of trial by jury.

Another generally recognized difference between direct and cross-examination is that for the most part the witness on direct examination should have the full attention of the trier of fact. The jury is supposed to conclude "[t]hat witness is right about . . . .." Often, the trial lawyer cross-examining the witness is not only on center stage but also is the central protagonist and "star" of the cross-examination. The jury will hopefully conclude "[t]hat lawyer is right . . . and that witness is wrong about . . . .."

Despite these prevailing views of different advocacy styles in direct vs. cross trial, lawyers should not fear to take control of and advocate during direct. Direct exam of any witness is an important opportunity to advocate your client's case. Jurors recognize that direct exam is a direct message from the lawyer who called the witness. If they don't, the defense will certainly raise their consciousness. As Herbert Stern says:

> The skillful advocate controls the examination. He is not the presenter of his pad of questions. He does not hold a pen or pencil, checking off as he 'covers' his questions or makes his points. Nor is he a passenger sitting in the rear of a toboggan hurling along under the hand of his witness. The advocate uses questions to control the pace of the examination, varying the amount of information coming from the witness to avoid ennui. To be sure, sometimes the answers will be longer, sometimes shorter—but always at the election of the advocate.

Stern, "Direct Examination—The Forgotten Advocacy Tool," 15 Trial Dip. J. 1, p. 29 (Jan/Feb 1992).

In most jurisdictions, "cross-examination will be limited to the matters testified to on direct." This majority rule is not rigidly enforced; most times, after plaintiff/plaintiff's witness is examined on direct, cross-exam is "no holds barred" credibility contest.

The essential design of every direct exam is to let the jury know where you are going with the witness, where you have been, and how that direct testimony relates to the theme(s) of your client's case. Direct exam is part of the overall storytelling process.

II. THE BASIC ABCs OF DIRECT EXAMINATION

As many trial attorneys and consultants have said about trial advocacy, the cardinal rule is PREPARATION, PREPARATION, PREPARATION. For direct exam, I add: PRACTICE, PRACTICE, PRACTICE! . . . and PRIORITIZE your witnesses, their order, and your proofs.

In this regard, to prepare any witness adequately to conduct effective direct examination and prevent a destructive cross, pretrial preparation and simulated practice are important.

A. Preparation

1. Prepare . . . Yourself for the Witness

To prepare properly, you must organize your file and your understanding of the facts and the applicable law of the case and the witness' recalled facts and opinions and bases thereof. Know the facts, opinions, and supporting data and how each witness fits into this case's universe.

2. Prepare . . . Your Trial Notebook for the Witness

Whether you use trial file/folders or three ring trial notebooks, your deposition digests, fact sheets, witness summaries, statements, and any materials or exhibits needed for each witness' trial appearance should be placed in an easily accessible location for your use.

3. Prepare . . . The Witness

Thoroughly review with the witness any and all prior statements, testimony, or opinions made or attributed to that witness. This "database" must be available to avoid contradiction, confusion, and worse—intentional misrepresentation by the witness—lay or expert. Example: client/witness version of fall down injury is totally in conflict with Police/ER/Doctor notes; or the liability or damages expert's opinions may have changed or become stronger based on recent medical treatment, research, or discovery since the expert's deposition.

B. Practice

1. Practice . . . With the Witness

The interaction between the examiner and the witness usually instills confidence and imparts facts and impressions more than just the words spoken. The interaction between witness and proffering lawyer on direct may be negative or positive to some degree. Communication by the witness on direct examination is much more than what is actually said.

Knowing a witness has certain positive/negative characteristics of voice and demeanor, the direct examiner should always try to keep the witness from exhibiting undesirable traits and attitudes to the jury or judge. If that is impossible and the witness is absolutely necessary, then the trial lawyer must do what is second nature to experienced trial advocates: try to turn negative(s) into positive(s).

If any witness—even experts—is uncomfortable with courtroom "conversation," it is very helpful, I have found, to orient the witness to your style of questioning.

The direct examiner should not only prep the witness before trial but should remain alert during direct and cross to tone, gestures, and overall demeanor of experts.

2. Practice . . . With Video of the Witness

If the witness with whom you are working does not readily understand some negative characteristic which you are seeking to limit or totally eliminate, use of videotape "replay" is most helpful. With clients, videotape can be used with little threat of the attorney-client and work product privileges being breached.

3. Practice . . . With A Mock Jury

Another good indicator of a witness' ability to communicate is to use a mock jury. With clients, this has low risk of being discovered due to attorney-client privilege; more care and circumspection needs to be given to lay or expert witnesses. Videotaping the witness and presentation of videotaped testimony to a focus group is the safest method to avoid discovery of your preparation of the nonclient and nonconsulting witness.

C. Prioritize

1. Prioritize . . . Your Order of Proofs

Well in advance of trial you, staff and client should decide order of witnesses and other evidence. How and in what order your client's story unfolds with witness' input can make big differences in jury's initial reaction and final understanding. Note psychological/advocacy principle of Primacy (items first discussed/impressions made are best recalled) & "Recency" (last words spoken/ thoughts/images provoked are best remembered). Use a trial calendar (Monday, end of week, etc.) and clock (very first witness in morning, right before/after lunch, end of day) to best position witnesses to communicate best to the jury.

2. Prioritize . . . Your Expert Witnesses

Some witnesses are better communicators than others; some better recall; some have "less hair (credibility problems)" than others. Choose in advance witnesses who are truly necessary and who are not and who have a higher value in your client's case. From this analysis, you should begin to develop your trial calendar and order of expert witnesses.

3. Prioritize . . . Your Questions of Each Expert Witness

For each witness, prepare at least an outline of areas of your inquiry and possible issues for cross-exam. From this master menu of topics, you should decide the important points your direct of the witness will cover. Then you should choose a sensible and interesting order to you direct examination. Again, utilize the principles of Primacy (first series of questions) and Recency (the last question & answer) to best persuade the jury.

III. SOME BASIC A TO Z SUGGESTIONS REGARDING WITNESS PREPARATION [omitted]

. . .

IV. SOME MORE BASICS REGARDING EXPERT WITNESS PREPARATION [omitted]

V. EXPERT DIRECT EXAM AT ITS BEST: VIVA VOCE AL DENTE

Just as with a good pasta, direct examination of an expert should leave the listener with the satisfaction that it was not overdone and yet not undercooked: just right to the jury's taste—al dente (literally "to the teeth") The expert should leave the jury with an overall impression of credibility and also an understanding that what the expert said was not only an honest present recollection but is also probably and/or certainly what actually occurred as opposed to "this was an honest witness but honestly mistaken in his/her opinion about what occurred."

Preparation of the expert or any witness by the attorney is essential. While much can be done by paralegals, it is vital that the trial attorney meet with expert witnesses to determine character, communication ability, skills, and, more importantly, an ability to interreact. Pretrial conference must be scheduled between the expert and trial attorney so the examiner can become familiar with the expert's habits and tendencies.

VI. CONCLUSION

To paraphrase Warren Spahn, one of the greatest left-hand pitchers in the history of major league baseball: "Hitting, (like direct examination), is based on rhythm. Pitching (like a cross-examination), is based upon upsetting rhythm."

SELECTED BIBLIOGRAPHY

Baldwin, S., Edem, E., Weitz, H. "Direct Examination" Chapter XIII, Excellence in Advocacy, p. 581-628 (ATLA Press 1992)

Baldwin, Scott, Direct Examination, Art of Advocacy Series (Matthew Bender, 1983)

Belli, Melvin, "Examining Witnesses," Modern Trials, 2d. Ed., Chap 63 (West 1982)

Hamlin, Sonya, What Makes Juries Listen?, (Law & Bus. Inc., 1985)

Herman, Russell, "Direct Exam of Lay Witnesses," Trial, V. 24, p77-9 (Feb 1988)

Lisnek, Paul, "Direct & Cross: The Keys to Success," Trial Dip. J., Vol. 18, No.5, p. 263

Oliver, Eric, "Embodying the Story," 17 Trial Dip.J. 4, p. 177

Stern, Herbert, "Three Techniques of Cross," Trial Dip. J., Vol. 16, No. 2, p. 49

Stern, Herbert, "Direct Examination — The Forgotten Advocacy Tool," Trial Dip. J., Vol. 15, No. 1, p. 29

EFFECTIVE USE OF DEMOS: DOCUMENTS, DIAGRAMS, PHOTOS, AND MORE: AN ADDED DYNAMIC TO DIRECT EXAMINATION

I. INTRODUCTION

The advantages of using exhibits/demos during any trial are too numerous and obvious to even begin to enumerate in this paper. Suffice to say, without some visual and tangible demonstrative or real evidence to relate to and discuss, the jury is left with only a memory of oral testimony and an impression of the witnesses. Exhibits/demos in every imaginable form—documents, photographs, overheads, slides, videos, sound recordings, animations, charts, graphs, diagrams, x-rays, models, medical illustrations, etc.—are the pieces of evidence which the jury can take back into their deliberations and inspect, use, read, and work with to decide the issues. "Demonstratives" or "demos" can be a more inclusive term, i.e., "demos" include audio visual aids, demonstrations, and jury views which the trial attorney can use with or without witnesses; "demonstratives" may not be admitted in evidence. Notwithstanding admissibility as exhibits, "demonstratives" may be referred to and used by the trial lawyer in summation. For example, some trial courts do not allow in evidence experts' charts as "unfairly highlighting the testimony." But plaintiff's attorney is still permitted to refer to the expert's "demonstratives" chart and audio visual aids in closing. Exhibits/demos, and any AVA, give jurors something to "play with" to make one or more decisions about a case. Exhibits/demos can make the plaintiff's case come alive and take concrete form rather than leave jury with a fleeting memory of testimony. Exhibits/demos can also backfire and result in adverse reactions.

The following discussion is a practical overview of suggestions to make the use of exhibits/demos during direct examination of witnesses more effective and useful to the plaintiff's trial lawyer. The categories of audio visual aids are numerous. The pros and cons of each category of exhibit, "demonstratives," or presentation mediums are not discussed in this paper. But see the attached chart of "Advantages and Disadvantages." Kirby Dial, "Demonstrative Evidence and Technology in the Year 2000," ATLA Annual Convention Paper, 2000.

The objective for using exhibits/demos is not just to make an interesting direct examination but also to understand the importance of and develop an "integrated" visual and oral strategy. Trial attorneys should use multiple modes of communication with witnesses on direct exam, i.e., use oral testimony, printed words, and visual exhibit/demos to improve the effectiveness of direct, making both testimony and demo a memorable part of the plaintiff's overall trial and increasing the likelihood that the exhibit/demo used or points made in direct examination will be used by the jury in deliberations to arrive at a fair verdict for the plaintiff. It is of little benefit to have produced and used in direct examination the most beautiful "demonstrative," model, or illustration if when the jury deliberates they ignore, criticize, or, worse, find an adverse use for it. While the principles and ideas discussed herein will be applicable to all exhibits/demos, this is a small reflection of one important piece—exhibits/demos used in direct examination—within a much larger mosaic—trial of a plaintiff's personal injury case.

II. WHAT CONSTITUTES AN EFFECTIVE EXHIBIT DURING DIRECT?

From experience with judges, jurors, focus groups, and jury consultants, the following are half dozen tips for planning, preparing, and using exhibit/demonstrative effectively during direct exam. Effective exhibit/demos in plaintiff's direct should be:

1. Objection-proof
2. A time saver
3. Easily understood
4. Memorable
5. Interesting and useful to the jury
6. Incapable of boomeranging

1. Objection-proofing: Anticipating, Avoiding, and Overcoming Any Possible Objections

As much as practically possible, exhibits/demos to be used in direct examination should be "immunized" from a sustainable objection. That is, the proponent should have the exhibit/demo identified and shown to the adversary in advance of its use. This may be accomplished by disclosing the exhibit/demo and/or making it available for inspection during discovery or pretrial conferences. Another good practice is to premark the exhibit/demo and give the defense a list of all exhibits/demos prior to trial. If during discovery or pretrial any objections are raised by any adversary, then a good practice is resolve the objections by a motion in limine prior to the start of trial in order to brief the issues with the trial judge and resolve the use of the exhibit/demo. At the very least, if there is any doubt about its admissibility, the exhibit/demo should be disclosed, out of the presence of the jury, prior to its use during direct examination. If the defense makes any objection, then an application can be made to the trial judge to rule upon its relevance and unlimited or limited admissibility. Fed. R. Evid. 105. "Bullet-proofing" exhibits/demos in advance of the direct exam gives the plaintiff's trial lawyer a static free environment for a much smoother presentation with the witness. Avoiding sidebars or shuttling the jury out of the courtroom should be an important goal for the direct examiner. For the plaintiff's trial lawyer, it is probably more important than for the defense to avoid distractions. This is because plaintiff has the burden of proof. To persuade a jury, plaintiff's case in chief should be credible, convincing, and motivational rather than disjointed, dubious, and dull.

2. Saving Time: Moving Direct Exam Along While Ingratiating, Not Aggravating

One of the biggest criticisms from judges and jurors about trial presentations by some lawyers is "they waste a lot of time." In direct exam, it is important for plaintiff's advocate to use exhibits/demos or "demonstratives" in a crisp and expeditious manner, with little or no "wasted time." One frequent criticism easy to avoid is "the marking ritual." Handing an exhibit/demo (or worse, multiple exhibits) to court clerk/reporter for placement of sticker and inscription of a "P- Number" is not high drama for anyone. It is like watching paint dry to be forced to watch these mind-numbing ministerial misdirections of a witness' testimony. The scattered attention of such time warps can also distract and upset the witness on the stand. Another common faux pas is to introduce a witness—usually an expert—who has a slide show, video program, or some other electronic visual aids presentation without first testing to see if machinery works. This will produce "dead time" in court room or another unnecessary "break" for the jury while court room attendants, lawyers, and "techies" try to get the exhibit/demo to work.

The best effect produced by expeditious use of exhibit/demo during direct is to have everyone in court, including the adversary, openly admit or secretly admire the conservation of time achieved. Use of exhibit/demo, whatever its form, should result in less time for the witness being on the stand and therefore less time for jurors to be involved with that witness. E.g., rather than have the jury read from or listen to a witness reading over long entries in medical records, some trial attorneys expedite the presentation by hiring nurses or using the hospital personnel to read summaries or synopsized charts of the records pursuant to Fed.R.Evid. 1006:

> The contents of voluminous writings or photo which cannot conveniently be examined in court may be presented by a qualified witness in form of a chart, summary, or calculation. The originals, or duplicates, shall be made available for examination or copying, or both, by other parties at a reasonable time and place. The judge may order that they be produced in court.

Fed.R.Evid. 1006.

Another common time saver is using a photo or scale diagram to describe what something looked like rather than waste time having a witness describe something in minute detail. Having a witness describe or narrate what is being shown on video, e.g., "Day in the Life" video, may be a more dynamic, efficient use of the witness' and jury's time rather than simply showing the jury a silent movie and have the witness on direct exam orally elaborate in detail to what has been or will be seen by jury. Some evidentiary foundation testimony and interest-peaking preliminaries may be necessary, but if the judge and jury are rolling their eyes, whispering to themselves "GET ON WITH IT ! SHOW US ALREADY!" then your preview of coming attractions has lost its appeal. Preludes should not preempt exhibits; overtures should never overwhelm main event.

3. Perspicacity: Making the Exhibit Easily Legible, Understandable, and Meaningful

There have been many papers, lectures, and entire seminars dedicated to the production of exhibits/demos which are visible and understandable to jurors. Jurors, like any human beings, process information both consciously and unconsciously.

How Do Jurors Process Information?

1. Conscious, analytical processing involves searching for, sorting, and weighing information to arrive at a decision. Jurors engage in this process only if they are sufficiently motivated to do so. Jurors become motivated to analyze case issues if they perceive the issues as relevant to their own personal life experiences. To maintain their motivation, jurors must have:

    a. Access to what they view as adequate information;

    b. The intellectual capacity and skill to process the information; and

    c. Methods, provided by lawyers and witnesses, to code the messages (including visual representations, metaphors, comparisons, etc.)
    If jurors cannot find any direct comparison in their own life experience for the concepts presented, they may lose motivation and stop searching for information. Responding irrationally, they may fall back on the closest comparisons they can find in their own experience and thus bring irrelevant information into the decision process.

2. Lawyers must assume, in any case, that jurors will apply some unconscious as well as conscious reasoning to the case issues. With unconscious reasoning, jurors tend to generate their own series of little rules for categorizing information. They may take mental shortcuts, which can make their thinking inaccessible to correction. Although they may use intuitive reasoning in place of a more objective reasoning, they will believe

their conclusions are accurate. The unconscious process occurs in response to:

a. A fact pattern that does not personally motivate the jurors; or

b. Overwhelming or confusing information." Rodney Jew, "Motivating The Jurors: A New Paradigm for Trial Communication," ATLA Paper

Another preliminary consideration for exhibit/demo during direct exam is to project and imagine what local venue jurors will bring with them as general background attitudes and beliefs and what is physical set up in the actual court room. As saying goes, "Ya gotta know the territory!" An example of juror bias re exhibits/demos would be if the planned exhibit/demo used an image, symbol, or phrase which the local population had come to strongly associate or identify with in a positive way—such as a business logo, symbol, or slogan well respected in the community—then that exhibit/demo would have more impact than an exhibit/demo which created a negative reaction amongst locals—such as a symbol or slogan used in a bad local TV advertisement.

What Factors Affect Jurors' Perceptions and Response?

Jurors' perceptions and response are affected by the following:

1. Socioeconomic filters and personal life experience. Preexisting beliefs held by the cultural group and the individual affect how jurors see and hear a case, what they are willing to believe, and what they decide.

2. Attention level and memory capacity. A lawyer's ability to sustain and direct jurors' attention and help jurors remember the case's key points is critical to a successful presentation. Many variables—such as fatigue, anxiety, age, and amount and variety of stimulation—can affect jurors' attention to, and retention of, key information.

3. Physical considerations. Lawyers must also take into account environmental conditions in the courtroom (spatial layout, sources of lighting, and so forth), jurors' aural and visual acuity (affected by age, fatigue, color blindness, and so on), and the legibility of exhibits." Rodney Jew, "Motivating The Jurors: A New Paradigm for Trial Communication," supra.

Understanding how jurors process information, and some of the factors that may affect jurors' perceptions and response, is a prerequisite to planning a strategy for trial and particularly direct examination. The strategic use of an exhibit/demo should address two other questions: 1. What do jurors want to know from the witness, and 2. how can the plaintiff trial lawyer help the jurors understand the witness by using an exhibit/demo(s).

The easiest way to test whether or not your exhibit/demo is perceptible and comprehensible is to try it out with a focus group or mock jury. Another way is to check the courtroom in advance and put yourself in the juror's seats to see if the visual images are clear. For example, if you intend to use a blowup of a deposition or any chart with words, set it up where you intend to use it with the witness on direct examination, and then position yourself or someone else in the jury box to check whether the writing is clear and legible for someone with normal eyesight. While using exhibits/demos in trial, it is proper to look at and recognize jurors' needs, and then ask the trial judge to question whether any of them have difficulty seeing the exhibit/demo, whether because of lighting, glare, smallness of the letters, etc.

4. Lasting Impact: Making the Exhibit Memorable

Research and experience teaches the most memorable exhibits/demos are visual. "Seventy-two hours after your oral presentation of evidence, jurors will remember only 10 percent, and what 10 percent are they remembering? When your oral presentation is paired with a demonstrative, jurors will remember 60 percent of the evidence (6 times the rate when there is no demonstrative). Although you may be a mesmerizing orator, if your jurors cannot marshal the facts needed for deliberations, you may not be successful." Philip Miller, "What Makes Exhibits Work: Psychological Principles," ATLA Annual Convention Paper, 2001.

In addition to making the exhibit/demo readable and understandable to jurors, a good exhibit/demo used in an effective manner with any witness should be capable of being recalled by the jury. Sometimes referred to as "anchoring," the concept to remember when using an exhibit/demo on direct examination is that whatever the witness has said or demonstrated by the use of the exhibit/demo may become so unconsciously and indelibly imprinted upon the sense of the jury that by simple reference, mention, or even looking in the direction of the exhibit/demo, the "anchored" message can be recalled for the jury. To make a lasting impression, an exhibit/demo used by a witness during direct should incorporate all of the avenues of juror learning. That is, neurolinguistic experts tell us that everyone learns through visual, auditory, or tactile senses. Therefore, effective exhibits/demos should create a visual, auditory, and, if possible, a kinetic impact upon the jury. Examples of exhibits/demos used by a witness during direct exam which apply all three NLP (neurolinguistic programming) approaches to "anchoring" into the jury's memory is a jury view or an actual piece of real evidence. For instance, using the heavy piece of lumber that killed the plaintiff. Having a witness physically lift and drop such a heavy wooden beam in front of the jury while describing its size and weight, or physically allowing the jury to "view" such dangerous instrumentality while a witness describes its features, has a three-way path to "anchoring" and creating a lasting effect on jurors. Such demonstrative use of an exhibit/demo allows jurors to see, hear, and get "a feel" for its size, weight, and dangerous qualities. It is much more of a memorable exhibit/demo than using a drawing or photograph with the witness.

To make any exhibit/demo "memorable" it is important that the exhibit/demo is prepared properly and then used by the witness on direct in an "integrated visual communication."

Why is integrated visual communication essential? While each type of communication has its functions and advantages, when color, pictures, symbols, printed, and spoken words are effectively combined, the impact they achieve as a whole is—not surprisingly—greater than the sum of the parts. Information presented in more than one sensory modality is understood more easily and retained longer.

In both recognition and recall, picture memory exceeds word memory in all age groups. But if pictures are used in combination with spoken words to tell a story, people will remember more than with either pictures or words alone. Data retention after 72 hrs is:

with oral presentation	10%
with visual presentation	20%
with both oral and visual presentation	65%

The improvement in recall is even greater if visual stimulus is presented before verbal stimulus. Further, when jurors are presented with a combination of spoken and written words and pictures, they have much greater short-term recall than if only spoken words and pictures are presented. Effects of multi-sensory imagery on recall are cumulative." Rodney Jew, "Motivating the Jurors: New Paradigm for Trial Communication," supra.

5. Attention Enhancement and Utility: Make Exhibit/Demo Interesting and Useful to Jury

When planning exhibits/demos with a witness, consider what will be important for the jury to refer to when they deliberate. Try to prepare exhibits/demos that will help the jurors to decide issues in favor of your client; e.g., on issue of liability it is always useful to give the jury some type of scale drawing, model, or aerial photo of the scene of a vehicular crash. Such an exhibit/demo is usually referred to by the investigating police officer and eyewitnesses to illustrate the evidence found at the scene or the happening of the crash. Conversely, use of a "rough sketch" not to scale, or use of distorted photos which leaves out or confuses issues of liability, will be a relatively useless exhibit/demo during the direct exam of investigating officers or eyewitnesses. For damages a useful exhibit/demo is to create a list of medical bills, or preserve the nature and extent of the immediate and acute injuries with video and/or photos of the initial stages of treatment.

Another way to approach the planning and preparation of useful exhibits/demos is to conduct a focus group or other brain-storming session to decide what piece of tangible evidence will help the jury to resolve any issue about which the witness will be challenged. For example, if you can reasonably predict that the defense will make a foreseeable argument that an eyewitness to an auto crash did not have sufficient time to see what they claim to have witnessed, it would be useful for the jury to have the witness show them on a scale drawing or aerial photograph the distance over which the cars moved while the witness was at an unobstructed vantage point.

Planning the exhibit/demo and its use during direct examination with the witness in an integrated and interesting manner will usually result in an expansion of the jurors' interest in what the witness will be talking about. One approach to an overall visual strategy is to try to remember the "set up, link and payoff" method of demonstrations. Without going into this very deliberate and thoughtful process for which many days of ATLA Colleges and seminar have been dedicated, it is a good introduction to the new lawyer and reminder to the veterans that each exhibit/demo should be tied into an overall case strategy. Included in any case strategy should be some attempt to "link" or "anchor" exhibits/demos, that is to offer exhibits/demos on a subject of liability which complement each other and the testimony of the liability witnesses. A classic example is for the eyewitness' diagram to be "linked" to another exhibit/demo, such as a computerized reenactment which the vehicular crash reconstruction expert will use to explain the cause of the collision. The exhibits/demos used on one subject, such as liability, may also be "setups" for the "payoff" exhibit/demo. That is, the photographs, diagrams, and scale model of the crash site may be used by plaintiff's counsel as "setups" for the direct examination and "payoff" computerization, video reenactment, or chart by the plaintiff's liability expert.

Building an Effective Case Strategy

Exhibits that are not linked—to oral testimony and to the visual presentation as a whole—can confuse jurors. Such exhibits may present a lot of information but fail to show jurors how to pull all the information together to support the case.

If jurors lack guidance to reach a conclusion through logical analysis, they will pursue their own intuitive reasoning to arrive at erroneous conclusions not open to revision. It is, therefore, essential to provide not only data, but also a context in which to fit the data—a system for interpreting it. Along these lines, all witnesses' testimony must be linked in a unified structure, and witnesses must be prepared, before trial, to fit their testimony into the overall schema. This crucial structure requires more than just an oral link—it must be supported visually. If the overall structure is weak or lacking, jurors may miss key points of testimony or view the witnesses' testimonies as disjointed or unbalanced.

(A) The Building Blocks

In a strategic presentation, each exhibit is assigned one or more strategic functions within a tight but dynamic framework. An exhibit must:

1. Convey critical, credible content, help jurors tie all the content together, and navigate the case road map;

2. Support the affirmative case, or neutralize issues (referred to as "land mines") that may work against the case; and

3. Function in one or more of a series of setups and payoffs that together build the case. Within each setup and payoff, an exhibit may function as:

    a. Anchor;

    b. Link; or

    c. Payoff.

The concept of the setup and payoff is critical.

(B) The Setup and Payoff

The anchor and link exhibits together can be thought of as a setup for a payoff exhibit. A payoff exhibit is an exhibit that delivers a critical concept. Anchor and link precede payoff, paving the way for jurors to fully understand the impact of payoff. Rodney Jew, "Motivating The Jurors: A New Paradigm for Trial Communication," supra.

6. Avoid Adverse Inferences: Making Exhibit/Demo a Positive Factor, Not Boomerang

A good exhibit/demo is usually one that is not captured by the opposition and used as a weapon against the proponent. One very bad thing that can occur is having an exhibit/demo turned around on the witness and used in a negative fashion during cross-examination or summation. In the example of an eyewitness with whom you will show the jury an exhibit/demo of the collision scene, the exhibit/demo should not be capable of exposing the witness to attack. For example, if one point to establish is the witness was in a good position to see the collision, then the photo(s) given the witness to use on direct examination should not be so confusing or ill prepared that the defense can use it (them) to argue with the witness about whether there appears to be some tree or other sight obstruction between the crash site and the witness' vantage point.

To avoid exhibit/demos "backfiring" and make exhibit/demos an effective part of direct exam it is necessary to develop overall effective case strategy which integrates and "links" the exhibit/demo into a unified case structure. To form successful integrated strategy of testimony + exhibit/demos there is no better primer than Rodney Jew's AAJ paper: "Motivating the Jurors: A New Paradigm for Trial Communication," supra.

An important practical tip during, and especially after, direct examination, is to be prepared to object to any effort by the defense to alter, deface, or change exhibits/demos used by or created by the witness. For example, many times an eyewitness will create a drawing or annotate upon a prepared diagram/photograph. The witness may simply mark "X" for the point of impact. Then on cross-examination the opponent may try to get the witness to alter the exhibit/demo by erasing, moving, enlarging the "X" or placing another "X" or some other markings on the exhibit/demo. As much as possible DO NOT ALLOW this tactic to dilute or destroy what has been illustrated clearly by the witness during direct examination.

A way to preempt such tactic is to move the exhibit/demo into evidence. Ask for introduction of the exhibit/demo into evidence immediately after the witness has finished using and testifying about it, or just before ending direct examination of that witness. This will allow the plaintiff attorney to meet and address any objections to the exhibit/demo's admissibility by the defense before the witness is turned over for cross or excused from the witness stand.

Whether the exhibit/demo has been formally admitted into evidence or not, the proponent of the exhibit/demo should object to any physical alteration of the exhibit/demo. Suggest that the opponent use another photo or drawing that is available in order to present and preserve any markings the defense believes are necessary; however the exhibit/demo produced during direct examination should be preserved in a manner consistent with the witness' testimony. Any contrary "proofs" or exhibits/demos should be the burden of the opponent to produce. The court should not allow the defense to piggy-back upon the plaintiff's work product.

III. "SPONSORSHIP" AND "SCARCITY"

There are two important psychological principles that should be considered when using exhibits/demos in trial and specifically during direct examination. "Sponsorship" is a theory which warns us as trial advocates that overuse of exhibits/demos, overproving a point, or overtrying a case can produce negative reactions from the jury. When the sponsorship theory is used to guide use of exhibits/demos, the theory can be explained best by the following syllogism:

1. Jurors expect you to be an advocate for your client
2. Jurors expect you to present the strongest evidence for your client
3. Jurors expect any exhibit you use is necessary or you would not present it
4. Jurors assume if additional exhibits are used, the prior exhibit was insufficient

> Jurors cannot remember everything, but they are most likely to remember what they see, and what involves them emotionally. What happens when they are presented with hundreds of visuals? First, they will remember more of the facts than they would without a visual, but so what? Unless the fact is critical to your case, the effect of multiple demonstratives may be to crowd out one fact for another that is far less important. Sponsorship theory is one explanation of the hazards of over-proving a case, with or without demonstratives . . .
>
> Two consequences of sponsorship theory impact the use of demonstratives. First, when an evidentiary point is proven, then proven again, the assumption is that the initial proof was by itself insufficient. In other words, you discount the value of evidence on a point by introduction of additional, weaker evidence on the same point. Second, if you introduce proof of facts that are not case critical, the jurors will assume they are just as critical to

the case as other facts, or you would not have introduced (sponsored) them.

Knowledge of sponsorship theory and juror memory, should cause question as to e number of exhibits that can be used effectively. There is no simple rule of thumb, but demonstratives must be tied to juror takeaways, not noncritical case facts.

Philip Miller, "What Makes Exhibits Work: Psychological Principles" ATLA Convention Paper 2001.

Another psychological principle to remember when planning the use of exhibit/demos during direct examination is "scarcity." This simple means:

Most people will place more importance on evidence they perceive to be scarce or banned. When you possess the only copy of a photo/document (or one of limited set), emphasizing that fact suggests the photo/document is important.

Philip Miller, "What Makes Exhibits Work: Psychological Principles," ATLA Convention Paper, 2001.

IV. COLOR, PICTURES, SYMBOLS, TEXT, AND WORDS

Basic components of trial communication, in order of their impact on jurors, are:

1. color
2. pictures
3. symbols/icons
4. printed words
5. spoken words

Jurors perceive color and pictures before symbols and icons; they will perceive symbols and icons before words. Therefore, to communicate more effectively with exhibits/demos during direct examination, plaintiff lawyers must first get the jury's attention and then tap into their emotions, beliefs, and life experiences. The most effective way of doing this is to combine the various modes of communication. Spoken words alone are not enough. Visual exhibits/demos will help, but exhibits/demos which are not strategically linked may not connect with or be of use to the jurors. Integrated exhibits/demos with spoken and written words provide the most effective means of conveying important information to the jury.

Plaintiff trial lawyers who rely only, or primarily, on spoken words by a witness on direct examination to impart critical information to the jury rely too heavily on the most ineffective and least impactful communication tool. To communicate effectively in the courtroom, it is necessary to present cases visually as well as orally; select colors, shapes, images, pictures, symbols and icons with the same care as words; and understand the unique advantages of each.

1. Color. Color helps make information memorable; it increases attention and retention. It grabs the eye first—before pictures, symbols, or words. Color should be used judiciously to draw attention to key information, enhance the visibility and legibility of exhibits, and reinforce thematic connections (with color-coding and color symbolism). Text should appear in most legible or visible color combinations. (Black text on white is most legible because it provides the greatest value contrast; black text on yellow is most visible, because yellow is the most readily perceived hue.) Colors that cannot be distinguished by color-blind viewers should not be used to show key distinctions. (About 8% of males, for example, are unable to distinguish red and green; and half of those who are color blind do not know it.) Colors may have a variety of connotations and evoke either positive or negative responses among different groups of people. It is critical to use colors that will evoke appropriate responses from jurors.

2. Pictures. Like colors, pictures grab jurors' attention before symbols or words. They evoke immediate emotional responses. Inherently more memorable than words, pictures increase jurors' recall . . . The old adage is true: The right picture = a thousand words.

3. Symbols and icons. Symbols and icons identify and help discriminate among topics. They reduce the amount of text needed to be read, increase data scanning and retrieval speed, and augment readability of information for those with limited linguistic skills.

4. Printed words. Words are excellent for naming concepts and things, defining terms, classifying elements, and allowing discussion of abstractions. Words on exhibits are best kept few and simple, to enable jurors to readily grasp them. Text items are ideally presented in groups of three, as people tend to remember things in threes. A neutral title should identify each exhibit (letting the jurors know what they are looking at). A subtitle that is a

rhetorical question should stimulate jurors to scan the information on the exhibit to determine a response. Rhetorical questions increase jurors' involvement by stimulating a higher level of information processing. Printed words, together with supporting visual images, can isolate key concepts and keep them in jurors' view, to ensure that the concepts, and their significance, are not missed.

5. Spoken words. Spoken words, on the other hand, although often the primary or only communication vehicle used to convey key concepts in trial, are not always the most effective. If jurors are even briefly distracted, they may miss key portions of spoken testimony (particularly if a witness rambles). Even if jurors hear the crucial words, they may overlook their importance, unless the oral testimony is reinforced with strategic exhibits.

Rodney Jew, "Motivating the Jurors: A New Paradigm for Trial Communication," supra

V. A DOZEN WAYS TO IMPROVE EXHIBIT EFFECTIVENESS

1. Know the Goal. As discussed above, it is important to see the "Big Picture" of the trial and see where the witness and planned exhibit/demo fit into that integrate trial strategy. One method to use in deciding upon what the issues and points to be made by the direct exam and use of exhibits/demos is by "Reverse Engineering the Verdict." This is a method by which exact language is taken from jury instructions and verdict forms and is integrated into the exhibits/demos and graphics used in trial. Samuel Solomon, "The Basics of Creating Technological Presentations at ADR and Trial: 'Ten Commandments of Persuasion,'" ATLA Annual Convention Paper, 2001.

2. Know the Witness. Before attempting to use any exhibit/demo with any witness, you should know how and in what manner that witness will best interact with the jury. It may be that a simple drawing is better for the witness to tell the story and make the point rather than an elaborate chart or video presentation.

3. Know the Adversary and the Judge. Before attempting to introduce an exhibit/demo or use a demo, try to anticipate the trial judge's reaction or comfort level to the exhibit/demo. Likewise, try to reduce or eliminate defense objections to the use of exhibits/demos in advance with conferences or motion practice.

4. Know the Audience. As discussed above, it is important to try to under-

stand the attitudes and life experiences which the average juror will bring into the trial. How they will react to the exhibit/demo is key to whether the demonstrative will be useful, useless, or hurtful. Try to anticipate what the jury will want to know.

"What Do Jurors Want to Know? What jurors want can be distilled to the following:

1. Why are the issues presented in the case important?

2. What comparisons—objective standards—can be used to evaluate the defendants' actions?

3. What is the history of the defendant's actions?

4. What does the defendant admit? Rodney Jew, "Motivating The Jurors: A New Paradigm for Trial Communication," ATLA Paper

5. Give Jurors What They Need to Know as Efficiently as Possible. The old saying is true: less is more. Remember the discussion above concerning "Sponsorship" and "Scarcity." There can be a tendency in preparing exhibits/demos to give jurors too much information. Too much data, or information that is not prioritized, can overwhelm jurors' efforts to analyze the issues of a case. Therefore, provide only what is the necessary information, but not too much for jurors to absorb.

6. Help Jurors Focus Upon and Remember the Exhibit/Demo. In addition to giving the jury the necessary information, help jurors focus on and remember the key points by:

    a. Directing attention to key information with color and placement;

    b. Eliminating distractions—avoiding data-dense presentations, omitting anything extraneous, keeping formats consistent;

    c. Clustering elements (grouping similar/contrasting features) aids learning + retention;

    d. Controlling sequence: put the most critical information at the beginning and end; and

    e. Building on previous knowledge and using repetition appropriately to reinforce learning and aid in retention." Rodney Jew, "Motivating The Jurors: A New Paradigm for Trial Communication," ATLA Paper

7. "The Seven Stakes:" Select Exhibits/Demos Which Relate to the Jurors' Life Experiences or Psychologically Connect. To motivate jurors to analyze

the issues you present by way of exhibits/demos during direct examination you should show them the significance and relevance of those issues. For example, in a negligent security or fall down case get the jurors to think about the experiences they, or their family or acquaintances have had—or have not had—with similar premises.

Additionally, to "connect" with jurors—or anyone—we know from psychologist Abraham Maslowe the "Seven Stakes" which explain what drives people, what people want, and what is "at stake" if people, like jurors, do not get it.

Great stories place these basic needs in jeopardy in order to raise the level of concern and identification with the jury.

1. Survival. This is a basic instinct common to all mammals. We all want to survive and will go to great lengths to do so. We identify with the life-and-death stakes. The conflict is always clear, involving us, and bringing ultimate identification to the situation. This is why is wrongful death cases, the jury does not need to be motivated to understand the matter involved is very serious and of important consequence to the plaintiff family.

2. Safety and security. People need to feel they are in a place that is safe, secure, and protective. This is the safe haven or a place to call home.

3. Love and belonging. People need to connect; it is natural to desire a sense of family. This can take the form of yearning for a nuclear family or a sense of community. This can also include the search for a mate or the need to belong to someone.

4. Self-esteem and self-respect. People desire to be looked up to and recognized for their skills and contributions. This includes the need for confidence and reward.

5. The need to know and understand. We are born with a sense of curiosity. We have a natural desire to know how things work and are on a constant quest for knowledge.

6. Aesthetic need. People have a need for balance or being connected to something greater than themselves. It is a recognized need although perhaps the least universal.

7. Self-actualization. We have a need to express who we are by actualizing our talents, skills, and abilities. That need comes alive in a story for someone people find worth rooting for." Jacob Virgil, "Psychologically Preparing

the Witness to Connect with the Jury," ATLA Annual Convention Paper, 2001.

8. Give the Jury Strategic Shortcuts. Anticipate jurors' unconscious and analytical processing of the case. Assume jurors will take some mental shortcuts in digesting the data presented. Prepare for this tendency by providing visual landmarks or "setups" to help guide jurors' intuitive and logical processing and lead them in the right direction.

9. Strategically Integrate Visual and Oral Communication
Integrated, effective visuals will increase the credibility and emotional impact, as well as the clarity, of any exhibit/demo use.
Visual communication has many advantages over oral communication. Adding the visual component:

   a. Heightens emotional involvement;

   b. Speeds communication;

   c. Makes it easier for jurors to perceive complex relationships; and

   d. Supports a more flexible processing of information: Visual aids allow jurors to have some control over the pace and sequence of information access.
   Visual presentation in trial is more critical at this time than ever. The growing complexity and magnitude of cases requires more effective communication tools. Further, in our increasingly visual culture, people attune to learn through visual means.
   Visuals are especially helpful to communicate with diverse language and ethnic groups in our country. Given current demographics, it is rare to encounter homogeneous groups of jurors. Colors, pictures, and symbols can often transcend verbal barriers. In addition, research has shown that the use of demonstrative exhibits conveys to jurors that lawyers (1) have faith in their case and (2) care about jurors' understanding of the case. It is no wonder that many lawyers now use demonstrative exhibits in trial." Rodney Jew, supra.

10. Understand How to Use the Multiple Modes of Communication. Remember the order of communicative impact your jurors. The order by which people obtain information is worth repeating and remembering for the use of exhibits/demos:
    There is a hierarchy that applies to the speed and the order in which humans perceive information. First is color—it is the first things people see. Second are pictures, followed by shapes, and then text. Spoken words

are fifth in line. While this hierarchy suggests that demonstratives should be used, it also suggests what should be included in demonstratives. Color will be the first thing jurors see on a demonstrative. This can be both good and bad. If color is used to focus jurors on the juror takeaway, it may be very useful. Unfortunately, color can also distract jurors from your point. If it affects the readability of the demonstrative (e.g., black on a red background), uses colors that cannot be seen by those who are color blind, uses colors that produce a negative response, or distracts from a critical part of the exhibit, the color use is counterproductive. Color must be used carefully.

Pictures are valuable components of demonstratives because they can communicate key information without words, and they can create emotional responses that make evidence memorable. Pictures, like any portion of a demonstrative, must be strategic. Jurors will remember the picture. If it does not anchor a takeaway, it can be counterproductive. Likewise, if the picture has not been carefully selected, jurors may see things or interpret the picture in ways you never anticipated.

Text is next to last in line for recognition (but before spoken words). Since it is last in line for demonstratives, care must be given to avoid demonstratives that rely too heavily on words. Nontechnical, nonlegal terms are the rule. The use of complicated terms or too many words on a demonstrative may completely undercut its effectiveness. Philip Miller, "What Makes Exhibits Work: Psychological Principles," supra.

11. Code Information in Language and Imagery the Jurors Understand. The best way to integrate visual and oral communication in any case is to present a compelling story in pictures and words. A well-crafted story should emotionally involve the jurors while providing a way to organize case facts and themes and build upon what the jurors know. The story serves as a kind of dynamic road map for developing and linking case themes and leading jurors to the desired conclusions. It will help provide familiar signposts for new areas and will allow the jury to make a mental U-turn and circle back to reinforce associations between new and previously processed information. Making a case intellectually and emotionally manageable for jurors also requires dividing its presentation into carefully linked segments. Effective use of exhibits/demos during direct examination functions as the building blocks for this strategy. Rodney Jew, supra.

12. Rehearse and test. Using either focus groups and/or the clients and/or the entire plaintiff trial team, including the legal assistants, trial lawyers

should test the effectiveness of any important exhibits/demos to see if the message being communicated is actually the same message the audience is receiving. Also, a "dry-run" or rehearsal with a witness is advisable. Nothing looks more disorganized and disingenuous than a witness not understanding or correctly using an exhibit/demo which is being introduced through him. Even a lay witness can be made to look confused and incredible if the trial lawyer shows them up by producing a drawing or a photo which they have never seen and which they have trouble orienting in order to use it.

VI. HOW TO AVOID REDUCING EXHIBIT EFFECTIVENESS

1. Overdoing It. Using too many demonstrative exhibits/demos can have a negative impact on the jury. The important message(s) may become lost in a sea of visual effects. Therefore, try to keep the exhibits/demos to a minimum necessary to make the witness during direct an effective part of the overall trial.

2. Assume the Exhibit/Demo Works. Without some "test" or reliable jury experience, never assume any exhibit/demo will "work" to the benefit of a witness, the jury, or your client.

3. Data Density. Some exhibits/demos are designed to include numerous facts and summaries of large amounts of data. The term "data dense" describes charts that include large amounts of data or many words. Although trial lawyers routinely review documents with large amounts of text and other data, this experience is not common among everyday jurors. When jurors are shown exhibits/demos with large amounts of text or data, it is almost impossible for them to know what is important. They will usually have no motivation to wade through all the detail. Data-dense exhibits/demos are ineffective because the juror may not understand what in the chart is important and therefore what to remember. Worse, the jurors may focus on some part of the data-dense exhibit/demo that is unrelated to "the strategic takeaway" sought by plaintiff's counsel. Philip Miller, supra.

4. Chart Junk. Many trial exhibits/demos are created and designed by nonlawyers who are unconcerned with and disconnected from the litigation. While well intentioned, many designers think their demonstratives are more valuable or effective because they are elaborate or "pretty." Chart junk refers to use of design elements that have nothing to do with communicating the point and purpose of the demonstrative. The ultimate

effect of chart junk is that they distract jurors from the message or "takeaway" you are trying to reinforce. Philip Miller, supra.

5. Misuse of Color. Just as exhibit/demo designers can err by filling exhibits/demos with "chart junk," they can also misuse color(s) trying to make exhibit/demo attractive or noticeable. Whenever color(s) distracts from juror "takeaways" must be questioned. Philip Miller, supra.

6. Naked and Unlabeled Charts. It is common to see photographs or other visual exhibits/demos presented as "naked charts," i.e., demonstratives without any label to describe them (e.g., "Photo of Scene," "Medical Bills," "Fetal Heart Rate"). The disadvantage of naked charts is that a juror whose attention has wandered may not know how or where to slot the exhibit/demo in his or her mental inventory of case evidence. A juror without direction may create his or her own reason and explanation for an unlabeled exhibit/demo. Philip Miller, supra.

7. Use of PowerPoint®, Elmos, & Animation. Many lawyers use "technological fixes" to communicate with jurors. Any of them can be effective if the lawyer is sensitive to the way jurors learn and acquire information. A PowerPoint® presentation for trial can include hundreds of slides. The problem is the witness and trial lawyer are limited to one slide at a time, and jurors can't raise their hands to ask the lawyer to go back so they can see an earlier slide. Also, when changing slides, the lawyer or witness may be overanxious and "move on" before all the jurors have had enough time to absorb the content of the current slide. If the trial lawyer or witness do not consider the jurors' ability to read and recall the slides, and if they "move on" before the jury is ready, then a PowerPoint® presentation can undermine its very purpose.

The "Elmo" or "document camera" can be used effectively with photos and most documents, but it is not a panacea. Unless focusing on a very few words, or text is in large type, documents put on Elmo are often unreadable. Making it the primary way to present documents makes it likely jurors will not be able to read your exhibits/demos.

Animations are often used in product liability and other cases. They can be powerful and memorable. They can also distract by doing too much. A common technique in animations is to do a 360-degree "fly by." This creates an interesting visual, but it may not be strategically necessary and cause jurors to be distracted from the real purpose and focus of the animation. When a juror is thinking "Oh, wow" during a flyby, is their attention on what is strategically important in the animation? In using animation, limiting the views shown to jurors, and producing stills of critical views, can reduce the chance of jurors being fascinated by the technology but unsure of the message. P. Miller, supra.

8. Ignoring the Environment of Use. To avoid delays and communication problems with the exhibit/demo, do not assume that the courtroom has the same lighting or sight lines as your office. Do not ignore the reality that the jury, judge, and even the adversary need to see the exhibits/demos. Therefore, be sure to visit and plan where in the courtroom the best viewpoint will be for the witness to use the exhibit/demo and communicate effectively to the jury.

9. Not Knowing Your Limitations. If you and/or the witness are not technologically adept, then recognize that/those limitations and arrange for a trial assistant or someone with technical skills to assist with overhead projector, laser disc, video, etc.

10. Not Asking "May I." It is the trial court's mandatory duty to control the "mode and order of interrogation and presentation" in the courtroom. Fed.R.Evid 611(a). Therefore, do not assume the trial judge, even with no objections, will allow you and your witness to walk about or use demonstrative aids or exhibits/demos in front of the jury in the manner you have planned. Always try to give your adversary and the judge the courtesy of advance notice if special lighting or demonstrative aids will be necessary before the witness is asked to start using a dynamic exhibit/demo.

VII. CONCLUSION

From all that has been said, written, and taught on the subject of direct examination and use of "demonstratives" and exhibits during direct, it should be painfully obvious to every conscientious plaintiff trial lawyer that presentation of the direct exam should not be an after-thought. Use of demos/exhibits during direct examination is not a matter of "off-the-cuff, catch-as-catch-can, or doing it "on the fly" with an unprepared witness. Do not simply leave direct examination exhibits/demos to the luck of the draw or whatever audiovisual tools are available in the particular courtroom. Effectively using exhibits/demos during direct examination takes time and effort. It takes "cerebration." It requires thoughtful planning, testing, and rehearing to be the most effective in the overall presentation of the client's case. Just as Mark Twain likened "word-smithing" or proper word choice to difference between "lightning and a lightning bug," the proper exhibit/demo during direct examination can be the difference between a masterpiece or a mud-pie in the collective minds and eyes of the jury.

VII. SELECTED BIBLIOGRAPHY

William S. Bailey, "Using Computer Technology to Prepare for Trial," TRIAL (1998).

David Bossart, "Direct Examination of Fact Witnesses" ATLA Convention Paper, 2000

Frank L. Branson, "Demonstrative Evidence," ATLA Annual Convention Paper, 2000.

Kirby Dial, "Demonstrative Evidence & Technology in Year 2000," ATLA Paper, 2000

Russ Herman, "Direct Examination of Lay Witnesses," ATLA Seminar Paper, 1993

Rodney Jew, "Motivating Jurors: A New Paradigm for Trial Communication" ATLA Paper 2001

Joshua Karton, "On Paper v. In Person," TRIAL, July 2002

Philip Miller, "What Makes Exhibits Work: Psychological Principles," ATLA 2001.

Howard Nations, "Predicate: Documentary and Demonstrative Evidence," ATLA Paper, 1997

M. Ogborn, "Making Your Case Come to Life: Storytelling & Theme Creation" ATLA 2001

Eric Oliver & Paul Lesnel, Courtroom Power, PESI, 2001

Brian Panish and Christine Spagnoli, "Taking Technology to Trial," TRIAL, July 2002

Kathleen Flynn Peterson, "High Tech or No High Tech: How to Present Medical Evidence To The Jury," ATLA Annual Convention Paper, 1998

Julie K. Plowman, "Multimedia in the Courtroom: Valuable Tool or Smoke and Mirrors?," 15 REV. LITIG. 415 (Spring 1996).

J. Stratton Shartel, "Jury Response Technology Revolutionizes Trial Preparation," 8(5) INSIDE LITIG. 34 (June 1994).

Samuel Solomon, "The Basics of Creating Technological Presentations at ADR and Trial: 'Ten Commandments of Persuasion," ATLA Annual Convention Paper, 2001

Jacob G. Virgil, "Psychologically Preparing the Witness to Connect with Jury," ATLA 2001

ADVANTAGES AND DISADVANTAGES OF EXHIBITS/DEMOS

By Kirby B. Dial[1]

Presentation Mediums	Advantages	Disadvantages	Notes
Overhead Projectors	Only advantage is the ability to clearly show an entire 8.5 x 11 document	Need a darkroom: every document must be made into a transparency	Very dated way to do business
Boards	Can become centerpiece of attention; gives higher comfort level for user; tangible for jury	Too many will create boredom; can become awkward if usable space in courtroom is too small	Boards can do different things using magnets, laminations, size, overlays, etc.
Television	Easily used to display a video image: VCR, documents on an ELMO	Untrustworthy for PowerPoint shows and unable to handle multimedia	What you see on computer screen not always what you get on a TV
Data Monitors	Higher quality imagery that is required for trial software packages	More expensive and more technical to set up	Must for high-end multimedia; requires skilled AV setup and several other components to work the best
LCD Projects	Cuts down on equipment in the courtroom	Courtroom lighting plays a role in visibility; must be perfectly positioned so everyone can see	No different than a data monitor–projectors have greatly improved, much brighter and clearer; resolutions have improved & rival data monitors
Multimonitor	Everyone is able	Creates multiple focus	This type of setup may be impractical
Configuration	To clearly see evidence and demonstratives as shown	Points around courtroom; not all courts big enough for these configurations	Extra power supply, multiple cords on the floor
Video Inputs	Advantages	Disadvantages	Notes
VCR	Everyone knows how to use— easy as cue and play	No instant access to clips unless preedited	New four-head VCRs capable of pause/displaying a clear image

---

[1] Kirby B.Dial of Zagnoli, McEvoy, Foley, Inc. from a paper entitled *"Demonstrative Evidence and Technology in the Year 2000,"* ATLA Annual Convention Paper 2000.

Presentation Mediums	Advantages	Disadvantages	Notes
Laser Disc Players	Instant access through bar codes to any image or video clips	Limited amount of space per disc	User must gain comfort with the bar code reader
Visual Presenters (e.g., ELMO)	Modern technology allowing visualization of anything that can fit on the base	Documents can generally only be shown as half pages and still be read	This is simply a small camera that shoots any object placed on its base
Computer	Advantages	Disadvantages	Notes
Trial Presentation Software	Instant access to all documents, depositions, deposition video clips, and any demonstrative	Requires much pretrial work, experienced techie, trial attorney willing to gain comfort level with it, and a logistically capable courtroom + backup	This software generally will be coupled with a multimonitor configuration
PowerPoint	Simple way to bring techno-feel to court; quickly edited	Low-end, limited abilities and interactivity	Most effective creating bullet-point/summary
Adobe Acrobat (PDF)	Strong application that is easy to learn	See Trial Presentation Software	Most computers have Acrobat Reader—ability to do presentations

aderire alla carne e patate

(stick to the meat and potatoes)

Chapter 9. INSALATA (Salad)

PART A. DOM'S RECIPES

FUOCO E INSALATA DI GHIACCIO
(Fire and Ice Salad)

INGREDIENTS (Serves 6 to 8):

2 Large honeydew, cantaloupe, crane, or other ripe melon or ½ watermelon

12 Italian cherry peppers

½ Cup Lime Juice

2 Tbsp Ginger

Parsley sprigs

DIRECTIONS:

Dice the melon into a bowl.

Add "THE FIRE"—Cherry peppers diced in same bowl.

Add "THE ICE"—Lime Juice.

Ginger diced into the bowl.

Toss in bowl; season with any salt, pepper, dressing + LOTS OF LIME JUICE.

Garnish with Parsley on top.

<u>BOCCONCINI</u>: *Ciliegio pepe* means "cherry pepper" in Italian; *pimiento or pimento* Spanish word (borrowed from Portugese) for cherry pepper. A variety of large, red, heart-shaped chili pepper, cherry peppers are large, red and green, pumpkin-shaped chili peppers; some varieties of cherry peppers are hot, and some are characterized by their mild, sweet, and aromatic flesh. Often found in salad bars, these peppers make a popular antipasto pepper; often they are stuffed with provolone and prosciutto as an appetizer.

The Vespers' Trial Cookbook

FIRE AND ICE SALAD VARIATION WITH TOMATOES AND CUCUMBERS

INGREDIENTS (Serves 4 to 6):

2 Tomatoes

2 Cucumbers

1 purple onion

½ cup Water

½ cup White vinegar

½ cup Sugar

DIRECTIONS:

Peel and slice cucumbers. Chop tomatoes and onion.

Combine all in a large bowl.

Mix dressing of equal parts vinegar, water, sugar (start with ½ cups; add more to taste).

Pour over vegetables and refrigerate.

BOCCONCINI: In Italian *cetriolo; cetrioli* are cucumber(s), which enjoy a long history in Italy. Emperor Tiberius, according to Pliny, had cucumbers on his table every day in both summer and winter. The Romans reportedly used artificial methods (greenhouses) to grow them for his daily table. Also, if you need to stock your medicine cabinet, the Romans reportedly used cucumbers to treat scorpion bites, bad eyesight, and to scare away mice. Ancient Roman wives wishing for children wore them around their waists, along with the midwives; they threw the *cetrioli* away when the child was born.

Cucumbers are cultivated creeping vine plants of the gourd family that bears cylindrical fruit edible when ripe. Three main varieties of cucumber are the slicing, pickling, and burpless. The cucumber is originally from Southern Asia. The word comes from Latin *cucumerem*. Interestingly, Old English *eortæppla* (plural) literally meant "earth-apples." Cucumbers are really "cool" fruits. The coomin phrase "cool as a cucumber" originated in the ancient folk knowledge confirmed by modern science in 1970, to wit: a field of growing cucumber on a warm day is 20 degrees cooler than the air temperature. COOL!

INSALATA DI CICORIA E FINOCCHIO
(Dandelion and Fennel Salad)

The base of fennel is very popular in Italy and can be eaten cooked or raw. Dandelion is part of the chickory family, and any greens in the chickory family can be used, like radiccio. The combination of the two vegetables makes a delicious salad.

INGREDIENTS (Serves 4 to 6):

1 head of fennel or finocchio

1 lb Dandelion greens

½ small Onion, minced

5 Tbsp Olive oil

3 Tbsp Balsamic vinegar

Salt and pepper to taste

DIRECTIONS:

Clean greens in cold water; discard discolored leaves; chop into 3" pieces and set aside.

Remove leaves from fennel and separate from bulb. Wash in cold water.

Slice fennel, white part only, into thin slices.

Combine greens, fennel, and onion in a salad bowl and mix.

In a separate bowl, mix oil, vinegar, salt and pepper until well blended.

Pour dressing over salad and toss until salad is well coated.

Refrigerate for 30 minutes and serve.

BOCCONCINI: Fennel is a hardy, perennial, umbelliferous herb plant, with yellow flowers and feathery leaves; indigenous to Mediterranean, it has become naturalized around the world, esp. on dry soils near the sea-coast and on riverbanks; it is highly aromatic and flavorful with culinary and medicinal uses; along with the similar-tasting anise, it is a primary ingredient of absinthe. "Florence fennel" or *finocchio* is a variety with a swollen, bulb-like stem base used as a vegetable. Always eaten in Vesper, Gallo, and Nicolella families after a big Sunday dinner as a "carminative." According to my Aunt Mary from Brooklyn "it helped yer Uncle's fluctuations" (she meant flatulence).

Finocchio is also big in Greek mythology: Prometheus used the stalk of a fennel plant to steal fire from the gods. Also, it was from the giant fennel, *Ferula communis*, that the Bacchanalian wands of the god Dionysus and his followers were made. And, just so you know, the Greek name for fennel is *marathon* (μάραθόν) or *marathos* (μάραθό?), and so, the famous Battle of Marathon and all subsequent sports event called "marathons" were and still are played not on a "Field of Dreams" but rather on "Field with Fennels."

INSALATA CAPRESE
(Tomato and Mozzarella Salad)

INGREDIENTS (Serves 4 to 6):

3 medium Tomatoes

1 (16 oz.) package Fresh mozzarella cheese

5 fresh Basil leaves, chopped

4 Tbsp Olive oil

Salt and pepper to taste

DIRECTIONS:

Slice tomatoes and arrange on a serving platter.

Slice cheese and lay one piece of cheese on each tomato.

Spread chopped basil on each slice of cheese.

Drizzle olive oil on salad making sure each slice is coated, use additional oil if needed.

Salt and pepper to taste. Sprinkle a pinch of red pepper flakes on each slice (optional).

BOCCONCINI: *Caprese* refers literally to something that comes from or is in the style of Capri—the Italian island off the coast near Naples. Insalata Caprese is a simple salad made of sliced fresh mozzarella, tomatoes, and basil, seasoned with salt, and olive oil. In Italy, unlike most salads, it is usually served as an antipasto, not a *contorno* (side dish).

Mozzarella comes from the Italian *mozza* (cut) or *mozzare* meaning "to cut off." It is a semi-soft, mild, fresh cheese, originally from southern Italy (our part), traditionally and originally made in Naples from Italian buffalo and later cow's milk by a method called *pasta filata* using spinning and cutting (hence the name)

Bocconcini (which we are using in this book as "tid bit") are small mozzarella cheeses the size of an egg. This cheese uses the Italian name for "small mouthfuls." Each cheese is about the size, shape, and color of a hardboiled egg. Baby or *Bambini bocconcini* can also be purchased; these are a smaller version about the size of large grapes. Whatever size you prefer, the taste is *delicioso*!

The Vespers' Trial Cookbook

INSALATA DI BACCALA
(Salad with Salted Cod)

INGREDIENTS (Serves 6):

2 lbs Dried salt cod (baccala)

1 cup Olive oil

4 Garlic cloves, minced

½ cup Lemon juice

2 cups Hot and sweet peppers from a jar, seeded and sliced

¼ cup Capers, rinsed, drained, and coarsely chopped

1 cup Pitted black olives

2 Tbsp Fresh chopped parsley

DIRECTIONS:

Soak the salt cod in water for 2 to 3 days to remove some of the salt. Change the water 2 to 3 times a day.

Bring 6 quarts of water to a boil in a large stockpot. Add the cod and cook until the fish is tender, about 15 minutes.

Drain the cod and set aside to cool. Remove and discard the skin and bones.

Break the fish into bite-size pieces.

In a small bowl, combine the oil, garlic, lemon juice, peppers, capers, and olives.

Add the cod and gently stir to combine.

Transfer the mixture to a serving platter and top with the chopped parsley.

Let the salad sit at room temperature for 1 hour before serving.

BOCCONCINI: *Baccalà* is the Venetian word for *stoccafisso*, meaning stockfish or cod. It's a traditional Christmas Eve favorite in Italy—a great appetizer, salad, or main course. It is salt-cured cod from the coast of Labrador and Newfoundland where it is fished, salted, and exported all over the world. The Campania region of Italy, which includes Naples, boasts the highest consumption of baccala in Italy. Legend has it that there are 365 different ways to eat baccala in Naples.

NOTE: Baccala must be soaked in clean fresh water for 48 to 72 hours, changing the water several times, before it can be eaten. This soaking is something most wives dislike . . . but, it is worth it!

The Vespers' Trial Cookbook

INSALATA DI POLPO
(Octopus Salad)

BACKGROUND: In Italy, as many countries, octopus is a delicacy. Cuz Dom and I like grilled octopi, unlike Korea where some small species are eaten alive as a novelty food—the live octopus is usually sliced up, and eaten while still squirming! Try our way:

INGREDIENTS (Serves 6):

1 (4—5 lb) octopus

4 Celery stalks, thinly sliced on the diagonal

Juice of 4 lemons

1 cup Pitted black olives, sliced

½ Medium red onion, chopped

1 Tbsp Fresh chopped parsley

¾ cup Olive oil

Salt and pepper

DIRECTIONS:

Put the octopus in a large stockpot, add water to cover it and then bring to a boil.

Simmer until tender, 1 ½ to 2 hrs. Test for tenderness by piercing tentacles with a fork.

Remove the octopus from the water and rinse under cold running water until cool. Once cool, clean the octopus. Remove the head and discard.

Skin the tentacles by rubbing them between your fingers; the skin will come off easily. Slice the tentacles on the diagonal about ¼" thick.

Put the octopus pieces in a large bowl. Add the celery, lemon juice, olives, onion, parsley, and olive oil. Mix well to combine.

Season with salt and pepper and serve at room temperature.

BOCCONCINI: An octopus has eight arms, usually bearing suction cups. The arms of octopuses are often distinguished from the pair of feeding tentacles found in squids and cuttlefish. Just so you know, "octopus" comes to us through scientific Latin, from ancient Greek word for "eight-footed"; and the usual plural in English is "octopuses"; *Merriam-Webster 11th Collegiate Dictionary*, lists "octopuses" and "octopi," in that order. However you say it, try it more than once and you will enjoy it in whatever dish you make at home.

INSALATA DI SUNGILLI
(Sungilli Salad or Salad with Sliced Conch)

INGREDIENTS (Serves 4):

1 (29oz.) Can sliced scungilli (preferably my friends' & clients' *LaMonica* family cans)

2 Stalks celery, chopped (you can also use lettuce of your choice)

½ cup Red onion, chopped

2 Tbsp Italian/flat leaf parsley, chopped (not curly!)

1 small can Sliced and pitted black olives (drained)

¼ to ½ cup of your best Olive oil

1 Lemon, juiced and strained

1 tsp Sea salt

¼ tsp Ground black pepper

Red pepper flakes (optional)

1 Clove garlic, chopped finely

DIRECTIONS:

Rinse the canned scungilli well, or better, soak for a minute and repeat one more time.

Mix all of the above ingredients in a medium mixing bowl and toss until mixed well.

Refrigerate for 30 minutes to let the flavors meld and enjoy!

BOCCONCINI: Scungilli is from Neapolitan *scuncigli,* plural of *scunciglio,* meaning conch; they are very large marine snails, firmly fixed in Italian-American cooking—whether served chilled in an *insalata di mare* or hot in a marinara sauce. Although they are not as popular as calamari, or even octopus and eel, scungilli is one of the dishes our *nonnas* prepared for a holiday spread, especially the "Feast of the Seven Fishes" on Christmas Eve or *Abbondanza* (feast of plentitude and bounty).

Cooking scungilli is *molto semplice,* BUT cleaning them is often described as penitential.

PART B. TOM'S TRIAL TIPS: CROSS-EXAMINATION

SALADS ARE SOMETIMES RUINED BY OUR EXCESSIVE "DRESSINGS": THE SEVEN DEADLY SINS OF CROSS-EXAMINATION: ETHICAL CONSIDERATIONS IN CROSS-EXAMS & IMPEACHMENTS

Most books and articles on cross-examination deal with methods and means of preparing for and conducting safe if not effective cross-examination. Most authors and lecturers address how to/not to cross-examine expert witnesses, hostile witnesses, and various types of lay witnesses including children. There are well known authoritative works how not to lose control of the witness during cross. One of my favorites is Professor Irving Younger's classic—the "Ten Commandments of Cross Examination." Younger, "A Letter in Which Cicero Lays Down the Ten Commandments of Cross-Examination," Winning Strategies & Techniques for Civil Litigators, Chapter 5, PLI (2001); Litigation, Winter 1997. But there is relatively little written on the ethics of the cross examiner. Very few written references explain how to avoid sanctions or reprimands for "crossing the ethical line" of cross-examination.

Surprisingly, there is no specific Code of Professional Conduct that deals with cross-examination. The closest analogous rules are RPC 3.4 Fairness to Opposing Party and Counsel and RPC 4.4 Respect for Rights of Third Persons:

> A lawyer shall not: . . . (e) in trial, allude to any matter that the lawyer does not reasonably believe is relevant or that will not be supported by admissible evidence, assert personal knowledge of facts in issue except when testifying as a witness, or state a personal opinion as to the justness of a cause, the credibility of a witness, the culpability of a civil litigant or the guilt or innocence of an accused; . . . RPC 3.4 (e)
>
> In representing a client, a lawyer shall not use means that have no substantial purpose other than to embarrass, delay, or burden a third person, or use methods of obtaining evidence that violate the legal rights of such a person.

RPC 4.4

From firsthand courtroom experience and second hand knowledge from discussions with trial lawyers and judges from many jurisdictions, I condensed a list of categorical transgressions that in most cases will cause an angry reaction, rebuke, and possible penalty from most courts. This short list is not meant to address the myriad mistakes—intentional or unintentional—that will in most trials cause an adverse jury reaction. Although some overlapping of ethical mistakes and negative advocacy exists, the following seven "sins" are primarily a matter of ethics and professional conduct; they are not directed to jury communication skills. If, from this menu of unprofessional conduct, trial practitioners find applications to or improvements upon personal styles of cross-examination, it may be an added benefit. However, the following are simply reminders to trial practitioners of some major ethical pitfalls which should be avoided.

An easily remembered acronym for the seven ethical faux pas of cross-examination coincidently spells out SLEAZIeS:

S. Shouting at witness

L. Laughing at witness

E. Embarrassing the witness

A. Abusing the witness

Z. Zero factual basis for question

I. Interrupting and exscinding

S. Spiteful and shiftless conduct

Normally, a "wide latitude" is allowed for advocates to cross-examine an adverse witness, especially the adverse party. On examinations of witnesses, see generally 2 G Hazard & W. Hodes, The Law of Lawyering 4.4:102(2d ed. 1991); 3A J. Wigmore, Evidence 986 (J. Chadbourn rev. 1970); C. Wolfram, Modern Legal Ethics 12.4.5 (1986). Most courts recognize cross-exam may be made difficult and wearing on witnesses. E.g., *Sowerwine v. Nielson*, 671 P.2d 295, 303 (Wyo. 1983); Restatement of Law Third—The Law Governing Lawyers, (2002 ALI) Ch 7. Representing Clients in Litigation. The enforcement of professional rules of conduct and finding a bright line between permissible and impermissible cross-exam is usually left to the trial judge or "hearing officer." The issue may arise upon an objection from the opposing attorney or sua sponte from the court. Many times, the cross-examiner is limited by the rules of evidence and the risk of incurring the antipathy of the fact finder.

Some "deadly sins" are subject to a situational ethic, that is, the demeanor, position of the witness on the stand, and the "trial setting" or attendant circumstances of the cross-examination. For example, if a witness is about to launch into a dissertation wholly outside the scope of the question and inject a subject which has been barred or should be barred as inflammatory and irrelevant, then in that situation most judges would welcome a firm but professional interruption of the witness. Some trial judges allow an attorney to "react" to a witness. For example, some trial judges permit an attorney to show some degree of disapproval, surprise, or humor during cross. However, as in any trial, the advocate is well advised to learn in advance or quickly ascertain what leeway the trial judge will allow during cross-examination. Some conduct is more clearly contemptuous. For example, it is never proper for an attorney during cross-examination of any witness to act spitefully, abusively or with no "good faith basis," or for the goal of improperly injecting inadmissible evidence or innuendo. Therefore, within certain reasonable degrees of flexibility for the personal sense of propriety of the trial judge and the situation confronting the examiner, the following guidelines are useful. Whenever a cross-examiner interrogates a witness and the manner of questioning degenerates into one or more of these seven areas, as will be explained below, the interrogator loses some degree of professionalism and is at risk that the trial judge will issue a stern rebuke for unprofessional or unethical conduct. Usually, if the offender continues to ignore the decorum and/or orders of the court, there can be reprimands and sanctions.

1. SHOUTING AT, CROWDING, AND OTHERWISE BULLYING A WITNESS

> Except where the circumstances make it wholly natural, there should be no place in cross-examination for indignation, shouting, belligerent hostility. A kindly voice and courtesy dig a better trap than high blood pressure. A jury regards the combat as unequal because of the skill and experience of the lawyer. Their sympathies are naturally with the underdog. They do not like to see him shouted at and brow-beaten. Generally speaking, the adroit cross-examiner will endeavor to have the witness destroy himself and waive his personal triumph, keeping his co-operation in the destruction well in the background. Wellman, F., The Art of Cross-Examination, 4th Ed (Collier Books), p. 217-218.

To shout at, charge into, crowd over, get in the face of, or otherwise act in any intimidating way to a witness is unprofessional. RPC 4.4. It is not showing "respect" for nor "obtaining evidence" from witness by honoring the witness' right to be free of assault, duress, or coercion. RPC 4.4. It employs "might makes right." It is thuggery.

Of course, some rules have exceptions. For shouting, a possible exception is the "natural course of conversation" exception. That is, when BOTH witness and examiner escalate the Q & A to a climax or crescendo due to a natural and emotional interaction between them. The most memorable exception to the nonshouting guideline is the well publicized and repeated scene from the movie A Few Good Men where the criminal defense lawyer (Tom Cruise) while cross-examining the key prosecution witness (Jack Nicholson) in reply to some sarcastic, loud, and belligerent remarks from the witness shouts back: "I WANT THE TRUTH!" Of course, in the movies, whether it is Tom Cruise, Raymond Burr (playing Perry Mason), or Andy Griffith (playing Matlock), the usual result of the shouting match is for the witness to stunningly concede or confess a crucial point. Unfortunately, what often befalls the overly emotional and unfocused advocate is that the shouting match ends unspectacularly and anticlimactically with a sustained objection and/or a stern rebuke from the trial judge. The safer course is to keep ones professional demeanor, not allow the witness to escalate the confrontation, and let your friends on the jury or the judge do the shouting.

2. LAUGHING, EDITORIALIZING, ASSERTING PERSONAL OPINION

> A distinction must be made between a jest vs. belittling a witness. An appropriate witticism may break the tension of the moment and find favor with jurors; but it should not be at the expense of witness. Rather, it should be of such a character the witness may join in the laughter and not feel he is the target of the remark. Friedman, Leo R., Essentials of Cross-Examination, 1968 (California Continuing Education of Bar).

The real "sin" committed whenever the cross-examiner is allowed to react to a witness' answers with feigned or nervously knee-jerked expressions, laughter, or commentary is violating RPC 3.4(e): the lawyer has ". . . assert(ed) personal knowledge of facts . . ., or state(d) a personal opinion as to . . . the credibility of a witness . . .." This unprofessionalism is not based simply upon the decorum of the courtroom or civility but more importantly is an act of improperly attempting to inject the opinion of the lawyer as to the facts and/or the credibility of the witness.

Some reactions by the cross-examiner may truly be a natural and normal human response. E.g., if the witness blurts out something truly surprising, a common reaction would be "what did you say?" But most judges (and jurors) recognize when theatrical ploys or histrionics are used by the interrogator. For example, to repeatedly comment on the witness' answers with such editorialization and dramatic asides as: "You really must be kidding," "Oh, now I see what you're trying to do," or "That's a very funny/crazy/false story." Also, to repeatedly snicker, laugh at, or mock witness' answers may be seen by judges as a deliberate attempt to argue with and interject an examiner's opinion into trial. Repeating answers in a mocking, sarcastic way may be viewed as more than "bad form." To repeat an answer solely to ridicule or mimic is not looked on by most judges as dramatic effect but rather as wasted time and an improper argument or repetitive question and is usually controlled by the judge per FRE 611 or its equivalent common law rule allowing the court to "exercise reasonable control over the mode and order of interrogating witnesses."

3. EMBARRASSING, HARASSING, AND NITPICKING A WITNESS

> Cross-examination as to credit has also its legitimate use . . . but this powerful weapon for good has almost equal possibilities for evil. . . cross-examination as to credit should be exercised with great care and caution, . . . Questions which throw no light upon the real issues in the case, nor upon the integrity or credit of the witness under examination, but which expose misdeeds, perhaps long since repented of and lived down, are often put for the sole purpose of causing humiliation and disgrace. Such inquiries into private life, private affairs, or domestic infelicities, perhaps involving innocent persons who have nothing to do with the particular litigation and who have no opportunity for explanation nor means of redress, form no legitimate part of the cross-examiner's art . . . .
>
> Counsel may have in his possession material for injuring the witness, but the propriety of using it often becomes a serious question even in cases where its use is otherwise perfectly legitimate. An outrage to the feelings of a witness may be quickly resented by a jury, and sympathy take the place of disgust. Then, too, one has to reckon with the judge, and the indignation of a strong judge is not wisely provoked. Nothing could be more unprofessional than for counsel to ask questions which disgrace not only the witness, but a host of innocent persons, for the mere reason that the client wishes them to be asked. Wellman, supra, at p. 196-197

There is a difference between this offense and mocking/laughing at (Sin # 2) or verbally abusing (Sin #4) a witness. This "sin" can be committed in the most respectful and polite way. It is a poison dart thrown at the witness in the form of a question for no other purpose than to embarrass. The question is intentionally framed to disrespect or "dis" a witness. Example of an "embarrassing" question is to nitpick a remote criminal conviction or personal problem—such as a divorce, bankruptcy, or job difficulty—which has little or no probative value to a witness' testimony or credibility. Trial courts will usually refer to Fed.R.Evid. 611 (a): "The court shall . . . (3) protect witnesses from harassment or undue embarrassment." Impropriety of this type assault upon a witness does not arise from impolite or unprofessional demeanor; rather, it is the content of the question that is offensive and improper. The attacking query may be true and factual, but the unworthy and irrelevant purpose makes it unfit. If the question or subject matter is persistently pressed after sustained objections, the interrogator may be sanctioned.

4. ABUSING THE WITNESS VERBALLY

> If the witness is uneducated, speaks with an accent, has difficulty making himself understood, or mispronounces some words, counsel must not use these short-comings to provoke laughter or to humiliate the witness. The jurors will resent such tactics. It is a common American trait to pull for and take sides with the underdog. If counsel makes the witness the butt of a joke, he puts the witness in the underdog position. Moreover, a juror himself or a member of his family may be poorly educated, or come from a foreign country and speak with an accent or mispronounce some words. Friedman, Essentials of Cross-Examination, supra.

This professional mistake occurs when the cross-examiner, either deliberately or unconsciously, tries to overpower a witness with superior vocabulary or syntax, i.e., the lawyer tries to get the witness confused, mistaken, or turned around by using words or forms of questions above the intellectual ken of the witness. Frequently, this occurs with lay witnesses who by reason of age, infirmity, or lack of education are easily confused or misled. What occurs if unprotected is the witness is made to look incredible, confused, or unsure of an issue. A classic example of this improper exposition of verbal power is to take advantage of an uneducated witness' inability to pronounce a technical term or phrase. Another egregious example is exposing a witness' foreign accent, uneducated phraseology, or inarticulate expression to ridicule. Because a witness cannot eloquently describe a painful memory does not mean it will be ignored or discounted by the jury.

Most lawyers commit this sin by sheer force of habit. Lawyers talk legalese. Most jurors and witnesses do not. There are also offenders who are just plain arrogant and condescending to everyone including witnesses. They may be totally ignorant of the negative effect they create in court. Such examiners usually enjoy showing off skill they never honed. They relish a "battle of wits" even if the struggle is one sided. One good exception to this ban on semantic jousting is when the witness tries to inject some intellectually dishonest word play to avoid answering. Then they may become fair game for a lawyer's rapier wit and word wisdom.

5. ZERO BASIS: MISREPRESENTING FACTS/OPINIONS, INTRODUCING UNPROVEN, IRRELEVANT FACTS OR INNUENDO, AND "ASPERSING"

One of the worst predicaments for any trial lawyer is to be accused and found guilty of "misrepresenting the facts." This is particularly unflattering when the witness being cross-examined makes this point obvious in front of the jury and/or the trial judge.

> . . . we have gone upon the presumption that the cross-examiner's art would be used to further his client's cause by all fair and legitimate means, not by misrepresentation, insinuation, or by knowingly putting a witness in a false light . . . These methods doubtless succeed at times, but he who practices them acquires the reputation, with astounding rapidity, of being "smart," and finds himself discredited not only with the court, but in some almost unaccountable way with the very juries before whom he appears. Let him once get the reputation of being "unfair" among the habitués of the court house, and his usefulness to clients as a trial lawyer is gone forever. Honesty is the best policy quite as much with the advocate as any other walk of life. Wellman, supra, at p. 197

This is the sin of putting the witness in a "false light." It is immoral and unethical to knowingly misrepresent facts to a tribunal. RPC 3.3 (a). It is also unethical to make a false statement of material fact "to a third person." RPC 4.1 (a)(1). A lawyer should never try to trick a witness by misquoting, misrepresenting, or taking prior testimony out of context to cause a false impression to or about the witness. No advocate should "spin" truth so as to distort or mislead. To play such perverted games with witnesses is to ignore our role as seekers of the truth.

Another analogous evil is to ask a question with no good faith basis. That is, a question which insinuates a fact which does not exist and about which there is no good faith basis to assume its existence. Just as attorneys can be disciplined for "aspersing" character or reputation of a witness when the aspersion is irrelevant, see section III above, an attorney also faces sanctions for making false accusations or alluding "to any matter that the lawyer does not reasonably believe is relevant or . . . admissible evidence." RPC 3.4(b).

6. INTERRUPTING, ILLEGAL BLOCKING, AND EXSCINDING

> "A lawyer shall . . . treat with courtesy and consideration all persons involved in the legal process."
> RPC 3.2
> ". . .shall not: (a) unlawfully obstruct another party's access to evidence. . .."
> RPC 3.4 (a)
> ". . . shall not (f) request a person other than a client to refrain from voluntarily giving relevant information to another party unless: (1) the person is a relative or employee or other agent of a client: and (2) the lawyer reasonably believes that the person's interests will not be adversely affected by refraining from giving such information."
> RPC 3.4 (f)
> "A lawyer shall not: (c) engage in conduct intended to disrupt a tribunal."
> RPC 3.5

To interrupt the relevant response of a witness is not "bad form" because it is rude it is also potentially unethical as being discourteous, obstructing access to evidence, forcing a witness to refrain from testifying, and a disruption of the fact finding process of the tribunal. If the witness is giving an answer which is a fair response to the question posed, trial counsel should preferably await the complete answer and then apply for any irrelevant testimony to be stricken from the trial record by the judge and a curative instruction given to the jury to disregard the nonresponsive and/or improper answer given by the witness.

There are obvious situations which require the cross-examiner to be alert and to stop any discussion by the witness that is inadmissible and/or so prejudicial that a curative instruction would be useless. An example is when a hostile witness has been told by the judge, out of the presence of the jury, to refrain from mentioning a prejudicial fact because it has been deemed inadmissible; yet the witness spitefully tries to inject the excluded fact into an answer. In that situation, the trial court will likely agree and side with the cross-examiner's interruption.

Exscinding is a tactic some use to try to ignore and erase a bad answer to a bad query. If the answer was fairly responsive, then the lawyer's statement "I did not ask for that" is usually followed by the court's admonition "The witness did answer you" or "Yes you did . . ., you opened the door."

7. SPITEFUL OR SHIFTLESS CONDUCT, SUCH AS DELAYING, BADGERING, AND BURDENSOMENESS

Some measure of embarrassment, delay, and burden is inherent in litigation. However, when an advocate lacks a substantial purpose of conduct having those consequences, a disciplinary offense occurs (see 110). A ruling of a tribunal officer or a standing rule may impose specific time limitations within which prescribed action must be taken; a lawyer ordinarily must comply with them (see 105). For example, seeking delay in a trial date in order to gather additional relevant evidence is nonfrivolous. On the other hand, delaying a trial solely to permit a client to extract a nuisance-value settlement is an improper purpose. In seeking delay, a lawyer must assert positions only if nonfrivolous under 110(1), must avoid misstating facts (120(1)(b)) or using evidence known to be false (120(3)), and must comply with court rules and orders (see 105). Restatement of Law Third—The Law Governing Lawyers (2002) American Law Institute, Chapter 7.

To be guilty of "burdening, delaying or badgering" is to commit the cardinal sin of this century. To intentionally or for no legitimate purpose cause undue delay or demand unnecessary effort on the part of a witness during cross-examination is viewed by many currently sitting trial judges as the ultimate insult to the court and jurors. It is a trespass of time. It is the tort of wasting a valuable court resource—time. To "waste time" during cross-examination—by stalling or delaying the questioning of the witness, by taking excessive amounts of time-outs to get prepared or to proceed, by plodding over and over the same testimony—is to run the risk of offending the court's timetable. Besides transgressing upon the jury's attention span, the prodigal trial lawyer who frivols away the opportunity to ask relevant questions "falls from grace" in a public way when the trial judge rebukes: "let's move along counselor, . . . that question has already been asked and answered."

One of the most unprofessional displays of the "burdensome" cross-examination is to unnecessarily repeat and repeat the same question or variation thereof to a witness who has already honestly answered the inquiry. This is the classic "badgering" of a witness. For the lawyer to ignore that the answer has been given, that the witness will not change the answer despite reasonable opportunity, and that the judge's patience has worn thin is to invite public ridicule and sanction.

THE MORAL DILEMMA OF CROSSING THE TRUTHFUL WITNESS

For our brethren of the criminal trial bar, there are many written authorities on cross-examination, especially the cross-examination of the truthful witness. While the discussions of cross-examining a truthful witness found in a judicial dicta and academic scholarship address the criminal-defense counsel, this issue is of obvious relevance to civil litigation as well. See, e.g., A. Amsterdam, Trial Manual for the Defense of Criminal Cases 370 (5th ed. 1988); M. Freedman, Understanding Legal Ethics, ch. 8 (1990); Subin, The Criminal Lawyer's "Different Mission": Reflection on the "Right" to Present a False Case, 1 Geo. J. Leg. Ethics 125 (1987); Burger, Standards of Conduct for Prosecution and Defense Personnel: A Judge's Viewpoint, 5 Am. Crim. L.Q. 11, 14 (1966) (the rationale this is merely to "test truth of prosecution's case").

The often-cited statement in a concurring opinion of Justice White supports the general view that "a lawyer's belief or knowledge that the witness is telling the truth does not preclude cross-examination, but should, if possible, be taken into consideration by counsel in conducting the cross-examination." See *United States v. Wade*, 388 U.S. 218, 257–58, 87 S.Ct. 1926, 1947–1948, 18 L.Ed.2d 1149 (1967). Cf. ABA Standards for Criminal Justice, Defense Function Standards 4-7.6(b) (2d ed. 1982); id. (3d ed. 1991) (same except for deletion of "but" clause); contra, e.g., ABA Standards, supra., Standard 7.6 (1971) (lawyer "should not misuse the power of cross-examination or impeachment by employing it to discredit or undermine a witness if he knows the witness is testifying truthfully"). Although there is very little authority discussing the issue in the context of civil litigation, the Comment to The Restatement of Law of Lawyers states the prevailing norm to be the same as for the criminal trial lawyer. But see Selinger, The "Law" on Lawyer Efforts to Discredit Truthful Testimony, 46 Okla. L. Rev. 99 (1993) (disagreeing with position stated in earlier draft Comment). Restatement of Law Third—The Law Governing Lawyers, Chapter 7, ALI, 2002.

CAVEAT: SOME EXAMPLES NOT TO FOLLOW AS ROLE MODELS

From the Annotated ABA Model Rules of Professional Conduct and from various state disciplinary proceedings and ethics opinions, there are some outrageous examples of lawyers who went "over the edge" during cross-examination and in trial. Annotated Model Rules of Professional Conduct, ABA 1999; also Thomas Fleming, "Propriety and prejudicial effect of counsel's negative characterization or description of witness during summation of criminal trial—modern cases," 88 ALR 4th 209

Some examples of abusive treatment to opposing party, violating RPC 4.4, are: *In re Black*, 941 P.2d 1380 (Kan. 1997) (the trial lawyer criticized opposing party for wearing military uniform to pretrial hearing, calling him a disgrace to the uniform and asserting that he [the lawyer] would have superior rank and could cause opponent to stand at attention and remain mute; conduct violates Rule 4.4); *In re Golden*, 496 S.E. 2d 619, 623 (S.C. 1998) (lawyer in domestic relations matter called client's wife a "mean-spirited vicious witch: and stated he would like "to be locked in a room naked with [her] and a sharp knife"); *Louisiana State Bar Ass'n v. Harrington*, 585 So.2d 514 (La. 1990) (rejecting lawyer's defense that when he bullied opposing parties and threatened them with police action he was merely being "abrasive"); *In re Bechhold*, 771 P.2d 562 (Mont. 1988) (lawyer rudely contacted claims company employee 7 or 8 times per day for several days about denial of client's claim; his "method of inquiry served only to embarrass and burden" employee). Annotated Model Rules of Professional Conduct, ABA 1999.

Unethical conduct towards a witness can also implicate Rule 4.4: *In re Golden*, 496 S.E.2d 619 (S.C. 1998) (lawyer demonstrated deposition conduct that was sarcastic, malicious, combative, and intimidating, and that had no purpose other than to embarrass, delay, or burden third person); *Florida Bar v. Schaub*, 618 So.2d 202 (Fla. 1993) (prosecutor accused defendant's psychiatric expert of charging $600 per hour when he knew witness charged $150 per hour, repeatedly insulted him on the stand, and ignored judge's rulings on defense objections); Pa. Barr Ass'n Comm. on Legal Ethics and Professional Responsibility, Op. 93-135 (1993) (lawyer seeking to impeach witness may not accept his expert's offer to examine witness's statutorily confidential psychiatric records, which happened to be maintained at expert's institution); cf. *Valassis v. Samelson*, 143 F.R.D. 118 (E.D. Mich. 1992) (noting that Rule 4.4 prevents lawyers from inquiring about privileged matters). Annotated Model Rules of Professional Conduct, ABA 1999.

A SAMPLING OF SANCTIONS FOR X-TREME CROSS

Cases where lawyers were sanctioned for cross-examination abuses tend to be instances of extreme harassment although the "X" factor may be a relative matter of the court's discretion. Some of the optional sanctions illustrating the exercise of the power of a trial judge to protect a witness against harassment, pursuant to Fed. R. Evid. 611(a) ("The court shall exercise reasonable control over the mode and order of interrogating witnesses and presenting evidence so as to . . . (3) protect witnesses from harassment or undue embarrassment") include: *Pool v. Superior Court*, 677 P.2d 261 (Ariz. 1984) (prosecutor's abusive, argumentative, harassing cross-exam of accused warrants a mistrial); *In re Lichtenstein*, 637 N.E.2d 1258 (Ill. App. Ct. 1994) (criminal contempt for lawyer of wife to attempt to recreate client's version of events by having husband leave witness stand and put on jacket and then yanking on hood of jacket from behind); *Commonwealth v. Rooney*, 313 N.E.2d 105 (Mass. 1974) (witness has right to be treated fairly by counsel, and judge has power and duty to compel fair and reasonable treatment) . . . *Chapman & Cole v. Itel Container Int'l B.V.*, 116 F.R.D. 550, 557–58 (S.D. Tex. 1987), cert. denied, 493 U.S. 872, 110 S.Ct. 201, 107 L.Ed.2d 155 (1989) (fee-shifting sanction against lawyer for discovery abuse by groundless charges against dep witnesses in attempt to intimidate). On professional discipline, see, e.g., *In re Crumpacker*, 383 N.E.2d 36, 49 (Ind. 1978), cert. denied, 444 U.S. 979, 100 S.Ct. 481, 62 L.Ed.2d 406 (1979), appeal dism'd, 470 U.S. 1074, 105 S.Ct. 1829, 85 L.Ed.2d 130 (1985); *State v. Phelps*, 598 P.2d 180 (Kan. 1979), cert. denied, 444 U.S. 1045, 100 S.Ct. 732, 62 L.Ed.2d 731 (1980) (disbarment for badgering witnesses, among several offenses, in personal-vendetta litigation against court reporter); *In re Williams*, 414 N.W.2d 394 (Minn. 1987), appeal dism'd, 485 U.S. 950, 108 S.Ct. 1207, 99 L.Ed.2d 409 (1988) (6 months' suspension for conduct prejudicial to administration of justice in calculated attempts to intimidate/demean witnesses); *In re Vencenti*, 554 A.2d 470 (N.J. 1989) (challenging witness to fight; using loud, abusive, profane language toward witnesses) . . . *Bull v. McCuskey*, 615 P.2d 957 (Nev. 1980) (plaintiff's lawyer violated "offensive personalities" prohibition in Nevada lawyer's oath by denigrating comments about physician defendant in medical-malpractice action). Annotated Model Rules of Professional Conduct, ABA 1999.

Note the above cases reached the "published" stage. Remember, in addition to referring the matter to an ethics panel, there are an infinite number of sanctions to be imposed, subject only to the judge's imagination, when an attorney commits an ethical/professional breach of conduct during cross-exam. From raised eyebrow to a fine, from a caustic censure to the ultimate sanction of case dismissal, the extent of the penalty is irrelevant. Our professional honor must be preserved, from initial retainer throughout litigation, including, but not limited to, trial and the crucible of cross-examination.

DO THE MEANS JUSTIFY THE END?

As with any ethical or moral issue, trial lawyers must be sensitive to and cautious about "any appearance" of impropriety. Cross-examination is a dangerous ethical and emotional arena because it is one of the times during trial when the trial attorney finds there is "no safety net." Despite all the pretrial discovery, depositions, and prior statements from witnesses, the attorney cannot prepare the witness and control the desired answer. Moreover, the attorney must be prepared for the unexpected answer, no matter how well prepared and armed with prior statements/testimony. The anxiety levels and adrenalin of both the interrogator and witness are usually highest during cross. It is during the crucial cross of a key witness that any trial lawyer becomes vulnerable to an emotional virus that can adversely affect professional behavior. Feelings can get us hurt. Letting a natural feeling of anger or fear get the better of our professional demeanor and style can result in an unprofessional interaction with the cause of our emotional distress, to wit, the witness being crossed.

Sometimes, the competitive edge is too sharp. Sometimes, trial lawyers look at cross-examination as the end rather than a means to an end. Our overall purpose should be to obtain a just result for our plaintiff client. To do so, we need not mistreat witnesses. The litigation moral and flip-side to the question "what does anyone gain if they inherit the world but lose their soul?" is "what hast thou trial lawyer gained if the adverse witness is demolished upon thy cross, but the client loses the case?"

Witnesses can be belligerent, deceptive, taunting, and irritating. Whatever the circumstances, however emotionally charged or drained, the trial lawyer needs to stay on course during cross-examination so avoid crashing upon an ethical sandbar. Avoiding the seven SLEASIeS shoals during cross-examination will hopefully help in the overall presentation but will protect the trial lawyer from an ethical embarrassment. The above recommendations may not help win any case, but the avoidance of sin, or the "near occasion" of these seven evil spirits, will help prevent the trial lawyer from a "fall from grace"—at least in the eyes of the trial judge—during cross-examination.

CROSS-EXAMINATION: JMO: SO, KO, TKO, or RKO (Just My Opinion: Sit Out, Knock Out, Technical Knock Out, or Rebuttal KO) (Excerpt from AAJ Trial Notebook, by Tom Vesper)

I. JMO (JUST MY OPINION):

Cross has four General Strategic Approaches or Combos thereof:

1. SO (the Safety Option or Sit Out or Shut Out)—ask safe questions or none at all
2. KO (Knock Out) Cross ' Short, effective—destructive and/or constructive
3. TKO (Technical Knock Out) Cross ' Longer but methodical—destroy/affirm
4. PDR-KO Cross (Pin Down for Rebuttal + KO) + Set up for rebuttal witness

II. PHYSICAL DYNAMICS OF CROSS EXAMINATION

1. Make Eye Contact With Witness
2. Physical Presence/Closeness to Witness
3. Remember "Pacing"
4. Remember "Mirroring"

III. THREE PURPOSES FOR CROSS:

1. Destruction
2. Affirmation
3. Clarification and Set Up for Rebuttal or Summation

IV. THE 10 BASIC TACTICS FOR CROSS EXAMINATION CONTROL[1]

1. One Fact . . .. One Question
2. Repeat the Question . . .. "Broken Record". . ."Let 'Em Run"
3. Throw Out Trash . . ... And Repeat the Question
4. State the Opposite
5. That's a "Yes"? or Are you saying "No"?
6. Include Answer in Question

---

[1] These cross-examination "Basics" were developed by the authors in trial, successfully used in trials, then further refined in workshops at the ATLA (now AAJ) Cross Examination Colleges.

7. "Call Your Shots" . . . Whenever you change subject announce your change for the Jury's sake

8. Summarize and use "The Scoptur Scoop"

9. Use Exhibits: (Show the Witness Some Conclusive Evidence/Exhibit of One Fact)

10. Physical Gestures and/or Pointing . . . (Not to be used until you've "earned the right")

NOTE: Judicial Intervention: Try not to ask for help from the trial judge.

THE FIVE CROSS EXAMINATION QUESTIONS OF DEFENSE EXPERTS

By: Jim Perdue and Tom Vesper

1. Mr. Expert, would you agree any expert who is giving professional opinions about [any subject] should be unbiased, objective, and not attempt to be advocate for either side?

2. Would you agree to the extent a professional expert expresses any opinions showing a bias or failure to be objective those opinions should be discounted?

3. Would you agree that the more pertinent information the doctor/expert has the greater the likelihood that his medical/expert opinions will be accurate?

4. Do you believe that where there is a conflict of medical/professional expert opinions between doctors/experts of equal qualifications, the doctor/expert who has the benefit of greater information is more trustworthy?

5. Would you concede an expert opinion based on limited, single exam/inspection and limited medical/fact history has a greater opportunity for error than an opinion by expert familiar with details of [patient's treatment or whatever event is in question] and who has followed the [patient or factual dispute] over the course of time?

FOUR SAFE AREAS OF QUESTIONING FOR THE "SOFT CROSS"

"If the witness is harmless or ineffective, the cross-examination merely creates the opportunity for that witness to salvage his or her testimony . . . . (So) just say no to cross-exam." Mark Kosieradzki, "The Impressive Cross-examination," TRIAL magazine, Mar 2009, p. 45.

"On the other hand, when you really can't do much with a witness who has testified well for your opponent, . . . Your only option is to choose safe questions—those that you know will elicit answers that can do no damage . . .." Mark Kosieradzki, supra, at p. 45.

Mark's four suggested areas for the "Safe Cross" are:

1. COMMON SENSE. Fact/opinion which if denied contradict common sense.
2. UNDENIABLE PROOF: Fact/opinion of which you have conclusive proof.
3. LOGICAL FOLLOW UP: Fact/opinion logically implied by the witness.
4. PRIOR STATEMENT: Fact/opinion expressed before by the witness.

Some witnesses are unimpeachable. These can hurt you AGAIN and AGAIN on cross. And in the wise advice of my friend "The Koz"—"If it can hurt you, DON'T DO IT!"

CONCLUSION: CORRAGIO!!

Your client is your last chance to rebut a DME/IME. If plaintiff is credible, if prior work, family life, community/social activities, and overall good character are established early in trial, the DME's "non" findings/opinions will wipe away like hot breath on a cold mirror. A life speaks louder in rebuttal than "subjective v. objective findings," leg raises, MRI, EMG, CT Scans, and "IMEs." Real people don't give up life's joys and dignities to fool a jury and extort "blood money."

A pair of real people—a real doctor and a real victim—living with and treating real injuries will always beat a full house of DME/IME's. Be confident in that fact and in yourself . . . and . . . DON'T BE AFRAID TO CROSS-EXAMINE or REBUT THE IME! **GUNG HO!**

piacevole e facile lo fa sul condimento per l'insalata

(nice and easy does it on the salad dressing)

Chapter 10. DOLCE (Sweets/Desserts)

PART A. ARLENE'S RECIPES

Dolci per la mia dolce moglie

My wife Arlene was a great inspiration for this cookbook and was a great help in assisting Tom and me. We asked if she would contribute to our cookbook, and she agreed to provide recipes for the desserts course, "DOLCE."

Arlene has a real passion for cooking and baking and gets much pleasure watching friends and family enjoying her meals and baked goods. She has earned various awards for her baking at the New Jersey State Fair and other competitions she has participated in. She also taught cooking classes and Adult Education Classes in the evenings at various local high schools. Her classes were very popular and her adult students particularly enjoyed eating the food that was prepared in each class.

We have been married for 43 years and work very well together in the kitchen (as long as I remember that she is the "kitchen boss." My wife has always cooked enough food for three or four extra people and when I ask who is coming for dinner, her answer is always the same—"don't worry about it; we will eat the leftovers this week." However, someone usually stops by and leaves with food. When my children come over for a visit, the first thing they do is look in our refrigerator and then say "hello." If they find something they like, they usually eat it or take it home.

Bon Appetito! Arlene

ARLENE VESPER

DOM & ARLENE

THE VESPERS' TRIAL COOKBOOK

RASPBERRY LEMON TIRAMISU

BOCCONCINI: *Tiramisu* means "pick or lift me up." It is a popular coffee-flavored Italian dessert made of ladyfingers *Savoiardi* (Italian ladyfingers) dipped in coffee, layered with whipped mixture of egg yolks, egg whites, sugar and mascarpone cheese, and flavored with cocoa. Sometimes, strawberries are added to the ingredients of the cake. The recipe has been adapted into many varieties of puddings, cakes, etc. Creation of this wonderful dessert is disputed; but both challengers for the title are from Venice—Carminantonio Iannaccone on 24 December 1969, while he was head chef at Treviso, near Venice vs. Roberto Linguanotto, a baker and his apprentice, Francesca Valori, in Treviso in 1967.

INGREDIENTS (Serves 8 to 10):

Lemon Syrup

¼ cup Fresh Lemon Juice

¼ cup Water

1/3 cup Sugar

DIRECTIONS:

In a small saucepan, combine above ingredients over medium heat.

Bring to a boil, reduce heat, simmer for 2 minutes; stir occasionally until sugar dissolves.

Take pan off heat and let syrup cool.

Tirmsu

1 quart heavy whipping cream

5 Tbsp sugar (divided)

½ cup Raspberry Liquor (I like to use Chambord Liqueur)

48 hard ladyfinger cookies

½ cup Sliced almonds, lightly toasted (To toast nuts, use dry saucepan or skillet and toast until light brown)

1 Lemon, zested

1 pint Fresh raspberries for garnish (optional)

8 oz. Mascarpone cheese

DOLCE

8 oz. light Cream cheese

DIRECTIONS:

Whip heavy cream in large bowl until thick. Add 2 Tbsp of sugar and continue to whip until cream holds soft peaks.

In another bowl, cream together the mascarpone and light cream cheese with the remaining 3 tsps of the sugar until blended.

Mix ½ of the heavy cream into the mascarpone and cream cheese mixture using a rubber spatula, using under-over strokes until lightened.

Fold in the remaining heavy cream. Set Aside.

FINAL PREPARATION:

Use a 13x9x2" glass baking dish.

Place Liqueur in a small shallow bowl. Dip 16 ladyfingers into liqueur and line the bottom of a 13" x 9" x 2" pan. Spoon the remaining Liqueur over the ladyfingers.

Spread 1/3 of the mascarpone mixture over ladyfingers.

Place the lemon syrup in a small shallow bowl. Dip 16 ladyfingers into the lemon syrup and place on top of the mascarpone.

Spread another 1/3 of the mascarpone mixture over second layer of ladyfingers.

Dip remaining ladyfingers in remaining lemon syrup and place on top of mascarpone.

Spoon remaining lemon syrup over dipped ladyfingers.

Spread the remaining mascarpone over the third layer of ladyfingers.

You now have 3 layers of ladyfingers with the mascarpone mixture between each layer.

Garnish top with lemon zest, raspberries, and toasted almonds.

Cover with aluminum foil and refrigerate overnight. Remove the Tiramisu from refrigerator 1 hour before serving.

The Vespers' Trial Cookbook

ZUCATTA CAKE

BOCCONCINI: Zuccotto ("little pumpkin") is a semi-frozen, chilled dessert from Florence made with brandy, cake, and ice cream. It can be frozen and then thawed before serving. Traditionally it is made in a special pumpkin-shaped mold; Cuz Thomas says it was inspired by the dome of Firenze's Duomo (cathedral); other history majors say its shape resembles a cardinal's skullcap or *zucchetto*.

INGREDIENTS (Serves 8 to 10):

2 large Sara Lee® Frozen Butter Pound Cakes

32 oz. Heavy whipping cream

½ blueberries, washed and dried

1 pint Washed and sliced strawberries

3 Bananas, sliced and drizzled with 1Tbsp lemon juice

½ pint Fresh raspberries, optional

1 (12 oz.) pkg Semi-sweet chocolate chips, separated

2 Tbsp Crisco

2 small pkgs Vanilla instant pudding

½ tsp Almond extract

EQUIPMENT:

10 to 12 cup stainless steel mixing bowl

Parchment paper

Stand or hand mixer

Microwave safe bowl for melting chocolate chips

DIRECTIONS:

Turn stainless bowl upside down on top of a sheet of parchment paper. Draw a circle around bowl and cut out. Make 2 circles.

Cut pound cakes into ¼" slices cover and set aside.

Place one parchment circle in bottom of stainless steel bowl.

Using slices of pound cake, mold around the bowl, filling in any bare spaces with pieces of cake, fitting them in tightly. Set aside some slices of cake for the top of bowl.

Put heavy cream, bowl, and beaters in freezer for 10 minutes to get cold. Take out of freezer; pour the 32 oz. of cream in bowl. Add the 2 pkgs. of instant pudding mix.

Beat on slow speed until mixed, increasing speed until mixture is whipped thoroughly.

Add the strawberries, blueberries, banana slices, and $1/4$ cup of the semi-sweet chocolate chips, folding them lightly as to not deflate the whipped cream.

Pour mixture into the cake-lined bowl, filling to top of cake slices. Use remaining slices of pound cake to cover the top of cake, again filling in any bare spaces with cake.

Place a second sheet of parchment paper on top of cake. Place a heavy skillet or dish on top of the parchment paper to press down contents. Place bowl in freezer overnight.

DAY OF SERVING: Melt the rest of the chocolate chips with the Crisco in a microwave safe bowl. Use 50% power in 30-second intervals, stirring after each interval until chips are melted.

Remove cake from freezer and remove cake from bowl. Place frozen cake on metal rack over cookie sheet.

Pour the melted chocolate over the cake, working quickly to spread the chocolate all over the cake, as the chocolate will harden very quickly. Fill in any bare spaces with the melted chocolate using a metal spatula. Use raspberries around the bottom of cake for decorations, or decorate, as you like.

Refrigerate until ½ hour before serving so that the chocolate does not break when cut. Enjoy!

The Vespers' Trial Cookbook

AMARETTO RICE PUDDING

<u>INGREDIENTS</u> (Serves 8 to 10):

1 cup Raisins

½ cup Amaretto liqueur

½ cup Warm water

7 cups Whole Milk

1 cup Sugar

¾ cup Uncooked long grain rice

1 ½ tsps Vanilla Extract

4 Large eggs

1 cup Heavy whipping cream or can substitute Half N Half

Cinnamon

<u>DIRECTIONS</u>:

Combine raisins, liqueur, and warm water. Set aside to plump the raisins.

Combine milk, sugar, rice, and vanilla into a heavy saucepan.

Heat just under boiling, on medium heat, stirring frequently. Do not boil.

Cook for 45 minutes or until taste tested to be done and starts to thicken slightly.

Beat 4 eggs with the cream by hand. Add 1 ladle of hot rice mixture, stirring slowly, into the eggs.

Pour this back into rice mixture; stir constantly until mixture thickens, about 5 minutes. It will have the consistency of potato soup. Mixture thickens more overnight.

Drain raisins and fold them into the hot rice mixture. Pour into serving bowl. Cover with plastic wrap, letting wrap touch the hot pudding to avoid a skin forming. Let cool until warm but not hot, and refrigerate overnight.

Before serving, sprinkle lightly cinnamon on top. Refrigerate leftovers.

<u>BOCCONCINI</u>: AMARETTO v. AMARETTI v. AMARO v. AMMARONE: Amaretto is diminutive of Italian *Amaro* ("bitter"); this herbal mix does have a distinctively bitter flavor from the *mandorla amara,* bitter almond, drupe

kernel, or apricots. Not to worry; its bitterness is not unpalatable or toxic, and its flavor is enhanced by sweeteners, and even sweet almonds are put into final products. Amaretto is not to be confused with the Amaretti cookies, the Italian almond-flavored cookies. Amaro (not the Philadelphia Phillies GM), which is a different Italian liqueur that, while also sweetened, has an even stronger bitter flavor of herbs; its bitter-sweet, syrupy flavor is produced by macerating herbs, roots, flowers, bark, and/or citrus peels in alcohol, mixing the filtrate with sugar syrup, and allowing the mixture to age in casks or bottles. Amarone, a rich dry red wine from Valpolicella, a wine zone in province of Verona, Italy, east of Lake Garda.

<u>VESPER FAMILIA</u>: Even if you and/or your family do not like "puddings," this dish is worth your trying to see it is **NOT "YOUR AVERAGE PUDDING"** or dessert.

The Vespers' Trial Cookbook

AMARETTO APRICOT OATMEAL CHEWS

INGREDIENTS (Makes about 55 cookies):

1 cup All-purpose flour

1 tsp Baking soda

1 cup Butter or margarine

¾ cup Packed brown sugar

1 tsp Amaretto liqueur

½ cup Granulated sugar

2 ½ cups Regular or rolled oats

1 cup Snipped apricots

½ cup Finely chopped almonds

For The Glaze:

2 cups Sifted powdered sugar

2 or 3 Tbsp Amaretto liqueur

DIRECTIONS:

Stir together flour and baking soda and set aside.

In a large mixer bowl, beat butter or margarine until softened.

Add brown sugar and granulated sugar and beat until fluffy.

Add egg and 1 Tbsp of Amaretto and beat well.

Add flour mixture and beat until well mixed.

Stir in oats, apricots, and almonds.

Drop, by rounded tsps, onto an ungreased cookie sheet.

Bake in 375° F oven for 8-10 minutes or until done.

Cool on cookie sheet for 1 minute, then remove and set aside and cool thoroughly.

Stir together powdered sugar and enough of the remaining Amaretto liqueur to make an icing of drizzling consistency.

Drizzle over cooled cookies and allow to dry.

BOCCONCINI: Apricots are Armenian? I couldn't believe it!? But according to my Cuz Dom, the scientific name of this species of fruit, plum or prune is *Mala armeniaca* or "Armenian apple." "Apricot" came from a tree mentioned by Ancient Roman Pliny for these apples (mala); it also comes from *praecocia*, "cooked or ripened beforehand." And if you cook Arlene's cookies "beforehand," you will be a big hit in any orchard!

The Vespers' Trial Cookbook

JEWISH APPLE CAKE

This dessert is a kind of dense cake made with apples and sold mostly in Pennsylvania. It has few known connections to Jewish cuisine; most sources think this cake is actually a Pennsylvania Dutch culinary treat erroneously attributed to Jews because it seemed "old world." It may also be considered Jewish because it contains no dairy, and it may therefore be eaten with meals which contain meat, according to Jewish laws of kashrut. My family and friends enjoy this cake, and I bake the cake frequently. It is a great way to make use of apples other than pies.

INGREDIENTS (Serves 8 to 10):

5 or 6 Apples, peeled, cored, and sliced

2 tsp Sugar

2 tsp Cinnamon

3 cups Flour

2 cups Sugar

¼ tsp Salt

3 tsp Baking powder

1 cup Oil

4 Eggs

½ cup Orange juice or apple juice

2½ tsp Vanilla

DIRECTIONS:

In large bowl, mix apples with 2 tsp of sugar, and 2 tsp of cinnamon until all ingredients are well mixed, set aside.

Mix flour, salt, and baking powder, set aside.

In large bowl, mix eggs and sugar and slowly add oil.

Add ½ cup orange juice and all vanilla and continue to mix to consistency of cake batter.

In greased 10" tube pan, add half the batter and half of the apple mixture well drained.

Repeat with the remaining half of batter and remaining half of apple mixture.

Bake at 350° F. If using a dark tube pan bake at 325° F. The cake usually bakes about 75 to 90 minutes or until a toothpick inserted in center of cake comes out clean. Let cool. Remove from cake pan carefully.

Dom Vesper & Tom Vesper at Ellis Island

PART B. TOM'S TRIAL TIPS: SUMMATION

THE MAGIC OF STORYTELLING IN TRIAL: WITH ALL OUR TECHNOLOGY, THE KEY IS STILL PEOPLE

I. INTRODUCTION

Long before I met my first jury consultant, and years before I first knew about focus groups, jury demographics, mock/shadow juries, Power Point, or CGI, I knew my Italian family—my mother, father, aunts, uncles, cousins—had unlimited, irrepressible amounts of insight and understanding about people.

They each had accumulated in their collective lifetimes an inexhaustible, unfathomable wealth of stories stuffed with lessons and folk wisdom. Before I enrolled in any NCA College, OJB (Overcoming Jury Bias) Seminars, or AAJ (then ATLA) Jury Workshops, and even prior to my first jury trial, I tried to always rehearse or "test" my openings and closings in front of the toughest jury I knew—my own family. Whether I asked for their input or not, they would always tell me whether or not my case selection, legal logic, or circumstantial evidence made no sense; always demand I explain those things that confused them; unmercifully criticize me when my words/phrases sounded "like'a Bigga Shot." Through all of my family's self-started "support" and sage skepticism, one clear message stays in my trial bag of memories. No matter who I represented, no matter the damages, and no matter the facts, the overriding concern of my family was always: "tell me more about the kind of person Mr./Mrs. (Blank) is/was."

Today's liability defense strategy is one of finding "gaps," driving wedges into plaintiff's cases, and trashing the injured plaintiff. The "gaps" can be manufactured, imagined, or real defects in the facts about liability, causation, or damages. The defense will attack the credibility, character, and complaints of almost all plaintiffs. As Rick Friedman calls the "Polarization" of cases: the character of the plaintiff is always assailed by defense medical examiners who question the plaintiff's "secondary gain," exaggerated/magnified symptomatology, or motive to malinger. The credibility of the plaintiff's version of the "traumatic event" is attacked whenever prior inconsistent statements in police reports, hospital or medical histories, or depositions can be found or created. Our clients' complaints are treated with disdain and cynicism by defense, who label almost all plaintiff-reported symptoms "subjective" and therefore frivolous and unworthy of any compensation other than "nuisance value." Even catastrophic and disabling injuries are "independently" evaluated as having little or no "permanency."

Throughout personal injury litigation and trials, the one true constant remains despite an escalating amount of technological and digital assistance available to trial lawyers and courts for adjudicating personal injury and wrongful death claims: the dignity of the individual plaintiff. That is, the kind of person plaintiff was and the kind of person plaintiff has become as a result of injury or loss of a loved one. Whatever technological wizardry or magic we use today for litigation support, discovery, or trial presentation, we should never lose sight of the simple fact that it is the injured, the deceased, and the survivors of the wrongful death victim who are the keys to the case and also the center of the defense's attack and the main targets of opportunity for our adversaries. They either hold "the magic" for themselves or the defense.

II. VIDEOTAPING AND VIDEOCONFERENCING FOR DEPOSITIONS AND TRIAL

Videotaping of experts in advance of trial and preserving their testimony "in the can" has proliferated. Court rooms and lawyers' offices today are equipped for video-conferencing. Deps of far-away witnesses can be televised "live and in color" into conference rooms with lawyers doing remote control interrogations. Now, any out-of-state witness can be presented to juries by the use of videoconferencing. All of these new communication developments may save stress, delay, and perhaps even the costs and time of travel. But in order to use them effectively, we still must "reach out and touch" the jurors and persuade them of the justness of our client's cause.

Whether it is a de bene esse dep of a dying plaintiff, or a de bene esse videotaped dep, or live video-conference of a treating or examining physician who will be otherwise unavailable for travel to trial, I urge you to have some tangible exhibit which can anchor that individual witness' "virtual" testimony for the jury. Whether it is a photograph, a chart, an anatomical model, or orthotic device, the "anchor" should make the witness' testimony come alive for the jury during your summation. These trial anchors will make the videotaped, televised, or telephonic witness more than just a talking head on a TV screen or a far off voice on a conference phone.

Anchoring is a storytelling and communicating technique. That is, you can get the jury to associate a certain part of the court room, or a particular exhibit, with a recurring theme or issue in the case. If you have one chart that outlines the economic damages, you should use that one chart every time you talk about those elements of damage. As an example of an outstanding and unforgettable visual exhibit in a death case, Murray Ogborn "anchored" the testimony of a little girl with a single red rose which the child brought to court and placed upon the plaintiff's counsel table in the presence of the jury.

ANECDOTE 1: Sound Can Be An Anchor

The first time I ever used "teleconferencing" was in a jury trial in 1985 for a woman who had slipped on the contents of a broken bottle of Bubble Up in an Acme supermarket. After the defense doctor testified and the defense rested early Friday morning, I requested the trial judge allow me a single rebuttal witness on one "surprise" opinion given by the defense "IME" in his cross examination. The defense doctor had testified on direct that my client's herniated disc was really not herniated but rather was a "bulging disc," and it was his Board-certified orthopedic opinion that as time went on and she aged, the vertebrae in her spine would actually "settle" like a new house or pile of bricks. Therefore, he concluded her injured spine and daily pain would subside. In order to rebut this "junk" prognosis, I requested the right to recall the treating doctor and rebut the defense doctor's medical theory of "spinal structural settlement." The trial judge agreed; however, due to the treating doctor's hospital schedule, he was unavailable to personally appear in court until Monday of following week. But to my surprise, the treating doctor offered a very practical solution: he was available telephonically that very morning. The judge immediately recognized the "judicial economy" of the doc's idea; and since the judge had a conference phone available on his desk, with an extension cord that reached his court room (no one I knew had any cellular speaker phones then), the jury could hear the doctor's testimony that morning. We could sum up and finish the case that week, not hold jurors over to the next week. The defense agreed to telephonic rebuttal rather than prolonging trial. So, we took the treating doctor's rebuttal testimony over the phone in front of the jury.

What I and several jurors remember best about that treating doctor's rebuttal testimony was his immediate reaction when I read to him the defense medical expert testimony that his patient's herniated and/or bulging disc would actually get better over time as she got older, and her spine "would settle like a house." His laugh was instantaneous and memorable. It filled the entire court room. He laughed for only a second or two, but it seemed like an hour. His laugh was so wonderful it became infectious. The judge and several jurors started to chuckle, cover their faces, and shake silently with heads down. After his laughter stopped, he said, "That doctor must be joking. His opinion is not only laughable, but if he ever gave such an absurd prognosis to his own patient he would surely be sued for a flagrant act of malpractice and probably lose his license to practice medicine . . .. For any doctor to tell a patient with such a badly damaged back that she will probably get better is just crazy." He went on to explain medically how the spine of any 35 year old woman or man would not "settle like a house" and that by the time my client was in her 50s she would in all probability and certainty suffer severe arthritis and much more serious problems with her back. The rebuttal medical explanation was not as effective as the doctor's laughter. His piercing laugh awoke in the jurors something they took back into the jury deliberation room with them when it came time to discuss the credibility of the defense expert's testimony. They all concluded it was not only silly junk science; it was despicably arrogant for anyone to suggest that a severe injury would just spontaneously go on and heal itself over time.

III. COMPUTERIZED, REAL TIME TRANSCRIPTS FOR DEPOSITION AND TRIAL

With today's latest computer technology, court reporters are equipped with stenographic machines that can show, on a computer screen, each word of the Q & A as the words are spoken. This is often helpful when a witness tries to quibble over a phrase or the wording of a question. It helps the interrogator to quote the witness verbatim. What is important to remember with this new transcription technology is that we do not allow it to distract from one of the most important personal interchanges and confrontations that can occur during a dep or trial. That is, a face-to-face, eye-to-eye confrontation by trial lawyer with witness. Demeanor of witnesses, how they answer, how quickly/slowly, how/where they look, and how long it takes to get to the point in their answer, these human elements do not show up on pages of the computer screen.

While I strongly urge all trial attorneys to become computer literate and utilize up to date technology, especially real-time transcription, I would also caution all trial lawyers not to fall into the trap of becoming hypnotized by the pretty colored words on the computer laptop screen. If you are only looking at a computer screen, and there is no live/taped video, you and the jury will not see a witness look aside or look at his/her notes or make some indication with their eyes or face that there is more to their answer than what simply appears in the computerized transcript.

ANECDOTE 2: One look can tell a lot.

In one of my first jury trial confrontations with a deceptive defense doctor, I asked the defense medical examiner (DME) if he was certain my client had never complained to him during his 15 minute exam of constant, daily low back pain. The DME (we must never allow them to be called IME—by their counsel or judges) had denied "any low back complaints" in his direct examination. The DME reiterated that his written report did not reflect any lumbo-sacral problems whatsoever. At the time he answered my question, however, he was not looking down at his report which he had brought to the witness stand; rather, he was looking at the back of the court room where his attaché case had been left when he assumed the witness stand. Taking a chance, I asked if there were possibly any additional notes in his brief case. He reluctantly and sheepishly admitted he might have left some of his handwritten examination notes with his original file. However, he just did not want to "burden himself" with all that stuff when he took the stand; and he added he thought it might now take "too much time" to retrieve his hand written notes which, after all would be reflected accurately in his typed report he had signed. In front of the jury, I asked him to go "all the way back" to the last row of the court room to retrieve his original file. He did. There, in his original notes, in his original file, in his own original handwriting, was notation "LS pain-constant." No further questions. And when the trial judge denied defendant's motion for new trial, he recounted on the record about the defense doctor's loss of credibility to the jury.

IV. JUNK SCIENCE AND SCIENTISTS

In today's environment of M.I.S.T. (minor impact/soft tissue), insurance companies hire from their "defense stable" those intellectually dishonest experts who will testify that minor impacts cannot cause serious injury that plaintiffs suffer. Much "junk" is introduced into our court room. Tom Vesper, " M.I.S.T.: A National Insurance Defense Strategy and How to Counterattack, From A to Z," The Trial Lawyer, Vol 22, No 1, Jan-Feb 1999, at p. 47-58. Many biomechanical, engineering, and medical experts misuse and abuse their professional qualifications and education to mislead jurors into believing the popular but unscientific and fraudulent concept that a minor impact/slow speed collision or small amount of resultant property damage to vehicle can never cause nor be evidence of a serious injury. Such "expert" testimony can sometimes be debunked easily and clearly by use of what I call "shirt sleeve" experts—someone who has either practical knowledge, such as an auto mechanic who can explain how much serious force must have occurred for a car frame/bumper brackets to bend. Shirt sleeve experts may have education such as a high school or college physics professor, who can explain the "Newtonian Physics" formulas used by defense have no meaningful relationship to real world impact. "Shirt sleeve" experts may have as much practical experience and training as trauma doctors, who knows it is not the amount of force that causes injury but rather the suddenness of applied forces plus other factors, such as age, physical condition, and relative location of head, neck, and seat back/head restraint.

Again, as in any real-life situation, it is often the kind of person who is claiming to be an expert and the impression made upon the jury that carries the day. If the expert is one who is condescending, arrogant, and unpleasantly tutorial and pedantic, that expert is not necessarily going to be looked upon as helpful. On the other hand, an ordinary person with oil, grease, and dirt under their fingernails, who has worked on cars for 25 years and who is a master mechanic, may have more "people power" than the most highly degreed professor or professional engineer.

ANECDOTE 3: High School Physics Teacher Can Explain Physics.

In a product liability case against both the manufacturer and distributor of a forklift for negligent failure to provide a fender, the defect allowed for a rock to strike the fork lift operator in the hand, resulting in Reflex Sympathetic Dystrophy Syndrome (RSDS). The defense rested on Friday with the opinion testimony of a professional engineer who used "The Range Theory" of physics to "professionally reconstruct" how it was physically impossible for the incident to have occurred. By use of what he claimed was a "well known and often used range theory," he very logically proved, at least to the satisfaction of the judge when my futile cross-examination was over, that a rock thrown by the tire of a fork lift moving at 5 mph would also move at 5 mph. Therefore, if both the rock and the plaintiff continued to move through space at the same rate of speed, the rock could never possibly strike the plaintiff-forklift driver's exposed hand. Therefore, my client must be a fraud! Sweating out that weekend, I rediscovered "The Range Theory" with a high school physics teacher. The defense expert had smugly and confidently illustrated, written out, and charted the one line physics formula for me and the jury several times on cross-examination (I didn't have anything else to ask him about, so I kept asking him to hit me over the head again and again with whatever he had in his hand at the time). The formula, he repeated, was very well known and ". . . could be found and referred to in any high school physics book." Over that memorable weekend and before returning to court that Monday, my law partner Dara Quattrone found a high school physics teacher—her father. Very quickly, Professor Quattrone taught me the truth about the defense expert. He had been "intellectually dishonest or a very, very unprofessional engineer." The Physics Prof explained that "The Range Theory" only works in a vacuum. It was never used in any real world application. It was "theoretical formula" only. It was not applicable in real life because in real life there are things like "slippage." That is, the tires of a car, or fork lift, always turn faster than the car is actually moving when you back up or go forward. As the physics teacher told the jury in rebuttal, "did you ever back up your car and hear the stones hit the underside of your car? That's slippage." When the jury started bobbing heads up and down like little bottle-head dolls, I knew the high school physics teacher had outclassed and debunked the "professional forensic engineer." So did the trial judge, who contemplated imposing sanctions upon the defense.

V. HIGH TECH EXHIBITS

With the advent of computerized exhibits, electronic presenters such as the Elmo, Power Point, Smart Boards, and CGI presentations with lap tops and Trial Presenter programs, there are many exhibits and "visuals" we can use to help us explain and teach juries. One of the most effective uses of videotape I have seen is when trials are videotaped, and attorneys use videotaped highlights for their summations. Final arguments become like an 11 o'clock News broadcast. This, of course, presumes that your client's case has "highlights" as opposed to "low lights."

In addition to using Power Point, CGI, and WordPerfect for charts, graphs, and diagrams to project to the jury, there is still something to be said for good, old fashioned flip charts, photos, or foam core backed diagram. The ability of jurors to touch, feel, and use the exhibits in the jury deliberation room is a consideration you should make whether or not you also utilize computer or audiovisual assistance in illustrating your exhibits to the jury during the trial.

In addition to and more important than an audiovisual aide, the most powerful exhibits in my opinion in any court room are still the plaintiff and the plaintiff's lawyer. According to some trial lawyers, jury consultants, and experienced trial judges, their importance is not necessarily in that order. The client's personality; the likeability and credibility of the plaintiff; the ability to engender empathy and not contempt, scorn, or skepticism; and the client's "Worthwhileness" as David Ball calls it are all factors that cannot be created with a scale model or photograph, videotape or computer. The ability of the plaintiff's trial attorney to practice what some trial lawyers call the ABCs of advocacy (accuracy, brevity, and credibility) are still intangibles that cannot be created or engendered in another person through a lap top or a high tech trial exhibit.

ANECDOTE 4: A Bad Client Trumps Any CGI or Exhibit

In a recent legal malpractice trial, we prepared what our jury consultant and I believed to be a very clear, convincing, and credible time line. We believed our color coded chronology easily showed all the mistakes the defendant lawyer had made and the physical impossibility of our client to have corrected any of the lawyer's deviations from accepted practice. After the verdict, the jurors told us that many of them did not understand our color code or the significance of the chronology of letters and telephone calls. However, they quickly found the defendant lawyer was "guilty of malpractice" because they "just did not believe him from the get-go!" He was not honest, and they had immediately decided that fact. When we called the defendant to the witness stand as our very first witness, he could not answer a single simple question without rambling and trying to make himself look like a genius. The jury then and there decided he was unbelievable and "not a good lawyer." Therefore, a positive and/or negative first impression can outweigh and trump any exhibit.

VI. JURY STUDIES, WORKSHOPS, AND FOCUS GROUPS

Much has been written and said about today's jurors and their biases. Some of these modern and very negative trends that have been reported are listed below.

A. Some of The Current Juror Bias

1. Attribution. This phenomenon is also referred to as "defensive attribution bias." It is a way some jurors judge plaintiffs by attributing whatever adverse outcome to plaintiff's lack of due care or comparative fault. This type of judgmental analysis allows the defense to play on the theme of the failure of plaintiff to exercise "personal responsibility." This survival technique by some jurors leads them to say "I wouldn't be dying of cancer (or whatever plaintiff is suffering) because I would have followed up. I would have done something differently. I would not be in the plaintiff's position." Mandell, "Overcoming Juror Bias: Is There An Answer?," TRIAL, July 2000, p. 28-29.

2. Antiplaintiff Bias. The second attitude that is used to the disadvantage of plaintiffs is the antiplaintiff bias. AAJ focus groups have shown that frequently jurors unjustifiably assess fault to the plaintiff. This attitude exists even in cases where contributory negligence is absent. AAJ researchers, David A. Wenner and Gregory S. Cusimano, have documented a "blame the victim" effect that naturally occurs in the trial context. Shaver, "Defensive Attribution: Effects of Severity and Relevance on the Responsibility Assigned for an Accident," 14 J. Personality & Soc. Psychol. 101 (1970). Jurors may be inclined to blame your plaintiff/client to avoid thinking they might suffer a similar fate. Psychologists call this "defensive attribution."

3. Personal Responsibility. In a telling survey, Americans ranked 15 values in order of importance, with more than 95% reporting personal responsibility to be "very important." This phenomenon is consistent across gender, race, class, and political preference. Cherlin, "I'm O.K., You're Selfish," N.Y. Times, Oct. 17, 1999 6 at 44.

AAJ focus groups have shown that the "personal responsibility" theme emerges in every case. Right or wrong, the American public is fed up with what appears to be the refusal of people to take responsibility for their own actions. In AAJ focus groups, members have been videotaped subscribing to the idea of personal responsibility and harboring the suspicion that people who bring lawsuits do not accept such personal responsibility. If there is any perception that your client has not been personally responsible, then a preference to impose responsibility on the plaintiff tends to rise.

If we trial lawyers expect jurors to hold a defendant accountable, we must first demonstrate that the plaintiff was responsible. We should try our cases with the perspective that jurors apply a higher standard of personal responsibility to plaintiffs than to defendants. Personal responsibility is a bias that is firmly rooted in jurors' minds. We must claim it as our message.

4. Confirmation Bias. The confirmation bias refers to the tendency of jurors to search for evidence that confirms their beliefs. That is, to critically scrutinize unconfirming evidence and to interpret ambiguous evidence as consistent with their beliefs. AAJ case workshops consistently see jurors accept supportive facts and discount nonsupportive facts. To understand this bias, lawyers must understand the concept of "schemas."

People organize their knowledge, beliefs, theories, and expectations in cohesive units called "schemas." When people encounter a new experience, they have a cognitive framework for understanding that experience. Schemas influence perception. Juror schemas, thus, serve as framework for interpreting the evidence.

Your opening statement can be event schemas. It can help jurors understand how an event should unfold. If events have not occurred in the way jurors expect, they will look for the cause. The goal should be to discover how to describe defendant's conduct in a way inconsistent with juror schemas and plaintiff's conduct consistent with them. Trial must make defendant's conduct vivid so it is memorable in deliberations.

5. Belief Perseverance Bias. The "belief perseverance" bias refers to today's jurors tendency, once they have adopted a trial story, to cling to it even in the face of conflicting or discrediting evidence. Nisbett, Richard E., and Ross, Lee, Human Inference: Strategies and Shortcomings of Social Judgment (1980); Lee Ross et al, Perseverance in Self-Perception and Social Perception: Biased Attributional Processing in the Debriefing Paradigm, 32 J. Personality & Soc. Psychol. 880 (1975); Tversky, Amos and Kahneman, Daniel, Judgment Under Uncertainty: Heuristics and Biases, 185 Science 1124 (1974). We often see focus group jurors maintaining their trial story even when we show them evidence supporting that position is lacking. The early-adopted trial story is an interpretative framework for understanding subsequent evidence.

6. Availability Bias. The availability of information can influence perception. Jurors often mistakenly equate the availability of information with frequency, probability, and causality. David Wenner and Gregory Cusimano suggest that whatever most occupies juror attention during the trial will most influence what jurors focus on during deliberations and disproportionately use in rendering a verdict. Wenner, David A. and Cusimano, Gregory S., "Combating Juror Bias," TRIAL, June 2000, p. 30.

A good rule of thumb is that if your trial proofs are focused on the defendant's conduct, jurors will focus on that conduct in deciding the case. In contrast, if the trial focuses on causation, jurors likely will focus on causation. Likewise, if jurors focus on the plaintiff's conduct during trial, they will focus on the plaintiff during deliberation. That does not mean plaintiff trial lawyers can ignore our plaintiff's conduct if it is in issue, nor should we not inoculate against defenses. On the contrary, it just means that we should try to focus of the case and the jurors' attention on defendant's conduct.

B. One Way to Approach Today's Juror Bias: Focus More

While there are many predisposed negatives in minds of today's jurors, there are still themes that motivate and persuade today's jurors. If you and your clients cannot find these themes or cords to strike and motivate jurors, then you should conduct your own focus group or "workshop" your client's case with a professional jury consultant and real jurors in focus group/mock trial exercises at AAJ's Case Workshops. Mark Mandell, "Overcoming Juror Bias: Is There An Answer?," TRIAL, July 2000, p.28-29; Wenner, David A. and Cusimano, Gregory S., "Combating Juror Bias," TRIAL, June 2000, p. 30.

I believe somewhere between our LSAT's and our partnerships or shareholdings we lawyers misplace or forget our own ability to relate to real people. As we are so tuned into the law of our client's case, we forget the humanity of our clients and their cases.

Any trial that has any importance to your client, your office, and you should be focused or work-shopped so the issues that appeal to or alienate real people are identified, and the proper and meaningful words, phrases, and themes are employed to help our clients tell their story. This is not a matter of "spinning" the facts or tricking a jury by playing motivational mind games. A bad plaintiff, with bad facts, will lose more times than not regardless of the number of focus groups or mock trials. But sometimes, the presentation of our client's cases can be improved, and the defense can be made to see "ultimate risk" they face when we do employ a focus group and/or jury consultant and/or our friends and families to help frame and phrase our issues. Focus groups can help us develop very powerful themes, which themes can translate into an improvement of the odds for successfully settling or receiving a jury verdict.

VII. CONCLUSION

My mother, Carmella, and her sister, Connie, were born in Italy, in a small town in the hills of the Princia d'Abuzzi called Riccia. Their family consisted of three sisters and seven brothers. Only one brother graduated high school. My father, Rocco, was the oldest of eight children. He got to the sixth grade and dropped out of grammar school to help his father, Domenico Vespe, support their family after his mother died. (My grandfather Domenico added the "r" to our family name because the rail road would not hire any Italian immigrants. So he successfully passed himself off as the Frenchman, "Dominique Vesper.") My mother and father's brothers and sisters had very little formal education. But they understood people on a much deeper, basic level than I ever will. They had an amazing reservoir of practical, everyday experience. And they each had an overwhelming abundance of good common sense.

The things they wanted to know about were the same kind of things that judges, arbitrators, and mediators also want to know about, which, I believe, are still the same things that most real people who serve on our juries want to know. They want to know what kind of person our plaintiff really is or was. To present our clients and their character, credibility, and complaints to a jury, we need to remember what is important to the finders of fact. It is still the type of person, not the type of technological advancements that are employed by the trial lawyer, that will carry the day. When presenting experts, it is still the basic honesty and trustworthiness of the expert's methods, analysis, and conclusions, as well as the expert's manner of explaining the opinions, that is important, and not the number of slides or glitzy Power Point illustrations.

10 STEP "QUICK MIX" FOR SUMMATIONS

By Tom Vesper

1. **GENERAL vs. SPECIFIC DISCUSSION ABOUT LIABILITY:** start with some general discussion of defendant's fault and then get into the specific evidence thereof.
2. **TIME = 33% OF TOTAL SUMMATION on LIABILITY:** most of your

time in summation discuss and explain damages and how the jury can evaluate monetarily

3. **Use "FUNDAMENTAL ATTRIBUTION"**—E.g., DON'T call defendant "Good Lawyer who made a mistake" rather "a Lawyer who was too busy to do his duty."

4. **E-LIMINATE THE NEGATIVE & ACCENTUATE THE POSITIVE:** emphasize GOOD CHARACTER of Plaintiff vs BAD CHARACTER of defendant; e.g., an honest security guard vs. "Made in China" defective chair (which collapsed at 0300 AM)

5. **CHOICES** = the more choices the defendant had the more the LIABILITY AND DAMAGES are driven upward.

6. **PERCENTAGE OF TIME TALKING ABOUT PRESENT & FUTURE**—that is, more time spent talking about POST injury plaintiff = less money award. THE TRUE TEST = "COMPARED TO WHAT"—the greater the severity of the drop or decline in what plaintiff's life was before = the greater $ awarded. E.g., Moe Levine and the two homeless people, the homeless husband died, so what did the homeless woman lose?

7. **Use VIGNETTES**—ala Moe Levine, tell a little vignette—e.g., The homeless woman and the homeless man ate beans together every night in their cardboard box home.

8. **IF you use QUOTATION or ANALOGY**—be sure it "rings true" and not trite.

9. **IF you use PPT, Video Clips, Exhibits**—DON'T OVERLOAD jurors' senses; DO NOT DISTRACT from YOUR EYE CONTACT + CONNECTION with the jurors

10. **HELP THE JURY GET TO A "FAIR AMOUNT OF MONEY"**—try to suggest, depending on the law of your jurisdiction, a time-unit formula or what a fair range of dollars would be for the plaintiff's injuries and losses.

gustare la dolcezza del nostro cibo

(enjoy our food's sweetness)

Chapter 11. APERITIVO (Aperitif) & DIGERENTE (Digestifs): Before & After Dinner Special Drinks

PART A. TOM & DOM'S RECIPES

1775 Fortitude Rum Punch
AKA "THE MARINE CORPS PUNCH" (anytime)

BOCCONCINI: The Marine Corps Punch is a traditional beverage served to

Aperiti & Digerente

Marine Corps recruits starting on the Birthday of the Marine Corps, November 10, 1775, at Tun Tavern in Philadelphia, during the American Revolution.

INGREDIENTS (Serves: As many as you and your "mess" or "dining in" like):

Jamaican rum

Lime juice

Maple sugar

Grenadine

DIRECTIONS:

1 part Dark Jamaican Rum

4 parts Lime juice

Maple sugar and grenadine to taste

Mix and pour over cracked ice in a glass punch bowl

The Vespers' Trial Cookbook

NAVY GROG (mostly after dinner)

BOCCONCINI: "Grog" can refer to a variety of alcoholic drinks. Originally, it was a drink of water and rum introduced into the Royal Navy by British Vice Admiral Edward Vernon in 1740. Navy Grog began as refreshment for British sailors and as an enhancer/preserver of water stored on ship and for vitamins to fight diseases. "Old Navy Grog" was a mix of rum, water, honey or molasses, lemon, and cinnamon served hot or cold.

Modern grogs are made with hot or boiling water and sometimes include lemon juice, lime juice, cinnamon, or sugar. Rum with water, sugar, and nutmeg was called "Bumboo" and popular with pirates and merchantmen. Navy Grog was a popular rum-based drink served for many years at Polynesian-themed *Don the Beachcomber* restaurants and is still served in many tiki bars. First created by Donn Beach, who helped the tiki cultural fad of 1940s-'50s; later Trader Vic et al, sold it in exotic tropical settings. Not as potent as Beachcomber's famous Zombie, it was, nevertheless, limited to two per customer.

Navy Grog was Frank Sinatra's favorite drink at the Hollywood *Don the Beachcomber* restaurant where it was first served. Whatever the recipe, Grog traditionally is served very cold in a large, broad-based old fashioned glass into which a frozen snow cone of shaved ice is put, so you sip the Grog through a straw that runs down through the cone.

Total Time: 2 minutes (NB: it always takes Navy longer than Marines to do anything)

INGREDIENTS (Serves 1 Drink):

1 oz. White rum

1 oz. Demerara rum

1 oz. Dark rum

3/4 oz. Lime juice

3/4 oz. White grapefruit juice

1 oz. Honey syrup

Club soda

Orange slice and cherry for garnish

DIRECTIONS:

Aperiti & Digerente

Pour the rums, juices, and syrups into a cocktail shaker filled with ice. Shake well.

Strain into a collins glass filled with ice. Top with soda.

Garnish with an orange slice and cherry skewer.

Stir the sugar and water in a large saucepan over medium heat until the sugar dissolves, about 5 minutes. Cool completely.

BELLINI (SLOW VERSION) (anytime)

<u>BOCCONCINI</u>: The Bellini is a peachy version of a Champagne cocktail and makes a great brunch cocktail. Created in the 1930s at Harry's Bar in Venice, Italy, by bartender Giuseppe Cipriani, it was named after a favorite painter, Giovanni Bellini. Originally, it was intended to use sparkling Italian wine and is still made that way in Italy with Prosecco. Elsewhere, it is made with Champagne. Also try the mocktail version—the Baby Bellini.

<u>INGREDIENTS</u> (Serves 12):

2 cups Sugar

1 cup Water

1 (16 oz.) Bag frozen peaches, thawed

1 tsp Grated orange peel

1 (16 oz.) Bag frozen strawberries, thawed

1 (16 oz.) Bag frozen blue/blackberries, thawed

4 to 6 (750 ml) Bottles Prosecco/sparkling wine, chilled

Fresh strawberries, raspberries, blueberries, for garnish

Orange peel twists, for garnish

<u>DIRECTIONS</u>:

Stir the sugar and water in a large saucepan over medium heat until the sugar dissolves, about 5 minutes. Cool completely.

Puree peaches and orange peel in a blender with 1/2 cup of the sugar syrup until smooth. Strain through a fine-mesh strainer into a bowl. Cover and refrigerate.

In a clean blender, puree strawberries with 1/3 cup of sugar syrup until smooth. Strain through a clean fine-mesh strainer into another bowl. Discard seeds.

Puree blueberries in clean blender with 1/3 cup of sugar syrup until smooth. Strain through clean fine-mesh strainer into a third bowl. Discard seeds and solids.

Pour each puree into clear glass bowls/small pitchers.

Aperiti & Digerente

For each serving, pour 2 to 4 Tbsp of desired fruit puree into a Champagne flute. Slowly pour enough Prosecco into flute to fill. Gently stir to blend. Garnish with the whole berries, as desired, and serve.

BELLINI (2 MINUTE VERSION) (anytime)

INGREDIENTS (Serves 1 Drink):

2 oz. Peach juice or peach puree

4 oz. Prosecco, Champagne or sparkling wine

DIRECTIONS:

Pour the peach juice or peach puree into a Champagne flute.

Slowly add the Prosecco/Champagne.

BABY BELLINI (2 MINUTE VERSION) (anytime)

The classic peach and Champagne cocktail from the 1930s called the Bellini has this as the virgin version. The Baby Bellini is perfect for elegant entertaining and has the feel of a great Champagne cocktail and same great taste of the original but no alcohol.

INGREDIENTS (Serves 1 Drink):

2 oz. Peach juice or puree

Chilled sparkling cider

DIRECTIONS:

Pour the peach nectar into a Champagne flute.

Slowly add the sparkling cider.

The Vespers' Trial Cookbook

THE VESPER or THE VESPER MARTINI
(Aperitivo)

BOCCONCINI: James Bond fans will recognize the recipe below as the first martini James Bond ordered in the 1953 Ian Fleming novel, *Casino Royale*. Kina Lillet is today labeled as White or Blanc Lillet—a brand of dry vermouth made in France since the late 1800s, often called "the apèritif of Bordeaux." Bond's glass of choice for the Vesper is a deep Champagne goblet. In Chapter 8, "Pink Lights and Champagne," Bond names it "the Vesper" at his introduction to the beautiful Vesper Lynd (no relation to Dom or me), who tells him: "I was born in the evening, . . . on a very stormy evening . . ." so Bond asks to borrow it. "Vespers" or "evensong" is the sixth of seven canonical hours of the divine office and are observed at "violet hour," sunset.

Although Bond drinks many Vespers (six of them) in the 2008 film *Quantum of Solace,* we recommend you stick to 1 large (or 2 small) and predesignate a driver for yourself.

INGREDIENTS (Serves 1 Drink):

3 measures Gordon's Gin

1 measure Vodka

½ measure Kina (White) Lillet

Lemon peel for garnish

DIRECTIONS: The Vesper ala Ian Fleming and James Bond:

"A dry martini . . . one. In a deep champagne goblet . . . . Three measures of Gordon's, one of vodka, half a measure of Kina Lillet. Shake it very well until it's ice-cold, then add a large thin slice of lemon peel. Got it? . . .When I'm . . . er . . . concentrating . . . I never have more than one drink before dinner. But I do like that one to be large and very strong and very cold and very well-made. I hate small portions of anything, particularly when they taste bad. This drink's my own invention. I'm going to patent it when I can think of a good name . . . Excellent . . . but if you can get a vodka made with grain instead of potatoes, you will find it still better," and then adds in an aside, " '*Mais n'enculons pas des mouches*' " (But let's not bugger flies—vulgar French expression meaning "let's not split hairs")." Ian Fleming, *Casino Royale*, Chapter 7, "Rouge et Noir."

Esquire magazine printed the following updated variation of The Vesper recipe in 2006:

Aperiti & Digerente

Shake (if you must) with plenty of cracked ice, 3 oz. Tanqueray gin, 1oz. 50% (100-proof) Stolichnaya vodka, ½ oz. Lillet Blanc, 1/8 tsp (or less) quinine powder or 2 dashes of bitters; strain into chilled cocktail glass; twist a large swatch thin-cut lemon peel over top. Modern cocktail glasses, larger today than 1953, replace deep Champagne goblets.

The Vespers' Trial Cookbook

THE GODFATHER... GODMOTHER... and GODCHILD (digerente)

BOCCONCINI: The origin of this name is uncertain. Amaretto brand *Disaronno* claims the drink was the favorite cocktail of Marlon Brando, known for the titular character in the popular American film adaptation of Mario Puzo's *The Godfather*.

INGREDIENTS (Serves as many as you and your "family" would like):

3/10 part Amaretto di Saronno

7/10 part Scotch whisky

DIRECTIONS:

Pour the ingredients in an ice-filled Old Fashioned glass and stir well.

THE FEMALE (VODKA) VERSION—"THE GODMOTHER"

<u>INGREDIENTS</u> (Serves as many as you and your "family" would like):

3/10 part Amaretto di Saronno

7/10 part Vodka

<u>DIRECTIONS</u>:

Pour the ingredients in an ice-filled Old Fashioned glass and stir well.

"THE GODCHILD" (Replaces Scotch with Cream) APEROL SPRITZ (Aperitivo)

BOCCONCINI: Aperol is an Italian aperitif first produced by the Barbieri company, based in Padua; Aperol is now produced by the Campari company; created in 1919. Aperol did not become popular until after WW II. Its ingredients include bitter orange, gentian, rhubarb, and cinchona. While it looks, tastes, and smells like Campari, Aperol has an alcohol content of 11%, which is less than half Campari, with the same sugar content; Campari is slightly darker in color. Aperol is main ingredient in Spritz.

INGREDIENTS (Serves 1 drink):

2/10 part Aperol

8/10 part Prosecco

Seltzer

DIRECTIONS:

Fill a tumbler or a red wine glass with ice, pour Aperol, Prosecco and top it with Soda water. Garnish with a slice of orange.

THE NEGRONI (Aperitivo)

<u>BOCCONCINI</u>: The most widely accepted story of the origin is that it was invented in Florence, Italy, in 1919, at *Caffè Casoni, ex Caffè Giacosa*, now called *Caffè Cavalli* by Count Camillo Negroni who asked the bartender, Fosco Scarselli, to strengthen his favorite cocktail, "The Americano," by adding gin rather than normal soda water. The bartender also added orange garnish rather than typical lemon garnish of the Americano to signify its difference. The Negroni Family founded the Negroni Distillerie in Treviso, Italy, producing a ready-made version of the drink, sold as Antico Negroni 1919. One of the earliest reports of the drink is Orson Welles' correspondence with the Coshocton Tribune while working in Rome in 1947 where he described the new Negroni: "the bitters are excellent for your liver, the gin is bad for you. They balance each other."

As with the Martini, the recent trend is to use a larger proportion of gin mainly because the quality of the spirit is a lot better than it used to be, meaning, less need to dilute the gin to make it palatable. Most bars will serve the drink with double the quantity of gin.

Many bars treat the Negroni as a template involving a base spirit + bitters + vermouth.

<u>INGREDIENTS</u> (Serves 1 drink or as many as you like):

1/3 part Vermouth rosso

1/3 part Bitter Campari

1/3 part Dry Gin

<u>DIRECTIONS</u>:

Served on the rocks, use a medium tumbler or an Old Fashion glass, stir the ingredients directly in your glass and garnish with a half slice of orange and lemon peel.

NEGRONI SBAGLIATO (Aperitivo)

<u>BOCCONCINI</u>: Negroni Sbagliato, a popular cocktail, is the summer version of popular Negroni cocktail. Campari is one of Italy's most famous liquor companies, and its wide assortment of cocktails pleases most palates. This version of the Negroni is a great choice for summer, thanks to Spumante sparkling wine. *Sbagliato* means "wrong" and refers to the fact that in it, the original Negroni cocktail gin is swapped for Spumante.

Although it's thought that the Negroni originated from Florence, the Negroni Sbagliato is said to have been invented in Milan (where Campari comes from) back in the 1960s.

<u>INGREDIENTS</u> (Serves 1 drink—or as many as you like):

1 part Campari

1 part Martini Rosso

1 part Spumante

Orange slice

<u>DIRECTIONS</u>:

Pour all ingredients into a highball or lowball glass with ice and mix.

Garnish with a slice of orange.

The Vespers' Trial Cookbook

THE AMERICANO (Aperitivo)

BOCCONCINI: The Americano is an IBA Official Cocktail composed of Campari, sweet vermouth, and club soda. It was first served in creator Gaspare Campari's bar, *Caffè Campari*, in Milan in the 1860s; originally called the "Milano-Torino" because ingredients: Campari, bitter liqueur, is from Milan (Milano), Cinzano, the vermouth, is from Turin (Torino). One legend is that in the early 1900s, the Italians noticed a surge of Americans enjoying the cocktail; as a compliment to them, the cocktail was called the *"Americano."*

This was the first drink ordered by James Bond in the first novel in Ian Fleming's series, *Casino Royale.* In the short story, *"From a View to a Kill,"* 007 chooses an Americano as an appropriate drink for a café, saying: "in cafés you have to drink the least offensive of the musical comedy drinks that go with them." Bond always stipulates Perrier, for in his opinion, expensive soda water was the cheapest way to improve a poor drink.

INGREDIENTS (Serves 1 drink):

5/10 Vermouth rosso

5/10 Bitter Campari

Soda Water (or Perrier)

DIRECTIONS:

Stir directly in an Old Fashion ice-filled glass.

Top it up with soda water and garnish with a slice of orange.

The Vespers' Trial Cookbook

CAFFE SHAKERATO (anytime)

<u>BOCCONCINI</u>: One of the rising stars of Italian cocktails is Caffè Shakerato, and it is nonalcoholic or a "virgin." *Shakerato* is from English "shake"—a key to the process.

Caffè Shakerato's sole purpose is to boost energy with espresso while simultaneously lowering body temperature with its cool frothiness.

<u>INGREDIENTS</u> (Serves 1 drink):

1 Shot of fresh espresso

2-3 Tbsp Sugar (optional)

Ice cubes

<u>DIRECTIONS</u>:

Add all ingredients into a shaker and shake uncontrollably for 30 seconds.

Drain it without the ice into a maritin or white wine glass.

Garnish as you please: coffee bean, orange peel, sugared rim (optional).

The Vespers' Trial Cookbook

LIMONCELLO (Mostly digerent or anytime)

<u>BOCCONCINI</u>: The tart taste of limoncello is always a great way to end any meal. This lemon liqueur originates from the Isle of Capri; it is Italy's second most popular liqueur. Traditional limoncello is made from the lemons of Capri and Sorrento, thanks to the fruits' large size and thick peel. Locals enjoy limoncello most often between May and mid-September. This digestivo is served best extremely chilled. Traditionally, it requires at least 80 days of fermentation; but as Dom would say NONAUWORRY: four days will suffice, too.

<u>INGREDIENTS</u> (Yields about 60 shots/cocktails, 90 oz., 3 quarts, or 2.6 liters):

Peels from of 7 or 8 large organic lemons; be sure they're organic and washed thoroughly

1 (750 ml or 25 oz. or 17 shots/cocktails) bottle of vodka or pure grain alcohol

5 cups (40 oz.) Water

3 cups (24 oz.) Sugar

<u>DIRECTIONS</u>:

Remove the lemon peel with a vegetable peeler and trim off the white from the peels. Place peels in a 2-quart pitcher where they will swim in the vodka.

Cover the pitcher for at least 40 days at room temperature.

Dissolve the sugar in water over medium heat for 5 minutes, let this sugar syrup cool.

Add the sugar syrup over the peels and vodka. Cover and seal at room temperature for an additional 40 days.

Strain the limoncello through a strainer and discard peels.

Transfer the limoncello to bottles and seal the bottles.

Refrigerate/freeze it until cold overnight (Dom insists on 80 days of fermentation).

FERNET BRANCA & MIXTURES THEREOF
(Digerent or anytime)

<u>BOCCONCINI</u>: Fernet Branca is a bitter, aromatic spirit invented in Milan in 1845 by Maria Scala as a stomach medicine. She became Maria Branca through marriage, and thus, the product's name was born. Since then, the Fratelli Branca distillery produces the drink according to a secret family recipe with 27 herbs from five continents; Fernet Branca includes South African aloe, Chinese rhubarb, French gentian, galangal from India or Sri Lanka, chamomile from Italy and Argentina, saffron, myrrh, and elderflower. Aged at least one year in oak barrels; alcohol content is 39 or 40% in Italy and 43% in Austria. The same manufacturer, Fernet Branca, offers also a sweeter bitter, Brancamenta.

BAVORAK COCKTAIL

INGREDIENTS (Serves 1 drink):

1 1/2 oz. Fernet Branca® bitters

Tonic water

DIRECTIONS:

Fill glass with tonic, pour Fernet over spoon and add a straw. Serve in a Cocktail glass.

FERNET CON COCA (Fernet with Coca-Cola)

<u>INGREDIENTS</u> (Serves 1 drink):

1 part Fernet Branca® bitters

2 parts Coca-Cola®

<u>DIRECTIONS</u>:

Put ice in a cocktail glass. Pour the fernet and then fill with coke. No mixing required. Serve in a Cocktail glass.

The Vespers' Trial Cookbook

FERNET WITH COMPARI "BACK IN THE SADDLE" COCKTAIL

INGREDIENTS (Serves 1 drink):

1 Lime

1/3 oz. Campari

1 oz. Ginger beer

1/3 oz. Fernet Branca

1/4 oz. Agave syrup

1 Tbsp Orange bitters

DIRECTIONS:

In a mixing glass, add all ingredients with ice and shake hard for ten seconds. Strain into a cocktail glass and garnish with a lime twist or candied lime peel.

The Vespers' Trial Cookbook

FERNET FOOTBALL

INGREDIENTS (Serves 1 drink):

4 cl Fernet Branca® bitters

1 splash whipped cream

DIRECTIONS:

Fill a glass with Fernet Branca.

Drop in a splash of cream, either whipped or foamed, and serve. Serve in a shot glass.

The Vespers' Trial Cookbook

THE BOCCE BALL COCKTAIL

BOCCONCINI: This popular highball juice drink is one I had to include in our book not just because it has an Italian heritage but also because my Cuz Dom is a champion bocce tournament player. With its Amaretto and soda, it is a lot like what my Cuz calls a "Screwdriver on steroids." Its similarity to the Screwdriver makes this cocktail easy to remember.

INGEDIENTS (Serves 1 cocktail):

2 oz. Vodka

1 oz. Amaretto

Splash of orange or grapefruit juice

Splash of soda water

Orange slice, Maraschino cherry, or anything else you like for garnish

DIRECTIONS:

Pour the vodka, Amaretto, and orange juice into a collins glass filled with ice.

Add a splash of soda water.

Garnish with an orange slice, cherry, etc.

BOCCE BOCCONCINI: *Bocce* (pronounced BOT-chee) is the plural form of boccia meaning "bowl," often anglicized as *bocci* or *boccie*. It is a ball sport belonging to the boules sport family, closely akin to British Lawn Bowls and French Pétanque (meaning literally "feet together or feet anchored"), with a common ancestry in the ancient games of the Roman Empire. It is what Cuz Dom calls "Italian Horseshoes." Traditionally, it is played on clay, natural soil, or asphalt courts 90 feet long and 8.2 to 13 feet wide. Bocce balls are metal or plastic. A simple description of the game is, in bocce, the only object is for one or more of your team's balls to be closer than any of your opponent's balls to the pallina (small white target ball) at the end of every set. Rather than a time period, you can play a fixed number of ends and total the higher score to win or the first team to a predetermined score.The scoring team receives one point for each of their balls that are closer to the jackor pallino than the closest ball of the other team. The length of a game varies by region but is typically from 7 to 13 points.

Bocce players are permitted to throw the ball in the air using an underarm action. This is generally used to knock either the pallino or an opponent's ball away to attain a more favorable position. Tactics can get quite complex when players have sufficient control over the ball to throw or roll it accurately.

Può vincere la squadra migliore! (May the best team win!)

VIN BRULE

BOCCONCINI: *Vin brulé* is Italian for "burnt wine." This a great recipe for "mulled wine," a beverage made in most European countries usually with red wine and various mulling spices, raisins, and other fruits. Served hot/warm, alcoholic/nonalcoholic, it's a traditional winter drink, especially at Christmas, New Year's, Twelfth Night or Epiphany Eve, and Halloween. Port and claret are traditional choices for wines. Italian mulled wine is a standard in winter festivals in Northern Italy, and Vin brulé is traditionally served with panettone, a sweet bread loaf, which also has a story:

Panettone, a type of sweet bread originally from Milan, is one of the symbols of the city. Usually made and enjoyed for Christmas and New Year's in Italy, it comes with a varied history. "Panettone" is from "panetto," or small loaf cake; with Italian suffix "-one" the meaning becomes "large cake." Origins of this cake date back to the Roman Empire. One suggests it is from Milanese "pan del ton" or "cake of luxury." A 15th-century legend from Milan gives the invention to the noble falconer Ughetto Atellani, who loved Adalgisa, daughter of a poor baker named Toni. To win her, the nobleman disguised himself as a baker and invented this rich cake to which he added flour and yeast, butter, eggs, dried raisins, and candied lemon and orange peel. Cuz Dom prefers "the Sforza Legend"—Duke of Milan Ludovico il Moro Sforza, agreed to union of said nobleman Toni, and Adalgusa and encouraged the launch of the new cake: **PAN de TONI** (Toni's cake)—no, despite some of you thinking this is one of my "pun-legends" . . . you can look it up.

INGREDIENTS:

3 bottles Italian red wine (about 2.25 liters)

Zest of 3 lemons

3 Cinnamon sticks

3 Whole cloves

1 cup Sugar

DIRECTIONS:

Pour the wine into a large pot. Add the lemon zest, cinnamon, whole cloves, & sugar.

Heat until it just begins to simmer, but don't boil. Strain & serve in ceramic cups.

PART B. TOM'S TRIAL TIPS: NEGOTIATION, MEDIATION & SETTLEMENT

TO SPIKE THE APPETITE OR SETTLE STOMACHS—SETTLEMENT TIPS: TWIN-TOWERS OF SETTLEMENT: PRESENTATION + NEGOTIATION

PROVING DAMAGES THROUGH DISCOVERY: AAJ DEPOSITION & SETTLEMENT NOTEBOOK

A DOZEN THINGS TO GET PRESUIT, FILING SUIT, & DURING DISCOVERY

1. FIRST REPORT(S) of how the plaintiff's injury(s) occurred + what injuries were first treated

2. INVESTIGATE + DIAGRAM the "Mechanism of Injury"—i.e., how exactly did trauma occur

3. BE SURE ALL "TREATERS" are on "the same page" as to injury(s), causation + permanency

4. PHYSICAL THERAPIST and/or NURSES should be interviewed + if helpful videotaped

5. COMPLAINT should address the "Incident" and "Mechanism of Injury(s)" NOT "accident"

6. INTERROGATORY ANSWERS address Plaintiff's symptoms, impairments, lost enjoyments

7. GET "BEFORE & AFTER" (aka "Moan and Groan Witnesses) for Answers to Interrogatories

8. GET FRE 608 "CHARACTER WITNESSES" named in Interrogatory Answers

9. PREP FOR DME like it was the Plaintiff's Deposition
    a. Four Steps of Pain: clients list each pain's (1) Quality (2) Quantity (3) Duration (4) Relief

b. Lost Enjoyments of Life: let your clients use their own hand written lists of their losses

10. PREP CAREFULLY FOR DEP of Plaintiff + Spouse

   a. Notes, diagrams, timelines: let clients use their own hand made memory devices

   b. Four Steps of Pain: let clients use list (1) Quality (2) Quantity (3) Duration (4) Relief

   c. Lost Enjoyments of Life: let clients use lists

11. GET "REBUTTAL" OPINIONS to DME reports

12. USE "DOCUMENTARY VIDEOS" for settlement and trial

HOW TO MAKE CLIENTS "SAVOR" YOUR SETTLEMENT ADVICE?

12 THINGS TO DO PRESUIT, DURING DISCOVERY, & NEGOTIATIONS

1. FIRST MEETING "ADVICE" WITH CLIENTS: explain in detail how you will handle their case.

2. FIRST MEETING PROOF: show them some evidence of your experience with their type of case.

3. FIRST MEETING "GAME PLAN": let the client know how you intend on evaluating their case.

4. "STATUS REPORTS" AND/OR CC'ING YOUR CLIENT & REFERRING ATTORNEY: always report/copy your clients and referring attorneys on what you are doing in the case.

5. SHOW RESPECT: demonstrate your concern for the clients welfare and time by doing things at places and times convenient with your clients and not just yourself or your staff.

6. EXPLAIN AGAIN & AGAIN: if needed explain any perceived delays in the process of settlement.

7. EVALUATE THE CLIENT'S CASE <u>BEFORE</u> ANYONE ELSE DOES: do not wait for some arbitrator, mediator, judge, or other "uninterested authority" (that does not include the insurance adjuster or defense lawyers) to tell your client what a jury in your venue would give in verdict.

8. USE OBJECTIVE JVR (JURY VERDICT RESEARCH): show clients you

do not "pull numbers out of the air" but rather research what similar injuries have received from juries in your venue—Thomson Reuters has a jury research service; most state TLA/AJ's and AAJ have case evaluation workshops, which you can use as a reference.

9. USE "INDEPENDENT & RESPECTED OPINIONS": you may introduce your client and referral attorneys to retired judges, jury consultants, and trial lawyers respected for their case evaluation skills.

10. RECALCULATE IMMEDIATELY IF SITUATION WARRANTS: when facts or legal changes in case adversely or positively affect the jury verdict value immediately inform the clients thereof.

11. BE THOROUGH & THOUGHTFUL: show clients and referral attorneys you are interested in and willing to spend time to investigate/research any alleged damages claims, e.g., even if you know a treating doctor will not causally relate a condition to traumatic incidents, nevertheless go talk with that doctor; likewise, if lost earning capacity is claimed, you may consult an economist or CPA.

12. BE PREPARED TO WALK OUT & GO TO TRIAL: whenever it appears the defense is being unreasonable, and your client's case is not being evaluated fairly, you must be prepared to walk out of any settlement situation and be prepared to go forward with the jury trial with your client. Cuz Dom says: IF YOU WANNA MAKE SOMEBODY TRUST YOU—THEN YOU GOTTA SHOW THEM YOU'RE WORTH TRUSTING—YOU GOTTA EARN THEIR CONFIDENCE!

HOW TO MAKE INSURANCE COMPANIES & THEIR LAWYERS SETTLE:

12 THINGS TO DO TO "SPICE UP" YOUR SETTLEMENT DEMANDS

1. LIABILITY: show the opposition you have assembled very good, if not excellent 100% liability case against their insured; if possible show evidence that may arose jury's anger at defendant.

2. OBJECTIVE INJURY + LOSSES: show them your client's injury, permanency, and past and future economic losses are credible and easily understood and accepted by a reasonable jury if not objectively provable and viewable by the triers of fact.

3. HARD ECONOMIC LOSSES: show that any past and future lost income and past and future medical expenses are "hard" (credible) and not "soft" (speculative or questionable).

4. GOOD WITCHES v. BAD WITCHES: show your client as good person, worthy of jury's respect and empathy; if possible show defendant as a "bad witch" who will probably be punished by jury.

5. NOT TO BRAG BUT . . .: show/suggest you are more than capable of getting a large jury verdict.

6. QUALITY EXPERTS: show your medical/liability experts not only have better qualifications and access to more/better facts than defense experts, but your expert opinions also MAKE MORE SENSE!

7. JURY VERDICTS IN YOUR VENUE: show what your settlement demand is below or within a fairly predictable jury verdict range; I suggest using JVR services at Thomson Reuters for this.

8. PROFILE THE TRIAL JUDGE: show that the trial judge has in past made favorable rulings.

9. ANY LEGAL/EVIDENTIARY ISSUES: show any legal or evidence problems that the defense has, and of course, if the defense raises issues that would adversely affect the outcome and/or the jury damage award show any rebuttal to legal positions taken against your client.

10. AGGRAVATING/MITIGATING FACTORS: show any "aggravating" or "punitive" facts that would cause the jury to punish the defendant; likewise, show if there are any "mitigating" facts that would help to reduce any comparative fault on the part of your client.

11. LOGISTICS & PLAIN OLD PRACTICALITY: if the defense costs to defend, produce experts, or the sheer length of time of the trial might help tip the scale toward settling then "play that card"; and, be prepared to counter/trump defense arguments that you should "save the costs of trial" by showing the defense lawyer/adjuster that all of your costs have already been spent in preparation.

12. THE "$64 DOLLAR" QUESTION or ". . . COMPARED TO WHAT?" ONE OF THE MOST UNPREDICTABLE ELEMENTS OF DAMAGE is "lost enjoyments" of life. Even the insurance industry's computers cannot adequately predict this piece of the damage puzzle. Jury's will award bigger money verdicts when the plaintiff's life is seriously impacted. Therefore, it is crucial that this element of loss be proven by both expert

and lay witnesses: how is the plaintiff's condition now, different from what plaintiff's life was like before the traumatic event? You must compare the present with the past life or the past plans for future life of the plaintiff and plaintiff's family.

THE AAJ DEPOSITION & SETTLEMENT NOTEBOOK

(Excerpted from the new AAJ Deposition Notebook 4th Edition by Tom Vesper & Mark Kosieradzki)

I. THE VALUE OF A SETTLEMENT NOTEBOOK

II. THE NEED FOR A SETTLEMENT STRATEGY

III. THE THREE PART SYSTEM: HOW IT SHOULD WORK

    A. SETTLEMENT OVERVIEW

        1. STRATEGY

        2. CASE EVALUATION

        3. JURY VERDICT RESEARCH

        4. SETTLEMENT HISTORY

        5. FEE SHIFTING

        6. ADR/CDR

        7. LIENS

        8. RECOVERY MANAGEMENT

    B. SETTLEMENT DATA—THE INFORMATION TO COLLECT FOR SETTLEMENT BRIEFS

        1. PLAINTIFF BACKGROUND

        2. LIABILITY

        3. INJURY(S)

        4. ECONOMIC LOSS

        5. "HUMAN LOSS"

        6. $64 QUESTION

        7. CONSORTIUM

        8. PUNITIVE/BAD FAITH/FEE SHIFT

C. SETTLEMENT BRIEFS & PRESENTATIONS

D. WHAT YOU NEED TO KNOW ABOUT CASE SETTLEMENT STRATEGY

1. WHY YOU NEED A CASE SPECIFIC STRATEGY?
2. WHAT NOT TO CONSIDER WHEN PLANNING A SETTLEMENT STRATEGY
3. WHAT "GENERALLY" YOU SHOULD CONSIDER—HIGH GROUND & RISK
4. IS THERE ANY SCIENCE TO SETTLEMENT? YES . . . CHAOS!
5. WHAT DO INSURANCE COMPANIES USE? . . . COMPUTERS!
6. WHAT MAKES INSURANCE COMPANIES SETTLE . . . OR NOT?
7. WHAT ARE THE "LAND MINES" IN MEDIATION—AND HOW TO AVOID THEM
8. WHAT ABOUT HIGH-LOW SETTLEMENT AGREEMENTS?
9. THE EIGHT AREAS OF SETTLEMENT MALPRACTICE

E. HOW TO USE THE DATA EFFECTIVELY

IV. EPILOGUE

V. SELECTED SETTLEMENT BIBLIOGRAPHY

I. THE VALUE OF A DEPOSITION & SETTLEMENT NOTEBOOK

"I cannot forecast to you the action of Russia. It is a riddle wrapped in a mystery inside an enigma."
—Sir Winston Churchill

Trying to settle a case with some insurance companies and self insureds can be like trying to decipher a "riddle wrapped in a mystery inside an enigma." Unlike legal theories/strategies, procedural rules, causes of action, discovery plans, deposition protocols, case themes, and focus groups, the settlement of the case is one of the first and most important topics discussed between a plaintiff and plaintiff lawyer. Often, one of the first questions asked by prospective plaintiffs before or after retainer agreements and authorizations are explained and signed is: "so, how much do you think my case is worth?" The vast majority of the time, the most professional and honest answer is: "I don't know at this time, to offer any number would be totally misleading. However, I will gather all the information I need to evaluate your case and then I will be in the best position to give you my honest professional opinion as to a fair range of settlement value." One of the few exceptions to this generally acceptable and accurate answer is where the plaintive lawyer knows the exact amount of all liability coverages available, and it is obvious the client's case is so catastrophic that it is clearly an "excess liability situation." That is, where the economic and "non-economic" (human) damages will clearly exceed the total amount of available coverage. In those cases, it may be very reasonable as well as professional to advise your client in the initial interview that their case appears to exceed the amount of available coverage. However, other than those cases of clear "excess liability," it is usually not good practice to "throw out a number" or speculate as to the value of a plaintiff's case with nothing other than the client's version of liability, causation, and damages.

Notwithstanding the speculative and potentially inaccurate case evaluation often requested at the initial client meeting, it is important for the client and the plaintive lawyer to recognize that settlement is one of if not the primary client objective. Therefore, it is important at or shortly after the initial client interview for the trial attorney and the client to discuss an overall approach, philosophy, and methodology for achieving a fair and reasonable settlement. Your *AAJ Settlement Notebook* should have a self-contained and removable SETTLEMENT section which allows the trial lawyer and the client to discuss, record, and store all relevant information necessary to properly evaluate the client's case and then to plan and decide upon a strategy to achieve a fair value; this section also provides a checklist set up with the use of subdividers and tabs which can be very useful in assembling, organizing, and storing the data needed for any type of settlement presentation—be it a settlement demand letter, settlement brief (do not call them "brochures"), arbitration/mediation statement, or video/CD/DVD presentation.

There are many publications by many experts—both academic and practical—on the art and science of case evaluation, the various techniques of negotiation, the advantages/disadvantages of the various types of settlement presentations, the use/misuse/abuse of ADR/CDR (Alternative/Complimentary Dispute Resolution) methods, and the dangers, benefits, and tax consequences (or not) of various settlement or recovery management devices. (See Selected Settlement Bibliography (A) regarding Settlement & Negotiation.) This Guide and your *AAJ Settlement Notebook* will provide some insights by way of useful and up to date discussions about how to evaluate the fair jury verdict potential and settlement range of the client's case and then an archive for the settlement presentation data gathered and generated by discovery and use of focus groups or mock juries.

The *AAJ Trial and Deposition Notebooks*, published by West, have three large light green tabs to allow the trial lawyer and staff to gather and revisit the overall case evaluation and approach to settlement and recovery management (SECTION IX(A) SETTLEMENT OVERVIEW Divider with eight subtabs), as well as a place to archive and update data and exhibits for settlement presentations, discussions, conferences (SECTION IX(B) SETTLEMENT DATA Divider with eight subtabs) and a place to store all settlement presentations by any party (SECTION IX(C) SETTLEMENT BRIEFS & PRESENTATIONS Divider).

The AAJ Notebooks have an Appendix which contains some helpful forms you can adapt to your personal injury practice—an evaluation checklist, settlement brief outline, and samples of demand letters and settlement briefs are in APPENDIX B: Form 11—Checklist for Evaluating Plaintiff PI cases; Form 12A—Sample Demand/"Bad Faith" Notice Letter; Form 12B—Sample Settlement Demand + JVR + Offer of Judgment; Form 12B.1—Sample Offer of Judgment; Form 12C—Sample "Halpern H-Bomb" Settlement Demand + JVR + Release; Form 13—Settlement Brief Outline; Form 14A—Sample Mediation/Settlement Brief (Auto Wrongful Death); Form 14B—Sample Arbitration/Mediation Brief (Negligent Security); Form 21A—Sample Drew Britcher, Esq. TLC Settlement CD; Form 21B—Sample Mike Maggiano, Esq. Settlement Demand DVD; Form 21C—Sample Howard Nations Settlement DVD.

An organized system for planning, discussing, and then conducting case evaluation and settlement presentations and conferences will allow you to plan, record, and preserve all the settlement demands/offers, as well as the relevant information needed to intelligently and fairly discuss settlement with the client, adversaries, or neutral arbitrators/mediators/judges.

Your *AAJ Trial Notebook* should be supplemented with an entire section, color coded with three large light green tabs and 16 smaller light green subtabs for evaluating, planning, and preparing for, conducting settlement discussions and then considering the management of your client's recovery. These tabs and subtabs can be identical to those contained in the *AAJ Trial and Deposition Notebooks*. If you and your support staff do utilize other AAJ litigation tools for trial or discovery, you may wish to simply keep the SETTLEMENT section from your *AAJ Settlement Notebook* in its own three ring binder for standalone usage in another case being prepared for mediation or arbitration, or you may wish to merge all of the relevant information from your *AAJ Settlement Notebook* Sections into your *AAJ Trial Notebook* system.

Optimally, you should begin to address your client's case evaluation and the best strategy to accomplish your client's settlement goals from the moment you undertake the representation. By seeing what facts and issues are important to evaluate and ultimately settle the case, you and your staff can begin to draft more pointed discovery requests and place all relevant information in the framework of the settlement presentation. At an early stage in the litigation process, if you and your client become better aware of the potential jury verdict and case value, the better you will both become positioned to plan upon and execute your settlement or verdict recovery objective(s).

II. THE NEED FOR A DISCOVERY & SETTLEMENT STRATEGY

> "Plans are useless. But planning is essential."
> —General Dwight D. Eisenhower

Even if you know, with some reasonable degree of probability and certainty, what the probable jury verdict range will be for your client's case, and even if you both mutually agree upon a settlement amount less than the predictable jury verdict range, and even if you both agree to a sensibly discounted amount which accounts for savings of time and expenses, there is still no assurance you will ever reach agreement with your adversary to pay such a levelheaded settlement amount. In fact, with no understanding of the mind set, philosophy, and tactics of your adversary and/or the liability insurance company(s) at risk, you will be adrift and at sea, with no way to reach a safe and reasonable settlement. With no settlement strategy of your own, you and your client will be at the mercy of the defense. You will be without any control or means of directing the ultimate amount of the recovery. Without any forethought or planning, you will leave yourself and your client at a tremendous disadvantage during the very important negotiation process.

The general approach of liability insurers is to attempt to settle all claims for the least amount of money possible. Obviously, if insurance companies paid 100% of all claims at 100% case value, there would be very little profit at the end of the fiscal year. It is therefore axiomatic that insurers seek to pay less than what they perceive to be their "exposure" or the 100% case value. Insurers, except in excess or bad faith situations, always seek to buy out the risk of exposure to their insured at a "discounted" settlement figure. To put it another way, insurance companies believe in paying wholesale not retail value for settlements.

Understanding this general settlement approach by liability carriers, plaintiff lawyers who seek to achieve the best settlements for their clients need to address two important issues. That is, to achieve a settlement in the client's best interests, the plaintiff lawyer needs to know and recognize this simple formula: DVR—DD = DSR (Defendant's Verdict Range minus Defendant's Discount = Defendant's Settlement Range) The insurer's perception and/or accurate analysis of its total risk from a jury verdict (DVR) will be a number which is always discounted (DD) to arrive at some range of settlement authority (DSR). The approximate value or range of jury verdict values for the client's case is necessary for the plaintiff lawyer to know in order to present the client's case in such a way that the insurance company views its exposure at a sufficient level (DSR) which is at or in excess of the plaintiff and plaintiff lawyer's settlement value.

This is a very simplistic approach to any settlement strategy: 1) first find and agree upon the value (V1) of the client's case; 2) then, convince the insurer its exposure (V2) is far above that (V1) value; 3) finally, get the insurer to realize it is in its best interest to pay the first amount (V1) or more (V1+). It sounds so easy. But no one in the practice of plaintiff personal injury law—plaintiffs or defense attorney—would ever approach any case with such a child like game plan. Each client, each liability carrier has its own specific set of needs and goals. (See the Settlement Chapter III. B., below entitled "What You Need to Know About Case Settlement Strategy," for some ideas on formulating an overall settlement strategy.)

While the task of the plaintiff trial lawyer is very complex, it can however be dissected into four component and far from simplistic settlement processes: 1) The First Phase is "Case Evaluation"—to recognize and evaluate the facts and circumstances of the plaintiff's case; 2) The Second Phase is "Liability Insurance & Risk Analysis"—to recognize the "risk factors" and settlement concerns of the liability carrier(s); 3) The Third Phase is the "Settlement Presentation"—to prepare a settlement presentation or position which will motivate the insurer/self insured to make a reasonable and acceptable settlement offer; 4) The Fourth Phase is "Recovery Management"—to plan and consider how plaintiff clients will maximize their net recoveries and if necessary address the safe future use of their net settlement dollars.

An *AAJ Settlement Notebook* should have its SETTLEMENT SECTION tabs and subdividers set up to allow the trial lawyer, client, and staff to plan and prepare a settlement strategy placing the information and ideas developed in the First, Second, and Fourth Phases above into the eight subtabs of (A) OVERVIEW, with the data needed for The Third Phase being assembled in the eight subtabs of section (B) SETTLEMENT DATA and then stored for reference in section (C) BROCHURE/PRESENTATION.

Any *AAJ Settlement* should be designed so that it can be removed and placed in a separate three ring binder to be used only at settlement conferences, mediations, or arbitrations. There are three large bright green dividers to store all your input and plans for settlement and recovery management of the client's net proceeds, outline your settlement package or presentation, and also store any settlement brochures or demand letters.

III. THE THREE PART SYSTEM: HOW A SETTLEMENT NOTEBOOK & PRESENTATION SHOULD WORK

HOW A AAJ SETTLEMENT NOTEBOOK SYSTEM SHOULD WORK

This should be the command center and conning tower for case evaluation and settlement. Your client's final success in settlement can be planned, discussed, and decided upon working out of this portable "war room." The case evaluation, drawing board plans, assembly of data, and all settlement presentations and discussions can be started, redesigned, and recorded in this section. Your *AAJ Settlement Notebook* should be divided into three large tabs: (A) SETTLEMENT OVERVIEW, (B) DATA, and (C) BRIEF/PRESENTATIONS and 16 subdividers to help you, your consulting experts, and staff to design a flexible strategy, plan and develop a settlement presentation in written, video or computerized format, and then track and oversee the developing settlement prospects for your client.

In the life of every case, there comes a time when someone asks "can you/he/she/we settle this case?" Whether it be the client, insurance adjuster, defense attorney, or judge, someone will ask the plaintiff's lawyer a very pointed question about the potential for settlement. Your own personalized AAJ Settlement Notebook system should allow the plaintiff trial lawyer and the client to use an outline to begin some meaningful analysis of the settlement value, potential for settlement, as well as providing a safe, central, and easily usable dossier and organizer to keep the plans, ideas, and meaningful settlement information in a portable and retrievable place for use in any settlement discussion. Whether you meet with clients, insurance adjusters/supervisors, defense attorneys, trial judges, mediators/arbitrators, or structure settlement specialists, every fact and detail necessary for a meaningful discussion should be contained in your AAJ Settlement Notebook system.

The *AAJ Settlement Notebook* system should contain three large parts. The first part—section (A)—should be the "SETTLEMENT OVERVIEW." This OVERVIEW Section can become the "command center" of your *AAJ Settlement Notebook*. Into this first section your planning, case evaluation, jury verdict research, and notes for or during arbitration/mediation can be collected. Also, this section should contain the history of any offers and demands, .as well as the net recovery analysis for your client. That is, you and the client sooner rather than later should consider, discuss, and agree upon the repayment of liens, any fee shifting that would be allowed, as well as the potentially beneficial dialogue about the net recovery management of your client's money through structures, special need trusts, etc. The SETTLEMENT OVERVIEW section should contain eight subtabs to help organize your overall approach to an ultimate settlement in the best interest of your client.

The second part of the *AAJ Settlement Notebook* should be section (B) for SETTLEMENT DATA. This can be your settlement brief blueprint. I discourage use of the term "brochure" because of its Hollywood or Madison Avenue, glitzy, commercial, and retail connotation. Your work product has more to do with the law, the civil justice system, and your client's right to a fair recovery than it does to selling products. Car dealers and retail outlets use "brochures." Plaintiff trial lawyers should refer to their work product as trial or settlement briefs. This section of your settlement notebook allows you and your staff to collect, collate, and critically analyze all data that would go into a written, videotaped, or other formatted settlement presentation for your client. The SETTLEMENT DATA section should be broken down into eight subtabs into which the basic components of every plaintiff injury or wrongful death settlement can be divided, conquered, and then prepared for any type of settlement presentation or discussion.

The third part of your *Settlement Notebook* is a place into which you/your staff can file for easy access any settlement brief/presentation from any party—section (C) or a BRIEFS/PRESENTATIONS section.

Your *AAJ Settlement Notebook* can be broken down into the following three major tabs and 16 subdivision tabs:

IX(A)   OVERVIEW

	Tab 1	Strategy
	Tab 2	Case Evaluation
	Tab 3	Jury Verdict Research
	Tab 4	Settlement History
	Tab 5	Fee Shifting
	Tab 6	ADR/CDR
	Tab 7	Liens
	Tab 8	Recovery Management
IX(B)	SETTLEMENT DATA	
	Tab 1	Plaintiff Background
	Tab 2	Liability
	Tab 3	Injury(s)
	Tab 4	Economic Loss
	Tab 5	"Human Loss"
	Tab 6	$64 Question
	Tab 7	Consortium
	Tab 8	Punitive/Bad Faith/Fee Shift
IX(C)	BRIEFS & PRESENTATIONS	

A. The Settlement Overview

(this section and subsections of *AAJ Deposition Notebook, 4th ed.* were not selected for this paper)

TAB 1.	STRATEGY
TAB 2.	CASE EVALUATION
TAB 3.	JURY VERDICT RESEARCH
TAB 4.	SETTLEMENT HISTORY
TAB 5.	FEE SHIFTING
TAB 6.	ADR/CDR
TAB 7.	LIENS
TAB 8.	RECOVERY MANAGEMENT

B. Settlement Data; The Information to Collect in Eight Subdivision/ Tabs

This part of the *AAJ Settlement Notebook* is the mold into which to pour and then process all the persuasive information needed to make an effective settlement presentation for your client. These following eight subtabs can be removed and used as the tabbed index for your own personalized Settlement

Notebook and/or your client's settlement brief or mediation/arbitration statement.

The Appendix of both my AAJ *Trial and Deposition Notebooks* contains some helpful forms you for your negotiation and settlement work. A personal injury case evaluation checklist, settlement brief outline, and several samples of demand letters and settlement briefs are in the Appendix: Form 12A, Sample Settlement Demand/"Bad Faith" Notice Letter; Form 12B, Sample Settlement Demand + JVR+Offer of Judgment; Form 12C, Sample "Halpern H-Bomb Settlement Demand+JVR+Release; Form 13, Settlement Brief Outline; Form 14A Sample Mediation/Settlement Brief (Auto Wrongful Death); Form 14B, Sample Arbitration/Mediation Brief (Negligent Security); Form 15, Sample Settlement CD.

The SETTLEMENT DATA section of your *AAJ Settlement Notebook* should contain the following eight subdivisions:

TAB 1.	PLAINTIFF BACKGROUND
TAB 2.	LIABILITY
TAB 3.	INJURY(S)
TAB 4.	ECONOMIC LOSS
TAB 5.	"HUMAN LOSS"
TAB 6.	$64 QUESTION
TAB 7.	CONSORTIUM
TAB 8.	PUNITIVE/BAD FAITH/FEE SHIFT

(these sections of the **AAJ Deposition Notebook, 4th ed.** were not selected for this paper)

C. Settlement Briefs and Presentations

This section of your *AAJ Trial Notebook* can be provided for the central filing and storage of all settlement briefs and presentations by all parties. (See the Chapter below entitled "HOW TO USE THE DATA EFFECTIVELY" for discussion/analysis of the different types, styles, and methods of settlement briefs and presentations.)

Additional Tabs

Remember that you may wish to expand any section depending on your personal preference.

D. What You Need to Know About Case Settlement Strategy

1. WHY YOU NEED A CASE SPECIFIC STRATEGY?
2. WHAT NOT TO CONSIDER WHEN PLANNING YOUR SETTLEMENT STRATEGY: NEEDS-BASED NEGOTIATION
3. WHAT "GENERALLY" YOU SHOULD CONSIDER—HIGH GROUND & RISK
4. IS THERE ANY SCIENCE TO SETTLEMENT? YES . . . CHAOS!
5. WHAT DO INSURANCE COMPANIES USE? . . . COMPUTERS!
6. WHAT MAKES INSURANCE COMPANIES SETTLE . . . OR NOT?
7. WHAT ARE THE "LAND MINES" IN MEDIATION—AND HOW TO AVOID THEM
8. WHAT ABOUT HIGH-LOW SETTLEMENT AGREEMENTS?
9. THE EIGHT AREAS OF SETTLEMENT MALPRACTICE
10. WHAT ARE THE "LAND MINES" IN RECOVERY MANAGEMENT—AND HOW TO AVOID THEM
11. ANNUITIES VS. ACTIVE ASSET MANAGEMENT
12. FAQs (Frequently Asked Questions) & As (ANSWERS) ABOUT "PLAINTIFF STRUCTURED SETTLEMENTS"

1. Why You Need a Case Specific Strategy?

KNOW THINE ENEMY! AND BEWARE OF SOLIPSISM

'Know thine enemy as thyself.' —Sun Tsu, <u>The Art of War</u>

(this section of the **AAJ Deposition Notebook, 4th ed.** was not selected for this paper)

2. What Not to Consider in Settlement Strategy

NEEDS-BASED NEGOTIATION—THE CASE FOR ARACHNOPHOBIA

"'Come into my parlor', said the spider to the fly."

(this section of the **AAJ Deposition Notebook, 4th ed.** was not selected for this paper)

3. What "Generally" You Should Consider—High Ground and Risk!

(a) Taking "The High Ground" a General Settlement Strategy

LEARNING FROM GENERALS PICKETT AND ROMMEL

(this section of the **AAJ Deposition Notebook, 4th ed.** was not selected for this paper)

(b) Risk: How to Make Defenses "Appreciate" + Pay to "Avoid Risk"

By: Mark Kosieradski, Esq.

Cases settle because of risk. To be more specific, there is a direct correlation between the defendant's *appreciation* of its exposure to risk and the strength of the plaintiff's bargaining position. Key factors are the defendant's appreciation of the plaintiff's commitment to trying the case, the strengths of the plaintiff's case, and the weaknesses of the defendant's own case. Therefore, when negotiating, the defendant's risks must be exposed before you enter into any meaningful settlement discussions.

Although significant injuries create a risk factor, my work in nursing home litigation has taught me that damages alone are not the key factor in the value of a case. Rather, it is the exposure of the defendant's bad conduct that drives substantial awards. The greatest risk to a defendant is an angry jury. Jurors who are angered are often motivated to punish, to make social statements, or to get revenge.

It is not enough to focus on a negligent act alone. Jurors are seldom motivated by a "mistake" or "accident." Rather, the focus must expose why the defendant acted negligently. What were the "choices" and circumstances giving rise to the conduct. What decision making was involved. What were defendant's choices. This analysis often reveals underlying corporate malfeasance and/or administrative indifference.

By exposing the underlying reasons, the jury realizes the injury will happen again to someone else unless they do something. The jury will understand the case is not about an unfortunate accident. The case is about a *disaster waiting to happen*. The jury will understand the defendant could have easily averted the disaster by doing the right thing in the first place. It is through this knowledge that jurors become motivated to make a statement with their award. By making the case bigger than one event, bigger than one family's loss, the risk to a defendant is magnified. The impact of expanding the case beyond a single plaintiff is seen in nursing home cases. By showing calculated under-staffing at a level that prevents nurses from properly doing their job, we shift the focus from a single act of nursing negligence to a profit-motivated corporate decision to make the delivery of health care unavailable to the most vulnerable members of our society.

When the defendant appreciates that it will be defending against issues of corporate malfeasance—when the defendant has to explain itself instead of belittling the economic damages of an elderly person's injury—the formerly steadfast defendant is now motivated to discuss settlement.

Not only must the defendant's conduct be exposed; the defense arguments must also be neutralized. A plaintiff's "He said/She said" responses do not create risk for the defense. A plaintiff's excuses, explanations, and technical debates do not create risk for the defense. To create risk for the defense, the plaintiff must render the defendant's arguments factually implausible or irrelevant.

If a case is to be resolved, the real decisionmakers must be made to appreciates the risks. Today, defense lawyers have less influence on whether a case is resolved. Corporate entities, which control the checkbook, make settlement decisions, often against the advice of their litigation counsel. For negotiations to be effective, those persons must be exposed to all of the facts that create risk for the defense.

How do you get past the defense lawyer and limited-authority adjusters to influence the decision-makers' appreciation of risk? If the case is positioned for mediation, the morning of mediation is not the time to identify the risk to the decision makers. They seldom attend conferences. Settlement authority is established long before mediation starts. Although, the person with "absolute authority" is present, limits on that "absolute authority" has been set by someone not present. In the end, "the call" invariably needs to be made to the home office—in a different time-zone and about to close for the day in fifteen minutes.

If the decision-makers are to pay appropriately, they must understand the risks *before* the negotiation begins. They must know that you have uncovered the Achilles' Heel of their case. They must know that you are prepared to expose them to a jury. The message is not conveyed with words. It is conveyed through your conduct. Calculated, aggressive discovery efforts will disclose the facts that will motivate the jury. Depositions allow you to explore the true meaning of documents and conduct. Motions force the defense to the court room and force complete responses to your discovery. The litigation process forces the defense to assess their risk and report it to the decision makers long before there are discussions of settlement.

While not a "magic formula," my experience has taught me that this effort is a path that leads to a settlement that is fair and that can make the difference in the quality of your client's life.

4. Is There Any Science to Settlement? . . . Yes . . . Chaos!

HOW INSURANCE COMPANIES VALUE CASES TODAY: THE CHAOS THEORY & HOW TO DEFEAT THE COLOSSUS GAME PLAN AND SOFTWARE

Application of Chaos Theory and the Heisenberg Uncertainty Principle to Tort Negotiation

By: Richard G. Halpern

If your only tool is a hammer, every problem begins to look like a nail.
— Old Saying

(this section of the ***AAJ Deposition Notebook, 4th ed.*** was not selected for this paper)

5. What Do Insurance Companies Use? . . . Colossus

COLOSSUS—NOT A COLOSSAL WASTE OF TIME: HOW TO COMMUNICATE WITH TODAY'S COMPUTERIZED ADJUSTER

I. <u>KNOW HOW TO CARE FOR & "FEED" COLOSSUS & BEWARE THE 13 FRAUD RED FLAGS</u>

(this section of the *AAJ Deposition Notebook, 4th ed.* was not selected for this paper)

II. <u>KNOW WHAT PD ADJUSTERS DO TO HELP THE M.I.S.T. DEFENSES</u>

(this section of the *AAJ Deposition Notebook, 4th ed.* was not selected for this paper)

6. What Makes Insurance Companies Settle . . . or Not?

<u>WHAT MAKES INSURANCE COMPANIES SETTLE OR NOT SETTLE?</u>

(most of this section of the *AAJ Deposition Notebook, 4th ed.* was not selected for this paper)

III. <u>A DOZEN MEANINGFUL DETAILS FOR INSURANCE DEFENSE LAWYERS</u>

(the entirety of this section of *AAJ Deposition Notebook, 4th ed.* was not selected for this paper)

1. <u>NATURE OF LIABILITY</u>.
2. <u>THE INJURY AND RESULTANT LOSS</u>.
3. <u>HARD vs. SOFT ECONOMIC LOSSES</u>.
4. <u>QUALITY OF THE LITIGANTS</u>.
5. <u>QUALITY OF THE ATTORNEYS</u>.

6. QUALITY OF EXPERTS & EXPERT OPINIONS.

7. VENUE: DELAYS AND CONTROLS OF VERDICTS.

8. THE TRIAL JUDGE.

9. EVIDENTIAL AND LEGAL QUESTIONS.

10. DEFLATIONARY OR INFLATIONARY ISSUES.

11. PRACTICAL CONSIDERATIONS.

12. THE $64 QUESTION OR WORTHWHILENESS.

IV. RECOGNIZE & HEED THE 13 "RED FLAG" INSURANCE FRAUD INDICATORS

Many insurance companies have "fraud units" where certain claims are routed to be investigated and defended "to the fullest." Often, the "fraud unit" is simply a rubber stamp for an insurance company's "stone wall" or arbitrary refusal to settle in good faith. However, there are certain facts which do legitimately give rise to suspicion of fraudulent or exaggerated claims. Certain "red flag" fraud indicators or suspicious fact patterns should require from plaintiff counsel some heightened awareness and antifraud investigation. That is, if the plaintiff lawyer knows certain fact patterns—such as MIST or minor impact, soft tissue car crashes—lead to denials and vigorous defenses, then some preliminary steps should be taken to validate the plaintiff's claims and meet the defenses with the true set of facts. According to the insurance defense bar, there are 13 "red flags":

1. Claims for injury without any visible damage to the vehicles involved
2. Low or minimal impact
3. Delay in medical treatment
4. Inordinate/unreasonable amount of medical treatment
5. Unnecessary diagnostic testing for soft-tissue neck and back injuries
6. Multiple plaintiffs treating with the same medical provider for identical lengths of time
7. Reluctance of medical providers to provide records in response to duly served subpoena duces tecum or medical authorizations
8. Unwitnessed accidents and/or the absence of police, incident reports, or other documentary evidence memorializing that an accident occurred

9. Multiple prior or subsequent claims or suits

10. "Mobile" diagnostic testing equipment

11. Mutual ownership/financial interests between the referring provider and counsel

12. Over utilized and/or abusive billing codes on first party claims

13. Medical provider and/or counsel of "ill repute," such as those who are known to be "ambulance chasers," "mills," or unethical.

These indicators are nothing more than the tip of the iceberg in quickly identifying a potentially fraudulent case. Of course, staged thefts, property damage claims or bus/auto "jump in" accident victims are exceedingly difficult to detect without immediate and extensive investigation.

Ethical considerations come into play in representation of a client who may be guilty of insurance fraud. Plaintiff attorneys must distance themselves from engaging in any conduct involving "dishonesty, fraud, deceit or misrepresentation." Rule of Professional Conduct 8.4.

Plaintiff practitioners cannot seek refuge behind the attorney-client privilege, which does not apply to communications in legal service sought or obtained in aid of commission of fraud. It is an infinitely better practice to recuse oneself or decline to accept a case that factually appears suspicious rather than run the risk of compromising the Rules of Professional Conduct.

> Attorneys must arm themselves with sufficient investigative weapons, including outside vendors, and experts, to aggressively reverse the tragic trend of escalating insurance premiums due to insurance fraud. Nothing less will remove the scourge of insurance fraud from the legal landscape.

Mario Colitti, Esq., "Fighting the War on Insurance Fraud," 159 N.J.L.J. 517 (Feb. 7, 2001).

7. What Are The "Land Mines" in Mediation

"IN THE GNOME OF JUSTICE: A GRIM FAIRY TALE ABOUT THE DISTORTION & DESTRUCTION OF ADR"

(this section of the ***AAJ Deposition Notebook, 4th ed.*** was not selected for this paper)

8. What About High-Low Settlement Agreements?

(this section of the ***AAJ Deposition Notebook, 4th ed.*** was not selected for this paper)

9. The Eight Areas of Settlement Malpractice

DON'T GET YOURSELF BEHIND THE EIGHT BALLS OF LEGAL MALPRACTICE

(this section of the ***AAJ Deposition Notebook, 4th ed.*** was not selected for this paper)

E. Settlement Briefs and Presentations: How and Who to Use All the Data Effectively

1. Types of Settlement Presentations

a. Settlement Demand Letter with HEADLINES

In some cases, a simple demand letter may be all that is needed to get settlement negotiations underway. If you choose to use a demand letter, certain information should be included. We prefer to use demand letters with "headlines" or capitalized headings. These headlines make the letter easier to scan and refer to in future settlement discussions. You can use this opportunity to draft what Catherine James and Alan Blumenberg call "the 10 word telegram." That is, sum up in one short sentence or phrase what the particular section of your demand letter is about. For example: "I. Liability: A DRUNKEN DISREGARD FOR SAFETY," or I. LIABILITY: AN ACCIDENT WAITING TO HAPPEN: A BROKEN, OUT OF CODE STAIRWAY.

A good outline to follow in structuring a demand letter is the following:

I. **WHAT HAPPENED**: Factual summary of how the incident occurred. Photos/diagrams should be used.

II. **LEGAL FAULT**: Succinctly recite why the defendant is legally liable. Legal citations are helpful.

III. **INJURIES**: Itemize the injuries, and attach medical records, quote from and highlight hospital records and any treating/examining physician reports, and emphasize the nature and extent of the injuries. Photos/diagrams/medical illustrations are also useful to emphasize the seriousness of the client's physical injuries.

IV. **PERMANENCY**: Describe and document the plaintiff's permanent disabilities and impairments. That is, what things can the plaintiff not due at all at work or at home or in usual hobbies/recreations. Also, in what activities is plaintiff impaired, diminished, or only able to do with difficulty.

V. **OUT OF POCKETS**: Economic losses should be itemized and totaled. Remember that future medical bills, future lost wages, or lost earning capacity should be supported with medical and/or economic reports.

VI. **LOST ENJOYMENTS OF LIFE: THE $64/NEW NORMAL QUESTION**: Summarize plaintiff's loss of enjoyments of life. Ask the "$64 Question" or "New Normal" question: how has the incident significantly impacted your life? Or, "how has your life (pre-incident) been changed into a "New Normal"? Again photographs of the plaintiff's past active enjoyments and past times in hobbies are helpful.

VII. **DEMAND (or not) + JUSTIFICATION (or not)**: Demand a specific monetary amount, or perhaps decide to make no demand. And, consider adding jury verdict research from ***Carswell's Quantum Services and Case Evaluator***. See Selected Settlement Bibliography below, or perhaps choose not to.

VIII. **TIME LIMIT (or not)**: Set a time limit for any offer. This too is optional. Some attorneys do not like time limits because they view such "ultimatums" to be looked at with disfavor and/or totally ignored.

Especially in a potential "bad faith" case where the client's potential jury verdict will exceed the policy limits of the defendant, you should think ahead to the bad faith case. Remember that your demand letter may be ignored because the insurer is unreasonable; however, you are writing a letter to make a record that a judge and jury (in post judgment hearings and/or the bad faith trial) may later consider. Therefore, you should always draft your demand letter in a way that sounds both professional and reasonable. It will not only have a better effect upon the reader, but it may become a much better exhibit in a later jury trial.

b. The "Halpern H-Bomb" Demand Letter

One of the settlement strategies created and perfected by Richard Halpern is what I call the "H-Bomb" settlement demand letter. It combines the very essence of a powerful negotiation position—a real threat—with my late friend, Richard Halpern's "Chaos Theory"—do the unexpected. It is a very succinct but devastating tool to either move the insurer to settle or assume a commanding position throughout the litigation and if warranted at post trial hearing for sanctions or the bad faith trial for excess liability against the nonresponsive insurance carrier.

This special letter does not elaborate upon liability or damages. It is a short cover letter with one or two items of importance: 1) an independent/objective case evaluation or JVR (Jury Verdict Research) and 2) a properly executed original release from the plaintiff. The first item may or may not be provided. If it is, it may simply state that there is an objective evaluation of the case (which can or cannot be attached). If attached, this JVR report will confirm the amount of the probable jury verdict. This jury verdict evaluation or JVR can be obtained from sources such as Millennium Settlements or national, state, or provincial precedents or jury verdict research projects. The second and most explosive part of this demand letter is the attached release signed by your client with an expiration date. The effect of sending the insurance carrier a signed release for the specific amount of your demand is that for the time allotted (usually 20 to 30 days) for the carrier to accept this ultimatum, they have the ultimate power to save the insured from any further risk of excess liability. See Form 12C—Sample "Halpern H-Bomb" Settlement Demand + JVR + Release. The pressure and responsibility to act in good faith is thrust squarely upon the adjuster and the supervisor. It is a surprise maneuver when used properly that will precipitate a settlement.

Because this tactic of having the client execute a release for an amount within the insurer's policy limits is unique, it has the effect of setting you and your client's case apart from any others. It will most certainly result in a call or a letter from the adjuster. The only caveat to using this "H-Bomb" approach is that you must never bluff. That is, if you and your client do execute a release and the insurance company refuses to accept it, you and your client must be prepared to try the case and obtain a verdict or settlement for at least the amount of the "H-Bomb" demand. If you and your client capitulate and settle for anything less, you will never be able to use the "H-Bomb" method again because you will be perceived as a paper tiger, a blowhard, and a lawyer who has no credibility.

c. Settlement Briefs—Do NOT Call Them "Brochures"!

"The appearance of preparedness is as important as the preparation itself. A comprehensive and artfully drafted brochure will demonstrate to both the adjuster and the defense attorney a high degree of efficiency and commitment on your part . . .. when the settlement brochure is well prepared, the case can be tried right out of the brochure if settlement fails." James Fitzgerald and Sharon Fitzgerald, "Settlements" Chapter 33, *AAJ Litigating Tort Cases,* Volume 3, West Group (2003).

It is our recommendation that any settlement documents you prepare for your clients should not be offhandedly referred to as a "settlement brochure." The connation of a "brochure" is that you are trying to sell a product to the defense as opposed to presenting the merits, strengths, and "objective value" of your client's case. The term "brochure" is not as objective or serious as "brief." We therefore urge you and your staff to label and refer to all written presentations on behalf of your clients' settlement position as "settlement briefs."

Preparing a settlement brief forces you in your staff to prepare for trial. Once prepared, you will then be in a much better position to negotiate from a position of strength. For an excellent discussion on preparing the contents of the settlement brief, see Guide Chapter entitled "HOW TO USE THE DATA EFFECTIVELY" and subchapters "1. TYPES OF SETTLEMENT PRESENTATIONS" and " 2. EVALUATION & THEMES."

For an evaluation checklist, settlement brief outline, and samples of demand letters and settlement briefs, refer to some of the forms in *AAJ Trial Notebook* and *AAJ Deposition Notebook,* APPENDIX B: Form 11—Checklist for Evaluating Plaintiff PI cases; Form 12A—Sample Demand/"Bad Faith" Notice Letter; Form 12B—Sample Settlement Demand + JVR + Offer of Judgment; Form 12B.1—Sample Offer of Judgment; Form 12C—Sample "Halpern H-Bomb" Settlement Demand + JVR + Release; Form 13—Settlement Brief Outline; Form 14A—Sample Mediation/Settlement Brief (Auto Wrongful Death); Form 14B—Sample Arbitration/Mediation Brief (Negligent Security); Form 21A—

Sample Drew Britcher, Esq. TLC Settlement CD; Form 21B—Sample Mike Maggiano, Esq. Settlement Demand DVD.

While there is no limit on what can be included in a settlement brief, you should consider a shorter settlement presentation that will make a quick and decisive impression upon the reader rather than a long dissertation. One of the most essential features of the settlement brief is the cover. Whether using a three ring notebook, a bound book, or simply a book report cover with inserts, always place an enlarged picture or some illustration that will remind the adjuster of your client's case on the cover or inside cover of the settlement brief. Photographs showing before and after pictures of a horribly scarred or deformed plaintiff or a recent photograph a once happy family before wrongful death will be very effective in making your presentation memorable. While a settlement brief will contain basically the same information as a demand letter, it should be filled with diagrams photographs and other illustrations such as excerpts from a day in the life of video to show the reader that your settlement brief is really only a preview of what is coming.

The "thousand word picture," diagram, timeline, or medical art/illustration can go a long way toward making you position and your client's injuries, disabilities, impairments, and pain more understandable and potentially "risk laden" to the insurer or self-insured. Two of the best creative minds I have worked with to capture the intangibles of plaintiff's lives are Peter Antonuccio, of Certified Medical Illustrations, in Lawrenceville, N.J. an experienced videographer and designer of medical illustrations, and Patricia Iyer, an experienced medical and nursing expert and author from Med League Support Services, in Flemington, N.J. Their insights and work products have helped me and many other plaintiff trial lawyers better identify and present our clients, cases at trials, and arbitration/mediation, particularly the pain, suffering, and significant losses of life's enjoyments. For some excellent samples of medical illustrations, timelines, and graphic presentations of pain and suffering, see *AAJ Trial Notebook* and *AAJ Deposition Notebook* APPENDIX B: Form B.15A—Sample Medical Illustration – Back Surgery (Created by Peter Antonuccio); Form B.15B – Sample Medical Illustration—Cervical Fusion (by Antonuccio); Form B.15C—Sample Medial Illustration—Shoulder Surgery (by Antonuccio); Form B.16A—Sample Treatment Exhibit – Diagnostic Testing (Created by Patricia Iyer); Form B.16B – Sample Treatment Exhibit—A "Medication Clock" (by Iyer); Form B.16C—Sample Treatment Exhibit—A "Treatment Calendar" (by Antonuccio); Form B.17A—Sample Medical Time Line – Pressure Sore Timeline; Form B.17B—Sample Medical Time Line—failure to Diagnose (by Antonuccio); Form B.17C – Sample Medical Time

Line—failure to Treat Cancer (Created by Dara Quattrone, Esq. & Antonuccio); Form B.17C—Sample Medical Time Line—Treatment (by Antonuccio); Form B.18A—Sample Pain Illustration—Level of Consciousness (by Iyer); Form B.18B—Sample Pain Illustration—The 1 To 10 Pain Scale (by Iyer); Form B.18C—Sample Pain Illustration—Increased Pain Timeline (by Iyer).

Another important part of your settlement brief should be its appendix. Any reports, records, or other material such as answers to interrogatories, model civil jury charges, or case law should be tabulated for easy reference by the reader. Whenever you make a statement of fact or law in your settlement brief, you have documented them by attaching the supporting material in your settlement brief's appendix.

d. Settlement Video/CD/DVD/Computerized Presentations

A well done videotape settlement demand has been referred to as "a guided missile that goes around defense counsel and the adjuster assigned to the case and is aimed at the claims committee." Fitzgerald and Fitzgerald, *supra*. This kind of settlement presentation graphically shows undeniable damages your client has sustained. To do a good job, you can hire a local videographer, or you can film and edit the videotapes yourself. The most important thing about a videotape settlement demand is to keep it short and to the point.

Showing the adjuster excerpts of key witnesses is very effective. This is a unique opportunity to show off your trial exhibits. If damages or the bona fides of injuries are in question, videotaping members of the community who are or have been affected by your client's disability or death can be very powerful.

Remember that claims adjusters and major defense firms are used to seeing good quality settlement videotapes. We therefore recommend that videotape presentations be produced by experienced videographers. Professionals know more about lighting, setting, editing, and what goes to make a good visual presentation.

A computerized settlement presentation is very much like a videotaped settlement demand. It needs to be produced by someone who knows how to do it. If you are intending to present a computerized presentation during a settlement conference, it is a good idea to send a written settlement brief or demand letter along with it. It is also good advice to have someone available to run the computerized program for you. The computerized presentation can be slowed, fast forwarded, or skipped as you need.

A computerized settlement presentation has advantages over videotape because it is more flexible than any "fixed" videotape presentation. Unlike a videotape settlement presentation, the plaintiff trial attorney gets to make a live presentation, allowing him/her to advocate and discuss the client's case at any speed or in any given amount of time. Even a good videotaped settlement presentation is somewhat one-dimensional and rigid because it is awkward and disjointed to fast forward, rewind, and switch the tape on and off.

2. Evaluation and Themes

EVALUATION AND THEMEING SERIOUS INJURY & WRONGFUL DEATH CASES FOR SETTLEMENT AND TRIAL

I. INTRODUCTION: TRUE STORIES ABOUT REAL PEOPLE

Storytelling is important whether you talk to a jury, a reasonable adjuster, or an arbitrator. The art is older than human existence. Anthropologists tell us even in caves, Neanderthals gathered around fires, whispering about the gods and spirits or shouting about their victories in combat and prehistoric animal hunts. From prerecorded charcoal creations of cavemen through Aesop's Fables, the songs of troubadours of medieval times, Shakespeare plays, and up to the modern hosts of TV magazines, storytelling has always been a way to teach and educate.

From my experience with juries, judges, mediators/arbitrators, and jury consultants, I have come away with a personal philosophy and psychology in telling a client's true story in any injury or death case whether in trial, arbitration, mediation, or settlement negotiations.

An opening is crucial in the communication of the case story and theme. Plaintiff's trial counsel must, in the very beginning of the trial or settlement presentation of the case, present an accurate yet compelling version of the facts when the jury or settlement referee is most receptive and untainted. Each plaintiff trial lawyer must, therefore, become a storyteller according to the style and personality each has perfected.

From people, juries, and jury consultants, I learn that jurors and settlement referees (arbitrators/mediators) decide cases based primarily on their own personal experience and personal set of values as they apply law to the case facts. When the facts in a case galvanize those two forces and result in a positive impact, the jury, judge, or mediator will usually decide in favor of plaintiff. One not-too-distant example of an effectively correct case theme is Rodney

King II trial: jurors told TV interviewers and news reporters after they found the police guilty of same beatings a prior jury had found same not guilty: "eleven out of twelve of us are parents. We didn't have any formal training to be parents, but when we hit our children <u>we knew when to stop</u>!" Therefore, the prosecution in Rodney King II either intentionally or unintentionally touched a critical chord in the jurors (parenting) or created a compelling analogy which corresponded with the collective experience and values of the jury. The result: a positive verdict in favor of the prosecution.

According to my friend and jury consultant Diane Wiley of National Jury Project, jurors and mediators can be looked at as having three typographies or "ways of coming to make decisions."

1. <u>The Socially Responsible</u>. The socially responsible type decides what impact their decision is going to have on society—"If we decide against the defendant or for the plaintiff, what effect will this have on doctors and medicine in general?"

2. <u>The Moralist</u>. The moralistic juror/judge/mediator tends to think about what a person should have done and what they would have or not have done, "You should do this . . . you should . . . you should . . . ." They do not necessarily take into account the big picture or practical side of an issue.

3. <u>The Pragmatist</u>. Pragmatic people come from the perspective of "[w]hat the hell happened here, let's apply common sense, make a decision everybody can live with, that's the way life is."

From my experience dealing with adjusters, defense attorneys, mediators, and trial judges, one of the biggest difficulties encountered in clear liability cases where economic damages are extensive is an ingrained inertia or reluctance to "Think Big." The attitude expressed or alluded to is: "we know the case is worth more than a million dollars, <u>but</u> . . . ." For whatever reason, adjusters, defense attorneys, mediators, and some judges have told me either the victim, the jury, the jury's historic attitude, anecdotal verdicts, and horror stories, statistical jury verdict analyses, these "hard economic times," or the specific economy of the region all mitigate against a high verdict despite the fairness of the losses claimed. Normally, adjusters, defense attorneys, mediators, and judges react negatively to <u>the bottom line number</u>, be it $1 million or $10 million. The gross aggregate number always seems "too much." This is a natural human reaction, especially to people in whose lifetime that much money in one lump sum is never seen.

Understanding that adjusters, defense attorneys, mediators, and judges are human, one can also understand the fear and trepidation of a jury of lay people who collectively in one room would not represent a total earning capacity of a million dollars. You must appreciate the fact that a compelling reason must be given for <u>each individual component</u> of any damage presentation.

Telling your client's true life story in the very beginning of a settlement presentation or jury trial opening is important not only to interest the jury/judge/referee in the proofs but also to make the listeners understand what they will later see and hear in the content of what is important for proof of the elements necessary to establish the noneconomic and economic losses. By weaving the proper theme into your story, and by matching the facts with that theme, the theme should strike home with the referee's/jury's real-life experiences and also the decision making analogies used in their own every day value judgments. You should recover for the plaintiff as much compensation as is fairly and reasonably estimated to compensate for the economic value of the injuries, disabilities, impairments, suffering, pain, and lost enjoyments of life of a real person. Your case is about Mr. or Mrs. or Ms. Hertz, <u>not</u> about a "plaintiff/claimant" or an "executrix" or "administrator ad pros" or "decedent."

II. <u>WHERE TO FIND THE TRUE STORY?</u>

To find a theme for settlement and trial, you must know the legal outline of your quest. The general areas of compensable loss in a personal injury case are usually categorized as "non-economic" and "economic" losses. The "non-economic" or human damages include:

1. The nature and extent of each injury sustained
2. The temporary and permanent disability
3. The temporary and permanent impairment
4. Pain, suffering and anxiety
5. Lost enjoyments of life

The economic losses for an injured plaintiff include any out of pocket expenses which have been or will be incurred, such as:

1. Past and future medical expenses
2. Past and future lost income or earning capacity
3. Property damage

The three general areas of damage in wrongful death cases include:

1. Conscious pain, suffering, and loss of enjoyment of life.
2. Pecuniary loss to economic dependents.
   - Lost income, benefits, and inheritance
   - Lost household services
   - Lost advice, counsel, and companionship
3. Claims for serious emotional distress of bystander

To find the theme in a death case, you must first gather enough facts to analyze and evaluate the tangible and intangible economic losses of the specific wrongful death. To do so involves an extensive investigation. I recommend a conference be held at the home of the deceased's family or closest living relative. It will be at that location and not in your law office where you will gather sufficient information, stories, photo albums, and mental pictures that will assist in discovering your theme. Some of the items you should develop can follow a rough outline.

1. <u>Personal Data</u>. The date of birth of the deceased is necessary to compute life expectancy. But you should also get a broader picture of the deceased's life. Determine the place of birth and places where the deceased grew up. Educational background, from kindergarten through graduate school, professional licenses, certificates earned, and a history of employment should be developed. This will start to establish some background and history of the decedent's life.

2. <u>The Deceased's Family Status</u>. Knowing whether the deceased's grandparents, parents, brothers, and sisters lived to be a "ripe old age" can be useful to establish longevity in the family. Knowing the background of the deceased's spouse or prior marriage partners, any natural, adopted, or step children is just a preliminary to the more important relationship questions that need to be asked about the deceased.

3. <u>Prior Health of the Deceased</u>. Any medical treatment, hospitalizations, surgical procedures, and any occupational, recreational, or environmental risks to the deceased's health are necessary to establish whether the deceased in fact had a normal life expectancy. The family doctor's records and opinion that the deceased would have led a normal life expectancy are important facts in your search for a theme.

4. <u>Ante-mortem Conscious Pain, Suffering or Fear</u>. Analyze the facts of the fatal incident. Ask your-self or an accident reconstruction expert whether

or not, from the happening of the accident, there was any possibility of a painful sensation or a sense of impending doom, possibility of conscious fear or fright. This may involve a matter of seconds or many minutes.

In any case of conscious pain and suffering, the most important witness is the pathologist or medical examiner who determined the cause of death. That medical expert probably has a medical opinion as to whether there was any consciousness at all between the traumatic impact and unconsciousness and/or ultimate death. That medical professional or another forensic pathologist can be supplied eyewitness statements indicating the independent observations of the length of any conscious sensations, sounds, movements, or other indicators of pain, suffering, or consciousness. That medical expert can then translate those facts into a medical opinion expressing an estimate or range of time for the deceased's last conscious sensations and feelings. Also, a graphically accurate and compelling description can be given by the forensic pathologist as to the probable sensation and feelings to an individual suffering that type of sudden or lingering death. *Tirrell v. Navistar Intern., Inc.*, 248 N.J. Super 390 (App. Div. 1991).

5. <u>Loss of Enjoyment of Life</u>. In New Jersey and some other jurisdictions, a deceased's "unconscious," even comatose, premortem condition is entitled to be evaluated by the jury's award for lost enjoyment of life even if for a brief period of time.

6. <u>Financial Services Advice and Companionship to Dependents</u>. If the deceased left a spouse or child or financially dependent individual, you should first determine the legality of their entitlement to recovery. Then discover the date of birth of that individual, their life expectancy, background, and the true meaning of the relationship between the deceased and beneficiary in terms of time and quality of time. Corroborating facts of and witnesses to this relationship are something you should insist upon to verify the truth of the story you will ultimately tell the jury.

7. <u>Educational Achievements of the Deceased</u>. Knowing the educational level and any scholastic or extracurricular achievements of the deceased while in school is important in developing the work ethic and character of the deceased.

<u>Community Involvement, Achievements or Volunteer Activity</u>. If the deceased volunteered any services in the community, these type of services can be not only corroborated but also used as an indicator of his/her work ethic and character.

Lost Wages. Lost wages are fairly easy to compute. An employer will usually have an employee file, and regular and overtime earnings can be calculated on a weekly or annual basis. It is customary to try to obtain five of the prior year's earnings and to compute fringe benefits such as a pension plan; savings plan; life, accident, and health insurance and dependent coverage; retirement benefits; collective bargaining agreement; and any foreseeable promotions the decedent was expecting. Be sure to obtain copies of these documents.

If the decedent was a union member, usually, the hours worked or an average can be obtained through the union or pension board. Tax returns should also be culled from the client's records. If they are not available, immediately send a form to the IRS requesting same. If the decedent planned to retire, there should be some corroboration by witnesses or some documentation of these plans.

Even if the decedent was unemployed, e.g., a child or retired/out of work adult, career aspirations and goals should nevertheless be explored with family and friends. If the deceased had any bank accounts, IRAs, savings, stocks, bonds, and other investments, they should be explored to demonstrate the (savings(that would have been accumulated in the future. An item to explore, in some cases, is whether there was a lost inheritance. If the deceased had actually saved and planned to leave certain funds or money in trust for various beneficiaries, this should be discussed with family or close friends in order to prove a lost inheritance. *Weiman v. Ippolito*, 129 N.J. Super. 578, Amended 130 N.J. Super. 207 (App. Div. 1974).

Household Services. If the deceased was married, the average number of hours per day and

per week spent giving care, hands-on help, attention, and maintenance to the family home and properties and the nature and extent of any such "around the house" help should be itemized.

When describing household duties, it is important for you and your expert to explain to the jury the nature and extent of the deceased's family properties: the home, its yard, their pets, cars, vehicles, or other equipment requiring maintenance. Any special or skilled services performed by the deceased— nursing, gardening, painting, plumbing, carpentry, etc.—should be explored. If at present the surviving spouse has substituted services, either paid or unpaid, which were customarily performed by the decedent, that will be a good indicator of the type and value of services.

11. Daily Routine. A good way to approach a case after the surviving spouse or

family members have had a chance to reconcile with their loss is to talk with them about the daily routine or a typical daily weekday (using a typical 24 hour day) in the life of the deceased. A typical weekend Saturday and Sunday can also be written out. These daily routines will help show you some of the daily personal habits and family customs of the deceased.

12. <u>Lost Advice, Counsel, and Companionship.</u> In order to prove a loss of society, there must have been some companionship lost. The "society" or "companionship" referred to in this legal context is not one that exists between friends but the society of those living together for continuous period. You should explore where the deceased and family lived, for how long, the type of building, and how long the decedent actually lived with each individual claiming lost advice, counsel, or companionship. If there is a continuous "living together," that would prove continuous association. But, if by reason of occupation or otherwise deceased/claimants were accustomed to leaving the common residence for extended periods that needs to be verified before, you and your client are embarrassed by having overreached in evaluating the loss of companionship. Also, the harmony of the marital or family relationship needs to be examined. Marital or family problems between the deceased and claimants will, of course, be used by the defense if at all possible to deflate the claim. If there was discord, but it was only temporary, that should be explained openly and frankly.

13. <u>Common Interests</u>. When a husband and wife are disassociated because of separate career paths for separate and uncommon interests, that is usually apparent not only in the household but also in the neighborhood and among their closes circle of friends and family. When there is a close and supportive relationship, one way of showing such a companionship is by the many "common interests" shared, such as religion, social activities, hobbies, intellectual studies, art, entertainment, and travel. Develop these common interests in your search for a theme.

14. <u>Participation in Family Activities</u>. A habit of participation by the deceased and claimants in a common family activity tends to show a closely knit family circle. This is very important in establishing whether there are true damages for loss of society. Determine who the members of the family were and what activities each participated in separately and together.

15. <u>Teaching Special Skills</u>. If the deceased possessed any special skills, such as mechanical, artistic, sports, music, etc., and it was his/her habit to teach such special skills to the family, then each claimant who received such instruction has a legitimate claim for the loss of that special advice and society.

16. Family Participation in Religion. Evidence by way of photographs, church programs, etc. that the family participated in religious activities is a good indicator that the family was close knit. "Praying and Staying Together" is not an empty phrase.

17. Reputation and Character. The character, reputation, habits, kindness, and disposition of the deceased are all matters which a jury can and will take into consideration to decide upon the economic value of the service of the deceased. *Wimberly v. City of Paterson*, 75 N.J. Super. 584 (App. Div,. 1962); *Gerstenberg v. Reynolds*, 259 N.J. Super. 431 (Law Div. 1991).

18. Financial and Business Expertise. Another important factor in evaluating the quality and quantity of advice and counsel is advice and assistance in financial and business matters. The deceased, because of superior business ability or life experiences, may have been qualified and in fact gave valuable business assistance and advice to his family or to others. That is a good indicator that as the children grew older he would have rendered such valuable business assistance to them. The actual disposition and inclination of people differ. Where one person will be of great comfort to their family and counsel and advice will be of great financial benefit, another person may merely be supportive of a family's economic wants and although a good provider not necessarily a great assistance in financial matters. While not ignoring the weaknesses, it is your obligation as plaintiff's counsel to discover and develop the pluses of the decedent's character.

19. Caveat: Overreliance Upon Professional Forensic Experts. Using an economist is rather routine in wrongful death cases. Sometimes, however, the plaintiff's attorney will rely too much upon the economists or their form questionnaires to discover the economic facts which go into the mathematical calculations.

The wrongful death of an individual is not simply an economic event. The death of our clients should be treated as seriously as any personal loss in our own family. Strive to learn as much as you can about the deceased in order to properly evaluate the value of that individual's life, work, and relationship to those left behind. If legally capable of being evaluated, they should be, and in the process of learning more than just the lost wages and fringe benefits of the deceased, you will learn their life and time history. Therein, you may find the true theme for the story of that individual's death and the resulting losses to family and dependents.

20. Caveat: Relying Strictly Upon Written Reports of "Unconsciousness."

Often, I have found that EMT and ER reports of the deceased being "unconscious" at the scene are inaccurate, incomplete, or outright wrong! Always try to interview lay people as well as emergency medical personnel at the scene as to any consciousness.

III. HOW TO TEST THE STORY THEME

After discovering and developing some of the life, times, education, work, home, and family experiences of the deceased, normally, you will find themes. An individual may have been a credit to the community and an outstanding example for everyone in church, school, and town; another individual, despite a spotty work record and several marriages, may nevertheless have been a good father or mother to the children or a good volunteer fireman. An invalid may have been the "final arbitrator" of family disputes and the patriarch or matriarch of the family, the historian, and ultimate lawgiver of the tribe. Each family has its own sense of value of relationships, and in each family, there is a true story to be told. Finding it is one very important and time consuming quest. Testing the theme is another separate and time consuming quest.

From my experience, the best way to test the theme to see whether it will be accepted in mediation/arbitration or trial is to test a representative sampling of people from the community in which the case will be tried by way of focus group or mock jury. My experience with them has been positive and beneficial in the evaluation, settlement, and trial of a client's wrongful death case. An emotional "unloading" or "unpacking" of the family to test for themes may require some refinement or additional facts after mock jury presentment before that theme has positive impact on ordinary and impartial members of the community.

IV. WHO SHOULD TELL THE CLIENT'S STORY: DO YOU WANT A "DH"?

In a serious injury or wrongful death case, separate reasons may develop naturally or as a matter of strategy that negotiating and trying the case jointly with separate counsel for a consortium plaintiff is a benefit not only to the client but also to the attorneys.

For whatever reasons, separate claimants may need separate advice and counsel. Also, in preparation for mediation, arbitration, or trial, it may become apparent that separate claimants should have separate counsel to effectively communicate their claim to the mediator or jury. If the issue of separate trial counsel arises, it should be considered, discussed, and decided upon long before it is time to submit the final witness lists. Selection of separate trial counsel should not be made at the last minute, thereby causing a delay of the trial. *Hauck v. Danclar*, 262 N.J. Super. 225 (Law Div. 1993).

There may also be good reasons to "double team" settlement and trial. Consider consulting with and having a professional consultant available to act as an advisor as to negotiation tactics of specific insurance carriers/self insureds involved in the settlement process. There are experts like The Halpern Group and Elite Financial Services, who provide such specialized services to help the lawyer understand and counter the evaluation and negotiation tactics of the authorized claims professionals involved. I have found it most advantageous to have my own structured settlement expert with me or on telephone standby whenever the opposition brings its own in-house or "exclusive" annuity expert to the settlement conference table.

You may also wish to consider having another attorney from your own office act as the designated settlement negotiator or "DH" (designated haggler). Using a "DH" often allows me to concentrate on trial preparation rather than spending time in several rounds of settlement discussions. For more discussion of this "double team" strategy for settlement and trial, see this Guide Chapter and subchapter below entitled "3. ALTERNATIVE APPROACH TO WHO SHOULD NEGOTIATE & TRY THE CASE."

YOUR SACRED MISSION

Representing the survivors of a wrongful death or catastrophic injury is one of the most sacred undertakings for which a trial lawyer can be chosen. It requires a sensitivity and doggedness to gently but firmly pry open and probe into sensitive areas that require inspection to not merely avoid embarrassment but also provide insights which will be valuable to the survivors. Family meetings at the home of the survivors require extra effort, time, and commitment by a plaintiff's trial lawyer and the entire office staff. If you undertake this type of case, you should also undertake to give it your best. If you undertake to make an opening, it should be prepared with the full facts and background of the deceased in hand and with the best and most accurate history and the best and most compelling theme that you can tell.

Representing a handicapped person, family of severely injured person, or a deceased's family requires you to build the case from its foundation. You must build the true story from building blocks and materials you uncover, using the blueprint of your damages law. Do not be discouraged by the defense attitude that you are trying to make "too much" out of this case. As my friend from

AAJ, Greg Cusimano often says: "it takes a carpenter a long while to build the barn, but any jack ass can kick it down in a minute!"

3. Who Should Negotiate and Try The Case? An Alternative Approach

TRIAL BY JOINT VENTURE: A Synergistic Approach to Civil Trial Advocacy & Settlement

(this section of the *AAJ Deposition Notebook, 4th ed.* was not selected for this paper)

TEN REASONS FOR "AAJ (NOW AAJ) DOUBLE TEAM"

The following are my reasons for recommending to plaintiff attorneys that a joint venture with a fellow AAJ (now AAJ) trial attorney with credentials and experience to handle specialized matters, rather than refer the entire case, or both clients to another attorney:

1. The Clients Are Better Served.
2. The Synergistic Effect.
3. Improved Communication.
4. The Sharing of Resources.
5. Sharing of Responsibility.
6. Sharing Risks and Expenses.
7. Complementary and Offsetting Weaponry.
8. The Reduction/Elimination of Stress.
9. Improved Relationships With Your Clients and Your Peers.
10. Additional Assurance From Allegations of Malpractice.

CONCLUSION

Everyone should reflect on their own personal practice and how and why we make decisions to accept, reject, settle, litigate, try, refer, or keep cases. If you never consulted with settlement strategists and utilized the historical data on specific insurance companies/self insureds in their programs, I suggest you check out the other successful trial lawyers around North America, confer with them, and then test drive a successful vehicle for case resolution. It is certainly more advantageous for your clients, than relying upon a volunteer/paid mediator/arbitrator. If you have never "DH'd" (designated a haggler) and turned over settlement negotiations between your client and the insurer to a trusted partner or trusted lawyer, you should consider saving yourself the time, stress, and distractions. If you have never tried a case sharing the cockpit with a compatible cocounsel, I strongly urge that you try it . . . sooner than later. You may find that your clients like it! You may "try by joint venture" and like it yourself! You may even double your pleasure and enjoyment in settlement conferences, mediations, and the court room.

4. Identify and Prove Pain With Nurse/Expert Fact Witnesses and Summaries

IDENTIFYING AND PROVING PAIN WITH NURSE/EXPERT FACT WITNESSES

By: Patricia Iyer, MSN, RN, LNCC and Tom Vesper

(this section of the ***AAJ Deposition Notebook, 4th ed.*** was not selected for this paper)

AAJ SETTLEMENT NOTEBOOK EPILOGUE

Trial advocacy is often referred to as an art, not a science. There is more to trying a case for an injured victim than simply knowing the law and medicine, understanding the rules of procedure and evidence, and following a fixed formula for success. There are some general rules and principles, but there are very few situations that can be met with a mathematical application of pure logic. However, there is at least one general rule of advocacy on which trial lawyers agree: "*semper paratus*"—always be prepared!

The best trial lawyers become successful through experience, hard work, motivation, and discipline. All are different in their manner and style of trial presentation and preparation. Whether they are cool and unflappable or aggressive and theatrical, trial lawyers have one thing in common: a love and reverence for the legal arena—the courtroom.

Many court administrators, Supreme Court committees on civil case management, appellate and trial judges, and congressional representatives seek to change our democratic civil jury procedures to increase efficiency and expedite the "resolution" of civil cases. The changes they seek are to "ensure *faster*, *fairer, and more economic results for* . . . *litigants.*"[1] This is the familiar cry for predictability, uniformity, and consistency.

In 1984, one of these would-be judicial reformers, then United States Supreme Court Chief Justice Warren Burger, referred to trial lawyers as "procurers" and "hired guns."[2]

He also denigrated the civil jury system by suggesting that trial by a jury of citizens is antiquated and as functional as medieval trial-by-combat:[3]

> Our distant forebears moved slowly from trial by battle and other barbaric means of resolving conflicts and disputes, and we must move away from total reliance on the adversary contest for resolving all disputes. For some disputes, trials will be the only means, *but for many, trials by the adversary contest must in time go the way of the ancient trial by battle and blood.* Our system is too costly, too painful, too destructive, too inefficient for a truly civilized people. To rely on the adversary process as the principal means of resolving conflicting claims is a mistake that must be corrected (*emphasis added*).

These statements by the former U.S. Chief Justice are out of touch with the street-level reality of our system of justice. The civil jury trial preserves our democratic ideals and individualizes and humanizes our laws. The conscience of our community, not Big Brother, His Honor, or Mr./Mrs. Arbitrator/Mediator, should decide the value and quality of life and disputed facts in our civil courts. Trial judges are often influenced by real-life administrative or political pressures having nothing to do with the case or issues at hand. Jurors, on the other hand, have no "next case on the list"; their collective wisdom has no artificial time limit on reaching a fair and impartial decision. The jury is our guarantee of quality in dispensing justice.

During his tenure as president of AAJ, the late David Shrager wrote, "[T]he system of trial by jury is an immaculate expression of the democratic process by bringing to bear the conscience and sense of fairness of our citizens in every community in the land."[4]

---

[1] Administrative Office of the Courts, State of New Jersey, Press Release, *Civil Cases to Be Focus of 1984 New Jersey Judicial Conference* (Sept. 27, 1983) (emphasis added).

[2] W. Burger, *The State of Justice*, 70 A.B.A.J. 62, 66 (1984).

[3] *Id.*

[4] D. Shrager, *President's Page: "Mr. Chief Justice, I Dissent,"* 20 TRIAL 4 (Apr. 1984).

Shrager also criticized the remarks made by Chief Justice Burger at the 1984 ABA Convention:[5]

> [The Chief Justice] talks of frivolous lawsuits, seizing on some spectacular examples which are calculated to distort the fact that the overwhelming number of cases involve good faith disputes among our citizens which are rather promptly, benignly, and fairly settled daily in the courts of our country.

To meet the challenge of cynical Supreme Court justices, to bear well the constant management of bureaucrats, and to live up to the daily expectations of the trial bench, we must remember the classic code of the cavalry: quick decision, speedy execution, and calculated audacity; better a good plan executed now than a perfect plan next week. *"Mobilitate vigemus"* (in mobility lies our strength).

Socrates called advocacy "the most noble profession." In representing clients whose lives, hopes, and dreams have been altered or crushed, we carry on that noble heritage. Advocacy, from the Latin verb *advocare*, means "to call to one's aid." We trial lawyers are modern-day warriors, called to aid our clients in the everyday causes that arise from their personal or business lives. As champions of our clients' rights and duties, we must train rigorously and battle effectively and zealously in the courtroom.

Years ago, I stumbled across a passage attributed to George S. Patton, Jr.; that struck a deep chord within me, and I copied it down. It stirs my passion for trying to win a just jury verdict. Although Patton speaks in the context of war, his insight applies to other fields of human endeavor, including law, and he powerfully expresses the idea that an individual can have a great impact.[6]

> The history of war is the history of warriors; few in number, mighty in influence. Alexander, not Macedonia, conquered the world. Scipio, not Rome, destroyed Carthage. Marlborough, not the allies, defeated France. Cromwell, not the Roundheads, dethroned Charles . . .. Truly in war, "Men are nothing, a man is everything." . . . [T]he leader must be an actor . . .. [H]e is unconvincing unless he lives his part . . .. The fixed determination to acquire the warrior soul, and having acquired it, to conquer or perish with honor is the secret of success in war.

---

[5]*Id.*

[6]Patton, *Success in War*, 40 Cavalry J. 26, 28, 30 (Jan. 1931).

The Vespers' Trial Cookbook

This *AAJ Settlement Notebook* ideas are adaptable to your personal trial style. You who are shrewd enough to observe others with more experience, to adopt the best of what you see, and to make your trial notebook a worthwhile working case file will be well on your way to victor.

BEST OF LUCK FINDING FACTS SUPPORTING CLIENTS' FULL MEASURE OF JUSTICE

Tom Vesper

Chapter 12. SOME FINAL TOASTS & BLESSINGS TO ALL TRIAL LAWYERS

TOM'S TRIAL TIPS: Value & Role of "Trial Lawyer"

<u>**BENEDIZIONE e SALUTE e BRINDISI POTABILE or blessings & toasts (in honor of American jury system & tribute to true "trial lawyer value" to USA)**</u>

SOME "FINAL TOASTS"

(Excerpts from <u>Uncle Anthony's Unabridged Analogies, 4th Edition</u>)

Uncle Anthony: Here's to an American and always remember last two syllables—**I CAN!**

Uncle Anthony: Here's to all of us who admit we are not perfect—if we were our poor wives would have to go out and criticize perfect strangers!

Uncle Anthony: Women have many faults; we men have only two. / Everything we say, and everything we do!

Some Final Toasts to Trial Lawyers

Uncle Anthony: As we all start this [**EDITOR:** Birthday, New Year, whatever event] / let's get down on our knees / to thank God that we're on our feet.

Uncle Anthony: Here's to . . . May he live respected and die regretted.

Uncle Anthony: A wise man once said somewhere that every successful enterprise requires three men—a dreamer, a businessman, and an SOB—here's to all three of you!

Aunt Mary Carlo: Bless you/us all, and may y/our shadows never grow larger.

Aunt Mary Carlo: Like a fine wine I ain't gettin older, I'm just gettin more complex.

Aunt Mary Carlo: I only drink on days ending in "y."

Aunt Mary Carlo: Here's to dose who love us well, an dose dat don't can go to hell!

Aunt Mary Carlo [**ED.:** my Aunt was very devout—when she wanted to—in her Catholicism; and so she often called upon the Martyrs and The Saints of the Roman Catholic Church—esp. if they were Italian—to bless or blast someone; one of her favorites was St Lucy or Santa Lucia (283–304); venerated as saint by Roman Catholic, Anglican, Lutheran, and Orthodox Christians; her feast day in the West is December 13, which by unreformed Julian calendar is the longest night of year; with a name derived from lux, lucis "light"; one of only seven women, aside from the Blessed Virgin, commemorated by name in the Canon of the Mass; during the Emperor Diocletian's persecution, she consecrated her virginity to God, refused to marry a pagan, gave her dowry to the poor; her would-be husband denounced her as a Christian to the Roman Governor of <u>Syracuse, Sicily</u>, who took out her eyes with a fork; therefore, in some art, her eyes appear on a plate she is holding; and since she is patron saint of those who are <u>blind</u>, my Aunt Mary often would say): Hey! Please!! **Santa Lucia, please help us taka da crap outta his/her/their eyes!**

Dr. Martin Arrowsmith: (the country doctor hero in Sinclair Lewis' 1925 Pulitzer Prize winning novel *Arrowsmith*): God give me clear eyes and freedom from haste. God give me anger against all pretense. God keep me looking for my own mistakes. God keep me at it till my results are proven. God give me strength not to trust to God.

Brendan Francis Behan: I have a total irreverence for anything connected with society except that which makes to road safer, the beer stronger, the old men and women warmer in the winter, and happier in the summer.

Oscar Levant (as Sid Jeffers in the 1946 movie *Humoresque*, starring Joan

Crawford and John Garfield in an older woman/younger man tale about a violinist and his patroness, Sid advises): I envy people who drink. At least they know what to blame everything on.

Humphrey Bogart: The whole world is about three drinks behind.

William Jennings Bryan (a teetotaler himself, once toasted the British Navy with a glass of water, saying): **Gentlemen, I believe your victories were won on water.**

Lord Byron: Man, being reasonable, must get drunk; / The best of life is but intoxication.

Thomas Campbell (Drink Ye to Her): Drink ye to her that each loves best!

Jack Canfield (coauthor of *Chicken Soup for the Soul*): May you always work like you don't need the money; may you always love like you've never been hurt; and may you always dance like there's nobody watching.

President Jimmy Carter (June 25, 1979): To peace and friendship among all people.

Cervantes: I drink when I have occasion and sometimes when I have no occasions.

Chaucer: Now let's sit & drink and make us merry, / And afterward we will his body bury.

Chet (a professional college student played by Eric Stoltz, in 1995 movie *Kicking and Screaming*; about a group of college graduates who refuse to move on with their lives, each in his own peculiar way): If Plato is a fine red wine, then Aristotle is a dry martini.

Winston Churchill: I have taken more out of alcohol than alcohol has taken out of me.

Winston Churchill: My rule of life prescribed as an absolutely sacred rite smoking cigars and also the drinking of alcohol before, after and if need be during all meals and in the intervals between them.

John Dryden: His preaching much but more his practice wrought / A living sermon of the truths he taught.

Robert Duvall (as Captain Gus MacCrae, ex-Texas Ranger, in the 1989 TV mini-series *Lonesome Dove*): Here's to the sunny slopes of long ago.

W.C. Fields: Drink is your enemy—love your enemies.

Some Final Toasts to Trial Lawyers

W.C. Fields: Beauty is in the eye of the beerholder.

W.C. Fields: Never drink water—look at the way it rusts pipes.

W C. Fields: I can tell I've had enough to drink when my knees start to bend backwards.

Scott Fitzgerald: First you take a drink, then the drink takes a drink then the drink takes you.

Franklin: In wine there is wisdom, / in beer there is freedom, / in water there is bacteria.

Benjamin Franklin: He that drinks fast, pays slow.

Benjamin Franklin: There are more old drunkards than old doctors.

French Inscription (found by my mother Carmella on a convent in Paris, France, which she repeated often to me): ***Faie le bien pour le mal, car Dieu te le commande*** ' Do good for evil, for God commands it.

French Inscription (on a clock in the Hotel de Ville, Neuilly, France): ***Ma voix resonne, ecoute! Elle dit qu'il est l'heure de bien faire*** ' My voice resounds, listen! It says that it is the hour to do good.

French Toast (especially July 14 Bastille Day): ***Plus je bois, mieux je chante*** ' The more I drink, the better I sing.

L. R. Fulmer (Methodist preacher and teetotaler): May you live forever / And die happy.

Gaelic Toast: [between two good friends]: A) Here's to us. / B) None like us. A) (Shrugging) Damn few. / B) Aye, and they're dead.

David Garrick: Let others hail the rising sun, / I bow to that whose course is run.

Kahlil Gibran: Love one another, but make not a bond of love: / Let it rather be a moving sea between the shores of your souls.

Ancient Greek Custom: A pledge of three cups: one to Mercury, one to Graces, one to Zeus.

Irish Blessing: *Go mairir is go gathair* or May you live and may you wear it out.

Irish Blessing: Bless your little Irish heart and every other Irish part.

Irish Blessing: May the road rise up to meet you, may the wind be ever at your back. May the sun shine warm upon your face and the rain fall softly on your fields. And until we meet again, may God hold you in the hollow of his hand.

Irish Blessing: May God grant you always . . . A sunbeam to warm you, a moonbeam to charm you, a sheltering Angel so nothing can harm you. Laughter to cheer you. Faithful friends near you. And whenever you pray, Heaven to hear you.

Irish Blessing: May your days be many and your troubles be few. May all God's blessings descend upon you. May peace be within you; may your heart be strong. May you find what you're seeking wherever you roam.

Irish Blessing: May flowers always line your path and sunshine light your day. May songbirds serenade you every step along the way. May a rainbow run beside you in a sky that's always blue. May happiness fill your heart each day your whole life through.

Irish Blessing: May God give you . . . For every storm a rainbow, for every tear a smile, for every care a promise and a blessing in each trial. For every problem life sends, a faithful friend to share, for every sigh, a sweet song and an answer for each prayer.

Irish Blessing: For each petal on the shamrock, this brings a wish your way. Good health, good luck, and happiness for today and every day.

Irish Blessing: May St. Patrick guard you wherever you go, and guide you in whatever you do and may his loving protection be a blessing to you always.

Irish Blessing: May you have the hindsight to know where you've been, / The foresight to know where you are going, / And the insight to know when you have gone too far.

Irish Blessing [EDITOR: attributed to St. Patrick**]:** May the strength of God pilot us; / May the wisdom of God instruct us, / May the hand of God protect us, / May the word of God direct us. / Be always ours this day and for evermore.

Irish Blessing: May you always have / Enough happiness to keep you sweet; Enough trails to keep you strong; / Enough success to keep you eager; Enough faith to give you courage; And enough determination to / Make each day a special day.

Irish Blessing: May the Irish hills caress you. May her lakes and rivers bless you. May the luck of the Irish enfold you May the blessings of Saint Patrick behold you.

Irish Blessing: May you be in heaven a full half hour before the devil knows you are dead.

Irish Blessing: May you have warm words on a cold evening, a full moon on a dark night, and a smooth road all the way to your door.

Irish Blessing: May good luck be your friend in whatever you do, and may trouble be always a stranger to you.

Irish Blessing: May you always have walls for the winds, a roof for the rain, tea beside the fire, laughter to cheer you, those you love near you, and all your heart might desire.

Irish Blessing: May you have love that never ends, lots of money and lots of friends. Health be yours, whatever you do, and may God send many blessings to you.

Irish Blessing: May the friendships you make be those which endure and all of your grey clouds be small ones for sure. And trusting in Him to Whom we all pray, may a song fill your heart every step of the way.

Irish Blessing: May you always walk in sunshine. May you never want for more. May Irish angels rest their wings right beside your door.

Irish Blessing: May your pockets be heavy and your heart be light. May good luck pursue you each morning and night.

Irish Blessing: May the sun shine all day long, everything go right and nothing wrong. May those you love bring love back to you, and may all the wishes you wish come true!

Irish Blessing: May your thoughts be as glad as shamrocks, may your heart be as light as a song, may each day bring you bright, happy hours that stay with you all the year long.

Irish Blessing: May the good Saints protect you and bless you today, and may troubles ignore you each step of the way.

Irish Blessing: May the raindrops fall lightly on your brow. May the soft winds freshen your spirit. May the sunshine brighten your heart. May the burdens of the day rest lightly upon you, and may God enfold you in the mantle of His love.

Irish Blessing: When the first light of sun, Bless you. When the long day is done, Bless you. In your smiles and your tears, Bless you. Through each day of your years, Bless you.

Irish Blessing: May brooks and trees and singing hills join in the chorus too, and every gentle wind that blows send happiness to you.

Irish Blessing: May you always have work for your hands to do. May your pockets hold always a coin or two. May the sun shine bright on your window pane. May the rainbow be certain to follow each rain. May the hand of a friend always be near you. And may God fill your heart with gladness to cheer you.

Irish Blessing: May your joys be as bright as the morning and your sorrows merely be shadows that fade in the sunlight of love. May you have enough happiness to keep you sweet, enough trials to keep you strong, enough sorrow to keep you human, enough hope to keep you happy, enough failure to keep you humble, enough success to keep you eager, enough friends to give you comfort, enough faith and courage in yourself to banish sadness, enough wealth to meet your needs and one thing more, enough determination to make each day a wonderful day than the one before.

Irish Blessing: May those who love us, love us; and those who don't love us, may God turn their hearts; and if He doesn't turn their hearts, may he turn their ankles so we'll know them by their limping.

Irish Blessing: May your neighbors respect you, / Trouble neglect you, / The angels protect you, / And heaven accept you.

Irish Blessing: May the Irish hills caress you. / May her lakes and rivers bless you. / May the luck of the Irish enfold you. / May the blessings of Saint Patrick behold you.

Irish Blessing: May the luck of the Irish possess you, / May the devil fly off with your worries, / May God bless you forever and ever.

Irish Toast: *Sliocht sleachta ar shliocht bhur sleachta.* [**EDITOR:** English translation: **May your children's children have children**]

Irish Toast: *Go mbeirimid beo ar an am seo aris.* [**EDITOR:** English translation: May we be alive at the same time next year]

Irish Toast (May the Road Rise Up To Meet You): May the wind be always at your back. / May the sun shine warm upon your face, / The rains fall soft upon your fields. / And until we meet again, / May God hold you in the palm of his hand. [**EDITOR:** If you are looking for a longer "toast" look at the full text of this traditional Irish Prayer above]

Irish Toast: We drink to your coffin. May it be built from the wood of a hundred year old oak tree that I shall plant today.

Irish Toast: Health and a long life to you. / Land without rent to you. / A child every year to you. / And if you can't go to heaven, / May you at least die in Ireland.

Irish Toast: In the New Year, may your right hand always be stretched out in friendship but never in want.

Irish Toast: May we all be alive this time next year; if we're not better may we not be worse.

Irish Toast: May your thoughts be as glad as the shamrocks. / May your hearts be as light as a song. / May each day bring you bright happy hours, / That stay with you all year long.

Irish Toast: For each petal on the shamrock / This brings a wish your way. / Good health, good luck, and happiness / For today and every day.

Irish Toast: May your heart be warm and happy / With the lilt of Irish laughter / Every day in every way / And forever and ever after.

Irish Toast: Wherever you go and whatever you do, / May the luck of Irish be there with you.

Irish Toast: May your blessings outnumber / The shamrocks that grow, / And may trouble avoid you / Wherever you go.

Irish Toast: Here's to the land of the shamrock so green, / Here's to each lad and his darling colleen, / Here's to the ones we love dearest and most, / And may God bless old Ireland!—that's an Irishman's toast.

Irish Toast: If you're enough lucky to be Irish . . . / You're lucky enough.

Irish Toast: Health and a long life to you. / Land without rent to you. / A child every year to you. / And if you can't go to heaven, / May you at least die in Ireland.

Irish Toast: May you have: / No frost on your spuds, / No worms on your cabbage. / May your goat give plenty of milk. / And if you inherit a donkey, / May she be in foal.

Irish Toast: To Ireland, the place on earth / That heaven has kissed / With melody, mirth, / And meadow and mist.

Irish Toast: When we drink, we get drunk. / When we get drunk, we fall asleep. / When we fall asleep, we commit no sin. / When we commit no sin, we go to heaven. / So, let's all get drunk, and go to heaven!

Irish Toast: Here's to a long life and a merry one. / A quick death and an easy one. / A pretty girl and an honest one. / A cold beer-and another one!

Irish Toast: An Irishman is never drunk as long as he can hold onto one blade of grass and not fall off the face of the earth.

Irish Toast [ED.: might properly be taken as an insult with class or classy insult]: May the devil make a ladder of your backbone / While he is picking apples in the garden of Hell.

Irish Toast: May you live to be a hundred years, with one extra year to repent!

Irish Toast: Do more than exist, live. / Do more than touch, feel. / Do more than look, observe. / Do more than read, absorb. / Do more than hear, listen. / Do more than think, ponder. / Do more than talk, say something. / May you live as long as you want but never want as long as you live.

Irish Toast: Here's to your enemies' enemies!

Irish Toast: To the thirst that is yet to come.

Irish Toast (usually spoken at wakes and in honor of the deceased): May neighbors respect you; troubles neglect you; the angels protect you; and Heaven accept you.

Jeremy Irons: We all have our time machines. Some take us back, and those we call memories. Some take us forward, and those are called dreams.

Washington Irving (from *Rip Van Winkle*): Here's to your good health, / And your family's good health, / And may you all live long and prosper.

Italian Blessing: There are three beautiful things in life: birth, love, and this day. Best wishes and good fortune to you, (bride) and (groom), for all of your life.

Italian Blessing: *O Dio, / che ci concedi ogni giorno / il pane, il vino, e l'olio / saziandoci nella tua benevolenza. / benedici questo nostro stare a mensa / e donaci la gratitudine verso di te / e verso tutta la creazione* [**EDITOR:** Translation: O God, / every day you give us / bread, wine, and oil / satisfying us with your generosity. / Bless our being together at this table / and give us gratitude toward you / and toward all of creation.

Italian Blessing: *Signore del mondo, / il pane della terra ci sostiene, / il vino rallegra il nostro cuore / e l'olio illumina il nostro volto. / Sii benedetto per queste creature, / doni preziosi che vengono da te / per la consolazione di noi uomini.* [**EDITOR:** Translation: Lord of the World, / bread from the earth sustains us / wine gladdens our heart / and oil makes \our faces shine. / May you be blessed for these creatures / precious gifts that come from you / for the comfort of us human beings.

Italian Inscription and Toast (found on a little house by my mother Carmella in Tuscany, which she loved to repeat to me whenever I asked her to move from her little house in Pennsauken, NJ): *Casa mea, casa mea; piccola che sia, Sei sempre, casa mea* ' My house, my house; small as it is, still always my house.

Ancient Italian Tradition: In Rome, drinking to another's health became so important that the Roman Senate decreed all diners must drink to Augustus Caesar at every meal. Fabius Maximus declared that no man should eat or drink before he had prayed for him and drank to his health.

Italian Toast: *Alla giornato!* To the day!

Italian Toast: At the table, one does not grow old.

Italian Toast: It is well to remember the four reasons for drinking: 1. The arrival of a friend; 2. One's present or future thirst; 3. The excellence of the wine; 4. Or any other reason.

Italian Toast: *Amore, salud, dinero, y tiempo para gustarle* [**EDITOR:** English translation: love, health, money, and time to enjoy it].

Italian Wedding Toast: It is around the table that friends understand best the warmth of being together.

Jesuit Blessing (Jesuits or members of the Society of Jesus, S.J., were founded by St Ignatius of Loyola in 1534; he and his six Companions went to Montmartre, the Hill of Martyrs in Paris, and vowed themselves to poverty, chastity, and apostolic endeavors in the Holy Land or, if it proved not be possible, to whatever tasks the Pope required of them; unlike the Dominicans, the Jesuits do not pray as a community, wear a distinctive religious habit, undertake regular penances, or have a female branch of the Order; the Society is highly centralized with military discipline; the Motto of the Jesuit Order is): *Ad Majorem Dei gloriam* ' **ALL FOR THE GLORY OF GOD.**

Jewish Toast: Thank you my friend for your **"DEEDS OF LOVING KINDNESS."**

Pope John XXIII: People are like wine-some turn to vinegar but the best improve with age.

Ben Jonson (from his poem *To Celia*): **Drink to me only with thine eyes / And I will pledge with mine; / Or leave a kiss but in the cup / And I'll not look for wine. / The thirst that from the soul doth rise / Doth ask a drink divine; / But might I of Jove's nectar sup, / I would not change for thine. // I sent thee late a rosy wreath, / Not so much honouring thee / As giving it a hope that there / It could not wither'd be; / But thou thereon didst only breathe, / And sent'st it back to me; / Since when it grows, and smells, I swear, / Not of itself but thee!

Ben Jonson (*To Celia*): **Drink to me only with thine eyes, / And I will pledge with mine**; / Or leave a kiss within the cup, / And I'll not look for wine.

Ben Jonson (from *A Pindaric Ode*): He stood a soldier to the last right end, / A perfect patriot, and a noble friend.

Knight's Oath (spoken by Dennis Quaid who plays dragon slayer Bowen in the 1996 movie *Dragonheart,* starring the voice of Sean Connery): **A Knight is sworn to Valor. / His Heart knows only Virtue. / His Blade Defends the Helpless. / His Strength Upholds the Weak. / His Word speaks only Truth. / His Wrath Undoes the Wicked!**

St. Thomas More Society: A LAWYER'S PRAYER: May the Lord of law and of all lawyers make me, at your request, a little more like you than I was yesterday. Pray that for the greater glory of God and in the pursuit of His Justice, I may be able in argument, accurate in analysis, strict in study, correct in conclusion, candid with clients, honest with adversaries, faithful in my library. Stand beside me in Court, so that today I shall not, in order to win a point, lose my soul. Pray that each may find in me, what they have a right there to seek: humor and humility, cheerfulness and charity, an approach to wisdom, counselor, sound consolation, and a little bit of the shadow of you. Saint Thomas, brother lawyer, who by your membership have proven our profession both honorable and compatible with true sanctity. Pray for us now engaged in the struggle to imitate the Divine Master. Lord Chancellor, stand retained by us before the Infinite Lord Justice Who will preside when we are to be tried.

Newfoundland Toast: LONG MAY YOUR BIG JIB DRAW! [ED.: From their long, rich colorful maritime traditions Newfies wish for wind in their sail' good luck/sailing].

Newfoundland Toast (to Honorary Newfie Inductees): Though your head might feel logy right now, / Keep your new friends tight. / 'cause God help ye all, / yer one of us tonight

Gen. George S. Patton (the **Patton Prayer** began with telephone call to 3rd

Army Chaplain Msgr. James H. O'Neill, morning of December 8, 1944, when 3rd Army HQ was located in Nancy, France: "This is Gen. Patton; do you have a good prayer for weather? We must do something about those rains if we are to win the war." O'Neill typed out on a 5"x3" filing card): Almighty and most merciful Father, we humbly beseech Thee, of Thy great goodness, to restrain these immoderate rains with which we have had to contend. Grant us fair weather for Battle. Graciously hearken to us as soldiers who call upon Thee that, armed with Thy power, we may advance from victory to victory, and crush the oppression & wickedness of our enemies & establish Thy justice among men & nations.

Polish Blessing: May your hand be outstretched to all you meet. / And may all men say "Brother" when they speak of you. / May the land be fertile beneath your feet. / May your days be gentle as the sun-kissed dew.

Colonel Potter (acted by Harry Morgan in TV series *M*A*S*H*): To long lives & short wars.

President Ronald Reagan (to General Secretary Mikhail Gorbachev, Moscow, May 30, 1989): Allow me to raise a glass to the work that has been done. And let us also toast the art of friendly persuasion, the home of peace with freedom, the hope of holding out for a better way of settling things.

Myrtle Reed: May our house always be too small to hold all our friends.

Horace Rumpole (in 1978 episode *Rumpole and the Learned Friends*; toasting his wife Hilda): RUMPOLE: Here, I give you a toast. Here's to the future. HILDA: Our future! RUMPOLE: [*Laconically*] Which now shows every sign of being exactly like our past.

Homer (Simpson): Doh! A beer! I want a beer/Ray, the guy who buys me beer./Me, the guy who Ray buys beer. / Far, the way to go for beer./So, I think I'll have a beer / La, la la la la la la.ea?/ No thanks I'll have a beer . . . / And that brings us back to Doh! doh! doh!

Russian Toast: Only problem drinkers don't toast before drinking.

Russian Toast: *Na zda-ro-vye!* [**EDITOR:** This famous Russian phrase *Na zda-rɵvye!* or *На здоровьы!* is actually not a drinking toast; it is a reply to "Thank you!" when someone thanks for a meal or a drink].

Russian Toast: [**EDITOR.:** Russians drink "To your health!"; 'Health' *zda-rɵ vye* and 'to' *za*; Russians tend to skip the word 'to' and say just]: *vashee zda-rɵvye*—Your health! (being polite or addressing a group of people) or *tva-jo zda-rɵvye*—Your health! (informal)

Russian Toast: [**EDITOR:** In Russia, you often drink to your own health and say]: **Bo-deem zda-rovye**], which can be translated as "To our health!"

Russian New Year's Eve Toast: The Russians believe that the coming year is going to be as good or bad as the New Year's Eve. May this year be as happy as this party!

Russian New Year's Eve Toast: May this year bring us as many nice surprises as there are lights in all Christmas trees of the city!

Russian New Year's Eve Toast: Let us raise our glasses to the Grandfather Frost **Ded Moroz** and his granddaughter **Snegurotchka**! They never get old or sick and always have enough money for presents! May we be like them!

Russian Wedding Toast: Gorka! Gorka! [**EDITOR:** Выпыем за любовь! Горобко!.- *vyupyim za lyoo-bf. Go-ka*; word "Горобко!" is typical for Russian weddings. It means "bitter." In Russia the newlyweds have to kiss if someone calls *"Горобко!!"*]

Carl Schurz: To our country! When right, to be kept right. When wrong, to be put right!

Sir Walter Scott: 'Twas Christmas broach'd the mightiest ale; 'twas Christmas told the merriest tale; a Christmas gambol oft could cheer the poor man's heart through half the year. [**EDITOR:** a "gambol" is a British word for skipping about in play: frisk, frolic]

Scottish Blessing: If there is righteousness in the heart, / there will be beauty in the character. / If there is beauty in the character, / there will be harmony in the home. / If there is harmony in the home, / there will be order in the nation. / If there is order in the nation, / there will be peace in the world. / So let it be.

Scottish Tradition: *Skoal!* [**EDITOR:** A morbidly fascinating custom from northern Europe is that of drinking mead or ale from the skull of a fallen enemy; both the Scots and Scandinavians practiced this primitive form of recycling, and the Highland Scotch *skiel* (tub) and the Norse *skoal* (bowl) derive from it. Our modern toast, *skoal*, comes from the Old Norse term; this custom persisted through the 11th century, after which only an occasional skull was converted into a drinking vessel].

Scottish Tradition: [**EDITOR:** This Scotch custom, still surviving, is often practiced by this writer] To drink a toast with one foot on the table and one on the chair.

Scottish Toast (Here's Tae Us): Hare's tae us / Wha's like us / Damn few / And they're a' dead / Mair's the pity!

Scottish Toast: May the best ye've ever seen / Be the worst ye'll ever see. / May a moose [mouse] ne'er leave your girnal [pantry] / Wi' a tear drap in his ee. / May ye aye keep hale and hearty / Till ye're auld enough tae dee, / May ye aye be just as happy / As I wish ye aye tae be.

Scottish Toast: Lang may your lum [chimney] reek [smoke] . . . W'other folks coal

Scottish Toast: May opinion never float on the waves of ignorance, / May we look forward with pleasure, and backwards / Without remorse, / May we never crack a joke to break a reputation, / May we never suffer for principles we do not hold, / May we live to learn, and learn to live well, / May we live in pleasure and die out of debt, / A head to earn and a heart to spend, / Health of body, peace of mind, a clean shirt, and a guinea [a guinea was one pound, one shilling, or a little less than $2].

Scottish Toast (The Selkirk Grace, penned by Robert Burns and is a grace said before eating at many Scottish gatherings, especially the traditional Burns Suppers held throughout the world on January 25): Some hae meat, and canna eat, / And some wad eat that want it; / But we hae meat, and we can eat / And sae the Lord be thankit.

Scottish Toast (popular toast by Allan Ramsay of Ayr, called **There's Nae Luck Aboot the Hoose**): May the best you've ever seen / Be the worst you'll ever see; / May a moose ne'er leave yer girnal / Wi' a teardrop in his e'e. / May ye aye keep hale and hearty / Till ye're auld enough tae dee, / May ye aye be just as happy / As I wish ye aye tae be. [**EDITOR:** girnal ' meal chest; moose ' mouse].

Scottish Toast: I drink to the health of another, / And the drink I drink to is he, / In hope that he drinks to another, / And the other he drinks to is me.

Scottish Toast: Weel may we a' be / Ill may we never see; / Here's to the King / And the gude companie. / Here's a health to them that's away, / Here's a health to them that's away, / Here's a health to them that were here shortsyne, / An, canna be here today.

Scottish Toast: Here's to the heath, the hill and the heather, / The bonnit, the plaid, the kilt and the feather.

Scottish Toast: Here's to all those that I love. / Here's to all those that love me. / And here's to all those that love those that I love, / And all those that love those that love me.

Scottish (Inverary) Toast): *Semper tibi pendeat halec* ' May there always be herring in your net.

Scottish Toast: Here's to Scotland's heather hills, / Her bonny glens and braes / But dinna forget Scotch Whisky, / It's worthy o' oor praise, / It makes us feel so frisky, / Happy and full o' cheer, / Let's hope there'll aye be plenty, / For many an' many a year!

Scottish Toast: Here's to it: / The fighting sheen of it, / The yellow, the green of it, / The white, the blue of it, / The swing, the hue of it, / The dark, the red of it. / The fair have sighed for it, / The brave have died for it, / Foeman sought for it, / Heroes fought for it, / Honour the fame of it . . . . THE TARTAN.

Socrates (Plato referred to Socrates as the "**gadfly**" of the state because the gadfly stings the horse into action, so Socrates stung Athens; found guilty of corrupting the minds of the youth of Athens and sentenced to death by drinking a mixture containing poison hemlock; before his death Socrates said): A prayer to the gods I may and must offer, / That they will prosper my journey / From this world to the other world . . ..

Spanish Saying: Good wine ruins the purse; bad wine ruins the stomach.

Star Trek (Mr. Spock, in first *Star Trek* TV series starting in 1966): **Live long and prosper.**

Star Trek (Surak of Vulcan, in the TV series 1969 episode *The Savage Curtain*, stardate 5906.4): I am pleased to see that we have differences. May we together become greater than the sum of both of us.

George Sterling: He who clinks his cup with mine / Adds a glory to the wine.

Robert Louis Stevenson (Long John Silver in *Treasure Island*): Fifteen men on a Dead Man's Chest / Yo-ho-ho and a bottle of rum! / Drink and the devil had done for the rest, / Yo-ho-ho and a bottle of rum!

James Stewart (as George Bailey, in the 1946 classic movie *It's A Wonderful Life*): A toast a toast a toast to mother dollar and to papa dollar. And if you want to keep this old Building and Loan in business, you'd better have a family real quick.

Mother Teresa: Let us always meet each other with a smile, for the smile is the beginning of love.

William Makepeace Thackeray: I drink it as the Fates ordain it, / Come, fill it, and have done with rhymes; / Fill up the lonely glass, and drain it / In memory of dear old times.

Ernest Thesiger (playing Dr. Pretorius toasting the supernatural in the 1935 movie *Bride of Frankenstein*): To a new world of gods and monsters!

Lt. Col. William Barret Travis (writing to his wife March 5, 1836, the eve of last day of the Battle/Siege of the Alamo): My respects to all my friends, confusion to all enemies.

Aaron Douglas Trimble: Nothing's better than the wind to your back, the sun in front of you, and your friends beside you.

Ann Trzuskowski: Here's to the Irish! Only Irish Coffee provides us in one single glass all four essential food groups: alcohol, caffeine, sugar, and fat.

Thomas Tusser: At Christmas play and make good cheer / **For Christmas comes but once a year.**

Mark Twain: Let us toast the fools; but for them the rest of us could not succeed.

Mark Twain: Sometimes too much to drink is barely enough.

Mark Twain: We haven't all had the good fortune to be ladies; / We haven't all been generals, or poets, / Or statesmen; / But when the toast works down to the babies, / We stand on common ground.

Mark Twain: There is an old time toast which is golden for its beauty. "When you ascend the hill of prosperity may you not meet a friend.

Daniel Webster (May 10, 1847): The law: It has honored us; may we honor it.

Daniel Webster: It is my loving sentiment, and by the blessing of God it shall be my dying sentiment—Independence now and Independence forever!

Orson Welles (from the classic 1941 movie *Citizen Kane*): A toast—Jedediah—to life on my terms. These are the only terms anybody ever knows, his own.

John Wesley: Do all the good you can, by all the means you can, in all the ways you can, in all the places you can, to all the people you can, as long as you can.

Western Blessing: May your belly never grumble / May your heart never ache. / May your horse never stumble, / May your cinch never break.

Whig Toast: To the Liberty of the Press; it is like the air we breathe; if we have it not, we die.

Oscar Wilde: Work is the curse of the drinking class.

Oscar Wilde: We are all of us in the gutter. But some of us are looking at the stars.

Oscar Wilde (dying of cerebral meningitis in Parisian hotel room in 1900, he was offered a glass of champagne; his final toast): I am dying as I have lived, beyond my means.

World Toasts to Good Health/Long Lives/Happiness/Good Cheer:

Albanian: *Gezuar* (All good things to you); *Se haten* (To your health); *Hga mot gezuar* (Happiness for many years); *Rrofsah sa malet* (May you live as long as the hills); *Te kini shendene* (May you enjoy good health)

Angolan: *A sua felicidade!* (To your happiness!)

Arabian: *B'ism Allah* (In God's name); *Fi shettak* or *Fi sihtak* (To your health); *Kasak* (In your honor); *Sihatikom* (To your health); *Besehtak* (To your health! Good luck! Success! Happiness!); Hanya! (Good health!)

Argentinean: *Salud!* (To your health!)

Armenian: Genatzt (To your health)

Australian: Cheers!; Down the hatch!; Or "Here's looking up your kilt!

Austrian: (May it be to your health!)

Belgian: *Op uw gezonheid!* (To your health)

Bolivian: *Salud!* (To your health)

Brazilian: *Saude! Viva!* (Health); *Viva Felicidades; Una pro santo!*

Canadian: English: Cheerio! (Good times!)

Canadian: French: *A votre sante and a la votre!* (Tou health and to you!)

Canadian: Innuit Eskimo: *Chimo!* (Hail!)

Chinese: *Ganbei!* or *Kan pei!* (Bottoms up!); *Wen Lie!* (dry your cup); *Wen ule; Nien Nien nu e; Kong Chien; Ken bei* or *Kan pei* (Bottoms up!; *Yum sen* or *Yam seng!* (Drink to victory)

Colombian: *Brindo por [insert names]*; (I drink for [Insert names])

Czechoslovakian: *Na Zdravi!; Nazdar* (Health to you)

Danish: *Skal!* (A salute to you!)

Dutch: *Proost!* (health); *Geluk!* or *Geluch!*; *Op je gezondheid!* (To your health)

Egyptian: Fee sihetak (Your health); *Al salamu alaycum!* (Peace be with you!)

English: Cheers!; Bottoms up!

Esperanto: *Je zia sano!*

Estonian: *Tervist!* (Good health to you); *Parimat tulevikuks!* (Best for your future!)

Ethiopian: *Letanachin!* (To your health)

Farsi: *Salumati!* (To your health)

Finnish: *Kippis!; Terveydeksi!* (To your health!); *Maljanne*

French: *Santé!; A votre sante! Chin!* (To your health . . . followed by) *A la votre!* (And to yours!); *Bon Sante; Sante; Merde* (Good health); *A votre sante, bonheur et prosperite* (To your health, happiness and wealth); *Cul sec* (Bottoms up); *Je leve mon verre a votre sante* (I raise my glass to your health); *Icia la ange avec un demander pour un diable! Moi!* (Here's to an angel with a yearning devil! Me!)

Gaelic: Sheed Arth! (May you enjoy good things of life!); Slainte mhath, slainte mhor! (Good health, great health!); Slaynt as shee as Aash dy vea, as Maynry's son dy Bragh (Health and peace and ease of life, and happiness forever)

German: *Prost!* (from Latin *"prosit"*—may it be good); *Auf ihr wohl* (best of everything); *Hopfen und Malz, Gott erhaltz!"* (Long live hops and malt!); *Ofen warm, Bier kalt, Weib jung, Wein alt* (Oven warm, beer cold, wife young, wine old); Ein prosit der Gemutlichkeit (A toast to easygoing, happy-go-lucky living.

Greek: *Ade yamas!; Eis Igian; Yasas!; Stin ijiasas!* Or *Stin ygia sou!* (To your health); *Ooopa!* (Hooray!; *Ygia-sou!* (Cheers!)

Greenlandic: Kasuguta

Gypsy: May you live until a dead horse kicks you!

Haitian: *A votre sante!* (To your health!)

Hawaiian: *Okole maluna; Hauoili maouli oe!* (To your happiness); *Meul kaulkama; Havoli maoli oe!* (To your happiness); *Huapala!* (To my sweetheart! *Kou ola kino* (To your health); *Kamau!* (Here's how!)

Hebrew: *Le'chaim!* (To life!) or *L'chayim; Mazel tov* (congratulations)

Hungarian: *Kedves egeszsegere; Egesegedre!* (Egg-esh-sheg-edra) (To good health)

Icelandic: *Santanka nu*

India: *Tulleeho!; Aap ki Lambi Umar Ke Liye; Aap ki sehat ke liye!* (To your health!)

Indonesian: *Selemat!*

Irish: *Sláinte!* (to your health)

Irish: *Cead Mile Failte* (a hundred thousand welcomes)

Italian: *A la salute!;Salute!* (Health!); *Per cent'anni!* (Good life, health and everything, for 100 years); *Cin Cin!* (All things good to you!); *Propino tibi* (I drink to you)

Italian Toast: *Alla giornato!* ' To the day!

Italian Toast: *A presto!* ' See you soon!

Italian Toast: *Fino a quel momento!* ' Until that time!

Italian Toast: *Propino tibi!* ' I drink to you! [**EDITOR:** actually this is in Latin]

Italian Toast: *Propino tibi salutem!* ' I drink to your health! (longer version of above)

Italian Toast: *Amore, salud, dinero, y tiempo para gustarle* ' Love, health, money, and time to enjoy it.

Italian Toast: It is well to remember the four reasons for drinking: 1. The arrival of a friend; 2. One's present or future thirst; 3. The excellence of the wine; 4. Or any other reason.

Italian Wedding Toast: It is around the table that friends understand best the warmth of being together.

Japanese: *Kampai!* (pronounced KAM-pie) (dry your cup); *Omedeto Gozaimasu!* (Congratulations!): *Kampai! Banzai! Campi!* (Bottoms up!); *Banzai! Banzai! Banzai!* (Our last farewell)

Korean: *Guhn-Bai!* (Bottoms up!); *Kong gang ul wi ha yo; Chu-kha-ham-ni-da* (Congratulations)

Lithuanian: *I sveikatas!* (To your health!)

Maori: *Kia Ora!*

Malayan: *Slamat minum*

Mexican: *Salud!* (To your health!)

Moroccan: *Saha wa'afiab*

New Zealander: *Kia ora*

Norwegian: *Skoll!* Or *Ska!l*

Pakistani: *Sanda bashi!*

Philippine: *Mabuhay!*

Polish: *Na Zdrowie!* (To health); *Vivat*; *Na zdrowie, azeby nasze dzieci mialy bogatych radzicow!* (To our health—may our children have rich parents!); *Sto lot!* (Another 100 years!); *Zdrowie twoje, w gardlo moje* (To your health, down my throat)

Portuguese: *A sau saude!* (To your health); *Saude e gozo* (Health and enjoyment); *A sua felicidade!* (To your happiness!)

Romanian: *Noroc!* (Good luck); *Pentru sanatatea dunneavoastra*

Russian: *Za vashe zdorov'ye!*; *Na zdorovia!* (To your health); *Budem zdorovy!* (Let's be healthy!); *S priyezdom!* (Happy arrival!); *S otyezdom!* (Happy journey!); *Da dna!* (Bottom's up!);

Scottish: *Slainte* (pronounced SLAN-jay; meaning Here's to your health)

Spanish: *Salud!*; *Salud, pesetas y amor . . . y el tiempo para gustarlos!* (Health, money and love . . . and time to enjoy them!); *Salud, pesetas y par de tetas*; *Salud y amor sin suegra!* (Health and love without a mother-in-law!); *Amor, salud, dinero, y tiempo para gustarle* (Love, health, money, and time to enjoy it.)

Swedish: *Skål!* (Health!)

Thai: *Sawasdi!* (Your best!); *Chai yo!* (To your health and well-being!)

Turkish: *Sherefe!* Or *Serefe!*

Ukrainian: *Boovatje zdorovi!*; *Na zdorovya!* (To your health!)

Welsh: *Iechyd da!* (health)

Yiddish: *Zol zon tzgezhint!* (To your good health!); *Mazel tov!* (Congratulations!)

ITEMS OF INTEREST: using a fact of Italian life, times & uniqueness may enrich & embed your appreciation of the food or drink; therefore, we researched interesting facts for some of our recipes. To use a very old analogy—when you add an interesting tidbits of fact or fiction/fable to a meeting or meal—it is like adding spicy flavorful sauce on your proverbial pasta, making it memorable to you/your guests. **BON APETITO!**

godere il rinvigorimento delle nostre bevande e la dolcezza del nostro cibo!

(enjoy the invigoration of our drinks and sweetness of our foods!)

Selected Bibliography

BOCCONCINI SOURCES & SELECTED CIBI E BEVANDE (FOOD & BEVERAGE) BIBLIOGRAPHY

SELECTED BIBLIOGRAPHY & SOURCES

<u>La Bar Liquore e Cantina Casa</u>

Brian St. Pierre, <u>The Wine Lover Cooks Italian: Pairing Great Recipes with the Perfect Glass</u>, Chronicle Books (2005)

Colleen Graham, <u>Essential Bar Tools: What No Bartender Should Be Without</u>, http://cocktails.about.com/od/stockyourbar/tp/essential_bartools.htm; see also Colleen Graham's on line Newsletter at http://cocktails.about.com/gi/pages/stay.htm

Eric Granata, *How to Stock a Home Bar, The Art of Manliness,* website customized by Eric Granata at http://www.artofmanliness.com/2011/07/07/how-to-stock-a-home-bar/

Frederic A. Birmingham, Editor, <u>Esquire Drink Book</u>, Harper & Row (1956)

Hugh Johnson, <u>The World Atlas of Wine</u>, Simon & Shuster (1977)

Madeline Puckette, <u>Types of Wine Glasses (Infographic) for Beginners, Wine Folly</u>, https://www.google.com/search?q=basic+wine+glasses&biw=1093&bih=483&tbs=ppl_ids:—109876745131766422228-,ppl_nps:Madeline+Puckette,ppl_aut:1

Money Instructor®, <u>The Best Bar-Bar None: How to set up a Home Bar for Entertaining</u>, at http://content.moneyinstructor.com/82/the-best-bar-bar-none-how-to-set-up-a-home-bar-for-entertaining.html

Steven J. Schneider, <u>The International Album of Wine</u>, Holt, Rinehart & Winston (1977)

Serena Sutcliffe, Wine Master, <u>The Wine Handbook</u>, Simon & Shuster (1982)

Terry Robarbs, <u>The New York Times Book of Wine</u>, Avon Books (1976)

Wikibooks, Bartending/Drinkware/Glassware, http://en.wikibooks.org/wiki/Bartending/Drinkware/Glassware

Wine Folly, LLC, Creative Commons BY-NC-SA, What Types of Wine

Glasses Do You Really Need? http://winefolly.com/tutorial/types-of-wine-glasses/

Aantipasti Freddo (Cold Appetizers)

Artemas Ward (1911), *The Grocer's Encyclopedia*; *The Grocer's Encyclopedia* online is a part of Feeding America: The Historical American Cookbook Project, a collaboration between the Michigan State University Library and the MSU Museum.

Carla Capalbo, Kate Whiteman, Jeni Wright & Angela Boggiano, *The Italian Cooking Encyclopedia*, Hermes House (1999)

Clifford A. Wright, *History of the Sicilian Caponata*, at his website http://www.cliffordawright.com/caw/food/entries/display.php/id/57/ (2014)

David Tannis, *Heart of the Artichoke and Other Kitchen Journeys*, Artisan (2010)

George E. DeLallo Co., Inc., *Antipasti: Meal, Social Gathering or Both?* website at http://www.delallo.com/articles/antipasti-meal-social-gathering-or-both

Harold McGee, *On Food and Cooking,* Scribner (1984)

John K. Crellin, Jane Philpott, and A. L. Tommie Bass, *A Reference Guide to Medicinal Plants: Herbal Medicine Past and Present*, Duke University Press (1989)

Michael T. Murray, Joseph E. Pizzorno, and Lara Pizzorno, *The Encyclopedia of Healing Foods*, Atria Books (2005)

Michele Scicolone, *The Antipasto Table*, Harper Collins (1998)

R. W. Apple, Jr., *A Prince of Pork: In Seattle, Recreating the Perfect Ham*, NY Times Dining & Wine, http://www.nytimes.com/2006/05/17/dining/17cula.html?_r=0

Stacey Printz, *Pestos, Tapenades, and Spreads: 40 Simple Recipes for Delicious Toppings*, Chronicle Books (2009)

Tony May, *Italian Cuisine: Basic Cooking Techniques*, Italian Wine & Food Inst (1990)

Wikipedia, Antipasto, http://en.wikipedia.org/wiki/Antipasto

Wikibooks, Artichoke, http://en.wikibooks.org/wiki/Cookbook:Artichoke

Wikipedia, Artichoke, http://en.wikipedia.org/wiki/Artichoke

Wikipedia, Caponata, http://en.wikipedia.org/wiki/Caponata

Wikipedia, Prosciutto, http://en.wikipedia.org/wiki/Prosciutto

Wikipedia, Tapenade, http://en.wikipedia.org/wiki/Tapenade

Aantipasti Cauldo (Hot Appetizers)

Ada Boni, *The Talisman Italian Cook Book*, Crown Publishers (1972)

Biba Caggiano, *Italy Al Dente: Pasta, Risotto, Gnocchi, Polenta, Soup*, William Morrow and Company (1998)

George E. DeLallo Co., Inc., *Antipasti: Meal, Social Gathering or Both?* website at http://www.delallo.com/articles/antipasti-meal-social-gathering-or-both

Jeff Smith & Craig Wollam, *The Frugal Gourmet Cooks Italian*, William Morrow and Company (1993)

John Mariani, *The Dictionary of Italian Food and Drink*, Broadway Books (1998)

Leah Zeldes, *Eat this! Polenta, a universal peasant food*, Dining Chicago website at http://www.diningchicago.com/blog/2010/11/03/eat-this-polenta-a-universal-peasant-food/

Lulu Grimes, *The Cook's Book of Everything*, Murdocks Books (2009)

Lynne Olver, *Food Timeline*, website at http://www.foodtimeline.org/foodbreads.html

Mary Reynolds, *Italian Cooking*, Crescent Books (1978)

Michael T. Murray, Joseph E. Pizzorno, and Lara Pizzorno, *The Encyclopedia of Healing Foods*, Atria Books (2005)

Michele Scicolone, *The Antipasto Table*, Harper Collins (1998)

Molly Watson, *Types of Sweet Peppers: The Many Colors of Bell Peppers*, at her website http://localfoods.about.com/od/peppers/tp/peppertypes.htm

Piergiorgio and Amy Hoch, *La Frittata: An Egg Dish with Endless Possibilities*, George E. DeLallo Co., Inc. website at http://www.delallo.com/articles/la-frittata-egg-dish-endless-possibilities

Wikipedia, Antipasto, http://en.wikipedia.org/wiki/Antipasto

Wkipedia, Bruschetta, http://en.wikipedia.org/wiki/Bruschetta

Wikipedia, Eggs, http://en.wikipedia.org/wiki/Egg_(food)

Wikipedia, Frittata, http://en.wikipedia.org/wiki/Frittata

Wikipedia, Omelette, http://en.wikipedia.org/wiki/Omelette

Wikipedia, Pepperone, http://en.wikipedia.org/wiki/Pepperoni

Wikipedia, Peppers, http://en.wikipedia.org/wiki/Pepper

Wikipedia, Polenta, http://en.wikipedia.org/wiki/Polenta

Zuppa (Soup)

Biba Caggiano, *Italy Al Dente: Pasta, Risotto, Gnocchi, Polenta, Soup*, William Morrow and Company (1998)

Carla Capalbo, Kate Whiteman, Jeni Wright & Angela Boggiano, *The Italian Cooking Encyclopedia*, Hermes House (1999)

Jeff Smith & Craig Wollam, *The Frugal Gourmet Cooks Italian*, William Morrow and Company (1993)

Judith Barrett, *Fagioli: The Bean Cuisine of Italy*, Rodale Books (2004)

Michael T. Murray, Joseph E. Pizzorno, and Lara Pizzorno, *The Encyclopedia of Healing Foods*, Atria Books (2005)

Norma Wasserman-Miller, *Soups of Italy: Cooking over 130 Soups the Italian Way, 1st ed.*, William Morrow (1998)

Wikipedia, Chickpea, http://en.wikipedia.org/wiki/Chickpea

Wikipedia, Minestrone, http://en.wikipedia.org/wiki/Minestrone

Wikipedia, Pasta e fagioli, http://en.wikipedia.org/wiki/Pasta_e_fagioli

Wikipedia, Risotto, http://en.wikipedia.org/wiki/Risotto

Pasta

Ada Boni, *The Talisman Italian Cook Book*, Crown Publishers (1972)

Alberto Capatti and Massimo Montanari, *Italian Cuisine: A Cultural History*, Columbia University Press (2003)

Alice Park, "The Supernut: Walnuts Pack a Powerful Dose of Antioxidants," *Time* magazine, March 29, 2011

Biba Caggiano, *Italy Al Dente: Pasta, Risotto, Gnocchi, Polenta, Soup*, William Morrow and Company (1998)

Canadian Pasta Manufacturers Association, *Pasta Facts: Facts About Pasta*, at its website at http://www.pastacanada.com/english/pastafacts/pastafacts.html

Carla Capalbo, Kate Whiteman, Jeni Wright & Angela Boggiano, *The Italian Cooking Encyclopedia*, Hermes House (1999)

Cindy Ott, *Pumpkin: The Curious History of an American Icon*, University of Washington Press (2012)

Diane Seed, *The Top One Hundred Pasta Sauces*, Rosendale Press (1987)

Dorothy Rankin, *Very Pesto*, Crown Publishing (2004)

History.com, The History of the Jack O'Lantern, http://www.history.com/topics/jack-olantern-history

Huffington Post, *HuffPost: What Are Capers And Where Are They From?* at its website at http://www.huffingtonpost.com/2012/02/14/what-are-capers_n_1276491.html

Jacob Kenedy, Caz Hildebrand, *The Geometry of Pasta*, Pan Macmillan (2010)

Jeff Smith & Craig Wollam, *The Frugal Gourmet Cooks Italian*, William Morrow and Company (1993)

John K. Crellin, Jane Philpott, and A. L. Tommie Bass, *A Reference Guide to Medicinal Plants: Herbal Medicine Past and Present*, Duke University Press (1989)

John Mariani, *The Dictionary of Italian Food and Drink*, Broadway Books (1998)

Marc Vetri & David Joachim, *Il Viaggio Di Vetri: A Culinary Journey*, Ten Speed Press (2008)

Mary Reynolds, *Italian Cooking*, Crescent Books (1978)

Michael T. Murray, Joseph E. Pizzorno, and Lara Pizzorno, *The Encyclopedia of Healing Foods*, Atria Books (2005)

Oretta Zanini De Vita, *Encyclopedia of Pasta*, University of California Press (2009)

Piero Sardo, Gigi Piumatti, and Roberto Rubino, *Italian Cheese: A Guide to Their Discovery and Appreciation, Two Hundred Traditional Types*, Slow Food Arcigola Editore (2001)

Silvano Serventi and Francoise Sabban, *Pasta: The story of a universal food (translated ed.)*, Columbia University Press (2002)

Simone Cinotto, *The Italian American Table: Food, Family, and Community in New York City*, University of Illinois (2013)

Tony May, *Italian Cuisine: Basic Cooking Techniques*, Italian Wine & Food Institute (1990)

Wikipedia, Caper, http://en.wikipedia.org/wiki/Caper

Wikipedia, Gnocchi, http://en.wikipedia.org/wiki/Gnocchi

Wikipedia, Italian Cheese, http://en.wikipedia.org/wiki/List_of_Italian_cheeses

Wikipedia, Pasta, http://en.wikipedia.org/wiki/Pasta

Wikipedia, Pesto, http://en.wikipedia.org/wiki/Pesto

Wikipedia, Pumpkin, http://en.wikipedia.org/wiki/Pumpkin

Wikipedia, Ricotta, http://en.wikipedia.org/wiki/Ricotta

Wikipedia, Walnut, http://en.wikipedia.org/wiki/Walnut

Intermezzo/Intermedio

Accidental Hedonist, *The History of Compari*, http://accidentalhedonist.com/history-of-campari/

Brian St. Pierre, *The Wine Lover Cooks Italian: Pairing Great Recipes with the Perfect Glass*, Chronicle Books (2005)

Colleen Graham, *Raspberry and Blackberry Cocktail and Mixed Drink Recipe Collection*, About.com website at http://cocktails.about.com/od/cocktailsbyflavor/a/Raspberry-Cocktails.htm

Dr. Gourmet, *Ask Dr. Gourmet: What's the difference between sorbet, sherbet, and ice cream?* http://www.drgourmet.com/askdrgourmet/sherbetvsorbet.shtml#.Usr8cbmA12E

Frederic A. Birmingham, Editor, *Esquire Drink Book*, Harper & Row (1956)

Gernot Katzers, Spice Page: Cardamom, http://gernot-katzers-spice-pages.com/engl/Elet_car.html

IDFA, International Dairy Foods Association, *What's in the Ice Cream Aisle?* http://www.idfa.org/news—views/media-kits/ice-cream/whats-in-the-ice-cream-aisle/

Jessica Harlan, *What's the difference between gelato and ice cream?* http://cookingequipment.about.com/od/icecreammachines/f/gelatovicecream.htm

John Mariani, *The Dictionary of Italian Food and Drink*, Broadway Books (1998)

LemoncelloQuest, A Personal Pilgrimage to Create Perfect Limoncello: How to Make Limoncello, http://limoncelloquest.com/limoncello-articles/how-to-make-limoncello

Luciano Ferrari, *Gelato and Gourmet Frozen Desserts—A professional learning guide*, Lulu.com (2005)

Melanie Barnard, *Williams-Sonoma: Frozen Desserts*, Simon & Shuster (2006)

Michael T. Murray, Joseph E. Pizzorno, and Lara Pizzorno, *The Encyclopedia of Healing Foods*, Atria Books (2005)

WHFoods.com, http://www.whfoods.com/genpage.php?tname=foodspice&dbid=25

Wikipedia, Blackberry, http://en.wikipedia.org/wiki/Blackberry

Wikipedia, Cardamom, http://en.wikipedia.org/wiki/Cardamom

Wikipedia, Compari, http://en.wikipedia.org/wiki/Campari

Wikipedia, Granita, http://en.wikipedia.org/wiki/Granita

Wikipedia, Gelato, http://en.wikipedia.org/wiki/Gelato

Wikipedia, Grapefruit, http://en.wikipedia.org/wiki/Grapefruit

Wikipedia, Italian Ice, http://en.wikipedia.org/wiki/Italian_ice

Wikipedia, Limoncello, http://en.wikipedia.org/wiki/Limoncello

Wikipedia, Mint Julep, http://en.wikipedia.org/wiki/Mint_julep

Wikipedia, Proseca, http://en.wikipedia.org/wiki/Prosecco

Wikipedia, Sparkling Wines, http://en.wikipedia.org/wiki/Category:Sparkling_wines

Wikipedia, Strawberry, http://en.wikipedia.org/wiki/Strawberry

Wikipedia, Sorbet, http://en.wikipedia.org/wiki/Sorbet

Pesce (Fish)

James Peterson, *Fish & Shellfish: The Definitive Cook's Companion*, William Morrow & Company (1996)

Mark Kurlansky, *Cod: A Biography of the Fish That Changed the World*, Walker Publishing Company (1997)

Michael T. Murray, Joseph E. Pizzorno, and Lara Pizzorno, *The Encyclopedia of Healing Foods*, Atria Books (2005)

Robert A. Germano, *The Eve of Seven Fishes: Christmas Cooking in the Peasant Tradition*, i-Universe (2005)

Silvio Suppa, *Cooking with Chef Silvio: Stories and Authentic Recipes from Campania*, State University of New York Press, 2010

Tony May, *Italian Cuisine: The New Essential Reference to the Riches of the Italian*, St. Martin's Press (2005)

Wikipedia, Calamari, Squid (food), http://en.wikipedia.org/wiki/Squid_(food)

Wikipedia, Conch, http://en.wikipedia.org/wiki/Conchm

Wikipedia, Cuttlefish, http://en.wikipedia.org/wiki/Cuttlefish

Wikipedia, Dried and salted cod, http://en.wikipedia.org/wiki/Dried_and_salted_cod

Wikipedia, Mussel, http://en.wikipedia.org/wiki/Mussel

Wikipedia, Octopus, http://en.wikipedia.org/wiki/Octopus

Wikipedia, Tilapia, http://en.wikipedia.org/wiki/Tilapia

La Verdura (Vegetables)

Georgia Chan Downard, *The Big Broccoli Book*, Random House (1992)

John K. Crellin, Jane Philpott, and A. L. Tommie Bass, *A Reference Guide to Medicinal Plants: Herbal Medicine Past and Present*, Duke University Press (1989)

John Mariani, *The Dictionary of Italian Food and Drink*, Broadway Books (1998)

Lynne Olver, *Food Timeline*, website at http://www.foodtimeline.org/foodbreads.html

Michael T. Murray, Joseph E. Pizzorno, and Lara Pizzorno, *The Encyclopedia of Healing Foods*, Atria Books (2005)

Molly Watson, *Types of Sweet Peppers: The Many Colors of Bell Peppers*, at her website http://localfoods.about.com/od/peppers/tp/peppertypes.htm

Robert A. Germano, *The Eve of Seven Fishes: Christmas Cooking in the Peasant Tradition*, i-Universe (2005)

Silvio Suppa, *Cooking with Chef Silvio: Stories and Authentic Recipes from Campania*, State University of New York Press, 2010

Tony May, *Italian Cuisine: The New Essential Reference to the Riches of the Italian*, St. Martin's Press (2005)

Wikipedia, Broccoli, http://en.wikipedia.org/wiki/Broccoli

Wikipedia, Endive, http://en.wikipedia.org/wiki/Endive (escarole is a broad-leaf endive)

Wikipedia, January King Cabbage, http://en.wikipedia.org/wiki/January_King_Cabbage

Wikipedia, Pepperone, http://en.wikipedia.org/wiki/Pepperoni

Wikipedia, Peppers, http://en.wikipedia.org/wiki/Pepper

Wikipedia, Rapini or Broccoli Rabe or Raab, http://en.wikipedia.org/wiki/Rapini

Wikipedia, Savoy Cabbage http://en.wikipedia.org/wiki/Savoy_cabbage

Wikipedia, Stuffed Peppers, http://en.wikipedia.org/wiki/Stuffed_peppers

Wikipedia, Zucchini, http://en.wikipedia.org/wiki/Zucchini

Wise Geek website, *What is Escarole?* http://www.wisegeek.org/what-is-escarole.htm#slideshow

Carne (Meat)

Bruce Aidells and Lisa Weiss, *Bruce Aidells's Complete Book of Pork: A Guide to Buying, Storing, and Cooking the World's Favorite Meat*, Harper-Collins Pubs (2004)

Jane C. Lawrence, *Easter Joy: Exploring the Origins of Easter Symbols*, CSS Publishing Company (1998)

Jerry Predika, *The Sausage-making Cookbook*, Stackpole Books (1983)

John Mariani, *The Dictionary of Italian Food and Drink*, Broadway Books (1998)

The Kitchen Project, *The History of Lamb on Easter. Why is Lamb popular during Easter?* http://www.kitchenproject.com/history/Easter/Lamb.htm

Marc Vetri, and David Joachim, *Rustic Italian Food*, Random House (2011)

Marion Eugene Ensminger, and Audrey H. Ensminge, *Foods & Nutrition Encyclopedia, 2nd Edition, Volume 1*, (Grades of Veal), CRC Press (1993)

Maryn McKenna, *How Do You Know Which Chicken to Buy? This Kickstarter Might Help*, http://www.wired.com/wiredscience/2013/05/buying-poultry-kickstarter/

NAMP, North American Meat Processors Association, *The Meat Buyers Guide: Beef, Lamb, Veal, Pork, and Poultry*, John Wiley & Sons, Inc. (2007)

Nora Narvaez Soriano, *A Guide to Food Selection, Preparation and Preservation*, Rex Printing Company, Inc. (2008)

Philip Hasheider, The Complete Book of Butchering, Smoking, Curing, and Sausage Making: How to Harvest Your Livestock and Wild Game, Voyageur Press (2010)

Wikipedia, Cacciatore, http://en.wikipedia.org/wiki/Cacciatore

Wikipedia, Lamb and mutton, http://en.wikipedia.org/wiki/Lamb_and_mutton

Wikipedia, Porchetta, http://en.wikipedia.org/wiki/Porchetta

Wikipedia, Scalopini, http://en.wikipedia.org/wiki/Scaloppine

Wikipedia, Veal, http://en.wikipedia.org/wiki/Veal

Insalata (Salad)

Alberto Capatti, and Massimo Montanari, *Italian Cuisine: A Cultural History*, Columbia University Press (1999)

Cesare Casella, and Jack Bishop, *Italian Cooking Essentials for Dummies*, John Wiley & Sons (2001)

Guido Garrubbo, Italian Cheeses (Formaggi), http://garrubbo.com/italian-cheeses-formaggi/

Insalate: Authentic Salads for All Seasons By Susan Simon

James Peterson, *Fish & Shellfish: The Definitive Cook's Companion*, William Morrow & Company (1996)

John K. Crellin, Jane Philpott, and A. L. Tommie Bass, *A Reference Guide to Medicinal Plants: Herbal Medicine Past and Present*, Duke University Press (1989)

John Mariani, *The Dictionary of Italian Food and Drink*, Broadway Books (1998)

Mark Kurlansky, *Cod: A Biography of the Fish That Changed the World*, Walker Publishing Company (1997)

Michael T. Murray, Joseph E. Pizzorno, and Lara Pizzorno, *The Encyclopedia of Healing Foods*, Atria Books (2005)

Patrick F. Fox, Paul L. H. McSweeney, Timothy M. Cogan, and Timothy P. Guinee (editors), *Cheese: Chemistry, Physics and Microbiology: Major Cheese Groups*, Elsevier Academic Press (2004)

Piero Sardo, Gigi Piumatt, and Roberto Rubino (Editors), *Italian Cheese: A Guide to Their Discovery and Appreciation, Two Hundred Traditional Types*, Slow Food Arcigola Editore (2001)

Robert A. Germano, *The Eve of Seven Fishes: Christmas Cooking in the Peasant Tradition*, i-Universe (2005)

Ruth Lively (editor), *Taunton's Complete Guide to Growing Vegetables and Herbs*, The Taunton Press (2011)

Smallwood & Stewart, *Peppers*, Andrews McMeel Publishing (1997)

Wikipedia, Calamari, Squid (food), http://en.wikipedia.org/wiki/Squid_(food)

Wikipedia, Capri, http://en.wikipedia.org/wiki/Capri

Wikipedia, Conch, http://en.wikipedia.org/wiki/Conchm

Wikipedia, Cucumber, http://en.wikipedia.org/wiki/Cucumber

Wikipedia, Cuttlefish, http://en.wikipedia.org/wiki/Cuttlefish

Wikipedia, Dried and salted cod, http://en.wikipedia.org/wiki/Dried_and_salted_cod

Wikipedia, Fennel, http://en.wikipedia.org/wiki/Fennel

Wikipedia, Mozzarella, http://en.wikipedia.org/wiki/Mozzarella

Wikipedia, Octopus, http://en.wikipedia.org/wiki/Octopus

Wikipedia, Pimiento (pimento, or cherry pepper) http://en.wikipedia.org/wiki/Pimiento

Wikipedia, Taraxacum (dandelion), http://en.wikipedia.org/wiki/Taraxacum

World's Healthiest Foods, WHFoods Organization, Fennel, http://whfoods.org/genpage.php?tname=foodspice&dbid=23

Dolce (Sweets/Desserts)

Anthony Parkinson, *Italian Desserts*, Lulu.com (2005)

Dwayne Ridgaway, *The Gourmet's Guide to Cooking with Liquors and Spirits*, Quarry Books (2010)

Italy Revisited.org website, *Lists of Italian Dishes and Desserts by Region*, http://www.italyrevisited.org/recipe/X_X_Lists_of_Italian_Dishes_and_Desserts_by_Region/672

Jonathan Deutsch Ph.D., and Rachel D. Saks, *Jewish American Food Culture*, Greenwood Publishing Group (2008)

Nick Malgieri, *Great Italian Desserts*, Little Brown & Company (1990)

Rosetta Costantino, Jennie Schacht, *Southern Italian Desserts: Rediscovering the Sweet Traditions of Calabria, Compania, Basilicata, Puglia, and Sicily*, Ten Speed Press, a Division of Random House (2013)

W. H.Lewis, and M. Elvin-Lewis, *Medical botany: plants affecting human health*, John Wiley & Sons (2003)

Wikipedia, Amaretto, http://en.wikipedia.org/wiki/Amaretto

Wikipedia, Apricots, http://en.wikipedia.org/wiki/Apricot

Wikipedia, Italian Desserts, http://en.wikipedia.org/wiki/Category:Italian_desserts

Wikipedia, Jewish Apple Cake, http://en.wikipedia.org/wiki/Jewish_Apple_Cake

Wikipedia, Tiramisu, http://en.wikipedia.org/wiki/Tiramisu

Wikipedia, Zuccotto, http://en.wikipedia.org/wiki/Zuccotto

Aperitivo (Aperitif) & Digerente (Digestifs)

Anthony Giglio, and Jim Meehan, *Mr. Boston Holiday Cocktails*, Wiley (2009)

Askmen.com website, Classic Italian Cocktails, http://www.askmen.com/fine_living/wine_dine_archive_300/362_classic-italian-cocktails.html

Brian D. Murphy, *See Mix Drink: A Refreshingly Simple Guide to Crafting the World's Most Popular Cocktails*, Little, Brown (2011)

Christopher O'hara, and William A. Nash, *Hot Toddies: Mulled Wine, Buttered Rum, Spiced Cider, and Other Soul-Warming Winter Drinks,* Clarkson Potter/Pubs (2002)

Food.com, *Mulled Wine Recipes*, http://www.food.com/recipes/mulled-wine

Frederic A. Birmingham, Editor, *Esquire Drink Book*, Harper & Row (1956)

Greg Rosewood, *Beverage Punch Recipes—The Ultimate Collection*, MaxHouse (2012)

Hannah Suhr, *The Best 50 Holiday Party Drinks*, Bristol Publishing Enterprises, 2004

Vintage Drinks. Fernet Cocktails, http://thevintagedrink.com/ingredients/fernet-branca-drinks-recipes

ItThing website, *10 Most Popular Holiday Drinks*, http://itthing.com/10-most-popular-holiday-drinks

Jessica Strand, *Holiday Cocktails*, Chronicle Books LLC (2003)

John Mariani, *The Dictionary of Italian Food and Drink*, Broadway Books (1998)

Joseph Scott, and Donald Bain, *The World's Best Bartender's Guide: Professional Bartenders from the World's Greatest Bars Teach You How to Mix the Perfect Drink*, The Berkley Publishing Company (1998)

Linda Doeser, Classic & Contemporary Cocktails, The Essential Collection, Parragon Publishing (2002)

Lois Sinaiko Webb, Lindsay Grace Roten, *Holidays of the World Cookbook for Students: Updated and Revised*, ABC-CLIO, LLC (2011)

Selected Bibliography & Sources

Paula S.W. Laurita, Guest Author for Peter F May, BellaOnline's Wine Editor website at http://www.bellaonline.com/articles/art28168.asp

Rob Chirico, *Field Guide to Cocktails: How to Identify and Prepare Virtually Every Mixed Drink at the Bar,* Quirk Productions, Inc. (2005)

Sally Ann Berk, *The Martini Book*, Black Dog & Leventhal Publishers, Inc. (1997)

Simon Difford, *Cocktails: Over 2250 Cocktails*, Sauce Guides Lmited (2007)

Stuart Walton, *The Bartender's Guide to Cocktails & Mixed Drinks: A Complete Encyclopedia of Spirits, Liqueurs, Wine, Beer and Mixers, with Instructions for Making 600 Drinks*, Hermes House (2006)

Wikipedia, Aperitif, http://en.wikipedia.org/wiki/Ap%C3%A9ritif_and_digestif

Wikipedia, Bitters, http://en.wikipedia.org/wiki/Bitters

Wikipedia, Digestif, http://en.wikipedia.org/wiki/Ap%C3%A9ritif_and_digestif

Wikipedia, Fernet, http://en.wikipedia.org/wiki/Fernet

Wikipedia, Fernet branca, http://en.wikipedia.org/wiki/Fernet_Branca

Wikipedia, Grog, http://en.wikipedia.org/wiki/Grog

Wikipedia, Navy Grog, http://en.wikipedia.org/wiki/Navy_Grog

Wikipedia, Mulled Wine, http://en.wikipedia.org/wiki/Mulled_wine

Zagat, A Bartender's Guide to Italian Spirits, http://blog.zagat.com/2013/01/a-bartenders-guide-to-italian-spirits.html

Index to Recipes

AGNELLO ARROSTO
  Recipe, **253**

AGRAVE SYRUP
  Back in the saddle cocktail, **375**
  Fernet with compari, **375**

AMARETTO
  Apricot oatmeal chews, **325**
  Bocce ball cocktail, **379**
  Rice pudding, **323**

AMARETTO DI SARONNO
  Godfather (cocktail), **353**
  Godmother (cocktail), **355**

AMARO
  Translation, **323**

AMERICANO (COCKTAIL)
  Recipe, **363**

ANTIPASTI
  Generally, **11 et seq.**
  Aperitif antipasti, **16**
  Arrosto peperone, **31**
  Bibliography, **448**
  Brushette, **29**
  Caponata, **17**
  Carciofi antipasto, **13**
  Cauldo, **29 et seq.**
  Cold and hot kinds, **15**
  Cold antipasto dishes, **11 et seq.**
  Diffusione di oliva, **19**
  Egg giambotta, **41**
  Eggplant, sweet and sour, **17**
  Freddi, **11 et seq.**
  Fried polenta or cornmeal, **45**
  Frittata ala Domenico, **39**
  Frittata ala salsiccia e spinaci, **37**
  Frittata ala tomasso vesper, **33**
  Frittata cooking tips, **41**
  Ham and melon, **11**
  Hot and cold kinds, **15**
  Hot appetizers, **29 et seq.**
  Insalata antipasto, **15**
  Italian ham, **11**

ANTIPASTI—Cont'd
  Marinated artichokes, **13**
  Olive spread, **19**
  Parma ham, **11**
  Prosciutto and melone, **11**
  Prosciutto crudo, **11**
  Roasted peppers, **31**
  Sausage and spinach omlette, **37**
  Serving tips, **15**
  Sweet and sour eggplant, **17**
  Tapenade, **19**
  Toasted bread, **29**
  Traditions, **16**
  Translation, **15**
  Vegetable omelet, **33**

APERITIF ANTIPASTI
  Generally, **16**

APERITIVO & DIGERENTE
  Generally, **341 et seq.**
  Amaretto di Saronno, **353, 355**
  Americano, **363**
  Back in the saddle cocktail, **375**
  Bartending tips, **5**
  Bavorak cocktail, **371**
  Bellini
    Generally, **345**
    baby bellini, **351**
    two minute version, **349**
  Bibliography, **447, 459**
  Bocce ball cocktail, **379**
  Caffe shakerato, **365**
  Campari, this index
  Champagne, this index
  Fernet branca, **369**
  Fernet con coca, **373**
  Fernet football, **377**
  Fernet with compari, **375**
  Godchild, **357**
  Godfather, **353**
  Godmother, **355**
  Kina Lillet, **347**
  Limoncello, **367**
  Marine Corps punch, **341**

APERITIVO & DIGERENTE—Cont'd
    Mint julep granita, **155**
    Navy grog, **343**
    Negroni, **359**
    Negroni Sbagliato, **361**
    Rum, this index
    1775 fortitude rum punch, **341**
    Toasts to trial lawyers, **425 et seq.**
    Vesper martini, **347**
    Vin brule, **381**
    Vodka, this index
    Wine, this index

APEROL
    Godchild (cocktail), **357**

APPETIZERS
    See Antipasti, this index

APPLES
    Jewish apple cake, **327**

APRICOTS
    Amaretto apricot oatmeal chews, **325**

ARROSTO PEPERONE
    Recipe, **31**

ARTICHOKES
    Varieties, **13**

BACCALA
    Insalata di baccala, **295**

BACK IN THE SADDLE COCKTAIL
    Recipe, **375**

BAR TIPS
    Generally, **5**

BASIL AND PINE NUTS SAUCE
    Recipe, **121**

BAVORAK COCKTAIL
    Recipe, **371**

BEANS
    Broccoli rabe with sausage and beans, **215**

BELLINI (COCKTAILS)
    Generally, **345**
    Baby bellini, **351**
    Two minute version, **349**

BEVERAGES
    See Aperitivo & Digerente, this index

BIBLIOGRAPHY
    Generally, **447 et seq.**
    Antipasti, **448**
    Aperitivo & digerente, **447, 459**
    Carne, **455**
    Cheeses, **452**
    Dolce, **452, 458**
    Insalata, **456**
    Intermezzo, **452**
    La verdura, **454**
    Pasta, **450**
    Pesce, **454**
    Zuppa, **450**

BITTER CAMPARI
    Negroni, **359**

BLACKBERRIES
    Intermezzo, **149**

BOCCE BALL COCKTAIL
    Recipe, **379**

BOCCONCINI
    Translation, **3**

BREAD
    Brushette, **29**
    Grissini, **12**
    Panettone, **381**
    Pasta with walnuts and bread crumbs, **123**
    Role in Italian cuisine, **4**
    Toasted bread, **29**

BROCCOLI RABE WITH SAUSAGE AND BEANS
    Recipe, **215**

CACCIATORA
    Polo alla cacciatora, **251**

CACCIATORE
    Translation, **252**

CAFFE SHAKERATO
    Recipe, **365**

CALAMARI POMODORA
    Recipe, **185**

CAMPARI
    Americano, **363**
    Back in the saddle cocktail, **375**
    Fernet with compari, **375**
    Negroni, **359**

INDEX TO RECIPES

CAMPARI—Cont'd
Negroni Sbagliato, **361**

CAPERS
Tapenade, **19**

CAPONATA
Recipe, **17**

CAPRESE
Insalata caprese, **293**

CARDAMOM
Sherry cardamom granita, **161**

CARNE
Generally, **247 et seq.**
Agnello arrosto, **253**
Bibliography, **455**
Chicken cacciatora, **251**
Polo alla cacciatora, **251**
Porchetta arrosto, **247**
Roast leg of lamb, **253**
Roast loin of pork, **247**
Salsiccia con peperoni alla scaloppini, **249**
Sausage cut thin with peppers, **249**
Veal in tomato sauce, **255**
Vitella scoloppini, **255**

CECI BEANS AND PASTA
Recipe, **67**

CETRIOLO
Translation, **289**

CHAMPAGNE
Bellini
Generally, **345**
two minute version, **349**
Granita, **159**

CHEESES
Bibliography, **452**

CHICKEN CACCIATORA
Recipes, **251**

CHICK PEAS AND PASTA
Recipe, **67**

CICORIA
Insalata di cicoria e finocchio, **291**

CILIEGIO PEPE
Translation, **289**

COD
Generally, **182**
Salad with salted cod, **295**

COMPARI
Fernet with, **375**
Sorbetto, **145**

CONCH
Salad with sliced conch, **299**

CON DI NOCI PASTA
Recipe, **123**

COZZE POMODORO
Recipe, **183**

CUCINA POVERA
Translation, **43**

CUTTLEFISH STEWED IN TOMATOES
Recipe, **185**

DANDELION AND FENNEL SALAD
Recipe, **291**

DESERTS
See Dolce, this index

DIFFUSIONE DI OLIVA
Recipe, **19**

DIGERENTE
See Aperitivo & Digerente, this index

DOLCE
Generally, **317 et seq.**
Amaretto apricot oatmeal chews, **325**
Amaretto rice pudding, **323**
Bibliography, **452, 458**
Granita, this index
Jewish apple cake, **327**
Raspberry lemon tiramisu, **319**
Zucatta cake, **321**

DRINKS
See Aperitivo & Digerente, this index

EGG GIAMBOTTA
Recipe, **41**

EGGPLANT
Sweet and sour, **17**

ESCAROLE AND BEANS
Recipe, **209**

Index to Recipes-3

FAGIOLINI
  Translation, **66**

FENNEL
  Dandelion and fennel salad, **291**

FERNET BRANCA
  Generally, **369**
  Back in the saddle cocktail, **375**
  Fernet with compari, **375**

FERNET CON COCA
  Recipe, **373**

FERNET FOOTBALL
  Recipe, **377**

FERNET WITH COMPARI
  Recipe, **375**

FETTUCINE ALA RICOTTA
  Recipe, **125**

FINOCCHIO
  Insalata di cicoria e finocchio, **291**

FIRE AND ICE SALAD
  Recipe, **287**

FISH
  See Pesce, this index

FLORILEGIUM
  Translation, **1**

FRIED POLENTA OR CORNMEAL
  Recipe, **45**

FRITTATA
  Cooking tips, **41**

FRITTATA ALA DOMENICO
  Recipe, **39**

FRITTATA ALA SALSICCIA E SPINACI
  Recipe, **37**

FRITTATA ALA TOMASSO VESPER
  Recipe, **33**

FRITTO
  Translation, **33**

FUOCO E INSALATA DI GHIACCIO
  Recipes, **287**

GELATO
  Intermezzo, **143**

GIAMBOTTA
  Translation, **41**

GIAMBOTTA ZUCCHINI
  Recipe, **207**

GIN
  Negroni, **359**
  Vesper martini, **347**

GINGER BEER
  Back in the saddle cocktail, **375**
  Fernet with compari, **375**

GNOCCHI CON DOLCE PATATA
  Recipe, **119**

GODCHILD (COCKTAIL)
  Recipe, **357**

GODFATHER (COCKTAIL)
  Recipe, **353**

GODMOTHER (COCKTAIL)
  Recipe, **355**

GRANITA
  Champagne, **159**
  Grapefruit campari granita, **157**
  Intermezzo, **143**
  Lemone granita alla siciliano, **153**
  Mint julep granita, **155**
  Sherry cardamom granita, **161**
  White wine granita, **159**

GRAPEFRUIT CAMPARI GRANITA
  Recipe, **157**

GRISSINI
  Translation, **12**

GROG
  Navy grog, **343**

INSALATA
  Generally, **287 et seq.**
  Antipasto insalata, **15**
  Bibliography, **456**
  Caprese, insalata, **293**
  Cetriolo, **289**
  Ciliegio pepe, **289**
  Dandelion and fennel salad, **291**
  Di baccala, insalata, **295**
  Di cicoria e finocchio, insalata, **291**
  Di polpo, insalata, **297**
  Fire and ice salad, **287**

INDEX TO RECIPES

INSALATA—Cont'd
  Fuoco e insalata di ghiaccio, **287**
  Insalata caprese, **293**
  Octopus salad, **297**
  Prosciutto in, **15**
  Salted cod, salad with, **295**
  Scungilli salad, **299**
  Sliced conch, salad with, **299**
  Tomato and mozzarella salad, **293**

INTERMEZZO
  Generally, **143 et seq.**
  Bibliography, **452**
  Blackberries, **149**
  Champagne granita, **159**
  Compari sorbetto, **145**
  Gelato, **143**
  Granita, this index
  Grapefruit campari granita, **157**
  Lemone granita alla siciliano, **153**
  Limoncello mint sorbetto, **147**
  Mint julep granita, **155**
  Sherry cardamom granita, **161**
  Sorbet, **143**
  Strawberry sorbetto, **151**
  White wine granita, **159**

ITALIAN HAM
  Antipasti, **11**

JEWISH APPLE CAKE
  Recipe, **327**

KINA LILLET
  Vesper martini, **347**

KITCHEN TIPS
  Generally, **3**

LAMB
  Agnello arrosto, **253**

LA VERDURA
  Generally, **207 et seq.**
  Bibliography, **454**
  Broccoli rabe with sausage and beans, **215**
  Escarole and beans, **209**
  Giambotta zucchini, **207**
  Peperone con ripieno, **213**
  Rapini con salsiccia e fagioli, **215**
  Riso con la verza, **211**
  Savoy cabbage with rice, **211**
  Scarola con fagioli, **209**

LA VERDURA—Cont'd
  Stuffed peppers, **213**
  Summer vegetables, **211**
  Winter vegetables, **211**
  Zucchini stew, **207**

LEMONE GRANITA ALLA SICILIANO
  Recipe, **153**

LIMONCELLO
  Recipe, **367**

LIMONCELLO MINT SORBETTO
  Recipes, **147**

MACARONI
  See Pasta in Italian Cuisine, this index

MARINATED ARTICHOKES
  Recipe, **13**

MARINE CORPS PUNCH
  Recipe, **341**

MARTINI ROSSO
  Negroni Sbagliato (cocktail), **361**

MERLUZZO DI POMODORA
  Recipe, **181**

MINESTRONE
  Translation, **72**

MINESTRONE CON POLPETTE
  Recipe, **71**

MINT JULEP GRANITA
  Recipe, **155**

MOZZARELLA
  Tomato and mozzarella salad, **293**

MUSSLES IN TOMATO SAUCE
  Recipe, **183**

MUTTON
  Agnello arrosto, **253**

NAVY GROG
  Recipe, **343**

NEGRONI (COCKTAIL)
  Recipe, **359**

NEGRONI SBAGLIATO (COCKTAIL)
  Recipe, **361**

NOODLES
  See Pasta in Italian Cuisine, this index

OATMEAL
　Amaretto apricot oatmeal chews, **325**

OCTOPUS SALAD
　Recipe, **297**

OLIVE SPREAD
　Recipe, **19**

ORZO
　Translation, **69**

PANETTONE
　Translation, **381**

PARMA HAM
　Antipasti, **11**

PARMESAN
　Risotto alla zucca, **127**

PASTA FAZOOL
　Translation, **66**

PASTA IN ITALIAN CUISINE
　Generally, **105]** et seq.
　Bibliography, **450**
　Decorative shaped pasta, **108**
　Different functions, understanding, **113**
　Extruded, **107**
　Fancy shapes, **108**
　Irregular shaped pasta, **110**
　Long noodles, **105**
　Minute pasta, **109**
　Pesto sauce, **121**
　Ribbon cut, **106**
　Short-cut, **107**
　Spicy pasta, **117**
　Strand pasta, **105**
　Stuffed pasta, **110**
　Thyme butter recipe, **120**
　Tiny pasta, **109**
　Tubular, **107**
　Varieties of pasta, **105**

PASTA RECIPES
　Basil and pine nuts sauce, **121**
　Con di noci pasta, **123**
　E ceci, **67**
　E fagiole, **65**
　Puttanesca, **117**
　With ricotta, **125**
　Risotto pasta with ricotta, **127**
　Sauce of the harlot, **117**

PASTA RECIPES—Cont'd
　Walnuts and bread crumbs, pasta with, **123**

PEPERONE CON RIPIENO
　Recipe, **213**

PEPERONI
　Salsiccia con peperoni alla scaloppini, **249**

PEPPERS
　Chicken cacciatora, **251**
　Ciliegio pepe, **289**
　Egg giambotta, **41**
　Frittata ala Domenico, **39**
　Fuoco e insalata di ghiaccio, **287**
　Giambotta zucchini, **207**
　Origin and use, **31**
　Polo alla cacciatora, **251**
　Roasted peppers, **31**
　Salad uses, **15**
　Salad with salted cod, **295**
　Sausage cut thin with peppers, **249**
　Stuffed peppers, **213**
　Vitella scoloppini, **255**

PESCE
　Generally, **181** et seq.
　Bibliography, **454**
　Calamari pomodora, **185**
　Cod, **182**
　Conch, salad with, **299**
　Cozze pomodoro, **183**
　Cuttlefish stewed in tomatoes, **185**
　Insalata di baccala, **295**
　Insalata di polpo, **297**
　Merluzzo di pomodora, **181**
　Mussles in tomato sauce, **183**
　Octopus salad, **297**
　Salad with salted cod, **295**
　Salad with sliced conch, **299**
　Squid stewed in tomatoes, **185**
　Tilapia con pomodora, **187**
　Tilapia with tomatoes, **187**
　Whiting in tomato sauce, **181**

PESTO SAUCE
　Recipe, **121**

POLENTA
　Fried polenta or cornmeal, **45**

POLO ALLA CACCIATORA
　Recipe, **251**

Index to Recipes

POLPETTA, POLPETTINE
Translation, **72**

POLPO
Insalata di polpo, **297**

PORCHETTA ARROSTO
Recipe, **247**

PORK
Roast loin of pork, **247**

PROSCIUTTO
Crudo, prosciutto, **11**
Salad uses, **15**

PROSECCO
Godchild (cocktail), **357**

PUMPKIN
Risotto alla zucca, **127**

RAPINI CON SALSICCIA E FAGIOLI
Recipe, **215**

RASPBERRY LEMON TIRAMISU
Recipe, **319**

RICE
Amaretto rice pudding, **323**
Savoy cabbage with rice, **211**

RICOTTA
Pasta with ricotta, **125**

RISO, RISOTTO, RISONI
Translations, **69**

RISO CON LA VERZA
Recipe, **211**

RISOTTO
Alla zucca, risotto, **127**
Pasta with ricotta, risotto, **127**
Zuccarrelli risotto, **127**

ROASTED PEPPERS
Recipe, **31**

ROAST LEG OF LAMB
Recipe, **253**

ROAST LOIN OF PORK
Recipe, **247**

RUM
Marine Corps punch, **341**
Navy grog, **343**

RUM—Cont'd
1775 fortitude rum punch, **341**

SALAD
See Insalata, this index

SALSICCIA CON PEPERONI ALLA SCALOPPINI
Recipe, **249**

SAUSAGE
Broccoli rabe with sausage and beans, **215**
Omlette, sausage and spinach, **37**
Peppers, sausage cut thin with, **249**

SAVOY CABBAGE WITH RICE
Recipe, **211**

SCALOPPINI
Salsiccia con peperoni alla scaloppini, **249**

SCAROLA CON FAGIOLI
Recipe, **209**

SCOLOPPINI
Vitella scoloppini, **255**

SCOTCH WHISKY
Godfather (cocktail), **353**

SCUNGILLI
Salad with sliced conch, **299**

SEAFOOD
See Pesce, this index

1775 FORTITUDE RUM PUNCH
Recipe, **341**

SHERRY CARDAMOM GRANITA
Recipe, **161**

SNACKS
See Antipasti, this index

SORBET
Intermezzo, **143**

SOUP
See Zuppa, this index

SPAGHETTI
See Pasta in Italian Cuisine, this index

SPICY PASTA
Recipe, **117**

SPINACH
Rice and spinach zuppa, **69**

SPINACH—Cont'd
Sausage and spinach omlette, **37**

SPUMANTE
Negroni Sbagliato (cocktail), **361**

SQUID
Stewed in tomatoes, **185**

STRAWBERRY SORBETTO
Recipe, **151**

STUFFED PEPPERS
Recipe, **213**

SUMMER VEGETABLES
Generally, **211**

SWEET AND SOUR EGGPLANT
Recipe, **17**

SWEETPOTATO GNOCCHI
Recipe, **119**

SWEETS
See Dolce, this index

TAPENADE
Recipe, **19**

THYME BUTTER
Recipe, **120**

TILAPIA
Con pomodora, tilapia, **187**
Translation, **187**

TIRAMISU
Translation, **319**

TOMASSO VESPER
Frittata ala tomasso vesper, **33**

TOMATOES
Brushette, **29**
Calamari pomodora, **185**
Chicken cacciatora, **251**
Cozze pomodoro, **183**
Cuttlefish stewed in tomatoes, **185**
Giambotta zucchini, **207**
Merluzzo di pomodora, **181**
Minestrone con polpette, **71**
Mozzarella and tomato salad, **293**
Mussles in tomato sauce, **183**
Pasta e fagiole, **65**
Pasta puttanesca, **117**
Polo alla cacciatora, **251**

TOMATOES—Cont'd
Salad uses, **15**
Salsiccia con peperoni alla scaloppini, **249**
Sauce of the harlot, **117**
Sausage cut thin with peppers, **249**
Spicy pasta, **117**
Squid stewed in tomatoes, **185**
Tilapia con pomodora, **187**
Veal in tomato sauce, **255**
Vegetable omelet, **33**
Whiting in tomato sauce, **181**
Zucchini stew, **207**

VEAL IN TOMATO SAUCE
Recipe, **255**

VEGETABLES
See La Verdura, this index

VERMOUTH
Americano (cocktail), **363**
Negroni, **359**

VESPER MARTINI
Recipe, **347**

VIN BRULE (COCKTAIL)
Recipe, **381**

VITELLA SCOLOPPINI
Recipe, **255**

VODKA
Bocce ball cocktail, **379**
Godmother (cocktail), **355**
Limoncello, **367**
Vesper martini, **347**

WALNUTS
Pasta with walnuts and bread crumbs, **123**

WHITING IN TOMATO SAUCE
Recipe, **181**

WINE
Bartending tips, **5**
Bellini
Generally, **345**
two minute version, **349**
Vin brule, **381**
White wine granita, **159**

WINTER VEGETABLES
Generally, **211**

Index to Recipes

ZUCATTA CAKE
  Recipe, **321**

ZUCCA
  Translation, **127**

ZUCCARRELLI RISOTTO
  Recipe, **127**

ZUCCHINI STEW
  Recipe, **207**

ZUPPA
  Generally, **65 et seq.**
  Bibliography, **450**
  Chick peas or ceci beans and pasta, **67**
  Di spinaci e riso, **69**
  Minestrone con polpette, **71**
  Pasta e ceci, **67**
  Pasta e fagiole, **65**
  Spinach and rice, **69**

Index to Trial Tips

ACCEPTANCE OF CASES
See Case Acceptance Decisions, this index

ACCIDENTS
Incident vs accident, effect of use of term on jurors, **219**
Reconstruction
   Generally, **47**
   expert use, **57**
Scene investigation
   Google Earth views, **51**
   preservation assumptions, **25**

AFFIRMATIVE DEFENSE TRAPS
Investigation and preparation, **21**

AGENTS
See Designated Representative Depositions, this index

ANCHORING THE EVIDENCE
Juries, this index
Memory, this index
Neurolinguistic programming approach, **267**
Opening Statements, this index
PowerPoint use, **241**
Real evidence, anchoring testimony with, **227, 270**
Sound as anchor, **330**
Storytelling and anchoring, **227**
Videotape use, **330**

ARGUMENT
Direct examination advocacy opportunities, **257**
Summation, this index

ASSUMPTIONS
Accident scene preservation, **25**
Causation assumption errors, **22**
Client history accuracy assumptions, **24**
Dangers of assuming too much, **27, 76, 88**
Drawings, scale accuracy, **26**
Expert witnesses
   background knowledge, **57**
   competence, **26**
Incident reports, accuracy, **23**
Juror understanding of key facts, **223**

ASSUMPTIONS—Cont'd
Liability assumption errors, **22**
Life expectancy, **24**
Police records accuracy and completeness, **23**
Prior claims, **24**
Real evidence admissibility, **282**
Records accuracy and completeness, **23**
Settlement assumption errors, **21**
Witness statement consistency, **25**

ATTORNEY'S FEES
Contingent fee representation, financing of costs, **52**

BIAS
Generally, **336**
Antiplaintiff, **336**
Approaching juror biases, **338**
ATLA jury bias project, **217**
Attribution, **336**
Availability, **202, 338**
Belief perseverance, **337**
Confirmation, **337**
Defense exploitation of biases
   client disabilities, **24**
   countering, **102**
Focus group studies, **336**
Frivolous lawsuit, **218**
Hindsight, **217**
Local bias affecting juror perceptions, **266**
Medical examiners', **130, 132, 196**
Mock jury use to identify, **191**
Perceptions of jurors, local bias affecting, **266**
Personal responsibility, **218, 336**
Stuff happens, **218**
Suspicion, **217**
Understanding juror biases, **191**
Victimization, **218**
Voir dire questions revealing, **190**

BLUFFS
Negotiation and settlement, **405**

BUSINESS ENTITIES
See Designated Representative Depositions, this index

CASE ACCEPTANCE DECISIONS
    Generally, **20 et seq.**
    Client history accuracy assumptions, **24**
    Decision tree approach, **20**
    Early investigation, importance, **57, 382**
    Expert witness costs considerations, **58**
    Liability assumption errors, **22**
    Mock jury case evaluations, **229**
    Preexisting conditions, **24**
    Prior claims, **24**
    Records accuracy and completeness, **23**
    Witness statement consistency assumptions, **25**

CAUSATION
    Assumptions about liability, **22**

CHAOS THEORY
    Demand letters, **405**
    Negotiation, **399**

CHARTS
    See Real Evidence, this index

CHOICES
    Defendant's, accentuating, **340**
    Effect of use of term on jurors, **204**

CLIENT AS DEPONENT
    Generally, **130 et seq.**
    Cliff notes for clients, **136**
    Credibility findings by medical examiners, **131**
    Demeanor improvement, **135**
    Diagrams use, **136**
    Disabilities questions, **134**
    Family member or friend support, **140**
    First language use, **138**
    Medical Examinations, this index
    Notes, use of, **136, 142**
    Pain questions, **135, 137**
    Preparation
        generally, **131, 383**
        standard questions, **134**
    Prior injuries/conditions questions, **134**
    Representation at medical examinations, **131**
    Role-playing exercises, **139**
    Structured lists, **138, 142**
    Timeline conflicts, **137**
    Translation assistance, **136**
    Unasked question issues, **139**

CLIENT AS WITNESS
    Direct examination practice, **258**
    Preparation, **139**

CLIENT CREDIBILITY ISSUES
    Generally, **196**

CLIENT DEMEANOR
    Depositions, **135**
    Juror considerations, **199, 206**

CLIENT DISABILITIES
    Defense exploitation, **24**

CLIENT ESCORTS
    Medical examinations, **132**

CLIENT HISTORIES
    Generally, **51, 229**
    Accuracy assumptions, **24**
    Medical examination use, **133**
    Prior incident surprises, **134**

CLIENT MEETINGS
    Generally, **383**

CLOSING ARGUMENT
    See Summation, this index

CONSULTANTS
    See Juries, this index

CONTINGENT FEE REPRESENTATION
    Costs, financing, **52**

CORPORATIONS
    See Designated Representative Depositions, this index

COSTS
    Conservation of trial costs, **54**
    Contingent fee cases, costs financing, **52**
    Defense cost estimates, assessing for settlement, **385**
    Discussing potential costs with clients, **56**
    Effective cost reduction methods, **63**
    Expert Witnesses, this index
    Jury consultant use, **139**
    Notebooks, costs savings, **60**
    Rebuttal experts use, **55**
    Settlement, defense costs assessments, **385**
    Strategic cost management, **56**

CROSS-EXAMINATION
    Generally, **300 et seq.**
    Abusing the witness verbally, **305**
    Abusive questions, **310**
    Aspersing questions, **306**
    Asserting personal opinions, **303**
    Badgering and burdensome conduct, **308**

CROSS-EXAMINATION—Cont'd
Bullying, **302**
Changing the subject, **313**
Contempt sanctions, **301**
Crowding, **302**
Defense cross-examination tips, **314**
Delaying conduct, **308**
Direct examination distinguished, **256**
Editorializing, **303**
Embarrassing questions, **304, 305**
Emotions, controlling, **312**
Ethical considerations, **300 et seq.**
Evasive answers, dealing with, **306**
Evidence rules
  generally, **300**
  examples of violations, **310**
Exhibits, anticipating cross-examination treatment, **271**
Experts, **314, 332**
Exscinding, **307**
Good faith bases for questions, **301, 306**
Harassing a witness, **304**
Illegal blocking, **307**
Impeachment, this index
Innuendo, **306**
Interrupting answers
  generally, **307**
  irrelevant or prejudicial responses, **307**
Introducing unproven or irrelevant facts, **306**
Junk science, debunking, **201, 331 et seq.**
Laughing, **303**
Medical examiners, **314, 332**
Misrepresenting facts or opinions, **306**
Nitpicking a witness, **304**
Over-the-edge questions, **310**
Physical dynamics, **313**
Prejudicial responses, interrupting, **307**
Purposes, **313**
Reacting to testimony, **301**
Repeating answers, **304**
Safe cross tips, **313**
Sanctions, **310**
Seven deadly sins of cross, **300**
Shouting, **302**
Soft cross technique, **314**
Spiteful or shiftless conduct, **308**
Stopping irrelevant or prejudicial responses, **307**
Surprising answers, reacting to, **304**
Syntax bullying, **305**
Tactics for cross-examination control, **313**

CROSS-EXAMINATION—Cont'd
Three purposes, **313**
Truthful witnesses, moral dilemma of crossing, **309**
Types of cross-examinations, **313**
Vocabulary bullying, **305**

DAMAGES
Concentrating and developing claims, **202**
Day in the life videos, **264**
Expert witness use in wrongful death cases, **412**
Human damages, jury understanding, **195**
Opening statement treatment of damages issues, **227**
Outlining for settlement, **407, 412**

DECISION TREES
Case acceptance decisions, **20**

DEFENSE COSTS
Assessing for settlement, **385**

DEFENSE EXPERTS
Reports, reviewing, **62**

DEFENSE MEDICAL EXAMINATIONS
See Medical Examinations, this index

DEFENSE STRATEGIES
Anticipating, **97, 198**
Wedge strategy, countering, **329**

DEMONSTRATIVE EVIDENCE
See Real Evidence, this index

DEPOSITION PRACTICE
Generally, **72 et seq.**
After action planning, **74**
Bracketing measurement opinions, **79**
Case analysis preparation, **102**
Cerebration tips, **73**
Client as Deponent, this index
Common civil practice rules problems, **74**
Commonsense standards of conduct questions, **102**
Computerized, real time transcripts, **201, 332**
Deathstar deposition notice, **97, 163**
Death star strategy, **93**
Defending depositions. See Client as Deponent, this index
Defense strategies, **97**
Demeanor of deponent
  capturing, **77**
  client as deponent, **135**

DEPOSITION PRACTICE—Cont'd
  Designated Representative Depositions, this index
  Dilatory discovery tactics, **101**
  Document use, **80**
  Domino principle, **76, 82**
  Evasiveness, preparing for, **103**
  Exhausting the deponent's knowledge, **77**
  Exhibit use, **75**
  Fact vs opinion answers of lay witnesses, **78**
  Federal protocols, **88**
  Final questions, **77**
  Focusing tips, **73**
  Form of question, objections as to, **89**
  Ground rules, **88**
  Hall Standards, **90**
  Impeachment material, preservation, **80**
  Instructions not to answer, **89**
  Interruptions, **89**
  Knowledge denials by representative deponents, **89, 95**
  Law of the case issues, **73**
  Making and updating the plan, **73**
  Measurement opinions, bracketing, **79**
  Medical examiner depositions, videotaping, **330**
  Miller mousetrap, **101, 163**
  Nailing down bases, **78**
  Nonparty document production, **92**
  Notebooks, this index
  Objecting to questions
    generally, **74**
    form of question, **89**
    preservation, **89**
  Obstructive tactics, **90**
  Pin down questions, **77**
  Planning for the deposition, **73**
  Preparation
    client as deponent, **131, 383**
    evasive deponents, **103**
  Preservation of objections, **89**
  Prior statements, development through, **80**
  Production demands, **91 et seq.**
  Protocols, deposition, **88, 164**
  Purposes of depositions, **97**
  Reasonable availability of documents, **100**
  Reasons for lay opinions, establishing, **78**
  Representatives as deponents. See Designated Representative Depositions, this index
  Settlement, discovery posture to motivate, **399**
  Standards of conduct questions, **101**

DEPOSITION PRACTICE—Cont'd
  Synopsizing transcripts, **75**
  Touching all bases, **78**
  Video depositions
    generally, **77**
    experts, **54**
    medical examiners, **330**

DESIGNATED REPRESENTATIVE (DCR) DEPOSITIONS
  Deathstar deposition notice, **97, 163**
  Duties, **94**
  Federal rules, **89**
  Knowledge denials, **89, 95**
  Production demands, **91, 93**

DIAGRAMS
  See also Real Evidence, this index
  Scale accuracy assumptions, **26**
  Settlement communications, **407**

DIRECT EXAMINATION
  Generally, **256 et seq.**
  Advocacy opportunities, **257**
  Anchoring, neurolinguistic programming approach, **267**
  Basic ABCs, **257**
  Confidence instilling interaction, **258**
  Cross-examination distinguished, **256**
  Documents, reading into evidence, **264**
  Experts, order of examination, **259**
  Integrating exhibits and demonstrative evidence, **268**
  Integrating visual and oral communication, **278**
  Interaction, confidence instilling, **258**
  Neurolinguistic programming approach to anchoring testimony, **267**
  Practice with the witness, **258**
  Preparation, cardinal rule of, **257**
  Prioritization, **259**
  Reading documents into evidence, **264**
  Rebutting surprises, **331**
  Surprising evidence, rebutting, **331**

DISCOVERY
  Auto crash investigation tools, **49**
  Client as Deponent, this index
  Costs control, **46**
  Creating exhibits, **53**
  Defense expert reports, reviewing, **62**
  Deposition Practice, this index

DISCOVERY—Cont'd
Designated Representative Depositions, this index
Dilatory discovery tactics, **101**
Exhibits, creating, **53**
Expert witnesses at discovery stage, **60**
Investigation expenses, **48**
Medical Examinations, this index
Nonparty document production, **92**
Notebooks, this index
Production demands, **91 et seq.**
Settlement
    assumption errors, **21**
    discovery posture to motivate, **399**
Strategy, **390**
Written discovery, **46 et seq.**

DOCUMENTS
See also Real Evidence, this index
Depositions, document use, **80**
Expert witness document review planning, **60**
Nonparty documents, **92**
Production Demands, this index
Reading into evidence, **264**
Reasonable availability, **100**

DOMINO PRINCIPLE
Deposition practice, **76, 82**

ETHICS
Cross-examination ethics, **300 et seq.**
Insurance fraud, **401**
Situational ethics, **88**

EVENT SCHEMA
Opening statements, use in, **337**

EVIDENCE
Anchoring the Evidence, this index
Documents, this index
Production Demands, this index
Real Evidence, this index

EXPERT WITNESSES
Accident reconstruction experts, **57**
Background knowledge assumptions, **58**
Competence assumptions, **26**
Cross-examination, **314, 332**
Damages experts use in wrongful death cases, **412**
Defense expert reports, reviewing, **62**
Demeanor, **333**
Depositions, videotaping, **54**

EXPERT WITNESSES—Cont'd
Direct examination
    order of examination, **259**
    practice examinations, **258**
Discovery stage, **60**
Document review planning, **60**
Fees
    budgeting, **59**
    costs considerations, **58**
    financing, **52**
    management, **56**
Field of play analysis of experts, **76**
Focussing the expert, **60, 62**
Investigations by experts, cost considerations, **57**
Junk science, debunking, **201, 331 et seq.**
Jury consultants. See Juries, this index
Legal research issues, **57**
Medical examiners, cross-examination, **314, 332**
Order of direct examination, **259**
Planning the expert's report, **61**
Rebuttal experts, **55, 62**
Rebutting surprises, **331**
Reports
    planning, **61**
    reviewing, **62**
Reviewing the expert's report, **62**
Selection assumptions, **26**
Shirt-sleeve experts
    generally, **333**
    costs considerations, **51**
    jury impacts, **63, 197**
Surprising evidence, rebutting, **331**
Synopses of opinions, **55**
Videotape
    depositions, **54**
    testimony, pretrial, **330**

EYE CONTACT
Opening statements, **199, 230**
Summation, **340**

FOCUS GROUPS
Exhibit and demonstrative evidence testing, **279**
Juror bias problems, **336, 338**
Notebook materials
    generally, **164, 168**
    organization, **176**
Opening statement testing, **328**
Summation testing, **328**

FRAUD INVESTIGATIONS
    Insurer practices, **401**

GOOGLE EARTH
    Accident scene investigation, **51**
    Exhibit creations, **53**
    Photograph source, **49**

HEISENBERG UNCERTAINTY PRINCIPLE
    Negotiation, **399**

HEURISTICS
    Jury communication, **216**

HINDSIGHT PRINCIPLE
    Jury communication, **216**

HISTORIES
    See Client Histories, this index

IMPEACHMENT
    Generally, **300**
    Deposition acquisition of impeachment material, **80**
    Truthful witnesses, **309**
    Unimpeachable witnesses, **315**

INCIDENT REPORTS
    Accuracy assumption errors, **23**

INDEPENDENT MEDICAL EXAMINATIONS
    See Medical Examinations, this index

INFERENCE TOOLS
    Jury communication, **216**

INFORMATION AVAILABILITY PRINCIPLE
    Jury communication, **217**

INSURANCE
    Fraud investigations, **401**
    Juror attitudes, **205**

INVESTIGATION AND PREPARATION
    Generally, **20 et seq.**
    Accident scene preservation assumptions, **25**
    Affirmative defense traps, **21**
    Auto crash investigation tools, **49**
    Causation assumption errors, **22**
    Client history accuracy assumptions, **24**
    Decision tree approach, **20**
    Drawing scale accuracy assumptions, **26**
    Early investigation, importance, **57**
    Expenses, **48**
    Experts, use to investigate, cost considerations, **57**

INVESTIGATION AND PREPARATION —Cont'd
    Expert witness selection assumptions, **26**
    Google Earth, accident scene investigation, **51**
    Liability assumption errors, **22**
    Life expectancy assumptions, **24**
    Paper trails worth tracking down, **23**
    Preexisting condition assumptions, **24**
    Prior claims assumptions, **24**
    Records accuracy and completeness assumption errors, **23**
    Records preservation assumption errors, **23**
    Settlement assumption errors, **21**
    Technical research, **57**
    Witness information assumptions, **25**
    Witness statement consistency assumptions, **25**

ISSUE FRAMING PRINCIPLE
    Jury communication, **217**

JOINT VENTURE REPRESENTATIONS
    Generally, **419**

JUNK SCIENCE
    Debunking, **201, 331 et seq.**

JURIES
    Generally, **188 et seq.**
    Accident, effect of use of term, **219**
    Aesthetic need as motivator, **194, 277**
    Analytical processing of the case, anticipating, **265**
    Anchoring as communication technique
        exhibit use, **227**
        neurolinguistic programming approach, **267**
        PowerPoint use, **241**
        testimony, **200**
        testimony use, **227**
    Antidote for apathy, **190**
    Antiplaintiff bias, **336**
    Approaching juror biases, **338**
    ATLA jury bias project, **217**
    Attention level of jurors, recognizing, **240**
    Attribution bias, **336**
    Availability bias, **202, 338**
    Bad conduct vs injury and juror motivation, **219**
    Belief perseverance bias, **337**
    Beliefs of jurors, speaking to, **216**
    Best voir dire questions, **188**
    Bias, this index
    Choices, effect of use of term on jurors, **204**
    Circle of life approach to juror selection, **194**

JURIES—Cont'd
  Client credibility issues, **196**
  Client demeanor, importance, **199, 206**
  Concentrating and developing damages, **202**
  Confirmation bias, **337**
  Connecting with the jury
    generally, **190, 199**
    jargon use, **203**
    voir dire, **201**
  Conscious and unconscious reasoning, **239, 265**
  Consultants
    generally, **188**
    costs, **139**
    information gaps, identifying, **236**
    juror bias problems, **338**
    techniques, **142**
  Costs, jury consultants, **139**
  Cross- vs direct examination, impacts distinguished, **257**
  Curiosity instinct as motivator, **194, 277**
  Decisionmaking, Paradox study, **192**
  Defense strategies, anticipating, **198**
  Demonstrations and exhibits, value of, **204**
  Emotion, controlling and using, **204**
  Environmental conditions affecting, **241**
  Event schema use, **337**
  Exhibits and demonstrative evidence as memory aids, **261**
  Eye Contact, this index
  Factors affecting jurors' perceptions and responses, **240**
  Focus Groups, this index
  Four minute drill and jurors' first impressions, **226**
  Frivolous lawsuit bias, **218**
  Go along approach to jury communication, **199**
  Heard vs said messages, distinctions, **221**
  Heuristics, **216**
  Hindsight bias, **217**
  Hindsight principle, **216**
  Human damages, understanding, **195**
  Indifference of otherwise nice jurors, combatting, **190**
  Inference tools, **216**
  Information availability principle, **217**
  Information gaps, identifying, **236**
  Information processing theory, **216**
  Injury vs bad conduct and juror motivation, **219**
  Insurance attitudes, **205**
  Issue framing principle, **217**

JURIES—Cont'd
  Jargon use, **203**
  Laws of the land approach to juror selection, **194**
  Linking. Anchoring, above
  Local bias affecting juror perceptions, **266**
  Love and belonging instincts as motivators, **193, 277**
  Make a difference approach to juror selection, **194**
  Memory, this index
  Men vs women jurors' priorities, **226**
  Mirroring use during voir dire, **201**
  Mistake, effect of use of term on jurors, **197, 204, 219**
  Mock Juries, this index
  Moralist jurors, typography of, **410**
  Neurolinguistic programming
    generally, **226**
    anchoring testimony through, **267**
  Noneconomic damages understanding, **195**
  Notebooks, mock jury materials, **164, 168**
  Older vs younger jurors, **204**
  Opening Statements, this index
  Pain and suffering, juror understanding, **195**
  Paradox study of decisionmaking, **192**
  Perceptions of jurors
    factors affecting, **240**
    local bias affecting, **266**
  Personal life experiences affecting jurors' perceptions and responses, **240**
  Personal responsibility bias, **218, 336**
  Point of view, importance in storytelling, **221**
  Pragmatist jurors, typography of, **410**
  Preconceptions of jurors, speaking to, **216**
  Preexisting beliefs affecting jurors' perceptions and responses, **240**
  Processing of information by jurors, **239**
  Real evidence, jury testing, **279**
  Recall and recognition, enabling, **224**
  Recognition memory, **224**
  Reptile theory, **190**
  Responses of jurors, factors affecting, **240**
  Safety and security instincts as motivators, **193, 277**
  Said vs heard messages, distinctions, **221**
  Seinfeld syndrome, **190**
  Self-actualization need as motivator, **194, 277**
  Sequence of presentation, importance, **221**
  Seven Stakes approach to juror selection, **193**
  Shadow juries. See Mock Juries, this index

JURIES—Cont'd
Shirt-sleeve experts use to impress, **197**
Shortening the trial, **202**
Socially responsible jurors, typography of, **410**
Socioeconomic filters affecting jurors' perceptions and responses, **240**
Stuff happens bias, **218**
Summation, this index
Survival instinct as motivator, **193, 277**
Suspicion bias, **217**
Ten voir dire ideas, **192**
Top three voir dire questions, **188**
Typographies of jurors, **410**
Unasked question issues, **139**
Unconscious and analytical processing of the case, anticipating, **278**
Victimization bias, **218**
Views, use of, **204**
Witness credibility, jurors' assessments, **199**
Women vs men jurors' priorities, **226**
Younger vs older jurors, **204**

LIABILITY
Assumptions about liability, **22**
Defendant choices and, **340**
General vs specific discussion about liability, **339**

LIFE EXPECTANCY
Assumptions, **24**
Computations, **412**

LINKING
See Anchoring the Evidence, this index

MEDIATION
Generally, **382 et seq.**
Decisionmaking by mediators, **409**
Typographies of mediators, **410**

MEDICAL EXAMINATIONS
Cancellations and no shows, **132**
Credibility findings, **131**
Cross-examination of medical examiners, **314, 332**
Defense strategies, **130**
Depositions of medical examiners, videotaping, **330**
Escorts for client, **132**
Histories, accuracy assumptions, **24**
Independent medical exam fictions, **130, 132, 196**
Instructions for client, **132**
Junk science, debunking, **201, 331**
Rebutting surprises, **331**

MEDICAL EXAMINATIONS—Cont'd
Representation of client at, **131**
Rules, establishing, **132**
Surprising evidence, rebutting, **331**
Videotaping depositions of medical examiners, **330**

MEMORY
See also Anchoring the Evidence, this index
Attention level and memory capacity, **240**
Exhibits, making them memorable, **267**
Exhibits and demonstrative evidence as aids, **261**
Jurors' memory capacity, recognizing, **240**
Jury communications, memory organization packages, **227**
Organization packages, memory, **227**
Recognition memory, **224**
Sponsorship of exhibits and, **272**

MILLER MOUSETRAP
Deposition practice, **101, 163**

MIRRORING
Use during voir dire and opening statements, **201**

MISTAKE
Effect of use of term on jurors, **197, 204, 219**

MOCK JURIES
Biases, identifying, **191**
Case evaluation, **229**
Direct examination practice, **258**
Exhibit testing, **267**
Notebooks, mock jury materials, **164, 168**
Opening statement rehearsal, **241**
Real evidence, jury testing, **279**
Visual strategies, improving, **53**

MULTIPLE CLAIMANTS
Representing, **417**

NEGOTIATION
Generally, **382 et seq.**
See also Settlement, this index
Bluffs, **405**
Chaos theory, **399**
Heisenberg uncertainty principle, **399**

NEUROLINGUISTIC PROGRAMMING
Anchoring the evidence, **267**
Jury communications, **226**

NOTEBOOKS
Generally, **162 et seq.**
Access tools, **163**

NOTEBOOKS—Cont'd
  Alternative/complimentary dispute resolution proceedings, **165**
  Briefs, settlement, **393**
  Costs savings, **60, 170**
  Data section, settlement, **393, 394**
  Deathstar deposition notice, **97, 163**
  Deposition notebooks
    generally, **167**
    designated representative depositions, **93**
    forms, **88**
    organization, **164**
    planning use, **74**
    protocols, **88, 164**
    use, **76**
  Designated representative depositions, **93**
  File sense approach to organization, **163**
  Florilegium, **1**
  Focus group materials
    generally, **164, 168**
    organization, **176**
  Folder organization systems compared, **174**
  Folder use compared, **75**
  Forms
    generally, **171**
    deposition notebooks, **88**
  Guides, **166**
  Main notebook, **167**
  Miller mousetrap, **101, 163**
  Mock jury materials, **164, 168**
  Opening statements use, **229**
  Organization
    file sense approach, **163**
    focus group materials, **176**
    folder organization systems compared, **174**
    settlement notebooks, **171, 388, 392**
    trial notebooks, **177**
  Overview section, **393**
  Paralegal updating responsibilities, **166**
  Paralegal use, **60**
  Presentations, settlement, **393**
  Protocols, deposition, **88**
  Recycling and reuse, **166, 170**
  Settlement notebooks
    generally, **167, 386**
    aids, **165**
    briefs, **393**
    data section, **393, 394**
    organization, **171, 388, 392**
    overview section, **392**

NOTEBOOKS—Cont'd
  Settlement notebooks—Cont'd
    presentations, **393**
    three-part system, **392**
  Staff updating responsibilities, **166**
  Supplementation, **164**
  Trial notebooks
    generally, **168**
    organization, **164, 177**

OPENING STATEMENTS
  Generally, **216 et seq.**
  Accident, effect of use of term on jurors, **219**
  Anchoring as communication technique
    exhibit use, **227**
    PowerPoint use, **241**
  ATLA jury bias project, **217**
  Attention level of jurors, recognizing, **240**
  Bad conduct vs injury and juror motivation, **219**
  Beginner mistakes to avoid, **233**
  Beliefs of jurors, speaking to, **216**
  Building an effective case strategy, **242**
  Choices, effect of use of term on jurors, **204**
  Color mistakes in use of, **237**
  Connecting with the jury
    generally, **199**
    jargon use, **203**
  Conspicuity problems, **239**
  Damages issues, **227**
  Darkside mistakes to avoid, **233**
  Defense strategies, anticipating, **198**
  Detail, using and avoiding, **220**
  Diffusion errors, **197**
  Dos and don'ts of storytelling, **222, 230**
  Emotion, controlling and using, **204**
  Environmental conditions affecting jurors, **241**
  Event schema use, **337**
  Excite the little child within us all, **225**
  Exhibit use, **227**
  Eye contact, **199, 230**
  Factors affecting jurors' perceptions and responses, **240**
  Facts statements, streamlining, **197**
  Focus group testing, **328**
  Four minute drill and jurors' first impressions, **226**
  Four storytelling rules, **220**
  Frivolous lawsuit bias, **218**
  Go along approach to jury communication, **199**
  Heard vs said messages, distinctions, **221**

OPENING STATEMENTS—Cont'd
    Heuristics, **216**
    Hindsight principle, **216**
    Ideations, **227**
    Importance of, **222**
    Inference tools, **216**
    Information availability principle, **217**
    Information processing theory, **216**
    Injury vs bad conduct and juror motivation, **219**
    Intermediate mistakes, **235**
    Issue framing principle, **217**
    Jargon use, **203**
    Juror beliefs and preconceptions, speaking to, **216**
    Linking. Anchoring, above
    Memory capacity of jurors, recognizing, **240**
    Memory organization packages, **227**
    Men vs women jurors' priorities, **226**
    Mirroring use, **201**
    Mistake, effect of use of term on jurors, **197, 204, 219**
    Mock jury rehearsals, **241**
    Natural motivational analysis, use of, **227**
    Neurolinguistic programming, **226**
    Notebook use, **229**
    Perceptions of jurors, factors affecting, **240**
    Personal life experiences affecting jurors' perceptions and responses, **240**
    Personal responsibility bias, **218**
    Perspicuity problems, **239**
    Pictures, mistakes in use of, **237**
    Point of view, importance in storytelling, **221**
    Positive and negative thoughts, **222**
    PowerPoint use
        generally, **230 et seq.**
        anchoring the PowerPoint opening, **241**
        defense use dangers, **243**
        staff training, **244**
    Preconceptions of jurors, speaking to, **216**
    Preexisting beliefs affecting jurors' perceptions and responses, **240**
    Preparation, **229**
    Present tense use, **226**
    Primacy, **223**
    Priorities for storytellers, **226**
    Processing of information by jurors, **239**
    Recall and recognition, enabling, **224**
    Recency, **223**
    Rehearsing, **198**
    Responses of jurors, factors affecting, **240**

OPENING STATEMENTS—Cont'd
    Said vs heard messages, distinctions, **221**
    Sentimentality, **222**
    Sequence of presentation, importance, **221**
    Socioeconomic filters affecting jurors' perceptions and responses, **240**
    Storytelling
        generally, **219 et seq.**
        see also Storytelling, this index
    Streamlining facts statements, **197**
    Stuff happens bias, **218**
    Suspicion bias, ATLA study, **217**
    Symbols, mistakes in use of, **237**
    Text, mistakes in use of, **237**
    Theme creation, **222**
    Victimization bias, **218**
    Visual aids, **230 et seq.**
    Women men jurors' priorities, **226**
    Written text, mistakes in use of, **237**

OPINIONS
    Expert Witnesses, this index
    Measurement opinions, bracketing, **79**
    Reasons for lay opinions, establishing, **78**

PAIN
    Client as deponent, pain questions, **135, 137**
    Conscious vs unconscious conditions based on medical reports, **412**
    Four steps of pain, **383**
    Juror understanding, **195**
    Settlement brief illustrations, **407**

PARADOX STUDY
    Jury decisionmaking, **192**

PHOTOGRAPHS
    See also Real Evidence, this index
    Google Earth as source, **49**
    Settlement communications, **407**

PLEADINGS
    Generally, **46 et seq.**

POLICE REPORTS
    Accuracy assumption errors, **23**

POWERPOINT PRESENTATIONS
    See also Real Evidence, this index
    Anchoring the PowerPoint opening, **241**
    Comparison of display modes, **284**
    Defense use dangers, **243**
    Opening Statements, this index
    Overuse, **281**

INDEX TO TRIAL TIPS

POWERPOINT PRESENTATIONS—Cont'd
Staff training, **244**
Summation, use in, **335**

PREEXISTING CONDITIONS
Assumptions, **24**

PREJUDICE
See Bias, this index

PRIOR CLAIMS
Assumptions, **24**

PRIOR STATEMENTS
Depositions, development in, **80**

PRODUCTION DEMANDS
Generally, **91 et seq.**
Deathstar deposition notice, **97, 163**
Enforcement, **94**
Nonparties, **93**
Response duties, **93**

REAL EVIDENCE
Generally, **261 et seq.**
Admissibility, **282**
Advantages and disadvantages, **284**
Anchoring exhibits, **270**
Anchoring testimony with, **227**
Building block analogy, **270**
Chart junk, **280**
Color
  communicative impact, **273**
  misuse, **281**
Comparison of display modes, **284**
Creating, **53**
Cross-examination use, anticipating, **271**
Data dense exhibits, avoiding, **280**
Deposition use, **75**
Display modes compared, **284**
Documents, this index
Drawings, scale accuracy assumptions, **26**
Effectiveness, improving, **273**
Elmo use, **281**
Focus group testing of effectiveness, **279**
Google Earth as resource, **53**
Icons, communicative impact, **273**
Improving effectiveness, **273**
Integrating in direct examination, **268**
Integrating visual and oral communication, **278**
Jury testing, **279**
Lasting impact exhibits, **267**
Linking to testimony, **242**

REAL EVIDENCE—Cont'd
Making the exhibit memorable, **267**
Memory aids, **261**
Mock jury exhibit testing, **267**
Naked charts, **281**
Objections, avoiding, **262**
Overdoing it, **280**
Permission to use, obtaining, **282**
Pictures, communicative impact, **273, 278**
PowerPoint Presentations, this index
Printed words, communicative impact, **273**
Production Demands, this index
Reading documents into evidence, **264**
Scarcity theory, **273**
Spoliation dangers, **47**
Sponsorship theory, **272**
Strategic functions, **270**
Summation, exhibits use, **340**
Symbols, communicative impact, **273**
Unlabeled charts, **281**
Videotape, this index
Views, use of, **204**

RECORDS
Accuracy assumption errors, **23**

RE-DIRECT EXAMINATION
See Direct Examination, this index

REFLEX SYMPATHETIC DYSTROPHY SYNDROME
Junk science, debunking, **334**

REPRESENTATIVE DEPOSITIONS
See Designated Representative Depositions, this index

RISK
Settlement risk analyses, **397**

ROLE-PLAYING EXERCISES
Generally, **139**

SCARCITY THEORY
Exhibit use, **273**

SEINFELD SYNDROME
Jury selection tips, **190**

SETTLEMENT
Generally, **382 et seq.**
See also Negotiation, this index
Appearance of preparedness, **406**
Assumptions about settlements, **21**
Bluffs, **405**

SETTLEMENT—Cont'd
  Briefs
    generally, **403**
    see also Notebooks, this index
    appearance of preparedness, **406**
    length, **407**
    pain illustrations, **407**
  Brochures, **393, 406**
  Computerized presentations, **408**
  Damages, outlining, **412**
  Defendant's settlement range, **391**
  Defense costs, assessing, **385**
  Delays, explaining to client, **383**
  Demand letters, **403**
  Diagrams use, **407**
  Discovery posture to motivate settlement, **399**
  Double teaming settlement and trial, **418**
  Evaluations and themes, **409**
  Financial analysis of case value, **391**
  Halpern H-Bomb demand letter, **405**
  Headlines in demand letters, **403**
  Joint venture representations, **419**
  Multiple claimants, representing, **417**
  Notebooks, this index
  Openings, **409**
  Pain illustrations, **407**
  Photographs use, **407**
  Preparedness, demonstrating, **406**
  Presentations
    generally, **403**
    see also Notebooks, this index
    computerized, **408**
    types of, **406**
    video, **408**
  Risk analyses, **397**
  Science of settlement, **399**
  Specific amount demands, **404**
  Spicing up settlement demands, **384**
  Storytelling
    generally, **409**
    testing the story theme, **417**
  Strategy, **390, 394**
  Types of presentations, **406**
  Video presentations, **408**

SHADOW JURIES
  See Mock Juries, this index

SPONSORSHIP THEORY
  Exhibit use, **272**

STORYTELLING
  Anchoring and storytelling, **227**
  Detail, using and avoiding, **220**
  Dos and don'ts of storytelling, **222, 230**
  Facts vs people as focus, **220**
  Four storytelling rules, **220**
  Memory organization packages, **227**
  Men vs women jurors' priorities, **226**
  Opening Statements, this index
  People vs facts as focus, **220**
  Point of view, importance in storytelling, **221**
  Present tense use, **226**
  Priorities for storytellers, **226**
  Settlement, **409, 417**
  Summation, this index
  Testing the story theme, **417**
  Vignettes use, **340**
  Women vs men jurors' priorities, **226**

SUMMATION
  Generally, **328 et seq.**
  Accentuate the positive, **340**
  Accident, effect of use of term on jurors, **219**
  Analogies, **340**
  Anchoring the evidence during, **330**
  ATLA jury bias project, **217**
  Attention level of jurors, recognizing, **240**
  Bad character issues, **340**
  Bad conduct vs injury and juror motivation, **219**
  Character issues, **340**
  Choices
    defendant's, accentuating, **340**
    effect of use of term on jurors, **204**
  Connecting with the jury
    generally, **199**
    jargon use, **203**
  Countering the defense wedge strategy, **329**
  Defense wedge strategy, countering, **329**
  Eliminate the negative the positive, **340**
  Emotion, controlling and using, **204**
  Environmental conditions affecting jurors, **241**
  Exhibits use, **340**
  Eye contact, **340**
  Factors affecting jurors' perceptions and responses, **240**
  Focus group testing, **328**
  Frivolous lawsuit bias, **218**
  Fundamental attribution arguments, **340**
  Future vs present impact of injury, **340**
  General vs specific discussion about liability, **339**

SUMMATION—Cont'd
Go along approach to jury communication, **199**
Good character issues, **340**
Heard vs said messages, distinctions, **221**
Heuristics, **216**
Hindsight principle, **216**
Inference tools, **216**
Information availability principle, **217**
Information processing theory, **216**
Injury impact, present vs future, **340**
Injury vs bad conduct and juror motivation, **219**
Issue framing principle, **217**
Jargon use, **203**
Liability
    defendant choices and, **340**
    general vs specific discussion, **339**
Memory capacity of jurors, recognizing, **240**
Mistake, effect of use of term on jurors, **197, 204, 219**
Perceptions of jurors, factors affecting, **240**
Personal life experiences affecting jurors' perceptions and responses, **240**
Personal responsibility bias, **218**
Point of view, importance in storytelling, **221**
PowerPoint use, **335**
Preexisting beliefs affecting jurors' perceptions and responses, **240**
Present vs future impact of injury, **340**
Priorities and time budgeting, **340**
Quotations, **340**
Rehearsing, **198**
Responses of jurors, factors affecting, **240**
Said vs heard messages, distinctions, **221**
Sequence of presentation, importance, **221**
Socioeconomic filters affecting jurors' perceptions and responses, **240**
Sound as anchor of evidence, **330**
Stuff happens bias, **218**
Suspicion bias, **217**
Ten-step quick mix for summations, **339**
Time budgeting and priorities, **340**
Victimization bias, **218**
Videotape use, **335**
Vignettes use, **340**
Wedge strategy, countering, **329**

TESTIMONY
Cross-Examination, this index
Direct Examination, this index
Exhibits, linking to, **242**
Expert Witnesses, this index

TESTIMONY—Cont'd
Witnesses, this index

TRANSCRIPTS
Computerized, real time transcripts, **201, 332**
Deposition transcripts, synopses, **75**

TREATING PHYSICIANS
Causation assumption errors, **22**
Records preservation assumption errors, **23**

TRIAL
Computerized, real time transcripts, **201, 332**
Cross-Examination, this index
Direct Examination, this index
Double teaming settlement and trial, **418**
Joint venture representations, **419**
Notebooks, this index
Opening Statements, this index
Shortening the trial, **202**
Summation, this index

VIDEO CONFERENCING
Generally, **330**

VIDEOTAPE
Generally, **330**
See also Real Evidence, this index
Anchoring value, **330**
Day in the life videos, **264**
Demeanor capture, **332**
Direct examination practice, **258**
Expert witness testimony, **330**
Settlement presentations, **408**
Summation, use in, **335**
Witnesses statement records, **25**

WEDGE STRATEGY
Generally, **198**
Countering, **329**

WITNESSES
Anchoring testimony, **200, 227**
Bracketing measurement opinions, **79**
Client as witness, preparation, **139**
Credibility, jurors' assessments, **199**
Cross-Examination, this index
Deposition Practice, this index
Direct Examination, this index
Exhibits, linking to testimony, **242**
Expert Witnesses, this index
Impeachment, this index
Information assumptions, **25**

WITNESSES—Cont'd
   Juror assessments of credibility, **199**
   Linking exhibits to testimony, **242**
   Measurement opinions, bracketing, **79**
   Memory organization packages, developing through testimony, **227**
   Practice examinations, **258**
   Reasons for lay opinions, establishing, **78**
   Statement consistency assumptions, **25**

WITNESSES—Cont'd
   Video records of statements, **25**

WRONGFUL DEATH
   Damages, outlining for settlement, **407, 412**
   Damages experts use, **412**
   Juror motivations, **193, 277**
   Life expectancy
     assumptions, **24**
     computations, **412**